Core Criminal Procedure

Core Criminal Procedure

Learning Through Multiple-Choice Questions

Kathy Swedlow

CAROLINA ACADEMIC PRESS

Durham, North Carolina

LCCN: 2017941361

ISBN: 978-1-63283-879-7
eBook ISBN: 978-1-63283-880-3

Carolina Academic Press, LLC
700 Kent Street
Durham, North Carolina 27701
Telephone (919) 489-7486
Fax (919) 493-5668
www.cap-press.com

Printed in the United States of America
2019 Printing

Contents

Preface

I was a law professor for fifteen years. During that time, my Criminal Procedure students would often ask me about supplemental materials to help them practice what they were learning in class—and as they were learning it. Responding to these requests was easy because there are a number of excellent hornbooks on the market.

But at the same time, my students anticipated the bar exam and wanted exposure to bar-style multiple choice questions. Bar preparation materials are plentiful, but are written with the assumption that students have already learned the material and are preparing for the bar exam. These materials are ill-suited for formative use for two basic reasons. First, they sample topics rather than presenting a comprehensive overview of the subject matter. Second, any given question might sample a sub-topic—or sub-topics—that a student enrolled in the class hasn't been exposed to yet.

The questions in this book were written to fill this gap: to provide bar-style multiple choice questions that can be used formatively, as students are progressing through a law school Criminal Procedure class.

The first half of the book consists of questions divided between three chapters—Fourth Amendment, Fifth Amendment, and Sixth Amendment—to parallel the materials covered in most law school Criminal Procedure classes. Each chapter has multiple subsections, and each subsection focuses on a separate topic.

Within each topic, the questions[1] begin with a basic concept and then go through many of the more predictable variations—using U.S. Supreme Court decisions to determine those variations. In some instances, facts patterns are even derived from Supreme Court cases. This is by design, so students can use the facts to help track and solidify the concepts they are learning in class.

The questions also follow the format used by the National Conference of Bar Examiners on the Multistate Bar Exam. Since the questions were written to present one concept at a time, instead of many concepts all at once, students may find it useful to go through these questions first and then move on to questions provided by bar review companies and released by the bar examiners.

The second half of the book presents concise answers for each question. The answers are intentionally brief and include relevant citations, so students can refer back to their casebooks for more detailed information. In many instances and for ease of reading, I excluded paren-

---

1. Unless a specific question indicates otherwise, students should assume that marijuana is strictly illegal.

thetical information describing omissions from a quotation, *e.g.*, footnotes, emphasis, internal citations, etc.

In writing this book, I've had a lot of help and support from my friends and colleagues. Special thanks go to Erik Altmann, Jeanette Buttrey, Terry Cavanaugh, Brad Charles, Tonya Krause-Phelan, Cathy McCollum, and Chris Trudeau. Former students Andrea Randall and Garett Curtis helped with editing.

I worked on this book while caring for my mother, Patricia Swedlow. Whether we were in Pennsylvania or Michigan, at home or in the hospital or hospice, my mother was by my side as I wrote most of this text. I dedicate this book to her: a person who so often had the right answer, no matter what the question.

Core Criminal Procedure

1

Fourth Amendment Questions

Fourth Amendment Searches

1. One afternoon, a woman came home and found a ticket for a moving violation in her mail. According to the ticket, a police camera mounted on a utility pole had captured a photo of the woman's car driving through a red light in a downtown area.

The woman called an attorney and asked for advice. The attorney explained that a recently enacted state law authorized the use of such cameras, but he told the woman that he would try to see what he could do to help her. The attorney filed a motion to quash the ticket, claiming that use of the traffic camera violated the woman's Fourth Amendment right to be free from unreasonable searches.

What is the prosecutor's best argument in response?

A. The motion should be denied because the woman has a reduced expectation of privacy in her car.

B. The motion should be denied because the camera recorded the woman committing the violation.

C. The motion should be denied because use of the camera did not infringe on the woman's privacy rights.

D. The motion should be denied because state law authorized the camera's use, and the law is presumed constitutional.

2. Police received a tip that a man was growing marijuana in his home. An officer reviewed the home's water bills from the prior six months and discovered that it was using four times the usual amount of water for a single family home.

The following day, the officer drove to the man's home and, staying seated in his patrol car parked across the street, pointed a thermal imager in the direction of the home. The imager gave an error code, indicating that it needed to be held closer. The officer got out of his car and walked onto the man's front lawn. Standing about five feet from the home, the imager gave the officer the information he was looking for: that one of the upstairs rooms facing the street was emitting a large amount of heat.

The officer applied for a search warrant, describing the tip, the water bills, and the thermal imager's readout in his affidavit in support of probable cause. The magistrate issued the warrant. When the warrant was later executed, marijuana was found in the same upstairs room that the imager had highlighted.

If the man files a motion to suppress, what is his strongest argument in support?

A. The anonymous tip did not provide an adequate basis for the officer's continued investigation.

B. The officer did not conduct a neutral investigation because he was looking for proof that the man was growing marijuana.

C. The anonymous tip and the water bills did not provide an adequate basis to justify use of the thermal imager.

D. The officer conducted a search when he used a thermal imager on the man's house while standing on the front lawn.

3. A man and a woman lived together in the woman's apartment for several months, but the man wanted to break up. While the woman was at work, the man packed most of his belongings and moved them to a friend's house, leaving one box behind. The man then wrote the woman a note explaining that he was leaving and telling her that she was free to sell the items in the box if she wanted to. The woman was heartbroken.

After drinking several glasses of wine, the woman went through the box. Near the top, the woman found a loaded revolver wrapped in a t-shirt. Scared of what else she might find, the woman closed the box and drove it to her local police station. An officer took the box to a back room and inventoried its contents. Among other things, the officer found a thumb drive with hundreds of pornographic images of children.

The prosecutor later charged the man with crimes associated with the photos. If the man files a motion to suppress, how should the court rule on the motion?

A. The motion should be granted and the evidence suppressed because the man clearly left the thumb drive in the box by mistake.

B. The motion should be granted and the evidence suppressed because the police only discovered the thumb drive due to the acts of a drunken, vengeful woman.

C. The motion should be denied and the evidence admitted because the man forfeited his Fourth Amendment rights when he broke up with the woman.

D. The motion should be denied and the evidence admitted because the man abandoned the box and its contents.

4.   Police in a college town were frustrated by a recent spike in the number of heroin overdoses. Hoping to solve the problem, the police chief developed a plan to post officers with drug-sniffing dogs throughout the town's downtown area. If the dogs "alerted" on any particular individual, the officer would then detain that person to investigate further.

One evening, two women were waiting in line at the movie theatre. An officer with a trained dog walked up to the women and the dog began sniffing at their feet. After several seconds, the dog sat down and began to whimper—which indicated to the officer that the dog had smelled an odor it equated with heroin. The officer took the women aside and out of earshot of the other people in line. He asked if they had any heroin on them. One of the women confessed that she did and handed a small baggie containing the drug to the officer.

If the woman is later charged with heroin possession and files a motion to suppress, what is the prosecutor's strongest argument in defense?

A. The officer did not "seize" the woman under the Fourth Amendment.

B. The dog did not "search" the woman under the Fourth Amendment.

C. The officer acted reasonably to preserve the woman's privacy.

D. The woman voluntarily handed the officer the baggie of heroin.

5.   One spring day, a police officer went to a residential neighborhood to investigate a tip that a middle-aged woman spent her afternoons sitting on a balcony outside her bedroom, smoking marijuana. Once at the house, the officer realized that he could not see the balcony because it was in the back of the house.

Undaunted, the officer asked a second officer to fly him over the woman's house in a police helicopter. From the air, the officer observed just what the tipster had described: a woman sitting on a balcony, smoking marijuana.

The officer requested a search warrant for the house, describing his own observations but intentionally omitting information about the tip. The warrant was issued and when the officer executed it, he found the woman sitting on the balcony, smoking marijuana. The woman was later charged with possession of a small amount of marijuana.

The woman's lawyer has filed a motion to suppress in advance of her upcoming trial. What is the most likely ruling from the court?

A. The evidence will be suppressed because the use of the helicopter was not justified for such a low-level charge.

B. The evidence will be suppressed because the officer intentionally left the tip out of the warrant application.

C. The evidence will be admitted because the officer did not violate the woman's Fourth Amendment rights in any way.

D. The evidence will be admitted because the officer acted reasonably when he flew over the woman's house in a helicopter.

6.   Acting on a tip, an officer began to investigate whether users were sharing pornographic images of children on a peer-to-peer file-sharing network. On the network, member users are able to share digital files with other member users, and the network stores the shared files on a central server instead of on users' individual computers. Using special software, the officer identified an IP address that had shared the child pornography files with the network, and he was then able to tie the IP address to a suburban house.

The officer obtained a search warrant which permitted the seizure of all personal computers in the house, including PCs, laptops, and tablets. The officer executed the warrant and found a single laptop; a subsequent search of its contents revealed several images of child pornography.

The laptop owner now seeks to quash the warrant, claiming that the use of the software violated his Fourth Amendment rights. What is the state's best argument in response?

A. The magistrate's signature on the warrant demonstrates that the officer had probable cause to search the laptop owner's house.

B. The officer's use of the software on the network files didn't implicate the laptop owner's Fourth Amendment rights.

C. The officer acted in good faith, and so any error in the officer's use of the software should not result in suppression.

D. The state's interests in stopping child pornography outweigh the laptop owner's interest in possessing child pornography.

7.   Police received a tip that a spa owner was using her business to launder money for a drug ring. The investigating officer managed to easily identify the members of the drug ring but was unable to tie the spa owner to any drug activity. Still, the officer had a hunch the tip was correct. The officer placed a GPS device on the spa owner's car to see if she made any contact with anyone in the drug ring.

Three weeks later, after monitoring the spa owner's car around the clock, the officer tracked the spa owner to a home repair store at the same time the leader of the drug ring was there. The officer used this information—together with other information from his investigation—to get a search warrant for the spa.

After executing the warrant and discovering large sums of cash, the spa owner was charged with conspiracy and other crimes. If she files a motion to suppress, what is her strongest argument in support?

A. The officer's placement of the GPS device on her car constitutes a Fourth Amendment search.

B. The officer's monitoring of the GPS device on her car constitutes a Fourth Amendment search.

C. The officer's placement and monitoring of the GPS device constitutes a Fourth Amendment search.

D. The officer's placement and monitoring of the GPS device constitutes a Fourth Amendment search and requires a warrant.

8.   Police suspected a man was growing marijuana in his home, but were unable to establish probable cause for a warrant. Frustrated, the lead officer waited until the man went out one night and then had a drug detection dog brought to the man's home. The officer told the dog's handler to have the dog sniff at the front door of the house and specifically told her to keep the dog away from the front and back yards.

The handler did as she was told and walked the dog up to the front door. The dog spent a few minutes sniffing at the front door and then sat down, alerting the handler he smelled an odor that he associated with marijuana. The officer used this information in his affidavit in support of probable cause for a search warrant for the home. The warrant was issued and executed, and the officer found marijuana inside the home.

If the homeowner moves to suppress, what is the most likely ruling on the motion?

A.   The motion will be granted because a government actor used a drug dog on the homeowner's curtilage, exceeding the implied license granted by the homeowner.

B.   The motion will be granted because a government actor physically intruded onto the homeowner's curtilage—a constitutionally protected area.

C.   The motion will be denied because the handler specifically restricted the dog to the part of the curtilage on which the homeowner might expect strangers to walk onto.

D.   The motion will be denied because a government actor's use of a drug dog in a public place does not implicate a privacy interest under the Fourth Amendment.

9.   Police received a tip that a farmer was growing marijuana on a distant corner of his property. Two officers were assigned to investigate. The farmer was not at home, so the officers walked onto his property and followed a narrow footpath toward the area identified by the tip. After walking approximately two miles on the footpath, the officers found a large patch of marijuana. The farmer had purposefully planted corn around the marijuana patch in order to hide the marijuana. The officers seized the marijuana.

If the farmer later challenges the officers' right to walk onto his property and seize his marijuana, what is the state's strongest argument in response?

A.   The farmer cannot claim a Fourth Amendment expectation of privacy in illegal activity.

B.   The officers only physically intruded on an open field, which is not a constitutionally protected area.

C.   The farmer granted an implied license for strangers to walk on his property because he had a footpath leading to the marijuana.

D.   The officers didn't exceed any implied license, because the farmer failed to post "no trespassing" signs.

10.   A drug patrol officer boarded a passenger bus after it pulled into a rest area for a 90-minute scheduled stop. The officer walked down the center aisle, squeezing the carry-on luggage that travelers had placed in the overhead rack. Halfway down the aisle, the officer squeezed a duffel bag and felt a brick-like object inside. The officer believed, based on his training and experience, that the object was a brick of packaged drugs.

The officer asked the man seated below the duffel bag if the bag belonged to him and the man said yes. The officer asked for consent to search the bag and when the man agreed, the officer opened the bag and found a brick of methamphetamine inside. The officer arrested the man and the prosecutor subsequently charged him with drug crimes.

The man has moved to suppress the drugs from his upcoming trial. What is the most likely ruling from the court?

A.   The motion will be denied because a public bus is not a "person, house, paper, or effect," and so is not a "constitutionally protected area."

B.   The motion will be denied because the officer's intrusion into the duffel bag only came after the man consented to the search.

C.   The motion will be granted because the officer had time to get a search warrant, and should not have relied on the man's consent to search.

D.   The motion will be granted because the officer's act of squeezing the duffel bag constituted an intrusion on the man's effect.

Fourth Amendment Seizures

11. A young man was walking down the street and decided to stop outside a diner to look at the menu posted in the window. While reading the menu, the young man noticed a police officer inside the diner, paying her bill at the cash register. The young man became very nervous because he had some marijuana in his pocket. As the officer walked out of the diner, she held the door open for the young man. Instead of walking through the door and inside the diner, the young man reached in his pocket, pulled out the marijuana, and handed it to the officer.

The young man was later charged with marijuana possession. At his suppression hearing, he argued that the marijuana should be suppressed as a fruit of an unreasonable seizure. What is the state's best argument in response?

A. This sort of casual encounter is not considered a seizure under the Fourth Amendment.

B. This sort of casual encounter is not considered an unreasonable seizure under the Fourth Amendment.

C. The young man was seized, but that he voluntarily handed the marijuana to the police officer.

D. The young man was seized, but the marijuana is admissible because the officer didn't search him.

12. Police received a call about a domestic disturbance at an apartment building. The caller reported arguing between a man and a woman and hearing the woman screaming and yelling, "no, please, no!"

An officer was sent to the address; he parked his car in the parking lot adjacent to the apartment building. As the officer was walking toward the building, he saw a man walking out of the building and toward the parking lot. The officer shouted to the man, "Hey, can you help me out here? I was just wondering if you'd seen or heard anything unusual around here in the past half hour or so?" The man responded, "Nothing unusual at all. My girlfriend picked another fight with me about my drinking, so I slapped her to get her to shut up."

The man was charged with battery and has moved to suppress his statement, arguing that it is a fruit of an unreasonable seizure. How should the court rule on the motion?

A. The man was not seized because the officer didn't prevent him from going to his car.

B. The man was not seized because a reasonable person would have felt free to ignore the officer's question.

C. The man was seized because he submitted to authority when he answered the officer's question.

D. The man was seized because no reasonable person would have felt free to ignore the officer's question.

13. A passenger bus was traveling across country when it made a scheduled stop midway through the trip. With the driver's permission, two police officers boarded the bus with the specific goal of asking passengers for consent to search their baggage. Only one of the passengers agreed to a search; that search yielded a kilo of cocaine and several ounces of heroin.

At a later suppression hearing, the officers admitted that they did not have any suspicion to believe that the passengers were transporting drugs. The officers also acknowledged that they did not inform the passengers that they could refuse the search.

If the passenger challenges her consent—and the subsequent search—as a fruit of an unlawful seizure, what test should the court use to evaluate whether she was seized?

A. Whether a reasonable police officer would have informed the woman that she had a right to refuse consent.

B. Whether a reasonable police officer would have requested consent to search in the absence of any suspicion of crime.

C. Whether a reasonable person would have submitted to the police officers' authority.

D. Whether a reasonable person would feel free to terminate the encounter with the police officers.

14. An officer on foot patrol noticed a young man standing on a street corner, smoking. The officer had no idea what the young man was actually smoking but she did know that there had been a recent spike in hospitalizations due to people smoking marijuana soaked in embalming fluid. The officer decided to investigate, and so she walked toward the young man and yelled out, "Hello, sir, I'm a police officer and I'd like to ask you a couple of questions."

The young man turned and ran in the opposite direction. As he did so, he dropped the item he had been smoking—a marijuana cigarette soaked in embalming fluid. The officer called for backup and chased the man, tackling him to the ground in the next block. After the backup officers arrived, the officer retrieved the marijuana cigarette from where the young man had dropped it.

If the young man is charged with drug possession and if he files a motion to suppress, how should the court rule on the motion?

A. The young man was seized when the officer called out to him and demonstrated her authority over him.

B. The young man was seized when the officer tackled him to the ground.

C. The officer had no right to approach the young man without reasonable suspicion or probable cause of wrongdoing.

D. The officer acted in the young man's best interest because she was concerned that he was smoking something harmful to his health.

15.   A driver was traveling home one evening around dusk, driving along a single-lane roadway. Ten miles from his house, the driver noticed that the car behind him had his lights switched to the "bright" position. As the second car got closer, the bright lights became distracting and so the driver decided to pull over and let the second car pass.

As he eased his car to the side of the road, the driver realized for the first time that the second car was a police cruiser. The driver panicked, grabbed a marijuana pipe from the console next to his seat, and threw the pipe out the window. The driver then got back on the highway and drove home. Unfortunately for the driver, the officer had witnessed him throw the pipe out the window. Moments later, the officer turned around and retrieved the pipe.

The driver was charged with possession of drug paraphernalia and his lawyer filed a motion to suppress the pipe. How should the court rule on the motion?

A.   The pipe is a fruit of a Fourth Amendment seizure because the driver submitted to the officer's authority when he pulled off the road.

B.   The pipe is a fruit of a Fourth Amendment search because the officer's headlights caused the driver to throw the pipe out of the window.

C.   The pipe is not a fruit of a Fourth Amendment search because the driver voluntarily threw the pipe out of the window.

D.   The pipe is not a fruit of a Fourth Amendment seizure because the driver did not submit to the officer's authority when he pulled off the road.

16.   A woman was watching television one evening when she heard a strange noise coming from behind her house. Looking out the back window, the woman saw a prowler in her backyard and so she called the police. Several minutes later, an officer arrived and began to investigate. Half a block down the street, the officer saw the prowler trying to break into the patio door of a second house. The officer called out and told the prowler to stop, but the prowler ran away. The officer again yelled for the prowler to stop, but the prowler kept running. Frustrated, the officer drew his weapon and shot the prowler in the back.

Later, the prowler's estate sued the officer for wrongful death and requested damages. How should the court rule on the issue of whether the officer seized the prowler when he shot him?

A.   The officer seized the prowler because he restrained the prowler's freedom of movement through the use of deadly force.

B.   The officer seized the prowler because a reasonable person, having been shot, would not be free to leave.

C.   The officer did not seize the prowler because the prowler ran away and did not submit to the officer's authority.

D.   The officer did not seize the prowler because the prowler unreasonably tried to run away from the officer's gunshot.

17.   A police officer was involved in a high-speed car chase with a suspected felon, but was unable to catch him. A second officer was tracking the chase and placed a tire "spike strip" on the road ahead of the speeding cars. The suspected felon did not see the spike strip in time and drove over it and the spikes ripped his tires to shreds. The suspected felon's car spun out of control and crashed into a wall, killing him instantly.

The suspected felon's estate filed a wrongful death suit against the local police, claiming that use of the spike strip constituted an unreasonable seizure. What is the state's best argument in response?

A.   The suspected felon forfeited his Fourth Amendment rights when he ran from the police.

B.   The suspected felon was not seized under the Fourth Amendment because no police officer actually touched him.

C.   The suspected felon was not seized under the Fourth Amendment because he did not submit to authority.

D.   The suspected felon was seized under the Fourth Amendment but the seizure in this case was reasonable.

18.   One day at a private high school, a police officer gave a presentation to a group of students about the dangers of drinking and driving. The students had been identified by their teachers as being at risk and the students were required to go to the presentation in lieu of attending their regular class. If they did not attend the presentation, students were told that they would receive an "F" for that day's class and would have to complete a week's worth of after-school detention.

The officer's presentation consisted of a series of slides depicting grisly car accidents caused by drunk driving. At the end of the presentation, the officer asked the students whether, after seeing all the gruesome photos, any of them would ever drink and drive. A teenager sitting in the front row responded: "I'm really drunk now, but after seeing this presentation, I'll be sure to get a ride home from one of my friends." The officer wrapped up his presentation and—after speaking with the teenager for a few moments to ascertain that he was drunk—arrested him for underage drinking.

At the teenager's upcoming suppression hearing, he plans to argue that his admission was a fruit of an unreasonable seizure. What is the state's best argument in response?

A.   The Fourth Amendment does not apply to "special needs" searches and seizures.

B.   The officer was not responsible for the teenager's attendance at the presentation.

C.   The Fourth Amendment has absolutely no application within private schools.

D.   A reasonable person would not have admitted to criminal conduct.

19. A patrol officer thought he saw a car with expired license tags and so he called his dispatcher to see if the owner of the car had submitted an application for renewal. The dispatcher told the officer that a proper renewal application was pending. The officer pulled the car over anyway. While the officer was interacting with the driver, he recognized the front seat passenger and realized that he was wanted for a recent parole violation. The officer arrested the passenger and searched him incident to arrest, discovering a syringe and a small amount of heroin in the passenger's coat pocket.

If the state concedes that the traffic stop was unreasonable, how should the judge rule on the passenger's motion to suppress?

A. The motion should be denied because only the driver was seized, as he was the target of the stop.

B. The motion should be denied because the officer lawfully searched the passenger incident to arrest.

C. The motion should be granted because the heroin was a fruit of the passenger's unreasonable seizure.

D. The motion should be granted because the officer did not verify that the passenger was a parole violator before arresting him.

20. One evening, an officer pulled a driver over to the side of the road. The officer admittedly did not have probable cause for the stop. However, because the officer saw the car weaving in its lane, he was concerned the driver might be impaired. Shortly after making the stop, the officer realized that the driver was not impaired and the weaving was due to the driver leaning over to change the radio station while she drove.

Before allowing the driver to leave, the officer asked her for permission to search her car, and the driver agreed. In the trunk, the officer found a baggie filled with a white powder, which later testing revealed to be cocaine.

If the driver is charged with cocaine possession and files a motion to suppress, what is the most likely ruling from the court?

A. The motion will be granted because the officer did not have probable cause to stop the driver.

B. The motion will be granted because the officer had absolutely no authority to stop the driver.

C. The motion will be denied because the officer had reasonable suspicion to stop the driver.

D. The motion will be denied because brief traffic stops fall outside of the Fourth Amendment.

Probable Cause and Reasonable Suspicion

21.   Police received a tip that a bartender was selling cocaine from the bar where he worked. According to the tip, the bartender received his drugs from a woman who lived in a neighboring town and the two met weekly at a local diner to exchange cash for cocaine. The tipster also explained that the bartender kept his cocaine supply in an empty cocktail shaker behind the bar.

An officer placed the bartender and the woman under surveillance; over the course of three weeks, he saw the two meet three times for breakfast at a local diner. Each time, the two sat at the same table and ordered the same food. As the bartender was driving away from the third breakfast, the officer pulled him over and searched his car. In the glove box, the officer found a large plastic bag with cocaine inside.

The bartender was charged with cocaine possession and filed a motion to suppress the cocaine seized from his car. The prosecutor defended the search, arguing that it was reasonable under the automobile exception. How should the court rule?

A.   The motion should be granted because the officer did not have probable cause to believe that any cocaine would be found in the bartender's car.

B.   The motion should be granted because the officer failed to corroborate the claim that the bartender kept the cocaine in an empty cocktail shaker behind the bar.

C.   The motion should be denied because the officer conducted a thorough investigation and the suspected cocaine was found in the car.

D.   The motion should be denied because the officer had probable cause to believe that the bartender had just purchased cocaine from the woman.

22.   A police officer pulled a driver over for speeding and wrote him a ticket. As the officer handed the driver the ticket, she requested permission to search the car and the driver agreed. After the driver and his two passengers — one sitting in the front seat and one sitting in the back — got out of the car, the officer searched the car and found a small baggie of cocaine under the armrest in the back seat. The officer confronted the driver and the two passengers with the cocaine and asked who owned the drugs, but the three men stayed silent. The officer arrested all three men for possession of cocaine.

Later, at the police station, the front seat passenger admitted that the cocaine was his. The officer then released the driver and the other passenger. Later, the district attorney filed cocaine possession charges against the front seat passenger.

If the front seat passenger files a motion to suppress his statement, how should the court rule on the motion?

A.   The motion should be granted because the officer lacked probable cause to arrest the front seat passenger and the statement was a fruit of that unlawful arrest.

B.   The motion should be granted because the cocaine most likely belonged to the back seat passenger and so the officer only had probable cause to arrest him.

C.   The motion should be denied because the officer had probable cause to arrest any or all three of the men riding together in the car.

D.   The motion should be denied because the front seat passenger voluntarily admitted that the cocaine was his.

23.   Two police officers stopped a driver for speeding. The first officer asked the driver for her license and registration; he noticed that the driver's hands were shaking as she removed her license from her wallet and the vehicle registration from the glove compartment. The first officer also saw that the driver had a cardboard air freshener dangling from the rear view mirror and that it was stamped with a drawing of a marijuana leaf.

While this was happening, the second officer walked a drug-sniffing dog around the exterior of the driver's car. The dog alerted at the trunk, signaling to the second officer that he smelled an odor he had been trained to associate with marijuana.

At the suppression hearing, the defense attorney established that the dog only had a 60% accuracy rate and falsely alerted the remainder of the time. What is the prosecutor's strongest argument in response?

A.   Regardless of the dog's accuracy rate, the driver's nervous behavior and the marijuana-leaf air freshener gave the officer probable cause to search the car.

B.   All the circumstances together—the driver's nervous behavior, the air freshener, and the dog's alert—gave the officers probable cause to search the car.

C.   The dog's accuracy rate shows that he is correct more often than not, which gave the officer probable cause to search the car.

D.   The driver does not have standing to challenge the dog's history of false alerts in unrelated cases that didn't involve her.

24.   Police received an anonymous call from a woman who identified herself as an "interested party" and who claimed that the social studies teacher at the local high school was having an affair with one of his underage students. The caller alleged that the affair had been going on for several months and that the teacher had been in sexual relationships with other underage students in the past.

An officer placed the teacher under surveillance. The very next day, she saw the teacher pick the student up at her house and take her to school; at the end of the day, the teacher drove the student home. After the teacher had driven a few blocks from the student's home, the officer pulled him over and arrested him for statutory rape. The prosecutor filed charges against the teacher two days later.

If the teacher later challenges his arrest, what is his strongest argument in support?

A.   The officer never investigated the anonymous caller's claimed "interest" in this situation, so she did not have probable cause to arrest the teacher.

B.   The officer failed to identify the anonymous caller's identity and knew nothing about her credibility, so she did not have probable cause to arrest the teacher.

C.   The officer never investigated the anonymous caller's claims about the teacher's past conduct, so she did not have probable cause to arrest the teacher.

D.   The information from the tip, coupled with the officer's own observations, did not provide probable cause to arrest the teacher.

25. As part of a lawful traffic stop but without any suspicion of other wrongdoing, an officer walked a drug-sniffing dog around the exterior of the stopped driver's car. When the dog got to the trunk, she alerted, signaling that she smelled drugs. Based on the dog's alert, the officer searched the car's trunk and found a large garbage bag of harvested marijuana inside.

The driver was charged with marijuana possession and filed a motion to suppress. At the suppression hearing, the prosecutor presented testimony about the dog's training and certification as a drug-sniffing dog. However, the prosecutor did not present any testimony about the dog's performance rate in the field, explaining that police did not keep records on the "misses," but only on the "hits." At the conclusion of the hearing, the defense attorney argued that probable cause from a dog sniff can only be established if there is proof that the dog performs well in the field, not just during training.

What is the prosecutor's strongest argument in response?

A. A drug dog's reliability can be established if there is adequate proof that the dog was properly trained and certified.

B. Dog sniffs are *sui generis* and so a positive alert from a trained dog will always establish probable cause to search.

C. A drug dog's reliability will always be established if there is adequate proof that the dog is properly trained and certified.

D. Dog sniffs are not searches under the Fourth Amendment and so there is no requirement that they be supported by probable cause.

26. A police officer was patrolling in a downtown area when he saw a woman walking along and carrying a paper-bag-wrapped bottle in her hand. Every few steps, the woman took a swig from the bottle. Because drinking alcohol in public is prohibited in this jurisdiction, the officer walked up to the woman and asked her what she was drinking. The woman showed the officer that the bottle contained apple juice. The officer thanked the woman and told her that she was free to go on her way.

Was the stop legally justified?

A. Yes, because the officer had a moderate chance of finding evidence of wrongdoing.

B. Yes, because the officer only detained the woman briefly, as permitted by *Terry v. Ohio*.

C. No, because the woman was drinking apple juice in public, not alcohol.

D. No, because the officer only had a moderate chance of finding evidence of wrongdoing.

27.   A police officer stopped a driver for defective brake lights on his truck. When the officer inspected the driver's license, he realized that the driver's listed address was identical to one where a search warrant had been executed the week before and where the officer had discovered methamphetamine and weapons. The driver explained that the address on his license was old, that he had moved from the listed address three weeks before, and that he hadn't yet updated his address with the department of motor vehicles.

The officer directed the driver to get out of the car. The driver complied and the officer frisked him. In the frisk, the officer found a handgun in the driver's pocket and a baggie of methamphetamine in the waistband of his jeans.

Was the officer justified in frisking the driver for weapons?

A.   Yes, because it was too much of a coincidence that the driver had just moved from a house where methamphetamine and guns had been found.

B.   Yes, because the driver's conduct during the traffic stop gave the officer reasonable suspicion for the frisk.

C.   No, because the officer only had a hunch that the driver was armed and dangerous and so lacked reasonable suspicion for the frisk.

D.   No, because the driver's conduct during the traffic stop suggested only that he was involved in drug crimes, not illegal weapons.

28.   An officer stopped a driver for failing to wear a seatbelt. When the officer explained to the driver why he had stopped her, she replied that she thought the seatbelt law restricted her personal liberty. The driver continued, explaining her belief that many other state laws were, in her view, similarly problematic—such as gun laws and vaccination requirements for children. The driver also told the officer that she didn't believe the state had the constitutional power to regulate when and where she carried her weapon. She concluded by asking, "how would anyone know if I was carrying anyway, because my weapon is always concealed from public view?"

The officer observed that as the driver spoke, she became more and more agitated. The officer directed the driver to get out of the car and she reluctantly complied. He then frisked her, and found a concealed weapon under her jacket, secured in a holster.

If the driver contests the officer's right to frisk her, what is the prosecutor's best argument in response?

A.   The officer had reasonable suspicion to frisk the driver because of her statements about personal liberty.

B.   The officer had reasonable suspicion to frisk the driver because of her increasing agitation.

C.   The officer had reasonable suspicion to frisk the driver because of the question she posed to the officer about her concealed weapon.

D.   The officer had reasonable suspicion to frisk the driver because the totality of the circumstances suggested that she was presently armed and dangerous.

29. Police received an anonymous call that a man was going to go into a bakery and shoot his estranged wife, who worked there. The caller explained that the man was standing beside a grey, four-door sedan parked on the street outside of the bakery, and that he was wearing a navy blue jacket, a white shirt, and tan pants. The caller also told the police that she knew the man well and that she sincerely believed that he was dangerous.

An officer rushed to the bakery and saw a man matching the caller's description, leaning against a grey four-door sedan. The man was talking on his phone and facing the bakery. The officer walked up to the man, frisked him, and found a handgun in his jacket pocket. When the man could not produce a weapons permit, the officer arrested him.

After the man was charged with illegal possession of a handgun, his attorney filed a motion to suppress the handgun. Will the court grant the motion?

A. Yes, because the officer lacked reasonable suspicion for the frisk.

B. Yes, because a large number of people could have been killed in a public shooting.

C. No, because the officer had reasonable suspicion for the frisk.

D. No, because the caller accurately predicted that the man had a gun.

30. Police received an anonymous call that a woman would be leaving an apartment building at a certain time, driving a certain model and color car, to deliver cocaine to someone at a motel five miles away.

The caller did not give the woman's name or say whether she lived in the apartment building. The caller did not give the name of the person the woman was going to meet, or state whether that person was staying in the motel, or worked there.

Two officers drove to the apartment building and parked on the street, just as a woman walked out of the building and began to walk toward the parking lot. The woman got into a car matching the caller's description and pulled out of the parking lot. The officers followed the woman in the car as she drove the most direct route from the apartment building to the motel. A quarter-mile from the motel, the officers pulled the woman over to the side of the road. The first officer explained to the woman why he had stopped her and requested consent to search the car. The woman agreed and the officer found cocaine in the car's trunk.

The woman was charged with attempted distribution of cocaine and has moved to suppress the cocaine. How should the court rule on the motion?

A. The motion should be granted; the police did not have reasonable suspicion to stop the woman because they did not know anything about the person she was meeting.

B. The motion should be granted; the police did not have reasonable suspicion to stop the woman because they pulled her over before she got to the motel.

C. The motion should be denied; the police had reasonable suspicion to seize the woman and her consent was otherwise voluntary.

D. The motion should be denied; the police
    had probable cause to seize the woman
    and her consent was otherwise voluntary.

Warrants

31. Acting on a tip, police began to investigate whether the owner of a local sandwich shop was using his business to sell drugs.

The lead officer on the case wrote and signed a lengthy probable cause affidavit and created a list of items police wished to seize from the sandwich shop. According to state law, all warrant applications are required to include a one-page form as a cover page; the form has spaces for the officer to write his name and the date of the application, and includes a checklist of items that are to be attached to the warrant application. The officer purposely decided not to use the one-page form.

The magistrate reviewed the warrant application and signed it. The officers executed the warrant the next day and found massive amounts of drugs and drug paraphernalia. The shop owner was then arrested and charged with drug crimes.

If the shop owner moves to suppress the drugs due to a Fourth Amendment violation, what is the most likely ruling from the court?

A. The motion will be denied because the officer acted in good faith.

B. The motion will be denied because the warrant was facially valid.

C. The motion will be granted because the officer purposefully decided not to use the form.

D. The motion will be granted due to the violation of state law.

32. A veteran police officer conducted a three-month investigation into allegations that a local daycare center was a front for a drug operation. At the conclusion of his investigation, the officer applied for a warrant to search the daycare center.

The officer's application relied on a one page pre-printed "warrant application" form used by police within the jurisdiction. The officer attached a detailed description of his investigation and a list of items he wanted to seize from the daycare center. At the bottom of the form was a line for the officer to sign and date the application and provide his badge number. The officer signed and dated the form but forgot to include his badge number.

The magistrate reviewed and signed the warrant application but didn't notice the officer's omission. The following day, the officer searched the daycare center, finding drugs and drug paraphernalia. Subsequently, the daycare center owner was charged with various crimes.

If the daycare center owner moves to suppress the evidence seized pursuant to the warrant, what is the most likely ruling from the court?

A. The motion will be denied because the officer conducted a lengthy investigation.

B. The motion will be denied because the warrant was facially valid.

C. The motion will be granted because the officer cannot claim good faith as an excuse for his forgetfulness.

D. The motion will be granted because a reasonable officer would not have forgotten to include his badge number.

33. Based on an anonymous tip, a police officer began to investigate whether a local natural foods store was also serving as a distribution center for a large, multi-state heroin ring. As part of his investigation, the officer spoke with two of the store's employees, who claimed that unidentified shipments were hand-delivered to the store on Sundays and then retrieved on Wednesdays by a known drug dealer.

Based on these statements, the officer placed the store under surveillance and observed that the drug dealer came to the store every Wednesday morning for six weeks in a row. Each time, the drug dealer walked into the store empty handed and then left some time later carrying a cardboard box in his hands. Through his investigation, the officer also learned that three of his confidential informants had purchased heroin from the drug dealer and that the drug dealer had bragged about his "connection" at the natural foods store.

After concluding his investigation, the officer applied for and received a warrant to search the natural foods store for heroin. What is the most likely reason the magistrate signed the warrant application?

A. Because probable cause to search was established by the statements from the store employees.

B. Because probable cause to search was established by the officer's ability to corroborate the store employees' statements.

C. Because probable cause to search was established by the information supplied by the confidential informants.

D. Because probable cause to search was established by the totality of the circumstances.

34. A mother reported to police that her six-year-old daughter had been sexually assaulted by a neighbor, a 45-year-old unemployed man. The mother had asked the man to babysit the girl one afternoon when the girl's regular babysitter was sick and the mother needed to run a quick errand. The girl told her mother that while the mother was gone on the errand, the man had sexually assaulted her in her bedroom.

The investigating officer discovered that there was an outstanding warrant for the man's arrest on an indecent exposure charge the previous month—the man had allegedly exposed himself while standing outside of the playground of a local school. The officer completed a search warrant application, requesting permission to search the man's house for "pornographic photos and/or images of children." A magistrate signed the warrant.

In a subsequent search of the man's home, the officer discovered a laptop computer with images of naked children on its hard drive. The man was charged with sexual assault of the neighbor and possession of child pornography and has filed a motion to suppress the evidence taken from his home.

What is the most likely ruling from the court?

A. The motion will be granted because the warrant application didn't specify that the officer was looking for a laptop computer.

B. The motion will be granted because the officer did not have probable cause to search the man's home.

C. The motion will be denied because the state's interest in catching child predators outweighs the man's interests in suppression.

D. The motion will be denied because the officer had probable cause to believe the man had committed a crime.

35. Acting on a tip, police began to suspect that the bartender at a neighborhood bar was also selling cocaine from the bar. According to the tip, the bartender stored the cocaine behind the bar. After placing the bartender under surveillance for several weeks, the investigating officer obtained a warrant to arrest him.

When the investigating officer entered the bar to make the arrest, she saw that there were two people behind the bar: the bartender and a waitress the officer had never seen before. Reasoning that the waitress would necessarily know about the cocaine if she worked behind the bar, the investigating officer arrested both the bartender and the waitress. In a subsequent search incident to arrest, the investigating officer found marijuana in the waitress's apron pocket.

If the waitress is charged with marijuana possession and her attorney files a motion to suppress, what is the strongest argument in support of the motion?

A. The investigating officer was looking for cocaine and not marijuana.

B. The investigating officer unfairly profiled the waitress as a drug dealer.

C. The investigating officer did not have probable cause to arrest the waitress.

D. The investigating officer did not have a warrant for the waitress's arrest.

36. Police received an anonymous letter that a high school teacher was selling marijuana to his students. The letter gave the teacher's home address, the make and model of his car, and alleged that the teacher always parked his car in a certain spot in the teachers' parking lot. The letter also explained that the teacher usually carried a briefcase to and from the school and that he carried the drugs in the briefcase. Finally, the letter said that the teacher often carried large amounts of cash with him.

An officer was assigned to investigate the tip. He was able to corroborate the teacher's address and the details about his car and that he used the same parking space every time he parked in the teachers' lot. The officer also followed the teacher several times when he left the school for lunch, and indeed, the teacher always paid cash for his lunch and always paid from a large roll of bills.

If the police officer presents this information in a warrant application and requests permission to arrest the teacher, what should the magistrate do?

A. The magistrate should refuse to issue the warrant because the officer cannot establish the identity of the anonymous letter writer.

B. The magistrate should refuse to issue the warrant because the officer cannot establish whether the anonymous letter writer has given accurate tips in past.

C. The magistrate should refuse to issue the warrant because the anonymous letter does not meet the *Aguilar-Spinelli* test.

D. The magistrate should refuse to issue the warrant because the officer cannot demonstrate probable cause to arrest the teacher for a crime.

37.   Acting on a tip, an officer began to investigate claims that the principal of the local high school was embezzling money from the school. The officer had the cooperation of the local school board, which had arranged for the officer to have access to the school's financial records.

The officer tried to complete her search warrant application but had significant difficulty understanding the school's financial documents. The officer brought everything to a local magistrate, who happened to have a degree in accounting. The magistrate went through the records with the officer and showed her how the principal had been taking money from the school but making it look — on paper — like the money was still in the school's accounts. The officer used this information to complete the search warrant application, and the magistrate authorized the warrant.

Later that day, the officer executed the warrant at the principal's home office. There, she found a large amount of cash and additional financial documents. The local prosecutor then charged the principal with embezzlement.

If the principal moves to suppress the evidence seized from his home, what is his strongest argument in support of that motion?

A.   The officer didn't understand the financial documents.

B.   The magistrate was not neutral and detached.

C.   The school board should not have given the officer access to the records.

D.   The prosecutor cannot prove that the cash from the principal's house came from school accounts.

38.   Police developed probable cause to believe that a cook in a local restaurant was selling heroin out of the restaurant's kitchen. According to the police investigation, the cook's supplier would hide the heroin in crates of vegetables that were delivered to the restaurant every morning. Usually, the vegetable crates were painted blue, but every third Monday, a red crate with heroin hidden inside was delivered to the restaurant.

The investigating officer completed a search warrant application and presented it to the local magistrate, who authorized the warrant. The officer then executed the warrant on a Monday afternoon and found a red crate with heroin inside. The cook was arrested and charged with crimes associated with the heroin.

Shortly before trial, the cook's defense attorney discovered that the magistrate who signed the warrant was not a lawyer and had never even attended law school. If the defense attorney moves to quash the warrant and suppress the evidence for this reason, what is the prosecutor's best argument in response?

A.   The magistrate need only be able to make the probable cause assessment, and need not be a lawyer or law school graduate.

B.   The magistrate's training and education are irrelevant as long as the police have probable cause.

C.   The magistrate would not have signed the warrant if she didn't think she was qualified to make the probable cause assessment.

D.   The magistrate's training and educational background is none of the defense attorney's business.

39. A rookie police officer was assigned to investigate an anonymous tip about a drug ring. The officer conducted a diligent investigation and spent hours drafting a warrant application, requesting permission to search the home of the drug ring's leader. The officer presented the application to an experienced local magistrate, who looked through the application very quickly and then handed it back to the officer, telling him that the application didn't establish probable cause.

Enraged by the magistrate's cursory inspection and confident in his work, the officer took the application to a second magistrate, who promptly issued the warrant. The officer then executed the warrant and found drugs and guns — as he expected — at the home of the drug ring's leader.

The drug ring's leader has been charged with various crimes and has filed a motion to suppress the evidence found in his home. What is the prosecutor's strongest argument in response?

A. The officer shouldn't have ignored the first magistrate, but the warrant was still based on probable cause.

B. The officer did nothing wrong, because drugs and guns were found in the search.

C. The officer was right to be enraged by the first magistrate's cursory inspection.

D. The officer might have been just a rookie, but he still conducted a diligent investigation.

40. The governing council of a small municipality was faced with a budget deficit. According to the municipality's accountant, the deficit could be resolved in three years if the pay structure for the municipality's magistrate was modified significantly. The accountant proposed eliminating the magistrate's annual salary; paying the magistrate on a contingency basis and only for the warrants she actually issues; and reducing the magistrate's health insurance and pension benefits. The council adopted these measures by a 3–1 vote.

Two weeks later, the magistrate signed a search warrant for a private home. The warrant was executed the same day and the police found the items listed on the warrant application.

If the homeowner moves to suppress the evidence, how should the court rule on the motion?

A. The court should deny the motion because the homeowner has no standing to inquire into the magistrate's compensation package.

B. The court should deny the motion because the magistrate's compensation package was changed through a democratic voting process.

C. The court should grant the motion because the magistrate who issued the warrant was not neutral and detached.

D. The court should grant the motion because the homeowner was adversely affected by the council's response to the budget deficit.

41. A 15-year-old boy confessed to his mother that he had been having sex with a 22-year-old teacher at his high school. The mother called the police and an officer was told to interview the boy. In the interview, the boy showed the officer photos on his phone showing him kissing the teacher and engaging in various sexual acts with her. The officer requested an arrest warrant for the teacher, but did not include a probable cause affidavit with his application. When the magistrate asked about the omission, the officer replied:

> Even though this kid doesn't realize it now, he's a molestation victim and there are very real psychological effects of what he's been through. He's going to have enough trouble in life without having to go through the shame and embarrassment of having the details of this sordid situation put into a court document. I interviewed the kid and saw the texts, and there's more than enough probable cause to arrest this awful woman.

After listening to this statement, the magistrate signed the arrest warrant. The teacher was then arrested, and she later challenged the validity of the arrest warrant. How should the court rule on the teacher's motion?

A. The warrant was invalid because the relationship between the teacher and student was consensual.

B. The warrant was invalid because it did not demonstrate probable cause for the teacher's arrest.

C. The warrant was valid because the officer made a legitimate point about protecting the child's privacy rights.

D. The warrant was valid because the officer assured the magistrate that there was sufficient probable cause for the arrest.

42. Police received a report from a hospital that a woman had been raped and was being treated in the emergency room. When an officer interviewed the woman after the medical exam, she identified her attacker as a work colleague who had recently been terminated. The woman said that the colleague came to her house and rang the doorbell; when the woman answered the door, she was surprised to see him but let him inside the house. The woman said that as soon as the door was closed, the colleague threatened to kill her and then raped her at gunpoint.

The officer returned to the station and performed a records search on the colleague, and was able to discover some basic biographical information about him. The officer then completed a warrant application, seeking permission to arrest the colleague and collect his DNA. In his affidavit in support of probable cause, the officer gave the colleague's name, date of birth, and address, and alleged that, earlier that day, the colleague had "talked himself into the home of the victim, threatened her, and raped her at gunpoint."

If the magistrate refuses to sign the warrant application, what will be the most likely reason why?

A. The officer did not verify the woman's claim that the colleague had been recently terminated from his job.

B. The officer did not provide sufficient information in the affidavit to demonstrate probable cause.

C. The officer did not interview the colleague and get his side of the story.

D. The officer did not interview the emergency room doctor to get information about the medical exam.

43. Police developed probable cause to believe that a man had a large collection of illegal weapons and related items — including grenades and rocket launchers — in his suburban home. The investigating officer wrote a detailed affidavit explaining the basis of his probable cause and requested permission to seize "all automatic weapons and devices related to automatic weapons." The officer also completed a warrant form, which, if signed by the magistrate, would be the actual search warrant for the house. The form required information about the "description of person or property to be searched/seized," and the officer filled in this area with the address of the house.

After review of these documents, the magistrate signed the warrant. When the warrant was executed, the police found the weapons they expected to find. The man was charged with various crimes and before his trial, he moved to suppress the weapons seized from his home.

How should the court rule on the motion?

A. The motion should be granted because the officer never specified where in the home he wanted to search for the weapons.

B. The motion should be granted because the warrant did not describe with particularity the items to be seized within the man's home.

C. The motion should be denied because the documents, when read together, described with particularity the items to be seized within the man's home.

D. The motion should be denied because the government's interest in keeping these types of weapons out of residential areas outweighs the homeowner's interests in keeping them.

44. Police obtained a warrant to search a residential house for drugs and guns. On the morning of the warrant's execution, two officers knocked at the front door. After waiting a second or two, the officers opened the unlocked front door and entered the house. As they entered, the homeowner came down the front stairs, bewildered to find the police inside his house. After showing the homeowner the warrant, the officers searched the house and found the drugs and guns as described in the warrant.

The homeowner now faces charges associated with the drugs and guns, and the prosecutor wants to use these items at the upcoming trial. If the prosecutor concedes that the officers violated the "knock and announce" requirement, what is his best argument against suppression?

A. The police only violated the homeowner's rights in a minimal way.

B. The evidence would have been inevitably discovered.

C. The police didn't know the homeowner was home at the time.

D. The evidence would have been destroyed had the officers not acted quickly.

45. A police officer developed probable cause to believe that a local bank president was embezzling funds from several charities. The officer submitted his warrant application to the local magistrate and, as required by state law, requested special permission to arrest the bank president at his home at night. The magistrate agreed that there was ample probable cause to make the arrest, but denied the officer's request for a nighttime arrest.

Purposely ignoring the magistrate's directive, the officer and his partner went to the bank president's house at 3:00 A.M. to make the arrest. The bank president met them at the door and was arrested without incident. In a subsequent search incident to the arrest, the officers found a bag of cocaine in the closet directly inside the front door, beside the exact spot where the bank president was arrested.

Later, the bank president challenged his arrest as unreasonable because the police came to his house at 3:00 A.M. If the prosecutor concedes that the officers should have made the arrest during the daytime, should the magistrate suppress the evidence found in the subsequent search incident to arrest?

A. No, because the officers had a lawful warrant for the bank president's arrest.

B. No, because the officers didn't cause personal injury to the bank president in making the arrest.

C. Yes, because the only way to deter this type of police misconduct is to provide a remedy to the bank president.

D. Yes, because the officers knew that they were violating the magistrate's order to execute the warrant in the daytime.

46. A police officer developed probable cause to believe that two men were growing marijuana in the basement of their shared home. After completing his investigation, the officer applied for and received a warrant to search the home for "live marijuana plants." The following day, the officer executed the warrant but did not find any marijuana plants. However, he discovered several unregistered handguns in a kitchen drawer and a kilo of cocaine wrapped in heavy plastic in the tank of a toilet located in the basement.

If the two men are charged with crimes associated with the guns and cocaine, what is their best argument to suppress these items?

A. The officer must have lied to the magistrate in his affidavit because plants were not found in the house.

B. The warrant did not demonstrate probable cause because plants were not found in the house.

C. The officer exceeded the scope of the warrant by searching in kitchen drawers and the toilet tank.

D. The warrant did not demonstrate probable cause because it did not reference the handguns and the cocaine.

47.　Police received a tip that a hairdresser was selling cocaine to her customers. According to the tip, the hairdresser worked at two different salons; she obtained the cocaine from a supplier at one salon and sold cocaine to customers at a second salon. Through surveillance, police confirmed that the hairdresser sold the cocaine at the second salon, but they were never able to establish how the hairdresser received the drugs.

Police then applied for and received a warrant to search the hairdresser's work area at the second salon. The following day, when police went to execute the warrant, they learned that the salon had been temporarily closed because of an electrical fire. Six weeks later, the salon re-opened and the police executed the warrant. In the hairdresser's work area, police found a can of hair spray with a false bottom; inside the can, police found several baggies of cocaine.

The hairdresser was charged with crimes associated with the cocaine, and has filed a motion to suppress. What is the most likely reason the judge will grant the hairdresser's motion?

A.　The police did not have probable cause at the time they searched the salon.

B.　The police were not able to ascertain the source of the cocaine.

C.　The police were not able to corroborate every aspect of the tip.

D.　The police didn't know the cocaine would be stored in a can of hairspray.

48.　Police developed probable cause to believe that a particular man had robbed a bank. According to a confidential informant, the man had hidden the proceeds of the robbery in the home he shared with his wife.

After obtaining a search warrant for the home, several officers went there to execute the warrant. When they knocked on the front door, a woman answered. The officers showed the woman the warrant and she explained that she and the man had been divorced six months before and that he no longer lived there. The woman also showed the officers a copy of her divorce papers. According to the papers, the man lived in an apartment across town. The police searched the house anyway. They didn't find any evidence relating to the bank robbery but they did discover a methamphetamine lab in the basement.

The woman has been charged with various drug crimes and has filed a motion to suppress. What is the strongest argument in support of her motion?

A.　The motion should be granted because no reasonable officer would have relied on such an obviously unreliable confidential informant.

B.　The motion should be granted because the information supplied by the woman rendered the warrant facially invalid.

C.　The motion should be granted because a reasonable police officer would have realized that the warrant's probable cause was inadequate.

D.　The motion should be granted because the warrant permitted a search for robbery proceeds, and not drugs.

49. Police obtained an arrest warrant for a bank president suspected of embezzling from his bank. The arresting officer drove to the bank president's home and noticed his car in the driveway. She knocked on the door twice, but no one answered. Standing at the front door, the officer could hear voices inside the house, so she entered through the unlocked door. In the vestibule inside the front door, the officer noticed an illegal short-barreled shotgun propped up inside an umbrella stand. The officer arrested the bank president and seized the weapon.

In addition to embezzlement, the bank president now faces a weapons charge; his attorney has filed a motion to suppress the weapon.

How should the court rule on the motion?

A. The motion should be denied because the bank president kept the shotgun in plain view, where anyone could have seen it.

B. The motion should be denied because the arresting officer had the right to enter the bank president's home to arrest him.

C. The motion should be granted because the arresting officer did not have a search warrant for the bank president's house.

D. The motion should be granted because the bank president never consented to the officer's entry into his home.

50. A police officer obtained an arrest warrant for a young man suspected of robbery. The officer went to the young man's apartment to arrest him, but did not find him there. Acting on a tip, the officer next went to the young man's girlfriend's apartment to look for him there. The officer knocked on the door and when the girlfriend answered, he walked inside the apartment and started searching for the young man. He found the young man in the bedroom watching television and snorting cocaine. After arresting the young man, the officer seized the cocaine and arrested the girlfriend.

The girlfriend has been charged with possession of cocaine and has filed a motion to suppress the drugs found at her apartment. What is her strongest argument in support of the motion?

A. The motion should be granted because the officer never established that the cocaine belonged to the girlfriend before arresting her.

B. The motion should be granted because the officer failed to tell the girlfriend about the arrest warrant when she answered the door.

C. The motion should be granted because the officer did not suspect the girlfriend of any wrongdoing prior to entering her apartment.

D. The motion should be granted because the officer conducted a warrantless search of the girlfriend's apartment without just cause.

Warrantless Arrests

51. A police officer arrested a woman for bank robbery, without first obtaining a warrant for the woman's arrest. The officer did not actually witness the woman robbing the bank, but he knew what she looked like because her photograph had been taken by the bank cameras and distributed to all local police officers. When the officer saw the woman on the street, he realized that if he took the time to get an arrest warrant, the woman would likely be gone by the time he returned.

At common law, would the officer have been permitted to arrest the woman under these circumstances?

A. Yes, because the woman committed a felony.

B. Yes, because the officer had probable cause to believe the woman committed a felony.

C. No, because the felony was not committed in the officer's presence.

D. No, because the common law did not permit warrantless arrests.

52. The president of a local school board suspected its treasurer of embezzling money from the school board's account. The president conducted an internal investigation and learned that on the last day of every month, the treasurer went to the bank and transferred funds from the school board account to her own personal account. The president reported his suspicions to the police.

After confirming the transfers between the two accounts, the investigating officer decided to see if he could catch the treasurer in the act. On the last day of the month, the officer posed as a bank employee and sat at a desk where he could see the bank teller's window.

The officer told the bank teller to give him a pre-arranged signal if the treasurer tried to transfer funds between the accounts. After about an hour of waiting, the treasurer came in the bank and requested that the teller transfer the funds. The teller gave the signal and the officer arrested the treasurer under a state law that permits warrantless felony arrests. In a subsequent search incident to arrest, the officer found a small baggie of marijuana in the treasurer's coat pocket.

The treasurer was charged with embezzlement and marijuana possession. Before her trial, she filed a motion to suppress. How will the court rule on the motion?

A. The motion will be granted because the officer arrested the treasurer without a warrant and the Fourth Amendment mandates warrants for all non-violent arrests.

B. The motion will be granted because the officer had no reason to believe that the treasurer posed a threat to his safety or the safety of the bank employees.

C. The motion will be denied because the officer was permitted to arrest the treasurer without a warrant since the suspected crime involved a breach of trust.

D. The motion will be denied because the officer had probable cause to believe a felony had been committed in his presence and arrested the treasurer pursuant to a valid statute.

53. Two hours after a bank robbery was committed, a police officer arrested a man for the crime, and without a warrant. The officer had relied on his dispatcher's description of the robber: a bearded man in a blue shirt. At the time of his arrest, the man had a moustache and no beard, and was wearing a red shirt.

Three days later, the prosecutor filed bank robbery charges against the man, and two days after that, the man was arraigned on the charges. At the arraignment, the judge accepted the man's not guilty plea and set bail at $100,000. Because the man could not afford his bail, he remained in the county jail until his trial.

Did the post-arrest process comply with the Constitution?

A. Yes, because the man appeared before the judge at arraignment and was permitted to enter his plea.

B. Yes, because the prosecutor's decision to charge the man demonstrates that the officer's probable cause determination was correct.

C. No, because the man only loosely matched the dispatcher's description of the bank robber, which is insufficient for probable cause.

D. No, because there has been no judicial determination that the officer had probable cause to arrest the man.

54.   A police officer arrested a college student without a warrant very late on a Thursday evening. The student had been part of a demonstration outside of the college president's house, protesting a recent tuition increase. The following Monday, the student's parents learned of their son's arrest. The parents hired a lawyer and with her help, the student was released late that night — shortly after the arresting officer brought the student to court for a probable cause hearing.

The student was later charged with disorderly conduct and the prosecutor notified the student's lawyer that he planned to use a statement from the student at the upcoming trial. When the lawyer inquired about the circumstances surrounding the statement, she learned that the student had made it on Sunday evening, about 24 hours before his release.

If the lawyer files a motion to suppress the student's statement, what is the most likely ruling from the court?

A.   The statement will not be suppressed because the arresting officer had probable cause for the warrantless arrest and the arrest was conducted in public.

B.   The statement will not be suppressed because the student was held less than 48 business hours before being brought before a magistrate for a probable cause determination.

C.   The statement will be suppressed because it was involuntarily made and was the product of coercion and duress.

D.   The statement will be suppressed because the student was held more than 48 hours before being brought before a magistrate for a probable cause determination.

55.   A woman attended a charity fundraiser where she drank two glasses of wine. On the drive home, the woman crashed her car into a guardrail. Police arrived at the scene and arrested the woman for DUI. Breathalyzer testing showed that the woman's blood alcohol level was well above the legal limit, but she told the arresting officer that she took several daily herbal medications and she believed that one of them had caused the high reading.

The next morning, the woman was brought before a magistrate who, after reviewing the police report, determined that the officers had made a proper arrest. Later that day, the woman's retained attorney arranged for her release. The woman was furious that the attorney had not been told of the proceeding before the magistrate and that she had not been given a chance to present her claim about the herbal medications. The woman asked her attorney to file a formal complaint with the magistrate's supervisor.

How should the attorney respond to the woman's request?

A.   He should file the complaint because the woman was denied her Sixth Amendment right to counsel.

B.   He should file the complaint because the woman was denied her Sixth Amendment right to cross-examine the witnesses against her.

C.   He should not file the complaint because the woman's claim about her herbal medication is better presented at trial, where it can be evaluated by a jury.

D.   He should not file the complaint because the woman is not entitled to an adversarial hearing to determine probable cause for arrest.

56. A college student was pledging a fraternity and as part of his initiation, was driven to a downtown plaza, told to strip down to his underwear, and dance. The student really wanted to be a part of the fraternity and so he complied. As the student danced, a crowd gathered and began to jeer at the student. A nearby police officer arrested the student for being a "disorderly person." In this jurisdiction, such an arrest requires that the arrestee be intoxicated and that he cause a public disturbance.

Later, after the student's parents hired him a lawyer, the lawyer told the district attorney that the arrest was unlawful because the student was not intoxicated at the time of the incident. The district attorney said that he'd continue with the prosecution anyway because the student could have been arrested for indecent exposure. The lawyer filed a motion to dismiss all charges.

If the judge agrees that the student's conduct doesn't meet the statutory definition for being a disorderly person but does meet the definition of indecent exposure, how should she rule on the defense motion?

A. The arrest was valid because the officer had probable cause to believe that a crime had been committed.

B. The arrest was valid because the charge of being a disorderly person is closely related to the charge of indecent exposure.

C. The arrest was invalid because the district attorney can't make up charges after the fact to justify a faulty arrest.

D. The arrest was invalid because the student kept his underwear on and so he can't be guilty of indecent exposure.

57. After an officer observed a car roll through a stop sign, he pulled its driver over to give him a ticket. When the officer approached the car, he realized that he had pulled over his neighbor. The officer did not like his neighbor and had argued with him previously about his overgrown lawn and how it might affect the property value of the officer's house.

The officer decided to arrest the neighbor for rolling through the stop sign. After handcuffing the neighbor, the officer searched him incident to arrest and found an unregistered weapon in the waistband of his jeans. The neighbor was later charged with possession of an unlicensed weapon and his attorney filed a motion to suppress the weapon from the search.

Two weeks later, at a hearing on the motion, the prosecutor conceded in court that state law does not permit an arrest for rolling through a stop sign. Based on this concession, what remedy should the court impose?

A. The court should grant the motion because the neighbor was unlawfully arrested and so the search incident to arrest was accordingly unreasonable.

B. The court should grant the motion because the officer only arrested his neighbor because of their past history, and not for any legitimate reason.

C. The court should deny the motion because the officer had probable cause to believe his neighbor committed an offense.

D. The court should deny the motion because the officer shouldn't be punished for having an opinion and caring about his property values.

58. One weekend afternoon, a police officer went to a private home to arrest the homeowner for possession of child pornography—a felony. When the homeowner answered the door, the officer stepped inside the home and placed the homeowner in handcuffs. He then searched her incident to arrest and found a baggie of marijuana in her pocket.

The homeowner was arrested pursuant to a state statute that permits warrantless felony arrests inside of private homes. The statute states that the arresting officer must "reasonably believe" that the person to be arrested is inside the home and must also "make a reasonable effort to give notice of his authority and purpose to an occupant" of the home prior to entering the home.

The homeowner concedes that the officer had probable cause to arrest her but argues that the arrest was unreasonable. How should the court rule?

A. The arrest was reasonable because it was made pursuant to a valid state statute and because the officer complied with the statute in making the arrest.

B. The arrest was reasonable because the officer had probable cause and so he would have been able to get an arrest warrant later.

C. The arrest was unreasonable because the officer failed to properly identify himself before entering the home and arresting the homeowner.

D. The arrest was unreasonable because warrantless activity in the home, absent exigency or consent, is presumptively unreasonable.

59. After witnessing a woman throw a soiled napkin on the ground, a police officer arrested her for violating a city ordinance against littering. The city ordinance authorized officers to make littering arrests although most officers usually gave verbal warnings or tickets for littering and rarely made arrests.

The arresting officer took the woman to the police station where she was photographed and fingerprinted; after a three-hour wait, the woman was released on her own recognizance. The woman asked her lawyer to fight the charges. Although she admitted that she had violated the littering ordinance, the woman was outraged that she had been arrested for such a low level offense—one that didn't even carry jail time. The lawyer filed a motion to dismiss the charges, arguing that the arrest was unreasonable.

What is the most likely ruling from the court on the woman's motion?

A. The arrest was unreasonable because littering does not carry jail time and there was no compelling need to take the woman into custody.

B. The arrest was unreasonable because the woman's actions did not even meet the common law definition of misdemeanor breach of the peace.

C. The arrest was reasonable because the officer witnessed the woman's littering firsthand and arrested her in public pursuant to a valid ordinance.

D. The arrest was reasonable because the woman's actions are the modern equivalent of common law misdemeanor breach of the peace.

60. An officer on patrol saw a man riding a moped down the street; the man was not wearing a helmet—a misdemeanor under state law. The officer turned on his lights but the man did not notice because the side mirrors on the moped were broken. Frustrated by the man's failure to slow down, the officer drove his cruiser up to the moped and intentionally hit it from behind. As a result, the man lost control of the moped and it skidded to the ground. The officer arrested the man for the helmet violation and then searched him incident to arrest, finding cocaine in his pocket.

After the man spent several weeks in the hospital with broken bones, the local prosecutor charged him with violating the helmet law and possession of cocaine.

What is the man's strongest argument to suppress the evidence found during the search incident to arrest?

A. The evidence should be suppressed because the man was arrested for a misdemeanor, which requires a warrant.

B. The evidence should be suppressed because of the extraordinary means by which the officer conducted the arrest.

C. The evidence should be suppressed because the officer should have turned on his siren before taking more drastic measures to stop the moped.

D. The evidence should be suppressed because the officer failed to get the man appropriate medical help before arresting him and searching him incident to arrest.

Exigent Circumstances

61. Police received a tip that a bartender was selling cocaine from the bar where he worked and that he kept his drug stash in his locker in the employee break room. Police had a confidential informant ("CI") make several controlled drug purchases from the bartender. With each sale, the CI reported that he saw the bartender fetch the cocaine from the break room before selling it to the CI.

Shortly after concluding the investigation but before getting a search warrant, the CI called the lead officer to report that the bartender had quit his job and was working his last shift at the bar—and that the shift was going to end in 20 minutes. The officer rushed over to the bar and, after verifying the CI's claims by speaking with the bar manager, searched the bartender's locker. Inside, the officer found two kilos of cocaine and thousands of dollars in cash.

If the prosecutor wants to use the cocaine against the bartender, what is the strongest argument to support the officer's actions?

A. The search was reasonable because the bartender had a reduced expectation of privacy in his workplace relative to his home.

B. The search was reasonable because the officer had probable cause to believe that cocaine and related evidence would be found in the locker.

C. The search was reasonable because the officer had probable cause to search the locker and inadequate time to get a search warrant.

D. The search was reasonable because the bartender had no expectation of privacy in the locker since he used it to store illegal drugs.

62. Acting on a tip that a man was selling cocaine from his house, police placed the house under surveillance. Over a one-hour period, the surveillance officers watched the man sell something—the officers could not see exactly what—to three different buyers. As the third buyer walked away from the house, one of the officers stopped him and verified that he had just purchased cocaine from the man.

The remaining officers then walked up to the house and rang the bell. When the man answered, the officers arrested him, searched him incident to arrest, and found a vial of cocaine in his pocket. The man was later charged with possession and sale of cocaine and his attorney filed a motion to suppress the cocaine found in the search. At the suppression hearing, the arresting officer explained that he went to the man's house without a warrant because he was concerned that since the third drug purchaser had been stopped so close to the house, the evidence might be destroyed by the time he got a warrant to search the man's house.

How should the court rule on the man's motion?

A. The motion should be granted because the officer did not have any grounds to believe there was an exigent circumstance.

B. The motion should be granted because the officer did not have probable cause to arrest the man for drug crimes.

C. The motion should be denied because the officer had probable cause to arrest the man and he opened his door to the police.

D. The motion should be denied because the officer had probable cause to arrest the man and could therefore search him incident to arrest.

63. Police received a report that a woman was screaming inside a house located in a suburban neighborhood. Two officers rushed to the house; as they approached the front door, the officers heard a woman screaming. The officers drew their weapons, loudly announced their presence, and walked through the screen door and inside the house. Lying on the couch in the room just inside the front door, the officers found a man sleeping. A large marijuana bong sat on the floor next to the couch and a horror movie was playing on the TV. One of the officers used the remote control to mute the TV while the second officer woke the man and arrested him.

The man was charged with marijuana possession and his attorney filed a motion to suppress. Should the judge suppress the marijuana evidence as a fruit of an unlawful entry?

A. Yes, because the officers should have tried to determine whether someone was actually in peril before entering the man's home without a warrant.

B. Yes, because the officers failed to wait a reasonable time before entering and if they had, they would have realized the screams were coming from the TV.

C. No, because even though no one was actually in peril, the entry can be alternatively justified on the basis that the officers were responding to a legitimate noise complaint.

D. No, because the officers had probable cause to believe that someone inside the house was in need of assistance and the officers didn't have time to get a search warrant.

64. After placing a law student under surveillance for several days, police developed probable cause to believe that he was selling cocaine out of his apartment. Police arranged for a confidential informant ("CI") to make several controlled purchases from the law student, and were confident that a magistrate would sign a search warrant for the law student's apartment.

On the day of the last purchase, the CI reported to the police that he had heard the law student was going to move out of his apartment, but didn't know when. That same day, the surveillance officer noticed that the law student had parked a van in front of his apartment building. Later, the surveillance officer saw the law student leave the building with a large cardboard box and place it in the van. The surveillance officer rushed into the apartment, searched it without a warrant, and found two kilos of cocaine.

If the prosecutor argues that exigent circumstances prevented the police from getting a warrant, what is her strongest argument in support?

A. Exigent circumstances existed because the CI reported that the law student was about to move out of his apartment.

B. Exigent circumstances existed because the surveillance officer saw the law student park a van in front of his apartment building.

C. Exigent circumstances existed because the surveillance officer saw the law student carry a large cardboard box from his apartment building to the van.

D. Exigent circumstances existed because of the totality of the circumstances.

65. Late one evening, a patrol officer pulled a driver over for speeding and driving over the center line. After speaking with the driver, the officer strongly suspected that she was drunk, so he asked her to take a breath test to measure her blood alcohol concentration ("BAC"). The driver refused. The officer then drove the driver to the local hospital and asked a phlebotomist to draw the driver's blood. When the blood was analyzed, the driver's BAC was measured at .19—far above the legal limit.

After the driver was charged with drunk driving, she filed a motion to suppress the blood test results and argued that the officer should have gotten a warrant to have her blood drawn. In response, the prosecutor argued that metabolization of alcohol in the bloodstream creates a *per se* exigency that never requires a warrant.

How should the court rule on the motion?

A. The motion should be denied because the prosecutor is right: drunk driving cases present *per se* exigencies, so warrants are never required for blood draws.

B. The motion should be denied because there is no proof that the driver refused to take the blood test, so there is inadequate proof that there was an exigency.

C. The motion should be granted because since the driver was so drunk, her BAC would still have been pretty high if the officer had gotten a warrant.

D. The motion should be granted because exigency cases are better decided on a case-by-case basis, rather than by applying *per se* rules.

66. A state trooper and her partner stopped a car full of teenagers for speeding; the driver was a 16-year old with a probationary license. As the trooper spoke with the 16-year old driver, she noticed that his eyes were glassy, his speech was slurred, and the car smelled like stale beer. The officer also noticed that the backseat passengers were sitting close together and had a sweatshirt draped over the area where their arms were touching.

The trooper directed all of the teenagers to get out of the car; as they did, the trooper saw that a bottle of vodka was hidden under the sweatshirt. While the partner stood with the teenagers several feet from the car, the trooper searched the car and found several miniature bottles of whiskey in the glove box and a case of beer in the trunk. All of the teenagers were then arrested.

The teenaged driver has been charged with various crimes and his lawyer wants to suppress the alcohol found in the car. What is the most likely ruling from the court?

A. The evidence will be suppressed because before the trooper searched the car, she did not demonstrate that she couldn't get a warrant for the search.

B. The evidence will be suppressed because before the trooper searched the car, she did not demonstrate that the evidence would be destroyed without a warrant.

C. The evidence will be admitted because the teenager gave implied consent to the search of his car by driving with a probationary driver's license.

D. The evidence will be admitted because the officer had probable cause to search the car and was not required to demonstrate an independent exigency to search.

67. A police officer chased a suspected drug dealer into an apartment building but did not see which apartment the dealer ran into. Instead, she heard a door slam at the end of the hallway and noticed that the hallway smelled like burning marijuana. The officer walked to the end of the hallway and saw two doors, leading to two separate apartments.

The officer decided that the marijuana smell was coming from behind the door on the left and so she knocked on the door and loudly stated that she was with the police. No one answered, but the officer could hear shuffling inside. The officer announced herself a second time and the shuffling noise continued. The door was unlocked so the officer opened it and walked inside. She found a young man putting marijuana into his garbage disposal. Later, the officer learned that the drug dealer had gone into the other apartment.

The young man was charged with marijuana possession and filed a motion to suppress. How should the court rule on the motion?

A. The officer created the exigency because she only had a 50% chance of getting the right door which is unacceptably low for a warrantless entry into the home.

B. The officer created the exigency because any reasonable person would destroy their marijuana if the police randomly knocked on their door.

C. The officer did not create the exigency because knocking at the door was not illegal and the young man could have answered the door but chose not to.

D. The officer did not create the exigency because the young man tacitly consented to the entry by leaving the front door unlocked while he smoked marijuana.

68. Hospitals in a small college town reported a sharp increase in overdoses of prescription pain medication. Concerned about the trend, the chief of police pledged that he and his officers would go "door to door" the following week in order to educate town residents about the dangers of drug abuse.

As part of this effort, a police officer knocked on the door of a young woman's house. The woman came to the door but did not open it; instead, speaking through the door, she told the officer to go away. The officer replied that he wanted to talk about drug abuse and the woman again asked him to go away. The officer persisted and told the woman that she would be arrested if she didn't open the door. The woman angrily refused and so the officer used a crowbar to force her door open. He found the woman standing inside the door, smoking marijuana and drinking a beer. The officer arrested the woman for disobeying an officer's order and seized her marijuana.

The woman was later charged with marijuana possession; she responded by filing a motion to suppress. If the prosecutor claims that the woman's refusal created an exigency, what is the woman's strongest argument in response?

A. The officer created the exigency by insisting the woman open the door and then forcing the door open when she refused.

B. The officer had no proof the woman was abusing prescription pain medication when he approached her door.

C. The officer was acting as a community caretaker and not as a law enforcement officer and so the woman was entitled to refuse his entry.

D. The officer was required by law to leave the house after the woman refused her consent to enter.

69. Police received a call about a domestic disturbance in a private home; two officers were dispatched to investigate. When the officers arrived at the house, they heard two men inside the house yelling at each other. The first officer knocked on the door and announced that he was a police officer, but the yelling continued. The officers then heard two gunshots and then the house became completely quiet.

Weapons drawn, the officers went through the front door and performed a quick sweep of the house. In an upstairs bedroom, they found a man lying on the floor, shot in the arm and the leg. A gun was on the floor next to him. A second man was sprawled on the bed, shot in the chest and with a gun clutched in one hand and a bag of cocaine in the other. The officers called for an ambulance and then seized the weapons and cocaine.

The man on the bed died from his injuries, but the man on the floor survived. The prosecutor charged him with murder and possession of cocaine. If the defense files a motion to suppress, how should the court rule?

A. The motion should be denied because despite the unlawful entry into the home, the evidence would have been inevitably discovered after the shooting.

B. The motion should be denied because the officers lawfully entered the house and restricted their search to the scope of the exigency.

C. The motion should be granted because the prosecutor cannot establish that the bag of cocaine belonged to the man found on the floor.

D. The motion should be granted because the officers impermissibly converted an investigation of a domestic disturbance into a search for drug evidence.

70. As part of a lengthy investigation, an undercover officer arranged to make a controlled drug purchase from a drug dealer at the drug dealer's apartment. The undercover officer's partner was working with him, posing as a janitor in the apartment building.

With the partner watching nearby, one of the apartment's occupants let the undercover officer inside; moments later, several shots were fired. The partner rushed inside the apartment and found the undercover officer dead. He called for an ambulance and backup and then walked through the apartment and found the drug dealer and two others, wounded but alive. After the backup officers arrived, they spent the rest of the afternoon searching the apartment and found a large amount of drug evidence.

The drug dealer has now been charged with murder and drug crimes and the prosecution wants to use the evidence seized from the apartment at the upcoming trial. If the drug dealer moves to suppress this evidence, what is the most likely ruling from the court?

A. The evidence will be suppressed because warrantless searches and seizures in the home are presumptively unreasonable.

B. The evidence will be suppressed because the backup officers searched the apartment without a warrant, exigency, or consent.

C. The evidence will be admitted because the drug dealer forfeited his Fourth Amendment rights by killing the undercover officer.

D. The evidence will be admitted because the backup officers acted under the homicide scene exception to the Fourth Amendment.

71. Police received a call from a middle-aged woman who explained that she lived out of town and that she had not been able to reach her elderly aunt for several days. The woman explained that she was her aunt's legal guardian, but the aunt lived alone and was in ill health. The woman was concerned that something might have happened to her aunt and asked the police if they could do anything to help.

Two officers went to the aunt's home and rang the doorbell several times, but the aunt did not answer. One officer peered in a window next to the front door and saw an elderly woman lying on the couch with some newspapers on the floor next to her. The officers called for an ambulance and broke down the door. When they got inside, they discovered that the aunt was not dead or ill; she was just napping on the couch.

The aunt has filed a complaint with the officers' supervisor, claiming that they had no legal right to enter her home without a warrant, consent, or exigency. What is the most accurate response that the supervisor can give?

A. The warrantless entry was reasonable because the middle-aged woman, the aunt's legal guardian, gave implied consent for the entry.

B. The warrantless entry was reasonable because the officers believed that the aunt needed medical attention, which is a legitimate exigency.

C. The warrantless entry was unreasonable because the officers reasonably believed that the aunt was dead and so there was no exigency.

D. The warrantless entry was unreasonable because the officers never bothered to speak to neighbors or friends to corroborate the middle-aged woman's story.

72. Police received a call from a woman who claimed that her neighbor was growing marijuana in his backyard. The woman gave her name and address, and invited the police to come into her back yard to take a look for themselves. An officer went to the woman's house, and—sure enough—while standing in her backyard, he was able to see several mature marijuana plants growing in the neighbor's backyard.

After thanking the woman, the officer went into the neighbor's backyard and seized the marijuana plants. When later asked by his supervisor why he took the plants, the officer explained that he was concerned that the neighbor might destroy the plants before he had time to get a search warrant for the backyard.

How should the supervisor respond to the officer's statement?

A. The officer's warrantless actions were reasonable because the homeowner could have learned of the woman's call to police, and destroyed the plants at any time.

B. The officer's warrantless actions were reasonable because the plants were mature and were likely about to be harvested—a form of destruction of evidence.

C. The officer's warrantless actions were unreasonable because even if the plants were harvested, the marijuana would just be altered and not destroyed.

D. The officer's warrantless actions were unreasonable because there was no proof of any exigency on these facts, just the prospect of possible future exigencies.

73. Late one night, a fire broke out at a furniture store. Firemen managed to put out the blaze, but the building was completely destroyed. As the firemen were putting out the last of the fire, the fire marshal walked through the building to conduct a preliminary investigation and discovered an empty metal gasoline container. Suspecting arson, the fire marshal seized the container. However, visibility was poor because of the residual smoke and so the fire marshal decided to leave and come back later.

Two days later, the fire marshal returned to continue his investigation. Walking through the damaged building, he took a series of photographs of areas that he thought showed that the fire had been intentionally set. One week later and acting on the fire marshal's recommendation, the prosecutor charged the building owner with arson.

If the building owner files a motion to suppress the evidence taken from the building, how should the court rule on the motion?

A. Only the photographs should be suppressed because the fire marshal took them after the exigency had ended.

B. Only the container should be suppressed because the fire marshal seized it as part of a criminal investigation and without a warrant.

C. All the evidence should be suppressed because the fire marshal searched the building without a warrant, exigency, or consent.

D. All the evidence should be admitted because a person who sets fire to his own building cannot claim an expectation of privacy in that building.

74. An undercover officer made a controlled purchase of cocaine from a dealer at the dealer's house. As he drove away from the house, the undercover officer called his partner and told him that the sale had been completed. The partner drove to the dealer's house and saw her standing on the sidewalk, speaking to a neighbor. The partner stopped his car, identified himself as a police officer, and told the dealer that she was under arrest.

The dealer turned and ran into her house, but the partner caught her in the vestibule, just inside the front door. In a subsequent search incident to arrest, the partner found cash and packets of cocaine in the dealer's pocket. Later, on the drive down the police station, the dealer remarked that she had been selling cocaine for several years but had never been arrested.

The dealer was later charged with cocaine distribution. The dealer's attorney filed a motion to suppress, arguing that the cocaine, cash, and statement were fruits of an unlawful entry into the dealer's house. What is the prosecutor's strongest response?

A. The partner had probable cause for the dealer's arrest and was in hot pursuit when he arrested her in her house.

B. The partner had probable cause for the dealer's arrest and the dealer resisted arrest by running into her house.

C. The partner had probable cause for the dealer's arrest and the dealer disobeyed the partner's direct order.

D. The partner had probable cause for the dealer's arrest and was required to recover the cash from the controlled purchase.

75. Police received a call from a woman claiming that the suspect in a recent gas station robbery and murder was staying with one of the tenants in her apartment complex. The woman told police that she had seen the suspect enter the apartment about thirty minutes prior and that she thought he was still inside the apartment.

Officers went to the apartment building and securely surrounded it. The lead detective then called the apartment where the suspect was alleged to be hiding; a woman answered the phone. The detective identified himself and told the woman that the suspect should come out of the apartment. During the conversation, the detective heard a male voice in the background say, "tell them I left." On the detective's orders, the officers entered the apartment and found the suspect hiding in a closet. The detective arrested the suspect and drove him down to the station; during the drive, the suspect made an incriminating statement.

If the suspect is charged with felony murder, what is his strongest argument to have his statement suppressed?

A. The statement should be suppressed because the detective didn't have probable cause to believe that the suspect was hiding in the apartment.

B. The statement should be suppressed because there were no exigent circumstances to support the warrantless entry.

C. The statement should be suppressed because the detective failed to corroborate the report that the suspect was in the apartment.

D. The statement should be suppressed because the detective did not first try to obtain consent before entering the apartment.

76. A homeowner called the police to report that there had been a shooting at her house. The homeowner told the dispatcher that her husband and teenaged son had gotten into a fight, the fight had escalated, and her son had used a handgun to shoot his father in the leg.

Two officers went to the house and arrived at the same time as an ambulance; the officers walked into the house, followed by the EMTs. In the kitchen, they found the homeowner sitting at a table, sobbing. A middle-aged man was sitting on the ground, bleeding from a wound on the leg. A handgun was lying on the floor next to him. One of the officers seized the handgun while the second officer began to take a detailed report from the woman. In the meantime, the EMTs provided medical assistance to the man.

The son was later charged with assault with a deadly weapon and the prosecutor announced that he would use the handgun as evidence at the son's trial. The son moved to suppress the handgun. What is the most likely ruling from the court?

A. The handgun is admissible because the homeowner gave implied consent to the entry when she called the police and reported the shooting.

B. The handgun is admissible because it was found in plain view, as the officers were responding to a legitimate exigency.

C. The handgun is inadmissible because there is no crime in a private person owning a handgun, and the officers just assumed it was illegal.

D. The handgun is inadmissible because the officers never requested consent to enter the private home, a protected area under the Fourth Amendment.

77. Late one evening, police received a call about a loud party in a fraternity house. Two officers went to the house and entered it after no one answered their repeated knocking at the front door. In the living room of the house, the officers found a group of college students dancing to loud music. One of the officers turned off the music and began to speak to the students about the noise their party was generating. As he did so, he noticed several kegs of beer at one end of the room, and so he asked the students to show him their IDs.

In the meantime, the second officer went upstairs to see if any underage drinkers were hiding upstairs. The officer didn't find anyone but he did find a scale and several pounds of marijuana sitting on the floor of a bedroom closet.

The officers later established the name of the 19-year old student who occupied the bedroom and arrested him. The prosecutor filed marijuana possession charges against him and the student's attorney filed a motion to suppress. What is the most likely ruling on the motion?

A. The court will deny the motion because legal minors do not receive full protection of the Fourth Amendment until they are 21 years old.

B. The court will deny the motion because the officer found the evidence in plain view when he looked in the closet for underage drinkers.

C. The court will grant the motion because the officer had no right to look upstairs and so the evidence was not found in plain view.

D. The court will grant the motion because officers may not make a warrantless entry into a home for a low-level violation like the one here.

78. Around 3 AM one morning, police received a call about a noisy party at a house in a residential neighborhood. Two officers went to the house to investigate. When they arrived, they found several teenagers standing in the driveway and drinking beer. The officers could also hear yelling coming from inside the house and so they bypassed the teenagers and approached the back of the house, where the yelling was loudest.

Standing at a screen door, the officers saw one teenager and several adults, fighting inside a kitchen. The officers saw the teenager punch one of the adults and continued to watch as the other adults tried to restrain the teenager. The officers knocked and announced themselves, but no one noticed them. The officers then entered the home, stopped the fight, and arrested the teenager and two of the adults.

The arrestees later filed a civil rights suit, challenging the officers' right to enter a private home without a warrant or consent. How should the court respond?

A. The warrantless entry was unreasonable because the officers were motivated, at least in part, by the desire to make arrests.

B. The warrantless entry was unreasonable because the officers were not permitted to enter unless they witnessed a concrete threat to human life.

C. The warrantless entry was reasonable because the arrestees forfeited their right to exclude the officers when they didn't respond to the officers' knock at the door.

D. The warrantless entry was reasonable because the officers witnessed an ongoing crime and otherwise behaved reasonably in entering the home.

79. Police responding to a noise complaint in a residential neighborhood found a car parked at an odd angle in the driveway; the car's front end was smashed in. The officers also saw that a couple of the fence posts along the driveway had been knocked over, there was blood on the driveway, and blood leading from the car to the front door of the house.

One of the officers knocked on the front door; a man came to the front door and yelled at the officer to go away. The man's hand was wrapped in a bloody towel. The man went back into the house and continued yelling. After waiting a few minutes, the officer went into the house to check on the man; the man pointed a shotgun at the officer, so the officer walked back out.

Later, the man was arrested and charged with assaulting a police officer. The prosecutor wants to use the officer's statement that the man threatened him, but the man claims that the statement is a fruit of an unlawful entry. Is the man right?

A. The man is right; no exigency existed because the officer suspected the man had a cut on his hand, which is not enough for a warrantless entry into a home.

B. The man is right; no exigency existed because a report of a noise violation can never be enough to support a warrantless entry into a home.

C. The man is wrong; an exigency existed because the man had smashed his car and fence posts and the officer had to enter the house to find out why.

D. The man is wrong; an exigency existed because the officer reasonably believed that a person might be in danger inside the house and that the man needed help.

80. An anonymous caller reported that he had just seen a car drive into a ditch. The caller said that he tried to keep the driver at the scene but she crawled out of the car and walked away.

When police arrived at the ditch, they found the car registration in the glove compartment and realized that the driver lived less than a mile away. The officers went to the driver's house and found the front door open. After ringing the doorbell several times without response, the officers walked inside. In the living room, they found a woman passed out on the couch. The officers arrested the woman and brought her to a hospital for a blood test to determine the blood alcohol concentration ("BAC") in her blood.

The woman was later charged with "drunk driving (first offense)" — a civil infraction in this jurisdiction — based on the results of the BAC test. The woman filed a motion to suppress the blood test results. What is the most likely ruling on the motion?

A. The motion will be denied; the officers had reasonable suspicion to believe the woman had been driving drunk which is a legitimate exigency to support the warrantless entry into her home.

B. The motion will be denied; the officers had probable cause to believe the woman had been driving drunk, which is a legitimate exigency for the warrantless entry into her home.

C. The motion will be granted; the woman was able to walk home from the accident, so there was no exigency to support the warrantless entry into her home.

D. The motion will be granted; the only potential exigency confronting the officers was the need to preserve the woman's blood, which is insufficient to support the warrantless entry into her home.

Plain View

81. A father and his teenaged son were having dinner at home when the son began to choke on something he'd eaten. The father stood behind the son and tried to dislodge the item by administering compressions, but the son continued to choke. The father called 911.

Two EMTs arrived in an ambulance moments later and stopped the son from choking to death. An officer on patrol arrived just as the EMTs were packing their equipment and getting ready to leave the house. When the officer walked into the house, she noticed a large marijuana bong sitting on a coffee table adjacent to the front door. Because the officer had come to the house on a medical call, she left the bong alone. Later, the officer asked her supervisor whether she would have been permitted to lawfully seize it.

What is the correct response to the officer's question?

A. The officer would have been permitted to lawfully seize the bong because she was responding to an exigency.

B. The officer would have been permitted to lawfully seize the bong because it was discovered in plain view.

C. The officer would not have been permitted to lawfully seize the bong because neither the father nor the son consented to her entry in the home.

D. The officer would not have been permitted to lawfully seize the bong because she was at the house on a medical call, not a crime-related call.

82. Police received an anonymous call that a homeowner was growing marijuana in his home. According to the caller, the home had a large window that faces the street and the homeowner had several potted marijuana plants sitting on a table, just inside the window.

An officer went to investigate and, standing on the sidewalk in front of the house, saw just what the caller had reported: several mature marijuana plants, sitting on a table next to the window. The officer returned to his precinct and applied for a warrant to search the house for marijuana plants. The warrant was issued and the officer later executed the warrant and seized the plants.

The homeowner was charged with cultivation and possession of marijuana. At a hearing on his motion to suppress, the homeowner's lawyer argued that the requirements of the plain view exception were not met. What is the prosecutor's strongest argument in response?

A. The plain view doctrine's requirements are met here because the officer viewed the marijuana plants while standing on a public sidewalk.

B. The plain view doctrine's requirements are met here because the officer saw the marijuana plants literally in plain view.

C. The plain view doctrine has no application here because the officer's viewing of the evidence didn't implicate the homeowner's Fourth Amendment rights.

D. The plain view doctrine has no application here because it exists to restrict police misconduct and the officer did nothing wrong.

83. Police received a complaint that a young woman was going door-to-door in a residential neighborhood, trying to collect money for a cancer charity. The caller complained that the young woman had refused to produce her identification, so the caller suspected that the young woman was not licensed by the city to conduct residential solicitations.

An officer was sent to take a report from the caller. When the officer arrived at the caller's home, the caller was on the phone. She invited the officer inside and told him to have a seat on the couch while she finished her call. Five minutes later, the caller returned to the living room to speak to the officer. However, while the officer had been waiting he had seized several marijuana cigarettes that were sitting in an ashtray on the coffee table in front of the couch. The officer took the caller's report and left. He later told his supervisor about the marijuana cigarettes.

The caller was charged with marijuana possession and filed a motion to suppress. What is the prosecutor's strongest argument in response to the motion?

A. The caller consented to the discovery of the marijuana when she invited the officer into her home.

B. The caller instigated the investigation and so has no standing to complain about the officer's discovery of the marijuana.

C. The caller didn't adequately hide her drugs and so has no standing to complain about the officer's discovery of the marijuana.

D. The caller consented to the officer's entry into her home and so the officer viewed the marijuana from a lawful vantage point.

84. Police obtained a warrant to search a private home for evidence related to a bank robbery: a black ski mask, canvas bags belonging to the bank, and weapons. Four officers were assigned to execute the warrant. Inside the house, one of the officers stayed with the homeowner and the other three fanned out, looking for the items listed in the warrant.

One of the officers was looking through a dresser in an upstairs bedroom when he saw a small square jewelry box, sitting in the corner of the drawer next to a pile of underwear. The officer opened the box and found a small plastic bag containing white powder. Suspecting that the bag contained cocaine, the officer seized the bag and then continued to look for evidence related to the bank robbery. Later testing revealed that the powder was, in fact, cocaine.

Police were unable to find anything related to the bank robbery, but when the prosecutor was informed of the cocaine, she filed drug possession charges against the homeowner. The homeowner moved to suppress. How should the court rule on the motion?

A. The evidence was not found in plain view because the warrant only permitted the officer to seize evidence related to the bank robbery.

B. The evidence was not found in plain view because the officer was not lawfully permitted to look in the jewelry box.

C. The evidence was found in plain view because the officer was lawfully permitted to look in the homeowner's underwear drawer.

D. The evidence was found in plain view because the homeowner failed to take proper steps to hide his cocaine from police view.

85. Police received an emergency call reporting gunshots in an apartment building. Two officers rushed to the given address, but no one seemed to be home. The officers broke the door down and did a quick sweep of the apartment; they didn't find any people or weapons inside the apartment.

As they were leaving, the officers noticed a pile of sheets next to the front door. Knowing that an armored car had been robbed two weeks prior, the officers were curious whether the pile might contain the canvas bags used to hold the cash from the robbery. The officers rifled through the pile and quickly found two canvas bags printed with the name of one of the banks. The officers went through the rest of the pile and discovered a total of six canvas bags, each printed with the bank's name.

The apartment tenant was later charged with bank robbery. If he files a motion to suppress, what is his strongest argument in support?

A. The canvas bags were not found in plain view because the officers' act of reaching into the pile constituted a Fourth Amendment search.

B. The canvas bags were not found in plain view because the officers' entry into the apartment without a warrant was presumptively unreasonable.

C. The canvas bags were not found in plain view because the officers' continued presence in the apartment after the exigency concluded was unreasonable.

D. The canvas bags were not found in plain view because the officers were not permitted to turn a shooting investigation into a bank robbery investigation.

86. After a woman was charged with embezzling from her local parent-teacher association, two officers went to her house to arrest her. The officers rang the doorbell and the woman answered the door. The officers showed the woman the arrest warrant and she reluctantly let them step inside so that her neighbors wouldn't see her being placed in handcuffs.

As the first officer was adjusting the handcuffs, he heard an unidentifiable noise from the back of the house. The officer asked the woman if anyone else was in the house and she replied, "Oh, that's just my husband. By the way, he'll kill you both if he sees me in these handcuffs." The second officer drew his weapon and walked to the back of the house. In the kitchen, he found a dog sleeping on the floor and a crack pipe on the kitchen counter. The second officer seized the crack pipe. The second officer then swept the rest of the house but did not find the husband.

The woman was later charged with possession of drug paraphernalia and her lawyer filed a motion to suppress the crack pipe from her trial. How should the court rule?

A. The crack pipe is admissible because the officer found it while conducting a lawful protective sweep of the house.

B. The crack pipe is admissible because the woman threatened the officers when she said her husband would kill them.

C. The crack pipe is inadmissible because warrantless activity within the home is presumptively unreasonable.

D. The crack pipe is inadmissible because a sleeping dog can't make any sort of noise that would support this type of warrantless search.

87. Late one night, a state trooper pulled a driver over for speeding. The officer approached the car and used his flashlight to see the driver while they spoke. The driver willingly supplied the officer with his license and registration but before the officer returned to his car to write the ticket, the officer shone the flashlight into the back seat. Sitting across the back seat was a sawed-off shotgun. The officer arrested the driver and seized the shotgun.

After the driver was charged with crimes associated with the shotgun, his attorney filed a motion to suppress it from the driver's upcoming trial. The attorney argued that the officer's use of the flashlight constituted a search under the Fourth Amendment and so the shotgun was not found in plain view.

What is the prosecutor's best response?

A. The shotgun was found in plain view because the flashlight didn't expose anything in the car that couldn't be seen by a random passer-by.

B. The shotgun was found in plain view because the flashlight didn't expose any personal information about the driver.

C. The shotgun was found in plain view because the flashlight exposed an illegal weapon and the driver cannot claim an expectation of privacy in illegal evidence.

D. The shotgun was found in plain view because the flashlight exposed an illegal weapon and the officer has a right to protect himself from danger.

88. After a lengthy investigation, police obtained a search warrant to search a private home for cocaine and heroin. While executing the warrant, one of the officers searched through the drawers of a dresser located in the master bedroom. In one drawer, the officer found an envelope marked "kids" on the outside, with several film negative strips inside. The officer picked up one of the strips, held it up to the light coming from a nearby window, and saw that the strip contained images of naked children. The officer seized the entire envelope and continued his search for drugs.

One week later, the officer showed the negatives to the local DA. The DA asked the officer why he had waited so long to hand them over and the officer replied that he'd been very busy and preoccupied at work. The DA then viewed the negatives, decided the images on the negatives were pornographic, and charged the homeowner with possession of child pornography.

If the homeowner seeks to suppress the envelope and its contents from his upcoming trial, what is his strongest argument in support?

A. The officer exceeded the scope of the warrant when he seized the envelope containing the film negatives.

B. The envelope and its contents belong to the homeowner's roommate.

C. The officer delayed in showing the evidence to the DA, which limits the DA's ability to link the negatives to the homeowner.

D. The envelope and its contents were not seized in plain view.

89. A police officer pulled a driver over for rolling through a stop sign. After speaking with the driver for a few minutes, the officer decided to give her a verbal warning instead of a ticket. As was his usual practice, the officer asked the driver to get out the car so he could administer the warning.

As the driver opened her car door, a prescription pill bottle fell out of the car. The officer leaned down to pick up the bottle; he noticed that it was filled with powder and that it didn't have a prescription label on it. The officer asked the driver what was in the pill bottle. She said nothing. He asked the question a second time and the driver replied that the powder was cocaine. The officer arrested the driver for cocaine possession, and she was charged with the crime the following week.

If the driver later files a motion to suppress, how should the court rule on her motion?

A. The motion should be granted because the officer could not identify the contents of the pill bottle on his own.

B. The motion should be granted because the officer only saw the contents of the pill bottle after he picked it up.

C. The motion should be denied because the officer found the cocaine in plain view.

D. The motion should be denied because the officer was following his usual practice when he asked the driver to get out of the car.

90. After a diligent investigation, an officer believed that he had probable cause to search an apartment for evidence related to a gas station robbery. In the officer's warrant application, he requested permission to search the apartment for weapons, credit card slips, and scratch-off lottery tickets. The magistrate authorized a search for weapons and credit card slips only, and told the officer that she didn't think he had probable cause to believe the lottery tickets were in the apartment.

Later that afternoon, the officer executed the warrant. While searching through a clothes closet for weapons, the officer saw several hundred lottery tickets scattered on the floor. The officer collected the tickets and continued his search. After contacting the state's lottery association, the officer established that the tickets had come from the robbery.

The apartment tenant was charged with robbery and theft of the lottery tickets. If he moves to suppress the lottery tickets from his trial, how should the court rule on the motion?

A. The motion should be granted because the magistrate told the officer that he hadn't established probable cause that the lottery tickets were at the apartment.

B. The motion should be granted because the officer suspected he'd find the lottery tickets in the apartment and so the plain view exception does not apply.

C. The motion should be denied because the tenant cannot claim an expectation of privacy in evidence he leaves out for anyone to see.

D. The motion should be denied because the officer discovered the lottery tickets in plain view, despite the fact that the discovery was not inadvertent.

91. A patrol officer saw a man smoking a cigarette and staring through the window of a jewelry store. The man then made a quick call on his cell phone. A few minutes later, a car drove by and stopped where the man was standing; the man nodded at the store with his head and the car drove away.

Thoroughly suspicious, the officer approached the man and asked him what he was doing. The man tried to walk away, but the officer placed his hand on the man's shoulder and stopped him. The officer then frisked the exterior of the man's clothing and felt two guns: one in each of the man's jacket pockets. The officer retrieved the weapons and arrested the man.

The man was charged with being a felon in possession of a firearm, and his lawyer filed a motion to suppress. What is the most appropriate ruling from the court?

A. The officer was not permitted to retrieve the weapons because, while the officer had a right to stop the man and frisk him, he only had reasonable suspicion to believe he felt weapons in the man's pockets.

B. The officer was not permitted to retrieve the weapons because, while the officer had a right to stop the man and frisk him, he did not have probable cause to believe he felt weapons in the man's pockets.

C. The officer was permitted to retrieve the weapons because the officer had a right to stop the man and frisk him, and had probable cause to believe he felt weapons in the man's pockets.

D. The officer was permitted to retrieve the weapons because the officer had a right to stop the man and frisk him because the man's actions showed that he posed a specific threat to the police officer.

92. An officer on highway patrol saw a car drive past him at a high rate of speed, far above the posted speed limit. The officer turned on his siren and lights, and pulled the driver over. While speaking with the driver, the officer noticed that the driver's eyes were glassy and that he spoke very slowly and repeated himself a couple of times. The officer asked the driver if he'd been drinking or using any drugs, but the driver said no. The officer didn't believe the driver, and directed him to get out of the car.

Once the driver was standing in front of him, the officer asked him if he was carrying any weapons; the driver replied, "maybe yes and maybe no." He then started to laugh. The officer quickly moved the driver up against his car and frisked him. Inside the driver's rear jeans pocket, the officer felt a small cylinder that rattled when the officer moved it. The officer reached into the pocket and pulled out a pill bottle filled with tablets. Later investigation revealed that the tablets were narcotics and the man did not have a prescription for them.

If, in a subsequent suppression hearing, the driver challenges the officer's right to retrieve the pill bottle from his pocket, what is his strongest argument in support?

A. The officer lacked reasonable articulable suspicion to believe that the driver was armed and dangerous.

B. The officer lacked probable cause to believe that the cylinder in the driver's pocket was a weapon.

C. The officer lacked the authority to order the driver to get out of the car because he stopped him for speeding.

D. The officer lacked probable cause to believe that the driver was armed and dangerous.

93. Police obtained a search warrant to search a private home for methamphetamine and related paraphernalia. When the officers went to execute the warrant, no one answered the door, so the officers forced their way inside. For their safety, the officers first conducted a protective sweep of both floors of the house and the basement. The two officers who swept the basement were immediately struck by a strong odor that, based on their training and experience, they believed was marijuana.

On closer inspection of the basement, the officers realized that the odor was coming from ten zipped duffel bags stacked along one wall of the basement. When the officers completed the search of the rest of the house, they returned to the basement and seized the duffel bags. Later, they opened the duffel bags and discovered that they each contained processed marijuana.

The homeowner was eventually arrested and charged with a long list of drug crimes; he later filed a motion to suppress. What is the most likely ruling from the suppression court?

A. The motion will be granted because the officers only smelled the evidence, and did not see it in plain view.

B. The motion will be granted because the officers did not open the bags in the house, so they did not know for certain what they contained.

C. The motion will be denied because the marijuana was detected in "plain smell," a variation of the plain view doctrine.

D. The motion will be denied because the officers had a good reason for exceeding the scope of the warrant.

94. Two patrol officers stopped a woman for driving 10 miles per hour over the posted speed limit. As the first officer approached the woman's car to request her license and registration, he noticed smoke coming out of the window of her car. When he got to the car, he smelled burning marijuana. The officer asked the woman if she had been smoking marijuana but she did not reply and just giggled. The officer directed the woman to get out of the car.

While the second officer stood with the woman a few feet from the car, the first officer searched the car and found an envelope with marijuana, resting in the console between the two front seats. He also searched inside the glove box and found a baggie of cocaine there. The officer seized both items and arrested the woman.

If the woman is charged with marijuana and cocaine possession and if she files a motion to suppress, what is the most likely ruling from the suppression court?

A. The motion will be granted; the officer turned a routine traffic stop into a drug search without a warrant, consent, or adequate suspicion.

B. The motion will be granted; the officer exceeded the scope of his suspicion when he searched the glove box for cocaine.

C. The motion will be denied; the officer detected the marijuana smoke in plain smell and the other evidence was found during a lawful automobile search.

D. The motion will be denied; the officer detected the marijuana smoke in plain smell and the other evidence was found in plain view.

95. A state trooper was on patrol when he spotted a luxury car without a license plate. The officer pulled the driver over and asked the driver for his license and the car's registration. When the driver could not produce the registration papers, the officer wrote down the car's Vehicle Identification Number ("VIN") and called his dispatcher to find out if anyone had reported the car stolen.

The dispatcher confirmed that the driver owned the car but also reported that the driver had a felony record and that a warrant for his arrest for drug trafficking had been issued two days prior. The officer arrested the driver and placed him—handcuffed—in the back of his patrol car. The officer then searched the car and found an unregistered weapon underneath the front passenger seat. The officer did not find any drugs.

If the driver is charged with being a felon in possession of a weapon and if he files a motion to suppress, how should the court rule on the motion?

A. The motion should be granted because the officer arrested the driver for drug trafficking but never found drugs in the car.

B. The motion should be granted because the officer had to check the VIN to see if the car was stolen, so the plain view exception doesn't apply.

C. The motion should be denied because the officer found the gun in plain view while conducting a lawful search of the car incident to the driver's arrest.

D. The motion should be denied because the driver, as a convicted felon, has no expectation of privacy when police suspect he possesses drugs.

Searches Incident to Arrest

96. Two police officers drove to a private home to arrest its owner, who had been charged with cruelty to animals. The officers rang the doorbell and the homeowner answered the door. The officers presented her with a copy of the criminal complaint and the arrest warrant. The first officer then arrested the homeowner, patting down the exterior of her clothing. As he was completing the pat down, the second officer opened a coat closet immediately inside the front door, and looked inside. Sitting on the floor of the closet, next to a vacuum cleaner, was a sawed-off shotgun. The second officer seized the weapon.

The homeowner now faces additional charges related to the weapon from the coat closet. If she files a motion to suppress it from her upcoming trial, what is the most likely ruling on the motion?

A. The motion will be granted because the officer lacked any suspicion that the coat closet harbored a person who posed a threat to him.

B. The motion will be granted because there was a very low likelihood the officer would find a wounded animal in the coat closet.

C. The motion will be denied because the authority to arrest carried with it the authority to conduct a limited, warrantless, and suspicionless search.

D. The motion will be denied because the officer was only protecting himself and his fellow officer by seizing the weapon.

97. Police received a call reporting a domestic dispute at a private residence. An officer responded to the call and knocked on the front door. A woman answered the door; she had a black eye and was crying. The officer requested permission to enter the home and the woman agreed and led him into the kitchen.

A man was sitting at the kitchen table, smoking a cigarette. The officer asked what had happened and the woman explained that the two got into a fight about their taxes. The man interrupted her and said that the couple owed a significant amount of money for their taxes but the woman had spent their savings clothes shopping. The man then admitted to punching the woman. The officer arrested the man for domestic assault. As part of a subsequent search incident to arrest, the officer looked inside a backpack which was sitting on a kitchen chair next to where the man had been sitting. The officer found a small stash of marijuana at the bottom of the backpack.

The prosecutor charged the man with marijuana possession and the man's attorney filed a motion to suppress. If the court decides to deny the suppression motion, what is the best reason for doing so?

A. The backpack may have contained evidence of other crimes.

B. The backpack may have contained a weapon.

C. The backpack may have contained information about the man's identity.

D. The backpack may have contained documents to corroborate the man's story.

98. A police officer was assigned to foot patrol at a community art fair. As he was walking down the street, he smelled the unmistakable odor of burning marijuana. The officer continued walking and noticed a man standing in an alley behind a bar smoking marijuana. The officer arrested the man and thoroughly searched the pockets of the man's jacket and pants. In the man's back pocket, the officer found a nearly empty plastic bag with a very small amount of marijuana.

The prosecutor filed misdemeanor marijuana possession charges against the man; the man moved to suppress the drugs found in his pocket. In his suppression motion, the man argued that the officer only had the right to frisk him for weapons, and nothing more.

What is the most likely ruling on the man's motion?

A. The motion will be denied because the search was permitted in this situation to preserve evidence of the crime.

B. The motion will be denied because the thorough search yielded evidence that established that the man broke the law.

C. The motion will be granted because the officer knew the man was unarmed and had no reason to search him more thoroughly.

D. The motion will be granted because this kind of thorough search is not permitted in low-level misdemeanor arrests.

99. One day at dusk, a state police officer saw a car being driven on the highway without its headlights on. Until recently, the officer had worked for a small municipality, and he had just joined the state police. Eager to impress his new supervisor by making lots of arrests, the officer pulled the car over and arrested its driver for violating a state law requiring use of headlights after sunset. In a subsequent search incident to arrest, the officer found a small baggie of cocaine in the driver's pocket.

The officer took the driver to the local barracks and began the booking process. As the officer was completing some initial paperwork, his supervisor walked into the room and began to laugh. The supervisor then said, "You idiot! Don't you know that state law doesn't allow you to arrest people for headlight violations?"

Regardless of the officer's mistake, the state attorney general charged the driver with possession of cocaine, and the driver's attorney filed a motion to suppress. How should the court rule on the motion?

A. The motion should be denied because the officer believed in good faith that he had the authority to arrest the driver.

B. The motion should be denied because the arrest was based on probable cause that a crime had been committed.

C. The motion should be granted because the arrest was made in violation of state law.

D. The motion should be granted because the officer made the arrest to impress his supervisor, not because he thought the arrest was appropriate.

100. A police officer was assigned to patrol the downtown area of a local college town on the night of a big football game. Shortly after the home team lost, people started leaving the bars to go home.

The officer saw a young man stumbling as he left a bar. After walking about 30 feet, the young man leaned over into some bushes and vomited. The officer approached the young man to ask if he was okay; as he did so, the officer realized that the young man was the teenaged son of a neighbor.

The officer wrote the young man a ticket for underage drinking, told him to go directly home and drink some water, and then go to bed. However, before permitting the teen to leave, the officer performed a quick search of his clothing and found marijuana in the teen's back pocket. The officer then wrote the young man a second ticket for possession of marijuana and sent him on his way.

The teen was later charged with possession of marijuana. If the teen's attorney files a motion to suppress the marijuana and the court grants the motion, what is the most likely reason for the court's ruling?

A. The officer did not arrest the teen, and so he lacked the authority to search him.

B. The officer did not have reason to believe that there would be evidence of underage drinking in the teen's possession.

C. The teen did not pose any sort of threat to the officer's safety.

D. The teen was clearly ill, and so the search was unwarranted.

101. After running a routine warrant check for a man stopped for a moving violation, the officer learned that the man was wanted for a bank robbery. The officer arrested the man without incident. Before placing the man in the patrol car, the officer also conducted a frisk of the man's clothing to check for weapons. Finding none, the officer drove the man to the police station, where, like all arrestees, the man was fingerprinted, photographed, and ordered to change from his street clothes into a county-issued jumpsuit. This process took about an hour.

Before putting the man's street clothes into storage, the officer went through the pockets of his pants. In a back pocket, the officer found a small sheet of paper with a hand-written list of four names, with times written next to each name. Subsequent investigation revealed the names to be those of the bank's security officers, and the times to be the officers' weekly schedule.

The man has filed a motion to suppress the sheet of paper from his upcoming trial. What is the most likely ruling on the motion?

A. The motion will be granted because the delay in conducting the search incident to arrest renders the search *per se* unreasonable.

B. The motion will be granted because the delay in conducting the search incident to arrest could have been avoided if the officer had searched earlier.

C. The motion will be denied because the delay in conducting the search incident to arrest was caused by the normal processing of the man at the jail.

D. The motion will be denied because the delay in conducting the search incident to arrest is unimportant when compared the evidentiary value of the paper.

102. After a university announced a steep increase in tuition, students held a protest outside of the university president's house. After two of the student protesters threw rocks at the windows of the house, two officers monitoring the protest arrested them.

Both arrestees were carrying backpacks. The first officer confiscated the backpacks and placed them in the trunk of police cruiser; the second officer placed the handcuffed arrestees in the cruiser's back seat. The officers then drove the arrestees to the police station for booking.

The following afternoon, the officers were out on patrol when the first officer asked the second officer if he had found anything when he searched the arrestees' backpacks. The second officer replied that he hadn't searched the backpacks because he thought the first officer had done so. The first officer, driving the cruiser, immediately pulled over and parked. The two officers pulled the backpacks out of the trunk and searched them. In each, the officers found a small stash of cocaine.

Both arrestees were charged with cocaine possession, and each has filed a motion to suppress. What is the most likely ruling on the motions?

A. The motions will be denied because the officers could have plausibly believed the backpacks contained weapons or evidence of crime.

B. The motions will be denied because the officers had the absolute right to search the backpacks incident to arrest, regardless of the unreasonable delay.

C. The motions will be granted because, due to the unreasonable delay, the officers no longer had the right to search the backpacks incident to arrest.

D. The motions will be granted because the officers had no reason to believe the backpacks contained weapons or evidence of crime.

103. Police received a call of an undisclosed disturbance in the downtown area, and an officer was dispatched to investigate. The officer found a woman standing on a street corner, yelling about how the government was spying on its citizens and collecting information for—what she referred to as—"the big experiment." The woman was very agitated and was carrying a large canvas bag.

The officer approached the woman and she punched him. The officer arrested the woman for assault of a police officer and placed her in his patrol car. Immediately after, the woman began to bang her head against the metal screen between patrol car's front and back seats, cutting her head in the process. The officer grabbed the woman's bag, put it in the trunk of the patrol car, and drove to the hospital. Once there, an emergency room physician sedated the woman and stitched up her head injury. While the woman was being treated, the officer went through the woman's bag and found several vials containing amphetamines.

The woman was later charged with assault and drug possession. Her attorney claims that the drugs must be suppressed because the officer did not search the bag at the time of the woman's arrest. What is the prosecutor's strongest argument in response?

A. The drugs should be admitted because the officer had reasonable suspicion to believe the woman was intoxicated, drugged, or both.

B. The drugs should be admitted because the officer had probable cause to believe the woman was intoxicated, drugged, or both.

C. The drugs should be admitted because the officer acted reasonably despite the delay in searching the woman's bag.

D. The drugs should be admitted because the officer was trying to assist the doctor when he searched the bag.

104. A patrol officer saw a car that was speeding and pulled the driver over. The officer asked the driver for her license and registration, which she supplied. In his cruiser, the officer ran a check on the driver's license and discovered an outstanding arrest warrant for failing to appear in an unrelated traffic matter. The officer returned to the driver's car and arrested her. The officer then searched the driver incident to arrest, but found nothing. He placed the driver in his cruiser and began to drive to the station.

As he was driving, the officer noticed that the driver was squirming in the back seat, moving her body in an unusual way. When the two arrived at the station, the officer handcuffed the driver's right arm to a desk chair, leaving her left hand free. The driver used her free hand to pick at her shirt in the area under her breasts. The officer asked a female officer to conduct a second search incident to arrest — and to pay particular attention to the driver's bra because she might be hiding evidence there. The female officer did as she was instructed and discovered a small packet of heroin hidden inside the driver's bra.

The driver was charged with possession of heroin and moved to suppress the evidence found in her bra, arguing that search interfered with her personal dignity. What is the most likely ruling on the motion?

A. The motion will be denied because the arresting officer made sure that a female officer conducted the search of the driver's bra.

B. The motion will be denied because the female officer conducted a permissible search incident to arrest.

C. The motion will be granted because the officers conducted two separate searches incident to arrest, and they were only permitted to conduct one.

D. The motion will be granted because the right to search incident to arrest does not extend to an arrestee's underwear.

105. Police received a report that a high school student had been robbed in an alley behind a restaurant where the student worked. The student gave police a detailed description of the man who robbed him, and told police that the man had taken his wallet. A responding officer quickly located a man who matched the given description exactly; the man was walking down the street, carrying a backpack.

When the man saw the officer drive up in his squad car, he began to run. The officer jumped out of his car and chased the man, catching him a block away and tackling him to the ground. In the meantime, a second officer drove up with the high school student. The student identified the man as the robber and so the officer told the man he was under arrest.

At the same time, the second officer noticed the man's backpack on the ground. The second officer searched the backpack and found the student's wallet inside.

The prosecutor charged the man with robbery, and wants to use the wallet as evidence of the crime. The man's attorney has moved to have the wallet suppressed. How should the court rule on the motion?

A. The motion should be granted because the second officer exceeded the scope of a permissible search incident to arrest.

B. The motion should be granted because the man did not consent to a search of his backpack, a constitutional "effect."

C. The motion should be denied because the man effectively abandoned the backpack when he walked off with the first officer.

D. The motion should be denied because the second officer conducted a permissible search incident to arrest.

106. A police officer was sitting in his cruiser, which was parked on a city street. All of a sudden, a car sped by and sideswiped the cruiser. The car's driver jumped out of his car and began to run. The officer chased after the driver on foot, tackling him to the ground about two blocks from the scene of the accident. As the two struggled on the ground, a baggie of marijuana fell out of the driver's pocket.

The officer arrested the driver for leaving the scene of an accident and marijuana possession, handcuffed him, and walked him back to the cars. The officer placed the driver in the back of his cruiser and searched the passenger compartment of the driver's car. In the console between the two front seats, the officer found a small amount of marijuana.

The driver was later charged with marijuana possession, and the prosecutor wants to use the marijuana from the driver's pocket and the marijuana from the car. The driver has moved to have the marijuana from the car suppressed. What is most likely ruling on the motion?

A. The marijuana from the car will be suppressed because the driver was arrested two blocks from his car.

B. The marijuana from the car will be suppressed because a third party could have put it in the car while the officer was chasing the driver.

C. The marijuana from the car will be admitted because it is evidence of one of the two arresting offenses.

D. The marijuana from the car will be admitted because the driver was a recent occupant of the car that was searched.

107. Early one morning, two officers came to an apartment building to arrest a woman charged with embezzling from a local charity. As the officers approached the front door of the building they saw the woman leave the building and start walking toward the parking lot. The officers followed the woman and caught up with her just as she was unlocking her car door.

The first officer explained to the woman that she was under arrest, handcuffed her and placed her in the nearby patrol car. The second officer began to search the passenger compartment of the woman's car. He found a folder of bank records under the front passenger seat.

The woman's trial has been scheduled, and the prosecutor wants to use the bank records against her. The woman's attorney has filed a motion to suppress. What is the most likely ruling on the woman's motion?

A. The motion will be denied because the officers had reason to believe that evidence of the embezzlement would be found in the woman's car.

B. The motion will be denied because the bank records provide positive evidence of the woman's guilt.

C. The motion will be granted because the woman did not have a chance of accessing the car or any weapon inside it.

D. The motion will be granted because the officers did not have a right to search the woman's car incident to her arrest.

108. A police officer pulled over a driver who was speeding down the highway. The officer, as permitted under state law, decided to arrest the driver for speeding. The officer placed the driver in handcuffs, put him in the back of his cruiser, and locked the cruiser door from the outside. The officer then searched the passenger compartment of the driver's car and found a vial of cocaine hidden under the armrest in the back seat. The driver was subsequently charged with cocaine possession and filed a motion to suppress the drugs.

At the suppression hearing, the prosecution argued that since the officer had the legal right to arrest the driver, he also had the legal right to search the passenger compartment of the driver's car incident to arrest.

If the judge rules against the prosecutor, what is the most likely reason for doing so?

A. The officer did not face any threat from the handcuffed driver.

B. The officer could not hope to find evidence of the arresting offense in the car.

C. The officer had no real reason to search the car incident to arrest on these facts.

D. The officer should not have arrested the driver for such a petty offense.

109. After a magistrate issued an arrest warrant for a mid-level drug dealer, an officer was asked to locate and arrest him. The officer first looked for the drug dealer at his house, but the house was empty. Driving away from the house, the officer passed the drug dealer driving toward the house. The officer pulled the drug dealer over and arrested him without incident. After the drug dealer was arrested, handcuffed, and seated in the back of the officer's car, the officer searched the drug dealer's car. In the trunk's spare tire compartment, he found a kilo of cocaine. The following day, the drug dealer was charged with drug trafficking.

The drug dealer's lawyer filed a motion to suppress the drugs from the upcoming trial; the prosecutor responded by arguing that the cocaine was found as part of a proper search incident to arrest.

How should the court rule on the motion?

A. The motion should be granted because the officer's search of the trunk exceeded the scope of a proper search incident to arrest.

B. The motion should be granted because the drug dealer was arrested without incident, so the officer had no reason to believe there were drugs in the trunk.

C. The motion should be denied because the drug dealer's arrest for drug crimes gave the officer probable cause to believe there were drugs in the trunk.

D. The motion should be denied because the drug dealer's arrest for drug crimes gave the officer reasonable suspicion to believe there were drugs in the trunk.

110. One summer evening, a state trooper pulled a woman over on suspicion of driving under the influence. The trooper directed the woman to get out of the car, and as she did, the trooper noticed that the woman was wearing a walking cast on her left leg. The trooper asked the woman if she'd been drinking, and she acknowledged that she'd had several glasses of wine in the past hour. The trooper conducted a variety of field sobriety tests, each of which the woman cheerfully performed—and failed. The trooper then arrested the woman for drunk driving, handcuffed her, and placed her in the back of his locked patrol car. While waiting for a tow truck for the woman's car, the trooper thoroughly searched the passenger compartment of the woman's car, and found an empty vodka bottle in the glove box.

If the woman is charged with drunk driving and if she files a motion to suppress the vodka bottle found in her car, what is the strongest defense argument in support of the motion?

A. The woman had been polite to the trooper and so there was no reason to believe she might access a weapon in her car.

B. The woman was wearing a walking cast and so wasn't able to move fast enough to access a weapon in her car even if she wanted to.

C. The woman was handcuffed in a locked car and so there was no reason to believe she might access a weapon in her car.

D. The woman had no known history of violence and so there was no reason to believe she might access a weapon in her car.

111. Police received a call from a distraught woman, claiming that her ex-husband was parked in a car outside of her house. The woman said that her ex-husband had recently threatened to kill her and so she had obtained a protective order, requiring him to stay at least 100 yards away from her. After verifying the existence of the protective order, two officers drove to the woman's house and found the ex-husband, sitting in his parked car outside the woman's house.

The officers parked their car and began walking toward the ex-husband's car. At the same time, the ex-husband got out of his car and walked toward the officers. The first officer arrested the ex-husband for violating the protective order and the second officer did a quick search of the passenger compartment of the ex-husband's car, finding a pistol resting on the front passenger seat.

Later, the ex-husband was charged with carrying an unlicensed weapon. The ex-husband filed a motion to suppress, arguing that the officer had no authority to search his car because he hadn't threatened the officers in any way. What is the prosecutor's strongest argument in response?

A.   The search was reasonable because, at the time it was conducted, the ex-husband could have accessed the car.

B.   The search was reasonable because, at the time it was conducted, the ex-husband was about to threaten the officers.

C.   The search was reasonable because, at the time it was conducted, the ex-husband was in violation of the protective order.

D.   The search was reasonable because, at the time it was conducted, the ex-husband had actually threatened the officers.

112. Police received a report that a man was selling drugs to high school students from a van parked by the local high school. An officer was dispatched to investigate. The officer quickly located the van and watched as the van's driver sold some marijuana to a teenaged boy wearing a football jersey. After the teenaged boy walked away, the officer approached the van and arrested the driver. After handcuffing the driver, the officer placed him in the back of his locked patrol car. Then, the officer searched the entire van, and found additional marijuana in a tackle box under the driver's seat.

The prosecutor charged the driver with drug crimes and plans to use the marijuana from the tackle box at the upcoming trial. The defense has filed a motion to suppress, arguing that the officer shouldn't have searched the van because the driver was securely locked in the patrol car at the time of the search.

What is the most likely ruling?

A.   The motion will be granted; because the officer only witnessed a single drug transaction, it was unreasonable for him to believe that additional drugs could be found in the van.

B.   The motion will be granted; because the officer arrested the driver for selling drugs, it was unreasonable for the officer to search the van without also arresting the buyer.

C.   The motion will be denied; because the officer witnessed a drug transaction, it was reasonable for him to believe that additional drugs could be found in the van.

D.   The motion will be denied; because the officer arrested the driver for selling drugs from the van, it was reasonable for him to believe that additional drugs could be found in the van.

113. A state trooper was parked by the side of a major highway and was using a radar gun to check the speed of passing traffic. Several cars passed by the officer, each driving the speed limit. Then, all of a sudden, a car whizzed by, and the radar indicated that the car's speed was 20 miles over the speed limit. The trooper pulled the car over.

After getting the driver's license and registration, the trooper ran a routine warrant check. That check revealed a year-old felony warrant for the driver's arrest, for forging checks. The trooper returned to the driver's car and arrested the driver. After placing him in handcuffs and in the back of his patrol car, the trooper thoroughly searched the passenger compartment of the driver's car and found a bundle of stolen checks under the driver's seat.

The prosecutor filed charges against the driver for possession of the stolen checks, and wants to use the checks at the driver's upcoming trial. The defense wants to have the checks suppressed. What is the strongest defense argument in support of suppression?

A. The trooper lacked probable cause to believe evidence of the arresting offense would be found in the car.

B. The driver never threatened the trooper in any way while interacting with the trooper.

C. The trooper lacked any reason to believe evidence of the arresting offense would be found in the car.

D. The driver could not have harmed the trooper from where he sat in the back of the patrol car.

114. A state trooper was driving down the road in her cruiser when she noticed a car on the side of the road with its hazard lights on. The officer pulled behind the car and got out of the cruiser. At the same time, the driver got out of his car, locked it, and began walking toward the officer.

The officer asked the driver what was wrong and the driver explained that he had pulled over to check some driving directions. As the driver spoke, he didn't make eye contact with the officer and instead looked off in the distance. The officer found this odd, and asked the driver if she could search him for drugs. The driver agreed and the officer patted down the exterior of the driver's coat. In one coat pocket she found a plastic bag filled with cocaine. The officer arrested the driver and secured him in the back of her cruiser. The officer then searched the driver's car, and found six more cocaine-filled bags in the car's glove compartment.

The prosecutor wants to use all the cocaine at the driver's upcoming trial on drug trafficking charges. The defense has filed a motion to suppress, arguing that the officer lacked probable cause to believe that there would be more cocaine in the car. What is the most likely ruling on the motion?

A. The motion will be denied because the officer correctly guessed that there would be additional drugs in the car.

B. The motion will be denied because the officer was not required to have any suspicion that there would be additional drugs in the car.

C. The motion will be denied because the officer had probable cause to believe that there would be additional drugs in the car.

D. The motion will be denied because the officer had reasonable suspicion to believe that there would be additional drugs in the car.

115. A state trooper parked by the side of the highway saw a car speed past him. The trooper pulled the car over and as he spoke with the driver, he began to suspect that she was intoxicated in some way. The officer asked the driver if she was impaired and she admitted that she had smoked "a little marijuana" a few minutes before she'd been stopped.

The trooper arrested the driver and placed her in the back of his cruiser. He then locked the cruiser from the outside and searched the driver's car. The officer found the driver's purse on the backseat and searched it. Inside, he found a small pill bottle filled with cocaine, nestled in a zippered cosmetic bag at the bottom of the purse. The driver was subsequently charged with cocaine possession. No marijuana was ever found.

The driver is considering whether to plead guilty to the cocaine charge, but her lawyer has suggested she wait for the court's ruling on a pending motion to suppress. How should the court rule on that motion?

A. The court should grant the motion because the officer was entitled to look briefly inside the purse, but not to search it as extensively as he did.

B. The court should grant the motion because the officer arrested the woman for smoking marijuana and he never found any marijuana in the car.

C. The court should deny the motion because the right to search a car incident to arrest extends to closed containers found within the passenger compartment.

D. The court should deny the motion because the right to search a car incident to arrest extends to all closed containers found anywhere in the car.

Terry Stop and Frisk

116. An off-duty police officer was at the bank one morning, standing in line to speak to a teller. While waiting, the officer noticed a man standing just inside the front door of the bank. The officer watched for a few minutes as the man looked back and forth between the bank teller, the bank security guard, and a video camera mounted on the wall above the bank teller. The officer also noticed that all the other customers in the bank were carrying papers—a checkbook, a bank statement, deposit slips—but the man did not have any paperwork with him and that he kept one of his hands shoved in his jacket pocket.

Concerned that the man was casing the bank for a future bank robbery, the off-duty officer stepped out of line and walked up to him. The officer pushed the man against the wall and patted down the exterior of the man's clothing. In the pocket of the man's jacket the officer found a gun and a baggie of cocaine. The officer arrested the man.

If the man is charged with carrying an unlicensed weapon and cocaine possession and if he moves to suppress the evidence found in his pocket, how should the court rule on the motion?

A. The motion should be granted because the off-duty officer did not have probable cause to believe the man was about to rob the bank.

B. The motion should be granted because the off-duty officer did not reasonably know when the bank robbery might occur.

C. The motion should be denied because the off-duty officer had probable cause to believe the man was about to rob the bank.

D. The motion should be denied because the off-duty officer reasonably suspected that the man was going to commit a crime.

117. An undercover officer was assigned to patrol a crowd during the governor's speech at a local university. During the speech, the officer stopped a man he thought looked suspicious; in a subsequent frisk, the officer discovered a handgun and a grenade in the man's jeans pockets.

The man was charged with weapons offenses and he filed a motion to suppress the weapons from his trial. At the suppression hearing, the officer testified as to why he stopped man in the first place:

> He seemed like he didn't fit in with the crowd. All the other people were watching the governor, but this guy wasn't. There was something about him I just didn't like. It's hard to explain, but he seemed strange.

Based on this testimony, how should the court rule on the motion?

A. The motion should be granted because the officer's testimony shows that he acted on a hunch and not on reasonable suspicion.

B. The motion should be granted because the officer's testimony shows that he only stopped the man because he didn't like him.

C. The motion should be denied because the officer's testimony shows multiple valid reasons for the stop.

D. The motion should be denied because the officer's testimony shows that the man didn't fit in with the crowd.

118. An officer pulled a driver over to the side of the road for speeding. When the officer asked the driver why she was in such a hurry, she explained that she was late to meet a friend at the shooting range. As the two spoke, the officer noticed that the driver seemed very nervous — she had difficulty maintaining eye contact, her hands shook when she retrieved her license and registration from her wallet, and she was speaking very quickly. The officer also noticed that the driver kept on looking over at her jacket, which was draped over the front passenger seat.

The officer reached into the car, lifted the jacket, and found a revolver sitting on the seat. He grabbed the revolver and arrested the driver for improperly transporting a firearm.

If the driver contests her arrest as a fruit of the unlawful search of her car, what is the prosecutor's best argument in response?

A. Reasonable suspicion to frisk the car was established by the driver's admission that she was on her way to the shooting range.

B. Reasonable suspicion to frisk the car was established by the driver's nervous behavior while interacting with the officer.

C. Reasonable suspicion to frisk the car was established by the driver's frequent glances over at the jacket on the front passenger's seat.

D. Reasonable suspicion to frisk the car was established by the totality of the circumstances.

119. Two police officers were on patrol in an area of town well known for drug sales and street violence. The officers turned a corner and saw a group of three young men, huddled together. As the cruiser approached, the men looked up at the car; suddenly, one of the men turned and ran away. The officers drove after the man and followed him into an alley. Cornered, the man stopped.

One of the officers got out of the cruiser, frisked the man, and found a weapon in his pocket. The man admitted that he didn't have a license for the weapon and so the officer arrested him. In a subsequent search incident to arrest, the officer found several bags of powder cocaine in the man's sock and jeans pockets.

The man was charged with crimes associated with this evidence, and he wants to have it suppressed from his upcoming trial. How should the court respond to his argument that the officer had no right to stop him in the first instance?

A. The stop was invalid because the man's presence in a high crime area, without more, did not provide reasonable articulable suspicion for the *Terry* stop.

B. The stop was invalid because the man's flight from the police was a sensible choice and did not provide reasonable articulable suspicion for the *Terry* stop.

C. The stop was valid because the men were huddled together in a high crime area, which gave the officers reasonable articulable suspicion for the *Terry* stop.

D. The stop was valid because the man's unprovoked flight from the police in a high crime area provided reasonable articulable suspicion for the *Terry* stop.

120. An officer on patrol was buying a sandwich at a deli when he noticed a known confidential informant ("CI") standing on the sidewalk outside. The officer knew that the CI had a heroin addiction. The officer paid for his sandwich and decided to follow the CI to see where he would go.

Over the next two hours, the officer watched the CI speak with three different men—each a known heroin addict. The CI met the first man in a nearby park and the two men spent about 30 minutes together, sitting on a bench and talking. The CI met the second man outside a coffee shop and the two men drank coffee together inside. The CI met the third man outside a convenience store and the two men smoked several cigarettes together. As the CI was walking away from the third man, the officer stopped the CI and frisked the exterior of his clothing. The officer found a handgun inside the pocket of the CI's jacket.

The CI is charged with being a felon in possession of a firearm and has filed a motion to suppress the weapon from his upcoming trial. What is the strongest argument in support of the motion?

A. The officer lacked reasonable articulable suspicion to frisk him.

B. Before frisking the CI, the officer should have asked if he was armed.

C. The officer lacked reasonable articulable suspicion to stop him.

D. Before frisking the CI, the officer should have asked questions to confirm or dispel his suspicion for the stop.

121. Police received an anonymous call that a woman was carrying an illegal weapon. The caller explained the woman was drinking coffee at a local coffee shop, that she was in her early 20s, had shoulder-length brown hair, and was wearing a tie-dyed shirt, faded jeans, and yellow sandals.

An officer went to the coffee shop to investigate and he quickly identified a woman matching the caller's description. As the woman was walking out the door of the coffee shop, the officer stopped and frisked her and found a handgun tucked into the waistband of her jeans. The woman admitted that the handgun was stolen. Two days after arresting the woman, the officer learned that the police ballistics lab matched the handgun to one used in a murder two weeks prior.

The woman has been charged with being an accessory to murder, and the prosecutor wants to use the handgun against her at trial. What is the woman's strongest argument for suppression of the handgun?

A. The officer failed to corroborate the tip before stopping and frisking the woman.

B. The officer lacked reasonable articulable suspicion to frisk the woman.

C. The officer took no steps to identify the anonymous tipster before acting on the tipster's information.

D. The officer lacked reasonable articulable suspicion to stop the woman.

122. A foot patrol officer was walking his beat one afternoon when he noticed two men standing on a nearby street corner. The men were standing close to one another and talking. The officer watched as the first man looked around him, pulled something out of his pocket and handed it to the second man—but the officer was standing too far away to see the item. The two men split up and walked away in separate directions.

Suspecting that the two men were involved in a drug transaction, the officer walked up to the second man and stopped him by placing a hand on his shoulder. The officer asked the man if he had any drugs in his possession and the man said that he didn't. The officer asked the man what had been handed to him, and the man pulled a ring of keys from his pocket. The man said that he had arranged to borrow the first man's truck so he could move some boxes from his apartment into a storage facility. Satisfied by this explanation, the officer permitted the second man to go on his way.

Believing that he had been stopped without just cause, the second man filed a formal complaint against the officer. What is the strongest legal argument in support of the complaint?

A. The officer had no right to stop the second man because the officer did not see what had been handed to him.

B. The officer had no right to stop the second man because the officer lacked reasonable suspicion to believe criminal activity was underway.

C. The officer had no right to stop the second man because the officer did not see any money exchange hands.

D. The officer had no right to stop the second man because the officer did not witness either man using drugs.

123. Two officers on their lunch break were sitting on a park bench, drinking coffee, when a young woman ran past them. A few seconds later, a young man ran by, chasing the young woman and yelling at her to stop. The officers chased after the two and quickly managed to stop them both. The young man explained that he and the young woman were friends and they were only joking around. The woman seemed visibly upset though, and looked like she might cry.

One of the officers took the woman aside to speak with her privately. After some discussion, the officer was satisfied that no crime had been committed and that the young woman was just unnerved by the whole situation. The officers allowed the two to go on their way. The entire episode took about ten minutes.

When the young man told his father about what happened, the father called the police to complain that the police detained his son for as long as they did. How should the police respond to this allegation?

A. The officers acted reasonably because the young man's actions gave them reasonable suspicion to stop him and investigate.

B. The officers acted reasonably because the young woman was at fault for acting nervous and upset.

C. The officers acted reasonably because the officers detained the young man as long as was necessary to dispel their suspicion.

D. The officers acted reasonably because the young man should have known that his actions were suspicious.

124. A police officer stopped a driver for turning left on a yellow light instead of stopping. As the officer approached the car, the driver was speaking on his cell phone and the officer asked the driver to end the call. After about 30 seconds, the driver complied. The officer asked the driver for his license and vehicle registration; while the driver was looking in his glove box for the registration, his phone rang and the driver answered the call. The officer again asked the driver to end the call, and the driver did—2 minutes later. During this time, the officer twice asked the driver to hang up and twice the driver refused. After ending the call, the driver then supplied his license and registration.

The officer returned to his cruiser and wrote the driver a ticket for the moving violation. When the officer returned to the driver's car, the driver was again on his cell phone. The officer asked the driver to get off the phone, but the driver said he needed to finish the conversation because he was speaking with his child's babysitter. About 3 minutes later, the driver finally hung up the phone. The officer returned to his cruiser and wrote the driver a second ticket—for failing to comply with an officer's order. The driver was pulled over by the side of the road for a total of 25 minutes.

The driver now contests the duration of the stop, claiming that the officer constructively arrested him because the stop took so long. What is the prosecutor's best argument in response?

A. The duration of the stop was largely due to the driver's actions.

B. Roadside stops that last less than 30 minutes are presumptively reasonable.

C. The driver is lucky the officer didn't detain him longer than he did.

D. Roadside stops can last as long as the officer needs them to last.

125. A police officer stopped a driver for having illegally tinted windows. The officer wrote the driver a ticket and then asked for consent to search the car. The driver refused and asked if she was free to leave. The officer told the driver that she would have to stay a bit longer and wait for a second officer to arrive with a drug-detection dog.

Ten minutes later, the K-9 unit arrived. The officer walked the dog around the perimeter of the driver's car and the dog alerted at the trunk, signifying that it detected the odor of cocaine. The officer used the driver's key fob to open the trunk and found a kilo of cocaine inside.

If the young woman is charged with cocaine possession and if she files a motion to suppress the cocaine from her trial, what is her strongest argument in support?

A. The dog's alert did not give the officer probable cause to believe there was cocaine in her car.

B. The cocaine found in the trunk is fruit of an unreasonable search.

C. The dog's alert only gave the officer reasonable suspicion to believe there was cocaine in the car.

D. The cocaine found in the trunk is a fruit of an unreasonable seizure.

126. Two police officers walked into a bar in order to conduct a spot check for underage patrons. One officer noticed a young woman who appeared underage and also a little drunk. The officer asked her for identification but she replied that someone had stolen her wallet earlier in the evening and so she didn't have any identification. The officer asked the bar manager if he could use his office so he could speak to the young woman in private, and the manager agreed.

The officer then took the young woman by the arm into the bar manager's office. After about 20 minutes of questioning, the young woman confessed that she was 16 years old and that she had lied about having her wallet stolen. The officer wrote the young woman a ticket for underage drinking and drove her back to her parents' house.

The young woman now contests the ticket, claiming that her admission of underage drinking is a fruit of her illegal seizure. What is the most likely ruling from the court?

A. The officer acted unreasonably when he moved the young woman to the office because the bar area was quiet enough for the two to talk.

B. The officer acted unreasonably when he moved the young woman to the office because he constructively arrested her by doing so.

C. The officer acted reasonably when he moved the young woman to the office because he wanted a quiet place where the two could talk.

D. The officer acted reasonably when he moved the young woman to the office because he was trying to protect her privacy from the other bar patrons.

127. A police officer on routine foot patrol received a call that a nearby jewelry store had just been robbed. As the dispatcher was providing a detailed description of the robber, the officer noticed a man matching the description about half a block away, walking quickly down the street. The officer ran after the man and caught up with him. The officer asked the man where he was going and the man mumbled something in response. The officer repeated his question but the man didn't respond and just stared back.

The officer noticed that the man's eyes were glassy and his pupils were dilated. The officer asked the man if he was currently under the influence of any drugs and the man confessed that he had smoked some crack cocaine a few minutes before. The officer asked the man if he was carrying any drugs, and the man said yes and pulled a small container with crack cocaine from his pocket. The officer arrested the man. The man was later charged with drug possession.

If the man moves to suppress the cocaine from his upcoming trial, how should the suppression court rule on the motion?

A. The motion should be granted because the officer's questions were not reasonably related in scope to the robbery investigation.

B. The motion should be granted because the officer's questions were designed to elicit an incriminating response.

C. The motion should be denied because the drugs were discovered during a lawful *Terry* stop.

D. The motion should be denied because the man matched the description of the person who had robbed the jewelry store.

128. An officer patrolling a county fair noticed three young men standing together near one of the concession stands. The men were passing a paper-bag-wrapped bottle between them and each was taking swigs from the bottle. Suspecting underage drinking, the officer approached to investigate.

When the officer got to the group, he asked the young men how old they were. One young man replied that he was eighteen. The officer then asked for the bottle and the young man handed it over. Pulling the bottle from the paper bag, the officer saw that the bottle contained whiskey. The officer arrested the young man for underage drinking.

If the young man moves to suppress his statement because the officer failed to provide him with *Miranda* warnings prior to asking his age, what is the prosecutor's strongest argument in response?

A. *Miranda* warnings are not required for preliminary, investigative questions.

B. *Miranda* warnings are not required when police ask questions to groups of people.

C. *Miranda* warnings are not required when questioning juvenile suspects.

D. *Miranda* warnings are not required during *Terry* stops.

129. A police officer approached a man he suspected of selling marijuana to high school students. The officer frisked the man and found the man's stash of marijuana—a large plastic bag, with 15 smaller plastic bags of marijuana inside. The officer arrested the man and the prosecutor later charged him with possession of marijuana with intent to deliver.

Prior to the man's trial, the man's attorney filed a motion to suppress the marijuana. At a subsequent hearing on the motion, the arresting officer testified:

> I frisked the guy because he's a drug dealer. You never know with these guys, but chances are, when there's smoke, there's fire. I just figured that if he's got drugs, he probably also has a gun.

Based on this testimony, how should the court rule on the suppression motion?

A. The motion should be granted because the officer classified the man as a "drug dealer" before he had been convicted of any crime.

B. The motion should be granted because the officer admittedly lacked the proper authority to search the man for weapons.

C. The motion should be denied because the officer suspected the man of selling drugs to minors, which provides an automatic right to search.

D. The motion should be denied because the officer correctly assumed that a drug dealer is also likely carrying a weapon.

130. A police officer was on foot patrol one evening, working in a small college town. The college football team had just won the final game of the season—and by a large margin. The officer saw a teenaged boy stumbling down the street, and the officer suspected that he had been drinking alcohol. The officer approached the teenager and asked for his identification; the teenager handed the officer his driver's license, which showed that he was 17 years old. The officer then frisked the teenager, and found a bag of pills in the waistband of his jeans.

What is the teenager's strongest argument to have the bag of pills suppressed from his upcoming trial?

A. The officer lacked the authority to approach him because there was only minimal suspicion to believe that he'd committed a crime.

B. The officer lacked the authority to stop him because there was no reason to believe that he had committed a dangerous crime.

C. The officer lacked the authority to frisk him because there was no reason to believe that he was armed and dangerous.

D. The officer lacked the authority to frisk him because underage drinking is a low-level summary offense.

131. A police officer noticed a young man standing outside a convenience store, looking through the window of the store. A second man came out of the store and joined the first man; the two men spoke for a moment, and then the second man went back inside the store. After the men repeated these steps two more times, one of the men pulled something shiny and silver from the waistband of his jeans and placed it in the pocket of his coat. The officer was convinced that the two were about to rob the store.

The officer walked up to the two men and asked them what they were doing. One mumbled an unintelligible response and the other tried to walk away. The officer stopped him, and pushed both men up against wall of the store. He frisked them both, and found that each was carrying a weapon in the pocket of his coat.

If the men are charged with weapons violations and if they move to suppress the guns found in their coat pockets, what is the prosecutor's strongest argument in support of the officer's actions?

A. The officer reasonably frisked the men because he had probable cause to believe they both were carrying weapons.

B. The officer reasonably frisked the men because he had probable cause to believe at least one of them was carrying a weapon.

C. The officer reasonably frisked the men because he had reasonable suspicion to believe they were about to rob the store.

D. The officer reasonably frisked the men because he had reasonable suspicion to believe that they were about to commit a crime.

132. A police officer received a report that a wine store had been robbed and the report included a detailed description of the would-be robber. The officer noticed a man matching the description standing on a street corner and smoking a cigarette; the officer approached him to investigate. When the man refused to answer the officer's questions and tried to walk away, the officer stopped him and frisked the exterior of the man's clothing. While frisking the man's upper body, the officer felt the contours of what he recognized as ammunition in the man's jacket pocket. The officer retrieved the ammunition. Then, continuing the frisk, the officer discovered a handgun tucked into the waistband of the man's jeans. The officer retrieved the handgun and arrested the man for carrying a concealed weapon.

The man was later charged with being a felon in possession of a firearm and ammunition. He has filed a motion to suppress both items from his trial. What is the most likely ruling from the court?

A. The motion will be granted because a *Terry* frisk is for weapons only, and the officer here discovered ammunition.

B. The motion will be granted because the officer exceeded the scope of a proper *Terry* frisk when he continued to frisk after discovering the ammunition.

C. The motion will be denied because the officer's actions did not exceed the scope of a proper *Terry* frisk.

D. The motion will be denied because the officer's discovery of the ammunition gave him reason to believe that the man would also be carrying a gun.

133. Police received a call from a motel manager, reporting that a man was "acting crazy" in the motel parking lot. An officer was sent to investigate. When the officer arrived at the motel, she saw a man standing in the parking lot, talking to himself in a loud tone of voice. The man kept on saying, "we'll all be dead, we'll all be dead." He had one hand in his jacket pocket and was waving the other in the air. The officer walked up to the man and asked him to pull his hand from his pocket but he ignored her and continued his talking. The officer repeated her request, but without success.

The officer pushed the man up against a car and frisked the exterior of his clothing. In the man's jacket pocket, the officer felt several small lumps, arranged close together. Using her fingers to slide the lumps back and forth, the officer realized that the lumps were crack cocaine. The officer reached into the man's pocket and pulled out a small baggie with crack cocaine inside. The officer arrested the man for drug possession.

If the man is charged with drug crimes and if he files a motion to suppress the drugs found in his pocket, what is the most likely ruling from the court?

A. The motion will be granted because the officer's actions exceeded the proper scope of a *Terry* frisk.

B. The motion will be granted because the officer felt the lumps of crack cocaine while conducting an improper *Terry* frisk.

C. The motion will be denied because the officer had reasonable suspicion to believe the man was using drugs, and acted reasonably to find those drugs.

D. The motion will be denied because the officer had probable cause to believe the man was using drugs, and acted reasonably to find those drugs.

134. A state trooper saw a driver speed past him on the highway and so he pulled the driver over. While speaking with the driver, the trooper noticed something silver and shiny in the console between the driver's and passenger's seats. The trooper did not know for certain that the object was a gun, but he was concerned that it might be.

The officer reached into the car and grabbed the object from the console — and it turned out to be a toy gun. But the driver was incensed by the officer's actions and got out of her car and began to yell at him. In fact, the driver became so worked up that she tried to punch the trooper, and so he arrested her for assaulting a police officer. In a subsequent search incident to arrest, the trooper found cocaine in the driver's jeans pocket.

The driver is charged with possession of illegal weapons and has filed a motion to suppress in advance of her upcoming trial. In the motion, she argues that the cocaine from her pocket is a fruit of the unlawful search of her car. What is the most likely ruling from the court?

A. The officer did not have a right to frisk the car because the right to search under *Terry* extends only to the person.

B. The officer did not have a right to frisk the car because he was not certain whether the object was a gun.

C. The officer had a right to frisk the car because officers can always search when they have a concern for their own safety.

D. The officer had a right to frisk the car because he had reasonable articulable suspicion to believe the object was a gun.

135. A state trooper and her partner were parked by the side of the highway when a car whizzed past them, driving at least 20 miles over the posted speed limit. The trooper switched on her lights and siren and sped after the car, pulling the driver over about two miles down the road. While the trooper was chasing the driver, she saw him leaning over into the middle of his car and she suspected that he was trying to reach into the glove compartment.

As the trooper and her partner approached the stopped car, the trooper instructed the driver to place both hands on the steering wheel. The driver did not and instead began to reach for the glove compartment. The trooper opened the driver's door, pulled him from the car, and frisked him for weapons. With the partner maintaining a watch over the driver, the trooper looked in the glove compartment, but did not find a weapon. The trooper then unlocked the trunk from the latch inside the car, and looked inside the trunk. There, she found a cache of stolen weapons.

The driver is charged with illegal weapons possession and has filed a motion to suppress. What is the most likely ruling from the court?

A. The evidence will be suppressed because the officer lacked reasonable articulable suspicion to believe the car trunk contained a gun.

B. The evidence will be suppressed because the officer exceeded the proper scope of a *Terry* frisk of a car when she looked in the car trunk.

C. The evidence will be admitted because the officer had reasonable articulable suspicion to believe the car trunk contained a gun.

D. The evidence will be admitted because the proper scope of a *Terry* frisk of a car includes any area where the driver might hide a gun.

Protective Sweeps

136. Two police officers were given a warrant to arrest a college student. The student was president of his fraternity and had presided over a party where alcohol was served to minors. The officers knew that the university had recently cut ties with the fraternity because of reports that members had used stun guns to play "Russian Roulette" with pledges as part of a hazing ritual.

The officers went to the fraternity house and arrested the student inside the front door. As the first officer was adjusting the handcuffs on the student's wrists, he heard sharp buzzing noises coming from inside the house. The second officer drew his weapon and did a quick sweep of the first floor looking for the source of the noise. He found it in the dining room: a fraternity brother was sitting at the table, smoking a marijuana cigarette and idly pressing the button on a Taser he was holding in his hand. The officer arrested the fraternity brother and seized the marijuana.

The fraternity brother was charged with marijuana possession and filed a motion to suppress. What is the prosecution's strongest argument in opposition to the motion?

A. The marijuana was found during a legitimate sweep of the house, conducted because of the recent allegations about fraternity hazing.

B. The marijuana was found during a legitimate sweep of the house, conducted to see if there might be minors in need of assistance inside.

C. The marijuana was found during a legitimate sweep of the house, conducted because the officer reasonably thought someone inside the house posed a threat.

D. The marijuana was found during a legitimate sweep of the house, conducted because of the need to control an obviously rowdy fraternity house.

137. After a prosecutor charged a doctor with Medicaid fraud, two officers went to the doctor's home to arrest him. The doctor lived in a large house in a wealthy suburban community. The officers parked their cruiser in the large, circular driveway, and the doctor answered their knock at the door. After showing the doctor an arrest warrant, the first officer placed handcuffs on him while the second officer walked through the first floor of the house to make sure that there was no one else in the house. While walking through the den, the second officer saw a crack pipe on the desk and seized it.

If the court suppresses the pipe as a fruit of an unlawful search of the doctor's home, what is the most likely reason for the court's ruling?

A. A sweep was not permitted in this case because the doctor was being arrested for a non-dangerous white-collar crime.

B. A sweep was not permitted in this case because the police lacked probable cause to believe that they faced danger from a third party in the house.

C. A sweep was not permitted in this case because the police lacked reasonable suspicion to believe that they faced danger from a third party in the house.

D. A sweep was not permitted in this case because the doctor did not suggest in any way that he posed a threat to the officers.

138. Two officers obtained an arrest warrant for a man charged with the murder of a police officer. From their investigation, the officers knew the man had a lengthy criminal history and had been convicted of several crimes of violence, including one conviction for assault of a police officer.

Once at the man's house, the officers knocked on the door; within seconds, the man answered. Both officers stepped inside and — as the man struggled and tried to get free — the officers frisked him and placed him in handcuffs. Once the man was handcuffed and in the first officer's control, the second officer did a sweep of the first floor of the man's house. In a bedroom in the back of the house, the officer found a handgun and seized it. Later testing on the handgun showed that it was the murder weapon.

The defense moved to suppress the handgun from the man's upcoming trial. How should the court rule?

A. The motion should be granted because the officers had no reasonable suspicion to fear an attack by a third party.

B. The motion should be granted because sweeps are not permitted after an arrestee is securely handcuffed.

C. The motion should be denied because the man's conduct at the time of arrest showed that he presented a danger to the officers.

D. The motion should be denied because the man's prior conviction of assault on a police officer gave the officers cause to fear an attack.

139. After a man was charged with murder, a judge issued a warrant for his arrest. Several officers went to the man's apartment and he was taken into custody without incident. The lead officer then asked the man whether he had any weapons in the apartment. The man nodded affirmatively and so two officers performed a quick protective sweep of the apartment, looking for weapons.

The officers found a machine gun in the cabinet under the bathroom sink and a handgun between the mattress and box springs in the bedroom. At the man's upcoming trial, the prosecutor plans to argue that the murder was committed with the handgun.

The man's attorney has filed a motion to suppress. What is his strongest argument in support of the motion?

A. The motion should be granted because the man did not threaten the officers in any way during the arrest.

B. The motion should be granted because in-home protective sweeps are for people, not physical evidence.

C. The motion should be granted because officers exceeded the scope of a legitimate protective sweep by looking where they did.

D. The motion should be granted because the officers clearly outnumbered the man and so didn't really face any threat from him.

140. Two officers arrested a man in his home on charges of being a felon in possession of a firearm. As one of the officers was searching the man incident to arrest and handcuffing him, the officers heard a banging sound coming from the back of the house. The first officer asked the man if anyone else was in the house and the man said that his roommate was at home, cooking breakfast. The man added: "He's a real mean guy and so you better watch your backs!"

The second officer drew his weapon and walked to the back of the house. No one was in the kitchen — it turns out that there was no roommate, and the banging noise came from an unlatched screen door, blowing in the wind — but the officer did find some ammunition in one of the kitchen drawers, which he seized.

The prosecutor amended the charges against the man to include the illegal possession of ammunition. If the man moves to have the ammunition suppressed, what is the most likely ruling on the motion?

A. The motion should be granted because the officer had no authority to conduct any search beyond the search incident to arrest.

B. The motion should be granted because the officer had no authority to search inside the kitchen drawers.

C. The motion should be denied because the officer only searched in the kitchen after hearing the man's statements about his roommate.

D. The motion should be denied because the officer was entitled to search the house for ammunition, given the arresting offense.

141. Two officers were assigned to arrest a woman in her home for growing marijuana. The officers knocked on the door and the woman answered, opened the door, and then walked back into the house. The officers followed the woman into the kitchen and after showing her the arrest warrant, arrested her. While there, the officers heard an irregular thumping noise coming from behind a door in the kitchen and smelled cigarette smoke. The first officer asked the woman if anyone else was in the house, but she did not respond and just stared at him. The thumping noise continued.

Concerned that there might be someone behind the door, the second officer opened the door, which separated the kitchen from an attached garage. Inside the garage, the officers found a man with a cigarette in his hand, standing in front of the source of the thumping noise: a hydraulic press that the man was using to package cocaine. The officers arrested the man. Later, with a search warrant, the officers seized the press and other evidence from the house.

If the woman is charged with crimes related to the cocaine and if she files a motion to suppress this evidence from her trial, what is most likely ruling from the court?

A. The motion will be denied because the officers were entitled to enter the garage, and so the fruits of that entry are admissible.

B. The motion will be denied because the officers had probable cause to search the garage for evidence of crime.

C. The motion will be granted because the officers unreasonably converted a lawful arrest into a search for evidence.

D. The motion will be granted because the officers were at the house for a marijuana arrest and they searched for cocaine.

142. Two police officers arrested a woman in her one-story home on charges of embezzling from the local school board. The home had a semi-open floor plan and, from where the officers were standing in the foyer inside the front door, they were able to see the living room and most of the adjacent kitchen and dining room.

Before handcuffing the woman, one officer searched her and discovered some marijuana in her pants pocket. The other officer then walked around the first floor of the house to the area of the kitchen and dining room he could not see, and found a bong and set of scales on the dining room table. He seized these items.

In addition to embezzlement, the woman now faces drug and paraphernalia charges. If the woman moves to suppress the evidence found at the time of her arrest, how should the court rule on the motion?

A. The motion should be denied in its entirety because the officers reasonably searched the woman and, given the floor plan of the house, the area within her reach.

B. The motion should be granted in part and the paraphernalia suppressed because the officers only had the authority to search the woman, but not her house.

C. The motion should be granted in its entirety because the officers arrested the woman for embezzlement and had no authority to search for drugs.

D. The motion should be granted in part and the drugs suppressed because the officers only had the authority to frisk the woman for weapons, not drugs.

143. Police developed probable cause to believe that a manager at a software company was selling cocaine and was using his office to store his supply. The lead officer obtained a search warrant for the manager's corner office, and together with his partner, he went to execute it.

While searching the manager's office, the officers heard some loud music down the hallway. Concerned about safety, the partner rushed out of the office with his weapon drawn, and followed the music to a conference room at the end of the hallway. He found two men sitting at the conference table, weighing and packaging marijuana. The music was coming from a portable stereo in the corner of the room. The partner seized the marijuana and scales and arrested the men. They were later charged with crimes related to the marijuana.

The men have filed a motion to suppress and the prosecutor has responded, arguing that the evidence was discovered as part of a legitimate protective sweep for dangerous people. How should the court rule?

A. The motion should be granted and the evidence suppressed because the partner was not entitled to conduct a protective sweep under these circumstances.

B. The motion should be granted and the evidence suppressed because the partner unreasonably converted a cocaine investigation into a general search for evidence.

C. The motion should be denied and the evidence admitted because the partner was entitled to conduct a protective sweep under these circumstances.

D. The motion should be denied and the evidence admitted because the officer had a legitimate fear for his safety.

144. Police had an arrest warrant for a drug dealer suspected of selling drugs from his house. As the officers arrived at the drug dealer's house, he walked out the door; the officers immediately arrested him. Moments later, two women ran out of the house, screaming and crying and trying to stop the arrest. It took several officers to restrain the women.

In the meantime, an officer opened the front door — located just a few feet from the place of arrest. The officer walked inside, loudly announcing that he was with the police and ordering anyone inside to come to the front of the house. The officer also performed a quick sweep of the house but found no one inside. He did, however, find a shotgun propped up against the wall, just inside the front door. At the subsequent suppression hearing, the officer testified that the weapon was not visible from the place of arrest outside the house.

What is the prosecution's strongest argument in support of the admissibility of the shotgun?

A. The sweep was reasonable even though the arrest occurred outside of the house because the women's actions gave the officer reasonable suspicion to believe there might be someone who posed a danger inside the house.

B. The sweep was reasonable because the arrest occurred on the curtilage of the house and so according to Fourth Amendment jurisprudence, the officer was technically inside the house when he conducted the sweep.

C. The sweep was reasonable even though the arrest occurred outside of the house, because the shotgun presented a danger to those on the arrest scene and was found in the officer's plain view.

D. The sweep was reasonable even though the arrest occurred outside of the house because the man had just come from the house and so the arrest occurred within the *res gestae* of the crime.

145. After a husband threatened several times to kill his wife, the wife decided to get a protective order against him. As part of her application, the wife explained to the judge that her husband kept several firearms in the house—all owned legally—and that he was a "mean drunk." The judge signed the order and two officers accompanied the wife to her house to serve the order and to keep watch while she gathered some clothes so she could move out.

When the officers and the wife arrived at the house, they found the husband sitting on the couch and drinking beer. When the husband saw the officers, he got off the couch and ran up the stairs. The first officer followed quickly behind and caught the husband on the landing at the top of the stairs—just as the husband was reaching for a handgun sitting on a small table. The officer arrested the husband and seized the handgun.

The husband was charged with assault and the prosecutor wants to use the handgun at the man's trial. What is the prosecutor's strongest argument for the admission of the handgun?

A. The handgun should be admitted because the officers were lawfully on the premises and had reasonable suspicion to believe the husband was dangerous.

B. The handgun should be admitted because the officers were at the house to serve the husband with a protective order, which is like an arrest warrant.

C. The handgun should be admitted because the wife gave implied consent to search the home when she allowed the officers to accompany her inside.

D. The handgun should be admitted because the husband gave the officer probable cause to arrest him, and the handgun was found in a search incident to arrest.

Automobile Exception Searches

146. A state trooper on routine patrol noticed a car pulled over by the side of the highway. The car was raised on a jack and one of the car's rear wheels had been removed and was propped up against the side of the car. The trooper parked his cruiser behind the car, expecting to help the driver finish changing her tire. Instead, as the trooper approached the car, he found the driver lying down on the backseat, smoking marijuana from a pipe. When the driver saw the officer, she sat up and tried to hide the pipe, but the officer grabbed it from her hand. He then searched the car and found a baggie of marijuana in the console between the two front seats.

Later, after the woman was charged with marijuana possession, she filed a motion to suppress the drugs found in her car. At the suppression hearing, the officer admitted on cross-examination that he could've called the district magistrate for a warrant to search the car—but he didn't.

What is the most likely ruling from the court on the suppression motion?

A. The motion will be denied because the officer was permitted to search the car without a warrant.

B. The motion will be denied because the officer reasonably feared the driver could have fixed her tire and driven away while he obtained a warrant to search the car.

C. The motion will be denied because the officer conceded that he could have gotten a warrant to search the car.

D. The motion will be denied because the officer reasonably feared the destruction of evidence, which is a recognized exigent circumstance.

147. Early one evening, a patrol officer pulled a car over for rolling through a stop sign and approached the car to ask the driver for her license and registration. When the officer got to the car, he smelled an odor that he believed was burning marijuana. The officer asked the driver whether she had been smoking marijuana and she admitted that she had "smoked just a little" to help her "mellow out after work." The officer searched the driver's car and found a stubbed-out marijuana cigarette in the ashtray.

At the pre-trial suppression hearing, the woman's attorney introduced testimony that in this jurisdiction, a magistrate is always on-call for telephonic warrants and that the telephonic warrant process takes, on average, four minutes.

What best supports the prosecutor's argument that this testimony is irrelevant?

A. The driver's car was readily mobile and she could have driven it away during the time the officer obtained the warrant.

B. The driver was high and could have become belligerent and dangerous during the time the officer obtained the warrant.

C. The officer did not have backup and so could not turn his attention from the woman to call the magistrate for a warrant.

D. The officer had no guarantees that the warrant process in this case would take four minutes, and it could have taken longer than that.

148. A traveling salesman was driving down the road one day when he was stopped for speeding. While the officer was speaking with the driver, she smelled marijuana. The officer asked the driver if he had been smoking marijuana or if he had any marijuana in the car and the driver admitted that he had some marijuana in the glove box. The officer looked in the glove box and found the marijuana.

The driver was charged with marijuana possession and his attorney filed a motion to suppress. At the suppression hearing, the driver testified that his sales territory included four states and that he usually spent between 12 and 14 hours a day in his car. For these reasons, the driver's attorney argued that the driver had a heightened expectation of privacy in his car relative to other people and so the officer should have obtained a warrant to search the car.

In consideration of this argument, how should the court rule on the driver's motion?

A. The motion should be denied because the driver cannot claim any expectation of privacy in a car with windows and that travels on public roads.

B. The motion should be denied because drivers have a reduced expectation of privacy in their cars.

C. The motion should be granted because the driver in this case has an increased expectation of privacy in his car.

D. The motion should be granted because the driver took steps to hide his drugs, which demonstrates his increased expectation of privacy.

149. Police developed probable cause to believe that a middle-aged man was using drugs to lure teenagers into his parked motor home, and was trading the drugs for sex. After waiting to make sure the man was alone in the motor home, two officers walked up to it and knocked on the side door. The man answered and the officers stepped inside and searched it. The officers found drugs and drug paraphernalia.

After the man was charged with various crimes, his attorney filed a motion to suppress. In the memorandum of law filed in support of the motion, the defense attorney argued that since the motor home was capable of being a home, the police were required to get a warrant for the search.

What is the most likely ruling on the suppression motion?

A. The motion will be granted because the motor home was capable of being a home and was thus deserving of higher protection under the Fourth Amendment.

B. The motion will be granted because the motor home was parked and immobile, so the police should have obtained a warrant or consent for the search.

C. The motion will be denied because the motor home was capable of mobility, so it should be treated as an automobile under the Fourth Amendment.

D. The motion will be denied because the danger associated with sexual abuse of minors outweighs the man's privacy interests in his motor home.

150. An officer stopped a car that was being driven erratically. When the officer approached the driver, she readily offered that she had a glass of wine about an hour before. But the driver insisted that she'd only had one glass, no more, and that she was no longer feeling the effects of the alcohol. As proof of her claim, the driver pulled a receipt of out her purse; the receipt was from a nearby restaurant, and it showed that the driver had paid for three glasses of wine an hour before — not one. When the officer asked the driver about this discrepancy, she could not provide an explanation. The officer then searched the driver's car and found a small baggie of marijuana in the glove box.

If the driver is charged with marijuana possession and if she moves to suppress the baggie of marijuana, how should the court rule on the motion?

A. The motion should be denied because the woman's lie gave the officer probable cause to believe evidence could be found in the car.

B. The motion should be denied because the woman's lie gave the officer reasonable suspicion to believe evidence could be found in the car.

C. The motion should be granted because the officer did not have reasonable suspicion to believe he would find evidence in the car.

D. The motion should be granted because the officer did not have probable cause to believe he would find evidence in the car.

151. An officer pulled a driver over for speeding. When the officer asked the driver where she was going in such a hurry, she replied that she was on her way to the shooting range. The officer asked the driver if she had a weapon in the car and she admitted that she had a loaded revolver in the glove box. She also told the officer that she didn't have a weapons permit but that she was planning on getting one the following week. The officer retrieved the revolver from the glove box and then using the fob on the driver's keychain, unlocked the trunk of the car. In the trunk, the officer found a kilo of cocaine and several rifles.

If the driver moves to suppress the evidence seized from her car, what is her strongest argument in support of the motion?

A. The motion should be granted because the officer did not have probable cause to believe that any evidence of crime would be found in the car.

B. The motion should be granted in part because the officer's probable cause was restricted to the glove compartment and he searched the trunk.

C. The motion should be granted because the officer should have asked the driver for consent to search car before beginning the search.

D. The motion should be granted because the officer had no reason to believe that the driver posed a specific threat to him.

152. Police received an anonymous tip that a young man was selling marijuana from his car. According to the tip, the young man would park his car outside a certain dry cleaning store on a pre-arranged day, for a two hour block of time. The young man's customers would then come to the car and buy drugs from him; the tipster claimed that the young man stored his drugs in the glove box and trunk of the car.

An officer assigned to investigate the tip watched as a young man parked his car in front of the dry cleaning store—just as the tipster had predicted. The officer also saw several people approach the car and give cash to the young man. Each time he received cash, the young man would retrieve something from either the glove box or the trunk, and then hand it to the other person. While waiting between customers, the young man would sit in the driver's seat and listen to the car radio. After about an hour of watching, the officer approached the young man and searched his car. The officer discovered cocaine in the glove box and methamphetamine in the trunk and under the driver's seat.

The young man was charged with drug possession and distribution. If he files a motion to suppress, how should the court rule on the motion?

A. The motion should be granted because the officer had probable cause to search for marijuana, not cocaine or methamphetamine.

B. The motion should be granted in part because the officer did not have probable cause to search under the driver's seat.

C. The motion should be denied because the officer had probable cause to search the entire car for drugs.

D. The motion should be denied because the officer witnessed the drug sales first hand, and did not rely on the anonymous tip.

153. The day before an air traveler was scheduled to fly across the country, police developed probable cause to believe that he would be transporting heroin in his suitcase. An undercover officer was posted at the airport and she watched as the traveler checked his bag. Six hours later, a second undercover officer at the traveler's destination city watched as he retrieved the bag from the baggage claim and walked to the parking garage, wheeling the suitcase behind him. The traveler placed the suitcase in the trunk of his car and drove away. A third officer then pulled the traveler over and searched the trunk of the car, including the suitcase. Inside the suitcase, the officer found the suspected heroin.

The traveler has been charged with various crimes associated with the heroin, and filed a motion to suppress. How should the court rule on the motion?

A. The motion should be granted because the police manipulated the law by purposefully waiting for the traveler to put the suitcase into the car.

B. The motion should be granted because the police clearly had ample time to obtain a warrant to search the suitcase.

C. The motion should be denied because the suitcase contained evidence of a crime.

D. The motion should be denied because the police had probable cause to search the suitcase and the suitcase was located in the traveler's car.

154. A police officer and his partner pulled a driver over for speeding. The officer asked the driver why he was in such a hurry and the driver replied that he and his passenger were late for a concert. In talking with the driver, the officer began to suspect that he might have been drinking alcohol and so the officer asked the driver when he had last had a drink. The driver admitted that he had snorted "a little cocaine" thirty minutes prior, but insisted that he was sober and able to drive legally. When the driver said this, the passenger began to laugh, but she quickly stopped herself.

The officer ordered the driver and the passenger out of the car, and the partner stayed with them, several feet from the car. The officer searched the glove compartment, and found a small baggie of cocaine. The officer then opened the passenger's purse—which she had left lying on the car seat—and found marijuana inside.

The passenger has been charged with cocaine and marijuana possession and her attorney has filed a motion to suppress. What is the prosecutor's strongest argument in opposition to the motion?

A. The motion should be denied because the driver's admission that he had recently snorted cocaine necessarily implicated the passenger in his crimes.

B. The motion should be denied because the passenger's inappropriate laughter gave the officer probable cause to believe that she had been smoking marijuana.

C. The motion should be denied because the officer had probable cause to believe that drug evidence would be found inside the passenger's purse.

D. The motion should be denied because the fact that the driver and passenger were on their way to a concert gave the officer probable cause to search the car.

155. An officer pulled a young man over for speeding. While speaking with the driver, the officer developed probable cause to believe that drug evidence would be found in the car. The officer searched the car and found three kilos of heroin and two loaded semi-automatic weapons hidden in the trunk. The prosecutor charged the driver with various crimes associated with this evidence and the young man's attorney filed a motion to have it suppressed.

At the hearing on the motion, the officer testified that the young man was friendly and cooperative during the stop, and that he was the calmest person he had pulled over in 20 years of policing. At the close of the testimony, the defense attorney argued that the officer's testimony established that there was no exigency on these facts and so the officer should have sought a warrant to search the car.

What is the prosecutor's strongest argument in response?

A. A warrant was unnecessary because the officer had probable cause to search the automobile for drugs.

B. A warrant was unnecessary because the driver was only acting calm because he knew he was transporting drugs and weapons.

C. A warrant was unnecessary because the quantity of drugs established exigent circumstances in this case.

D. A warrant was unnecessary because the loaded semi-automatic weapons established exigent circumstances in this case.

156. Based on a thorough investigation, police learned that the suspect in a jewelry store robbery was staying at a local motel. The investigation also revealed that the suspect was wary of the housekeeping staff at the motel, and so he kept the proceeds of the robbery in his car trunk. Two officers were sent to the motel to arrest the suspect; as they approached the motel, they spotted the suspect driving his car in the opposite direction. The officers pulled the suspect over and arrested him without incident. The officers also searched the suspect's car and found many of the stolen pieces of jewelry.

Three hours later, after the suspect's car had been impounded, the officers interrogated the suspect. During the interrogation, the suspect told the officers that the gun he used in the robbery was hidden in the dashboard of his car. One of the officers went to the impound lot where the car was parked and found the gun just where the suspect said it would be.

If the suspect challenges the search of his car at the impound lot, what is the correct ruling from the court?

A. The search was justified because the police had probable cause to believe that the car contained evidence of crime.

B. The search was justified because the car had been impounded and so the suspect had lost all expectation of privacy in the car.

C. The search was not justified because the car had been impounded and so there was no exigency to support the search.

D. The search was not justified because police are always required to obtain warrants to search cars after they are rendered immobile.

157. Police received a call from a mall security officer that a minivan had been parked in the corner of the mall parking lot for several days. The security officer provided information about the minivan's make and model, as well as its license plate. From that information, police were quickly able to establish that the minivan's owner was suspected of committing a bank robbery earlier in the week. According to police reports, the owner had been shot in the arm during the robbery and had fled in the minivan.

Officers went to the mall and searched the minivan. Inside, they found a canvas bag stamped with the name of the bank and smears of blood across the back seat. Lab technicians took samples of the seat upholstery and later testing revealed that the blood came from a human. Two months later, the minivan's owner was apprehended and DNA testing established that the blood on the backseat was hers.

The minivan's owner filed a motion to suppress, arguing that the search was unreasonable because she was nowhere near the minivan at the time it was searched. What is the prosecutor's strongest argument in response?

A. The search was reasonable because the woman abandoned the minivan and therefore she lacked standing to challenge the search.

B. The search was reasonable because police were responding to a legitimate exigency because they knew the woman had been shot.

C. The search was reasonable because police had probable cause to believe that evidence of crime was located in the minivan.

D. The search was reasonable because the woman abandoned the minivan and therefore had no expectation of privacy in its contents.

158. After pulling a driver over for speeding, a state trooper developed probable cause to believe the driver had been smoking marijuana while driving. While a backup officer stayed with the driver on the side of the road a short distance away from the car, the trooper searched the car. The trooper found a large bag of processed marijuana in the glove compartment and a second bag of marijuana in the backseat, hidden in the armrest. The trooper then searched the trunk, and found several dozen photos of naked children scattered throughout the trunk compartment.

The driver has been charged with possession of child pornography. If the driver files a motion to suppress the photographs, what is the most likely ruling from the court?

A. The motion will be denied because the government interest in catching child pornographers outweighs the driver's privacy interests in his car.

B. The motion will be denied because the trooper found the child pornography in plain view.

C. The motion will be granted because the trooper converted a routine traffic stop into a search for drugs and child pornography.

D. The motion will be granted because the trooper only had probable cause to search for marijuana, not child pornography.

159. Early one evening, an officer on routine patrol stopped a driver for speeding. When speaking with the driver, the officer developed probable cause to believe she had been drinking alcohol. The officer directed the driver to get out of the car and had her perform several field sobriety tests — which she failed. At that point, the driver admitted that she'd had a few drinks after work. The officer arrested the woman, searched her incident to arrest, and discovered a handgun and a baggie of cocaine in the pocket of her jacket.

After handcuffing her, the officer placed the woman in the back of his locked patrol car. He then returned to the woman's car, searched it, and found two more guns in the trunk. After the prosecutor discovered the woman had a felony record, she was charged with being a felon in possession of a firearm and cocaine possession.

If the woman argues that the evidence seized from her car should be suppressed, what is the prosecutor's strongest argument in support of the search?

A. The search was a reasonable automobile exception search because the officer had probable cause to believe that evidence would be found in the trunk.

B. The search was a reasonable search incident to arrest because the officer had reason to believe that evidence would be found in the trunk.

C. The search was a reasonable inventory search because the officer was required to inventory the contents of the car.

D. The search was reasonable *Terry* frisk of the car because the officer had reasonable suspicion to believe that a weapon was in the trunk.

160. Two officers stopped a driver for driving through a yellow light. The first officer wrote the driver a ticket. When she was done, the first officer and her partner asked the driver to get out of the car so the first officer could hand him the ticket. The driver complied, but as he got out of the car, the first officer saw that he was carrying a weapon in a holster inside his jacket.

The first officer frisked the driver and disarmed him. Then, as the partner stood with the driver a few feet away, the first officer searched the passenger compartment of the car and found a second weapon in the glove box. When asked, the driver admitted that he didn't have permits for either weapon. The first officer arrested the driver.

If the driver is charged with carrying unlicensed weapons and if he challenges the search of his car, what is the prosecutor's best argument as to why the search was reasonable?

A. The search was a reasonable automobile exception search because the officer had probable cause to believe that additional weapons would be found in the car.

B. The search was a reasonable search incident to arrest because the driver was a recent occupant of the car.

C. The search was a reasonable inventory search because the officer was required to inventory the contents of the car.

D. The search was a reasonable *Terry* frisk of the car because the officer had reasonable suspicion to believe the driver was armed and dangerous.

161. A police officer stopped a driver for failing to wear a seatbelt. The driver didn't contest that she wasn't wearing her seatbelt, but she explained to the officer that she thought it was unfair that she was going to be ticketed for a something that she believed should be determined by her own physical comfort and free will. The officer told the driver that he didn't care for her attitude and so he decided to arrest her—as he was permitted to do under state law. The officer handcuffed the driver and placed her in the back of his locked cruiser. The officer also called for a tow truck.

While waiting for the tow truck to arrive, the officer searched the driver's car and found hypodermic needles in the glove compartment and heroin in the console between the driver and front passenger seats.

When the officer's supervisor found out that he had arrested a driver for failing to wear a seatbelt, she was livid. The supervisor also asked the officer to justify the search of the car. What is his most plausible response?

A. The search was a reasonable search incident to arrest.

B. The search was a reasonable automobile exception search.

C. The search was a reasonable inventory search.

D. The search was a reasonable *Terry* frisk of the car.

162. A police officer was called to the scene of an accident involving a car and a motorcycle. When the officer arrived, emergency medical personnel were helping the motorcyclist, who had been thrown from his bike and who appeared to have extensive injuries. The driver of the car was uninjured. The officer walked over to the motorcycle—which was lying on the ground on its side—and began to go through the contents of the bike's saddlebags. In one of the bags, the officer found a vial of crack cocaine, which he seized.

After the motorcyclist recovered from his injuries, the prosecutor charged him with possession of cocaine. Prior to trial, the motorcyclist's lawyer filed a motion to suppress. The prosecutor responded, arguing that since the motorcycle is a type of vehicle, the search of its saddlebags was authorized by the automobile exception.

How should the court rule on the motion to suppress?

A. The motion should be granted because a motorcycle is different from an automobile and as such, it cannot be searched under the automobile exception.

B. The motion should be granted because even though motorcycles can be searched under the automobile exception, the officer lacked probable cause for the search.

C. The motion should be denied because even though motorcycles cannot be searched under the automobile exception, the officer conducted a lawful inventory search.

D. The motion should be denied because motorcycles and automobiles have enough in common that motorcycles fall within the automobile exception.

163. During the summer, local police patrol a lake north of the town center. The lake is ringed by vacation homes and motor boats are allowed to be used on the lake. Drinking and boating is strictly prohibited.

One weekend afternoon, an officer on lake patrol saw a motorboat being driven by a man who was drinking from a beer bottle. The officer steered his motorboat over to the man's motorboat and boarded it. The officer noticed a closed cooler on the deck, located near where the man was standing. The officer opened the cooler and saw that it was filled with bottles of beer. The officer towed the motorboat back to the shore and wrote the man a ticket for drinking and boating. Because this was the man's third drinking-and-boating ticket, he faced a large fine, loss of his boating license, and up to three days in jail.

If the man challenges the ticket, what is the most appropriate ruling?

A. The ticket should be dismissed because the officer failed to request permission to board the man's boat and search it.

B. The ticket should be dismissed because the officer had no way of knowing whether the man was drinking beer or a soda.

C. The ticket was properly issued because the officer didn't need any suspicion to board the boat or search the cooler.

D. The ticket was properly issued because the officer had probable cause to board the boat and search the cooler.

164. A police officer and his partner stopped a car for speeding; while speaking to the driver, the officer developed probable cause to believe that she had been smoking marijuana. The officer directed the driver and passenger to get out of the car. Both complied. Since it was a windy day, the passenger kept her jacket on when she left the car.

While the partner stood with the driver and the passenger, the officer searched the passenger compartment and trunk of the car, and found a small baggie of marijuana. The officer then walked over to where the driver and the passenger were standing and searched the passenger's jacket. In one of the front pockets, the officer found a baggie of marijuana, rolling papers, and a lighter.

The passenger was later charged with possession of marijuana and drug paraphernalia and she filed a motion to suppress. If the prosecutor defends the search as a reasonable automobile exception search, what is the most likely ruling from the court?

A. The search was reasonable because the passenger had been wearing her jacket in the car and the police had probable cause to search the car.

B. The search was reasonable because the officer's probable cause included both the car and its recent occupants.

C. The search was unreasonable because at the time of the search, the officer did not have probable cause to believe evidence was in the passenger's jacket.

D. The search was unreasonable because at the time of the search, the passenger's jacket was not located inside the car.

165. A member of the police gang surveillance unit was parked outside a residential house where a known gang member lived. The officer had probable cause to believe that the gang member sold drugs that he stored in a green backpack. The officer had considered getting a search warrant to look for the backpack in the house, but had decided that she didn't want to deal with the "red tape" associated with obtaining a warrant.

After the officer had waited for about an hour, the gang member walked out of the house carrying the green backpack over his shoulder. The officer watched as the gang member got into his parked car and pulled out of the driveway. The officer then began to follow the gang member, and when he failed to properly signal a right turn, the officer pulled him over. The officer then searched the backpack and found it packed with methamphetamine and cocaine.

The prosecutor charged the gang member with various crimes associated with these drugs; in response, the gang member's attorney filed a motion to suppress, arguing that the drugs were the fruits of an unreasonable search. How should the court rule on the motion?

A. The motion should be granted because the officer manipulated the law when she purposefully waited until the backpack was in the car.

B. The motion should be granted because the officer had time to obtain a warrant, but she intentionally decided not to get one.

C. The motion should be denied because the officer had probable cause to search the backpack and the backpack was located inside the car.

D. The motion should be denied because the officer knew the gang member was involved in dangerous activity.

Consent Searches

166. A police officer who had lawfully stopped a driver requested consent from the driver to search the trunk of her car. The driver said yes and used her key fob to open the trunk. The officer looked inside and found a kilo of cocaine sitting next to the driver's groceries. He arrested the driver and the D.A. filed drug charges against her. Prior to trial, the driver filed a motion to suppress the cocaine discovered in the trunk.

At the suppression hearing, the officer testified that he had no particular reason to suspect the driver had anything illegal in her car. Instead, he testified that he had asked for the driver's consent because he had been placed on probation at work for some paperwork errors and thought that his supervisor might be willing to remove him from probation if he "made a big arrest."

Based on these facts, how should the court rule on the suppression motion?

A. The motion should be granted because the officer admitted that he had no reason to suspect the driver of any crime.

B. The motion should be granted because the officer admitted that he wanted to search the trunk to advance his own professional interests.

C. The motion should be denied because the driver invited the search by unlocking the trunk with her key fob.

D. The motion should be denied because the driver consented to the search of the trunk of her car.

167. A man was traveling on a bus when it pulled into a rest stop for a scheduled stop. The man had several kilos of packaged cocaine in his bag. Two police officers boarded the bus and walked down the center aisle, asking individual passengers for consent to search their bags. Each time they asked, the officers also explained that passengers had a right to refuse their consent.

When the officers got to where the man was sitting, they asked him for permission to search his bag, but did not also explain that he had a right to refuse. The man agreed to the search, thinking that by giving consent the officers might leave him alone. The man was wrong; the officers searched his bag and found the cocaine inside. The officers arrested the man and he was later charged with drug crimes.

If the man files a motion to suppress the cocaine found in his bag, how should the court rule on the motion?

A. The motion should be granted because the officers did not tell the man he had a right to refuse consent.

B. The motion should be granted because the officers treated the passengers unequally by only telling some of them that they had a right to refuse consent.

C. The motion should be denied because the man voluntarily consented to a search of his bag.

D. The motion should be denied because the man knowingly consented since he knew his bag contained cocaine.

168. A college student was sitting on a bench in a public park in the center of town, taking a break between classes. A police officer walked up to the student and started a conversation with him about the weather. After several minutes of chatting amicably, the student took his backpack off the bench to give the officer room to sit down.

The two began to talk about the student's classes and career plans. Then, out of the blue, the officer asked the student for permission to search his backpack. The student was taken aback and said yes. The officer searched the backpack and found a baggie of amphetamines in the zipper compartment on the outside of the backpack.

If the student is charged with drug possession and files a motion to suppress, what should the court consider in determining whether the student voluntarily gave consent for the search?

A. Whether a reasonable person would have voluntarily given consent for the search.

B. Whether a reasonable person in the student's same situation would have voluntarily given consent for the search.

C. Whether the student, properly educated as to his rights, would have voluntarily given consent for the search.

D. Whether, under a totality of the circumstances, the student voluntarily gave consent to the search.

169. A police officer stopped a teenaged driver for speeding. The teenager told the officer that she was very nervous because she'd just gotten her driver's license two days before. The officer spent about ten minutes in his cruiser writing a ticket, and then returned to the teenager's car.

As the officer handed the teenager the ticket, she asked if she was free to leave. The officer replied that she was not and explained that, "according to state law," when an officer pulls a driver over for speeding, he is allowed to detain the driver for up to 30 minutes, even if the ticket process takes less time than that. (There was no such law.) The officer looked at his watch and said, "according to my clock, you and I have another 20 minutes together." The officer then stood by the side of the teenager's car and stared at her. After ten minutes of uncomfortable silence, the officer asked the teenager for consent to search the trunk of the car. The teenager readily agreed. The officer found a small amount of marijuana in the trunk.

If the teenager is charged with marijuana possession and if she files a motion to suppress, what is her lawyer's strongest argument in support of suppression?

A. The teenager's consent was involuntary because of her young age and inexperience with the traffic laws.

B. The teenager's consent was involuntary because the officer knew of her young age and inexperience with the traffic laws.

C. The teenager's consent was involuntary because the officer lied about the state traffic laws.

D. The teenager's consent was involuntary because of her age, inexperience with the traffic laws, the officer's knowledge of her age and inexperience, and his lie about state law.

170. An officer was on highway patrol when he saw a car speed past him, traveling at least 20 miles per hour over the posted speed limit. The officer pulled the driver over to the side of the road. After reviewing the driver's license and registration, the officer decided to give the driver a verbal warning.

The officer directed the driver to get out of his car. The driver complied and the officer gave him the verbal warning. The officer then handed the driver his license and registration and said, "I just have one question before you go … do you have any contraband in your car? Drugs? Weapons? Anything illegal?" The driver said no. The officer asked for consent to search the car and the driver agreed. In the trunk of the car, the officer found a bag of amphetamines and several illegal weapons.

Later, after being charged with crimes, the driver filed a motion to suppress. What is the most likely ruling on the motion?

A. The motion will be denied because the driver's rate of speed gave the officer reasonable suspicion to believe there were drugs in the car.

B. The motion will be denied because the request to search did not prolong the stop and because the driver consented to the search.

C. The motion will be granted because the officer was required to tell the driver that he was free to leave after giving him the ticket.

D. The motion will be granted because the officer is not permitted to convert a routine traffic stop into a search for evidence of crime.

171. Police suspected that a young man was selling drugs out of the house he shared with his elderly aunt. Three officers went to the house one afternoon and knocked on the door; the aunt answered the door and asked the officers what they wanted. The lead officer explained that they had a warrant to search the house and so the aunt opened the door wide and stepped out of the way saying, "well, then you better come inside and take a look around." The aunt returned to the kitchen to finish preparing her lunch and the officers searched the house. During the search, the officers discovered a kilo of cocaine sitting on one of the dining room chairs.

The young man was later charged with drug crimes associated with this cocaine. His attorney filed a motion to suppress, arguing—correctly—that police never had a warrant to search the house.

How should the trial judge rule on the motion?

A. The motion should be denied because the officers did not threaten the aunt, show their weapons, or harm the aunt in any way.

B. The motion should be denied because regardless of the lack of warrant, the aunt still consented to the search of the house.

C. The motion should be granted because the officers never actually asked for consent to search and so the aunt could not have given consent to search.

D. The motion should be granted because the aunt's consent was given in response to the officers' show of authority and is therefore involuntary.

172. Police received a tip that a mother of three young children was selling drugs to other area parents. The investigating officer went to the mother's house and requested permission to come inside and search her house for drugs. The mother refused. The officer then said:

> Look, there's been an accusation that you're selling drugs to the other moms and dads. If you let me inside to search your house and I find nothing, then this whole thing will go away. But if you say no and I have to go to a judge to get a warrant, I doubt a judge is going to be too happy about that. And if a judge takes your kids away because you were being so stubborn, you better not come crying to me....

The mother looked down at her feet for a few moments and then let the officer inside the house. In the kitchen, hidden inside a coffee pot, the officer found a large supply of amphetamines.

The mother was charged with drug crimes and filed a motion to suppress. How should the court rule on the motion?

A. The motion should be granted because the mother's consent was a product of coercion and duress.

B. The motion should be granted because the officer failed to corroborate the tip before going to the mother's house.

C. The motion should be denied because the officer's threat was too speculative to have any coercive effect.

D. The motion should be denied because the mother is only the victim of her own stupidity.

173. Police suspected a woman was growing marijuana in her house but were unable to develop probable case for a search warrant. Frustrated by the pace of the investigation, the lead officer decided to conduct a "knock and talk" at the woman's house, to see if he could garner any information that way.

The next afternoon, the lead officer went to the woman's house. He rang the doorbell and the woman answered. She opened the door wide and stepped to one side; the officer walked inside and immediately saw a marijuana pipe sitting on a table inside the front door. He seized the pipe and arrested the woman for possession of marijuana paraphernalia. Later, after she was charged, the woman filed a motion to suppress the pipe.

Should the woman win her motion to suppress?

A. Yes, because the officer admittedly lacked probable cause to search the woman's house.

B. Yes, because the woman never verbally consented to the entry into her house.

C. No, because the officer legitimately suspected the woman was involved in crime before he knocked on her door.

D. No, because the woman consented to the entry into her house.

174. A police officer received a tip that a woman was dealing drugs out of her bakery. The officer drove to the bakery and spoke to the woman about the allegations. She told the officer that she ran an honest business and didn't have anything to hide. The officer then asked the woman for permission to search the bakery and she agreed. Twenty minutes later, while searching in the kitchen, the officer found a stash of cocaine, hidden in a sugar bin. The officer seized the cocaine and arrested the woman.

Later, after the woman was charged with cocaine possession, her attorney filed a motion to suppress. In the motion, the attorney argued that when the woman gave consent to search "the bakery," she was limiting her consent to the actual bakery showroom and that her consent did not extend to the kitchen. As such, the attorney argued that the woman's consent was ineffective and the cocaine should be suppressed.

What is the prosecutor's strongest argument in response?

A. The cocaine should be admitted because a reasonable business owner would have understood the woman's consent as extending to the kitchen.

B. The cocaine should be admitted because a reasonable baker would have understood the woman's consent as extending to the kitchen.

C. The cocaine should be admitted because a reasonable person would have understood the woman's consent as extending to the kitchen.

D. The cocaine should be admitted because a reasonable bakery customer would have understood the woman's consent as extending to the kitchen.

175. A police officer seated in a coffee shop saw a transaction on the street that he believed to be a drug sale. The suspected drug purchaser got into his car and drove away; the officer relayed what he'd see to his dispatcher, along with a description of the man's car. A second officer in a police cruiser overheard the call and, seeing a car matching that description, began to follow it. The officer pulled the driver over a few minutes later, after he rolled through a stop sign without coming to a complete stop.

When the officer approached the driver's side of the car, he explained that he had pulled the driver over for a moving violation but that he also suspected the driver had drugs in his car. The officer then asked the driver for permission to search the car and the driver agreed, saying that he had "nothing to hide." In the subsequent search of the car, the officer found a paper bag on the floor of the backseat. The top of the bag was folded over, but the officer opened the bag and found half a kilo of cocaine inside. The officer arrested the driver.

The driver has been charged with possession of cocaine and has moved to suppress the drugs from his upcoming trial. What is the prosecutor's strongest argument in response to the motion?

A. The motion should be denied because the driver knew he had evidence to hide, contrary to what he told the officer.

B. The motion should be denied because the officer had reasonable articulable suspicion to search the car.

C. The motion should be denied because a driver's consent to search a car extends to all closed containers inside the car.

D. The motion should be denied because the driver's consent to search the car in this case extended to the paper bag.

176. A police offer pulled a driver over for speeding and wrote her a ticket. When the officer handed the driver the ticket, he asked her for consent to search her car. The driver agreed to the search, but explained that she was late for a business meeting and didn't have a lot of time to spare. She then said to the officer, "I've got about five minutes, so if you can do this quick, then it's okay with me."

The officer reached across the driver and using the fob on her keychain, unlocked the trunk. He then walked to the back of the car, searched the trunk, and found a bag of cocaine hidden underneath the spare tire. The officer arrested the driver and the D.A. later charged her with possession of cocaine.

If the driver files a motion to suppress, what is the most likely ruling from the court?

A. The motion will be granted because the driver did not give the officer consent to unlock the trunk of her car.

B. The motion will be granted because the driver placed limits on the scope of the search and the officer did not follow those limits.

C. The motion will be denied because the driver voluntarily consented to an unlimited car search and the officer complied with her consent.

D. The motion will be denied because the driver consented to the search and the officer complied with the driver's time limits for the search.

177. The state legislature voted to cut funding for a local public college. In response, students organized a protest at the state capitol and state police were directed to monitor the protest.

In the middle of the protest, an officer came up to one of the protesters and asked her if he could search her knapsack. The protester said yes and began to hand her backpack to the officer, but then pulled it back and started to walk away. The officer followed the protester and demanded that she hand him the backpack. The protester complied with the order and the officer searched the backpack. He found a small amount of cocaine hidden inside.

If the protester is charged with cocaine possession and moves to suppress the evidence found in her backpack, what is the most likely ruling from the court?

A. The protester revoked her consent, so the search of the backpack was unreasonable.

B. The officer interfered with the protester's First Amendment rights and so the search of the backpack was unreasonable.

C. The officer never actually interfered with the protester's First Amendment rights and so the search of the backpack was reasonable.

D. The protester gave consent to search, so the search of the backpack was reasonable.

178. An officer on routine foot patrol saw a man standing on a residential street corner, smoking a cigarette. The officer was familiar with the area and hadn't seen the man before. Concerned that the man might be planning a residential burglary, the officer approached him and asked him if he would mind if the officer frisked him for weapons. The man refused, and said that he'd prefer to finish his cigarette in peace. The officer quickly pushed the man up against the wall and frisked him, finding a screwdriver and a case of lock picks in his jacket pocket.

The officer arrested the man and the prosecutor charged him with possession of burglar's tools. Later, at the suppression hearing, the man's attorney asked the officer why he had frisked the man. The officer replied that the man's refusal provided reasonable suspicion for the frisk. The officer continued, "after all, if your client had nothing to hide, why wouldn't he just agree to the frisk?"

How should the court rule on the motion to suppress?

A. The motion should be denied because the officer was right: the man's refusal to consent to the frisk was suspicious.

B. The motion should be denied because the officer was right: he suspected the man was planning a burglary and the man had burglar's tools.

C. The motion should be granted because the officer drew an adverse inference from the man's exercise of a constitutional right.

D. The motion should be granted because the officer really had no reason to suspect the man was planning a residential burglary.

179. A police officer pulled a driver over for having a broken taillight. When the driver first began to speak to the officer he was very nervous and stammered when he answered the officer's questions. Later, when the officer had written the ticket and returned to the car to give it to the driver, the driver continued to stammer and would not make eye contact with the officer.

The officer asked the driver for consent to search his car. Looking straight ahead and not at the officer, the driver said no. As the driver spoke, he placed his right hand on a sweater on the passenger's seat, and he appeared to be grasping something underneath with his fingers. The officer pulled the driver from the car and looked underneath the sweater only to find a cell phone.

The driver's attorney filed a complaint with the officer's supervisor, claiming that the officer should not have been permitted to search the driver's car. What is the most appropriate response from the supervisor?

A. The driver's nervous behavior gave the officer probable cause to search the car.

B. The driver's nervous behavior gave the officer reasonable suspicion to frisk the car.

C. The driver's refusal to give consent gave the officer probable cause to search the car.

D. The driver's refusal to give consent gave the officer reasonable suspicion to frisk the car.

180. Police received a tip that two law students were selling drugs to their classmates. The two students were lived together in a house in a residential neighborhood. The officer assigned to investigate the tip decided to go to the house and see if he could speak to one or both of the students.

When the officer arrived at the house, one of the students—a man—was outside mowing the lawn. The student asked the officer if there was a problem and the officer asked if he could come inside the house and look around. The student agreed and showed the officer into the house. The officer walked into the kitchen and found a small methamphetamine lab. The officer arrested the student. Later, the officer arrested the second student—a woman—as she was coming out of the law school after class.

When the second student learned about the search of her house, she asked her attorney whether the evidence would be suppressed because she hadn't consented to the search. How should the attorney respond?

A. The evidence will be admitted because the male student had common authority over the kitchen and consented to the search.

B. The evidence will be admitted against the male student only because evidence discovered by a consent search can only be used against the consenting party.

C. The evidence will be suppressed because the officer never bothered to ask the male student whether he had common authority over the kitchen.

D. The evidence will be suppressed because the male student could only consent for a search of an area over which he had exclusive control.

181. After obtaining an arrest warrant, police arrested a teenager at his house for murder. The arresting officer asked the teenager where she could find his clothing from the night before—when the murder occurred—and the teenager pointed to a duffel bag on the floor. The officer asked the teenager for permission to search the duffel bag and he agreed. In the bag, the officer found clothing belonging to both the teenager and also his cousin.

Subsequently, police arrested the cousin and both the teenager and his cousin were charged with murder. Prior to trial, the cousin moved to suppress the clothing found in the duffel bag arguing that the teenager lacked common authority over the interior of the bag. According to the cousin's motion, the duffel bag was his and he had only given the teenager permission to use the outer zippered compartment and not the entire duffel bag.

What is the most likely ruling on the cousin's motion?

A. The motion will be granted because the teenager lacked common authority over the entire duffel bag.

B. The motion will be granted because the teenager waived his cousin's rights when he consented to the search of the duffel bag.

C. The motion will be denied because the cousin waived his rights when he permitted the teenager to use the bag.

D. The motion will be denied because the teenager had common authority over the duffel bag.

182. A middle-aged woman called police to report that she thought her husband was dealing drugs out of their shared house. An officer was sent to investigate and when he knocked at the door of the house, the woman invited the officer inside. According to the woman, she had been cleaning in her husband's home office and found a large bag of cocaine on the bookshelf, hidden behind some books. The woman brought the officer into the office and showed him the cocaine — which he seized.

Later, after a grand jury indicted the husband for cocaine possession and he was arrested, his attorney filed a motion to suppress. In the motion, the attorney argued that the room where the cocaine was discovered was his client's "man cave" and the woman did not have permission to enter the room, let alone clean it.

If the court accepts this assertion as true, how should it rule on the man's motion to suppress?

A. The motion should be granted because the woman lacked common authority to consent to a search of the room.

B. The motion should be granted because the man never consented to a search of his "man cave."

C. The motion should be denied because suppression courts have no business delving into marital business.

D. The motion should be denied because the officer reasonably believed that the woman had authority to consent to a search of the room.

183. An off-duty police officer was leaving the grocery store one day and was about to get into her car when she smelled the odor of burning marijuana. The officer looked around the parking lot and saw a teenager sitting in the passenger seat of a parked car. The officer approached the car, identified herself to the teenager, and asked him if he had been smoking marijuana. The teenager said no.

The officer then asked for consent to search the car for marijuana; the teenager hesitated for a moment and said, "I guess it'll be okay, but I don't think my friend will be happy when he finds out." Based on this statement, the officer searched the car and found several baggies of marijuana under the front seats and a smoldering half-smoked marijuana cigarette in the ashtray. As the officer was arresting the teenager, his friend came out of the grocery store. The officer arrested the friend as well.

The teenager and the friend were charged with marijuana possession and the friend filed a motion to suppress the evidence from the car. What is the friend's strongest argument in support of his motion?

A. The motion should be granted because by using conditional language, the teenager did not consent to a search of the car.

B. The motion should be granted because there is no proof that the friend constructively possessed the marijuana found inside the car.

C. The motion should be granted because a reasonable police officer would have realized that the teenager lacked authority to consent to the search.

D. The motion should be granted because the officer was off-duty and did not have the authority to conduct searches and seizures.

184. A wife was involved in a fight with her husband and called the police for help. When an officer arrived, the wife explained that her husband was a "big time cocaine user" and invited the officer to search the house to see the husband's cocaine supply for himself. The husband denied the claim and told the officer that he did not want the officer to come inside the house. However, based on the wife's consent, the officer searched the house, and found a kilo of cocaine inside a closet in the master bedroom.

The husband was charged with cocaine possession and the prosecutor wants to use the cocaine at the upcoming trial. How should the court rule on the suppression motion?

A. The motion should be denied because officer reasonably relied on the wife's consent to search the house.

B. The motion should be denied because the wife had common authority over the house and was entitled to give consent to search.

C. The motion should be granted because the wife's consent is ineffective in the face of the husband's refusal to give consent.

D. The motion should be granted because the officer unreasonably failed to ascertain whether the wife's name was on the deed of the house.

185. Police were chasing a robbery suspect and saw him run into an apartment building. When the officers entered the building, they couldn't tell which apartment the suspect had entered, but they heard shouting and yelling from behind one of the apartment doors. The officers knocked on the door and a woman answered; the woman's face was bleeding and she was crying. A man came up behind her and told the officers that he didn't want them inside his apartment and told them to leave.

One of the officers asked the woman if the man had hurt her and the man turned to glare at the woman; the woman did not answer the officer. The officer arrested the man for assault and took him to the police station. A second officer stayed with the woman while she calmed down. About thirty minutes later, the second officer asked the woman for permission to search the apartment. She agreed and the officer searched, finding evidence of the robbery on the kitchen counter.

The man was later charged with robbery, and the prosecutor wants to use the evidence from the search of his apartment against him. If the man moves to suppress, what is the most likely ruling from the suppression court?

A. The motion will be denied because the woman consented to the search.

B. The motion will be denied because the police had probable cause to arrest the man and the woman consented to the search.

C. The motion will be granted because the police unreasonably arrested the man in order to get the woman to consent to the search.

D. The motion will be granted because the man's refusal to give consent remained effective until he revoked it.

Inventory Searches

186. A police officer arrested a woman for shoplifting. The woman had been caught after she placed an expensive dress in a shopping bag filled with legitimately purchased clothing. After the officer handcuffed the woman, the shop clerk handed the officer the woman's shopping bag. The officer put the bag in the trunk of his cruiser and drove the woman to the police station. One hour later, the officer went through the contents of the bag and made a list of its contents.

What is the most likely justification for the officer's warrantless search of the shopping bag?

A. The officer conducted a lawful plain view search of evidence in his trunk.

B. The officer conducted a lawful inventory search of the bag's contents.

C. The officer conducted a lawful catalogue of the evidence to be used at trial.

D. The officer conducted a lawful but delayed search incident to arrest.

187. An officer arrested a driver for reckless driving. In the course of making the arrest, the driver acted erratically and the officer was concerned that she might be mentally ill and in need of immediate treatment. The officer brought the driver to the emergency room of a local hospital. After an evaluation, the treating physician determined that the driver was not mentally ill and was not in need of treatment. The officer took the driver to the police station for booking.

In the meantime, a second officer towed the driver's car to the impound lot—which was located 15 miles from the police station where the driver was being held. Five hours after the arrest, the arresting officer went to conduct an inventory search of the driver's car. The officer used the jurisdiction's inventory code to guide his search, and during the search, discovered a bag of opiate pills in the glove box. Later, after the driver could not produce a prescription for the pills, she was charged with drug possession.

The woman's lawyer has filed a motion to suppress the pills from her upcoming trial. What is the most likely ruling on the motion?

A. The inventory search of the car was unreasonable because it was conducted five hours after the officer arrested the driver.

B. The inventory search of the car was unreasonable because the car was 15 miles away from the driver at the time of the search.

C. The inventory search of the car was reasonable because the officer needed to find the reason for the driver's erratic behavior.

D. The inventory search of the car was reasonable because the officer searched the car according to the jurisdiction's inventory code.

188. A police officer arrested a driver for drunk driving, and had the driver's car towed to the police impound lot. At the lot, the officer's partner searched the car, using the municipality's "Inventory Search Protocol" to guide his search of the car. Inside the unlocked glove box of the car, the partner found a half kilo of powder cocaine. The partner seized the cocaine.

When the prosecutor learned about the cocaine, she charged the woman with possession of cocaine with intent to distribute. The woman's attorney filed a motion to suppress.

If the court denies the motion, what is the most likely reason for doing so?

A. The car might have contained evidence of other, unknown crimes that the driver might have committed and was trying to hide.

B. The car might have contained valuable items that could have be stolen from the car while it was parked in the impound lot.

C. The car might have contained information about the driver's identity that the officer could use to process the driver's arrest.

D. The car might have contained evidence of the alcohol the driver consumed prior to her arrest by the officer for drunk driving.

189. A police officer arrested a woman for speeding and the officer had the woman's car towed to the impound lot. After taking the woman through the booking process, the officer inventoried the contents of her car, following the procedures set forth in the department's inventory policy. In the glove box of the car, the officer found a baggie of methamphetamine, which he seized.

One week later, the prosecutor charged the woman with possession of methamphetamine and the woman's attorney filed a motion to suppress. In the motion, the attorney argued that the methamphetamine was perfectly safe in the glove box, that it did not pose any danger to the police, and that the woman wouldn't have reported it as stolen even if it had been taken by someone.

How should the court rule on the motion?

A. The motion should be denied because the officer conducted a lawful inventory search, following the department's routine inventory policy.

B. The motion should be denied because the methamphetamine might have been stolen from the car, had the officer not searched and seized it.

C. The motion should be granted because none of the rationales supporting warrantless inventory searches are present on these facts.

D. The motion should be granted because there was no reason to believe that evidence of the arresting offense would be found in the car.

190. A police officer pulled a driver over for speeding and the officer eventually arrested the driver for drunk driving. The driver's car was towed to the impound lot, where the officer inventoried its contents. While conducting the inventory, the officer found a revolver in the trunk, inside a small zippered bag next to the spare tire. The revolver was later linked to a homicide, and the driver was eventually charged with murder.

Prior to the driver's murder trial, he filed a motion to suppress the revolver. At the hearing, the officer testified that the police department did not have a written inventory protocol, but he explained that he had developed his own system for inventorying the cars of arrestees—beginning with the passenger compartment and then going into the trunk. Asked for his policy on the opening of closed containers within the cars he searched, the officer replied, "it depends on how I'm feeling that day."

Based on the officer's testimony, how should the court rule on the motion?

A. The motion should be granted because the officer did not follow any established police procedures in conducting his inventory search of the driver's car.

B. The motion should be granted because the officer impermissibly searched for a weapon after stopping and arresting the driver for a moving violation.

C. The motion should be denied because the officer's testimony establishes that he has, by practice, created an established procedure for inventorying cars.

D. The motion should be denied because the officer's supervisors are really the ones at fault for not establishing a written policy for inventory searches.

191. A police officer arrested a driver for vehicular manslaughter because of an accident involving a pedestrian. According to the applicable inventory code, an officer who arrests a driver has the discretion to decide whether to have the arrestee's car towed to a police impound lot or to leave it locked in a public place. If the officer elects the former option, the contents of the car will be inventoried; if he elects the latter, the car will not be inventoried. The code also sets forth several criteria officers are to use in determining whether to impound the car or not, including whether leaving the car in a public place would create a danger to the public or a risk of vandalism to the car and whether the car itself was used in the commission of a crime.

The officer decided to have the driver's car towed to the impound lot. Later, during the officer's inventory search of the car, he discovered a bag of cocaine in the car's glove box. After the driver was charged with possession of cocaine, his attorney filed a motion to suppress.

How should the court rule on the motion?

A. The motion should be granted because the inventory code impermissibly gives officers wide discretion as to whether to impound and search the cars of arrestees.

B. The motion should be granted because there is no showing that the officer fully considered and documented his decision to have the car impounded and searched.

C. The motion should be denied because the officer's subjective motivation is irrelevant here and the court should only consider objective, fact-based criteria.

D. The motion should be denied because although the inventory code gives officers some discretion it also provides standard criteria for exercising that discretion.

192. An officer saw a woman driving without her seatbelt and signaled for her to pull over. The officer had stopped the woman for moving violations several times in the past month and had a hunch that she was a drug trafficker. Each time he had pulled the woman over, he asked for her consent to search the car, and each time she had refused.

As permitted by state law, the officer arrested the woman for the seatbelt violation. After her car was towed to the police impound lot, the officer searched it according to the jurisdiction's inventory code. In the trunk, the officer found exactly what he thought he'd find: bags of drugs. The officer informed the district attorney of his discovery and she charged the woman with a variety of drug crimes. If convicted of these crimes, the woman will be incarcerated for life.

The woman's attorney filed a motion to suppress the drugs from the trunk. How should the court rule on the motion?

A. The motion should be denied because the officer conducted a lawful inventory search, following the jurisdiction's inventory policy.

B. The motion should be denied because the officer would have been able to search the car anyway under the automobile exception.

C. The motion should be granted because the officer's sole purpose for arresting the woman was to conduct an inventory search of her car.

D. The motion should be granted because the officer acted on a hunch and not on probable cause or reasonable suspicion.

193. During an inventory search of a car that had been towed to the police impound lot, a police officer used the driver's keys—taken from the driver at the time of the arrest—to unlock the car's glove box. According to the jurisdiction's inventory code, the officer was permitted to look inside closed and locked containers, "if the process of opening those containers would not destroy or damage them." Inside the glove box, the officer found a revolver and a bag of methamphetamine. The officer was later able to tie the revolver to a gas station robbery from the previous week.

After the car's driver was charged with armed robbery and possession of methamphetamine, his attorney filed a motion to suppress the items taken from the car. In the motion, the attorney conceded that the officer had a right to conduct an inventory search of the car. However, the attorney argued that the driver retained an expectation of privacy in the locked glove box and that the officer should have been required to obtain a warrant to open it and search inside.

How should the prosecutor best respond?

A. The glove box was not really locked because the officer had the car keys.

B. The car's driver cannot claim an expectation of privacy in evidence of crime.

C. The jurisdiction's inventory code permitted the officer to unlock the glove box.

D. If not secured, the weapon could pose a danger to the police and the public.

194. After arresting a driver for failing to wear a seatbelt, reckless driving, and other moving violations, the arresting officer searched the driver's car according to the jurisdiction's inventory code. The code instructed officers to collect and secure "all cash, valuables, weapons, and evidence associated with the arresting offense."

Following the code, the officer opened the car's trunk and found two laundry baskets inside, each filled with folded laundry. The officer rifled through the laundry, looking for items to inventory. At the bottom of one of the baskets, the officer found a clear plastic bag with a kilo of cocaine inside. The officer seized the cocaine.

If the prosecutor charges the driver with cocaine possession and if the driver files a motion to suppress, how will the court rule on the motion?

A. The motion will be granted because the cocaine is not cash, valuables, weapons, or evidence associated with the arresting offense.

B. The motion will be granted because the officer discovered the cocaine while searching the baskets, and plain view requires that an officer come across evidence, not search for it.

C. The motion will be denied because the officer found the cocaine in plain view while conducting an otherwise lawful inventory search.

D. The motion will be denied because the officer's discovery of the cocaine was inadvertent, so the plain view exception is inapplicable.

195. A police officer assigned to the impound lot was told to inventory the contents of a car that had recently been towed there. While searching, the officer found a plastic bag of cocaine pushed under the front driver's seat. The officer seized the cocaine and continued to search. In the trunk, the officer found a zippered canvas bag. The officer unzipped the bag and found a second large plastic bag of cocaine inside.

The owner of the car was later charged with cocaine possession and her attorney filed a motion to suppress. In the motion, the attorney cited to the jurisdiction's inventory code, which states, in relevant part:

> While conducting an inventory search, officers may not open any closed containers found within an automobile, unless the officer can determine, by visually inspecting the exterior of the container, that it contains a weapon. If, after visual inspection, the officer develops the belief that the container contains a weapon, the officer may open the container and secure the weapon.

How should the judge rule on the motion to suppress?

A. The motion should be denied because the officer could have believed that the zippered canvas bag contained a weapon.

B. The motion should be denied because the officer had probable cause to believe that the zippered canvas bag contained cocaine.

C. The motion should be granted because there is no evidence the officer believed that the zippered canvas bag contained a weapon.

D. The motion should be granted because the officer clearly exceeded the plain language of the jurisdiction's inventory code.

Special Needs Searches

196. A state enacted legislation mandating drug testing for all emergency call center operators. The testing was to be conducted through urinalysis and the testing protocol allowed operators a limited ability to select the date and time of their test. Once the test date and time were established, operators were required to report to a testing center where they would be met by a supervisor of the same gender. The supervisor would oversee the collection of the sample and was required to take steps to preserve the privacy of operators while the urine was being collected.

If an operator tested positive for any screened substance, he would be given an opportunity to provide an explanation for the results. If there was no satisfactory explanation, the operator would be terminated. However, the test results would not be released to the police without the operator's written permission.

An emergency call center operator wants to challenge the constitutionality of the legislation. If she consults with a lawyer about the possibility of a lawsuit, how should the lawyer respond?

A. The legislation is likely unconstitutional because the Fourth Amendment prohibits governmental searches without some form of individualized suspicion.

B. The legislation is likely unconstitutional because there is no compelling state interest for the suspicionless testing.

C. The legislation is likely constitutional because the state can offer a legitimate special need for the testing and the test protocol appears to be reasonable.

D. The legislation is likely constitutional because the suspicionless testing is rationally related to a legitimate governmental interest.

197. A state probationer was charged with possession of cocaine after his probation officer conducted a warrantless search of his home and found cocaine in a bedside table in the bedroom. The probationer was charged with cocaine possession and filed a motion to suppress.

At the suppressing hearing, the probation officer testified that he searched the home in accordance with a state statute that permits such searches if the officer has reasonable suspicion to believe that the probationer is in violation of the terms of his probation. The officer also testified that the statute was enacted to allow probation officers more discretion as to how closely to monitor their probationers. Finally, the officer testified that he had received a call from the probationer's ex-girlfriend, claiming that he had threatened her with a gun and that the gun was kept in the drawer of the probationer's bedside table.

What is the most likely ruling from the court on the probationer's suppression motion?

A. The motion will be granted because the probation officer only had reasonable suspicion to look for a gun in the bedside table, not cocaine.

B. The motion will be granted because warrantless activity within homes—even those belonging to probationers—is presumptively unreasonable.

C. The motion will be denied because supervision of probationers is a legitimate special need and a warrant would be impractical under these circumstances.

D. The motion will be denied because supervision of probationers is a legitimate special need that voids the probationer's Fourth Amendment rights.

198. A state senator introduced a bill requiring all candidates for state office to submit to mandatory drug testing as a pre-condition of having their name placed on the ballot. According to the preamble to the bill, the bill was being introduced because "voters have a right to be governed by elected officials who follow the law and who don't suffer from the impaired judgment that is commonly associated with illegal drug use."

At the first committee hearing on the bill, one of the state senator's political rivals argued against it, claiming that it would be a waste of the senate's time and taxpayer's money to enact obviously unconstitutional legislation. The state senator, who honestly believed in the bill's constitutionality, demanded an explanation.

What is the political rival's best response?

A. The bill is most likely unconstitutional because the Fourth Amendment prohibits searches without some form of individualized suspicion.

B. The bill is most likely unconstitutional because it exceeds the sovereign powers reserved to the states by the Tenth Amendment to the Constitution.

C. The bill is most likely unconstitutional because the First Amendment requires an opt-out provision to those who have religious scruples against drug testing.

D. The bill is most likely unconstitutional because it fails to articulate a legitimate special need for the suspicionless searches of political candidates.

199. The medical director of a public hospital's emergency room noticed that more and more drug-addicted pregnant women were visiting the hospital, seeking emergency services. After consulting with the local police chief, prosecutor, public health experts from a nearby university, and drug counselors, the medical director developed a policy for mandatory drug testing of any pregnant woman who sought emergency treatment from the hospital.

If the woman tested positive for the presence of an illicit drug, she would be referred for drug treatment at the hospital's expense. The woman's name and the drug report would be forwarded to the police, who would monitor the woman's treatment. If the woman refused or did not complete the treatment, her drug test results would be sent to the prosecutor, who would evaluate whether the woman should be charged criminally.

The medical director presented this plan to the hospital's general counsel for review before implementation. Can the policy survive a Fourth Amendment challenge?

A. No, because the articulated need for the testing is too closely aligned with the ordinary needs of law enforcement.

B. No, because the articulated need for the testing is not based on actual data, but instead on anecdotal impressions.

C. Yes, because the articulated need for the testing is based on an ongoing and widespread public health problem.

D. Yes, because the articulated need for the testing is based on a wide range of opinions from various experts.

200. The day after the enactment of a state statute requiring mandatory, suspicionless drug and alcohol testing of any police officer who discharged his weapon while on duty, the police officers' union filed suit to enjoin the statute. The statute had provisions outlining the methods of testing and steps to be followed to preserve the officer's privacy during and after testing.

In its complaint, the union conceded that the statute was based on a legitimate special need. However, the union also argued that the Constitution requires a minimum showing of reasonable suspicion of impairment before any testing can be performed.

What is the most likely ruling from the court?

A. An on-duty police officer has a reduced expectation of privacy in his body, so he can be subjected to suspicionless drug testing.

B. Requiring reasonable suspicion of an on-duty police officer's impairment prior to testing would place a significant burden on the state.

C. The state's compelling need for testing outweighs an on-duty police officer's right to be free from suspicionless drug and alcohol testing.

D. The proposed testing interferes with an on-duty officer's expectation of privacy and right to be free from unreasonable searches.

201. Doctors in a small town noticed an increase in the number of patients brought to local hospitals, beceause of opiate overdoses. The overdosed patients were often unable to tell doctors what drug they had taken and how much, which affected the doctors' ability to give aid. After a high school senior died from an overdose and the treating physician complained that he could have saved her life if he'd had access to better information about the drugs she was using, the doctors developed a protocol to get access to the information they needed.

According to the protocol, if a person suspected of an opiate overdose came to a hospital's emergency room and if the doctor needed additional information to effectively treat the patient, a police officer would be sent to the patient's home to conduct a warrantless search of the home for opiates. If the officer discovered opiates, that discovery would only be used for the patient's treatment, and it could not be used in any criminal prosecution. However, if the officer discovered other non-opiate criminal evidence in plain view, he would be permitted to seize that evidence and the prosecutor would have discretion whether to bring criminal charges.

Does the protocol correctly balance the government's special needs against the rights of the individual?

A. No, because the protocol permits a suspicionless and warrantless search of the home, the chief evil against which the Fourth Amendment is directed.

B. No, because the protocol presumes that critical information about the patient's drugs can be found in her home, and that information could be anywhere.

C. Yes, because drug users who overdose and then seek medical treatment only have themselves to blame if police search their homes without a warrant.

D. Yes, because as demonstrated by the high school senior's senseless death, the critical need for this evidence outweighs any privacy interest in the home.

202. A public residential high school has a standing policy that if a dormitory's adult resident assistant ("RA") develops reasonable suspicion to believe that a dorm resident has alcohol in her room, the RA may search the room — in the resident's presence — for alcohol. RAs receive extensive training on how to assess reasonable suspicion and the policy sets forth guidelines for conducting the search in a manner that best preserves residents' privacy.

After an RA searched a resident's room under this policy, the school's students banded together and filed a petition with the school president, demanding that the policy be rescinded. The president forwarded the petition to the school's general counsel, and requested a legal opinion about the policy and the petition's demand.

How should general counsel respond?

A. The policy must be rescinded because a dorm room is the equivalent of a home, and warrantless activity in the home is presumptively unreasonable without a warrant, exigency, or consent.

B. The policy must be rescinded because although underage drinking is against the law, residents drinking in dormitory rooms are not driving and thus do not present an immediate danger to others.

C. The policy can be maintained because although a dorm room is the equivalent of a home, reasonable suspicion of underage drinking creates a unique exigency that permits a limited warrantless search.

D. The policy can be maintained because the school has a legitimate special need for the warrantless searches and has created a policy that balances the residents' interests against those of the school.

203. After teachers noticed an increase in the number of public high school students smoking behind the football field, beyond the school property, the school adopted a policy permitting searches of students' lockers to look for cigarettes. The policy permitted searches by the principal and only if she had reasonable suspicion to believe that the student was storing cigarettes in the locker. The policy described factors that could be used to develop reasonable suspicion—witnessing the student smoking or holding cigarettes, smelling cigarette smoke on the student, or overhearing the student talking about smoking—and also required that locker searches be conducted in the student's presence.

Two days after the policy was adopted, the principal saw a sophomore, standing behind the football field and smoking a cigarette. After the sophomore returned to the building, the principal searched her locker and found a half-smoked pack of cigarettes on the locker's top shelf. When the sophomore told her parents about the search, they were angry and complained to the principal.

What is the principal's best defense of the locker search policy?

A. The locker search policy is based on a legitimate special need because cigarette smoking by teenagers is a violation of the law.

B. The locker search policy is based on a legitimate special need because cigarette smoking is dangerous, addictive, and filthy.

C. The search here was based on reasonable suspicion and limited in scope to the place where the cigarettes would plausibly be stored.

D. The search here uncovered cigarettes, so the parents have no basis to complain about what happened to their daughter.

204. After noticing a sharp increase in drug use and behavioral problems among its students, a school district enacted a drug-testing policy for all students involved in student athletics. As a condition of their participation in the school's athletic programs, students were required to sign a consent form, agreeing to random and suspicionless drug testing. Each week, a set number of students were randomly chosen for testing, and were required to provide a urine sample—which was then sent to a private lab for testing. When the student provided the urine sample, an adult monitor was required to stand nearby but was also instructed to take steps to preserve the student's privacy.

A ninth grade student who wanted to play on the shuffleboard team objected to the testing and refused to sign the consent form. As a result, he was barred from trying out for the team.

If the student and his parents file a legal challenge to the policy, what is the most likely ruling from the court?

A. The policy will be found unconstitutional because it permits suspicionless testing and school searches must be based on some form of individualized suspicion.

B. The policy will be found unconstitutional because by permitting suspicionless testing, it pre-supposes that the students selected for testing are active drug users.

C. The policy will be found constitutional because participation in student athletics is a privilege and not a right and so the student lacks standing for his suit.

D. The policy will be found constitutional because it reasonably balances the rights of students against the needs of the school, even though it permits suspicionless testing.

205. Based on reports from several students, a public middle school principal developed reasonable suspicion to believe that a particular student had contraband—over-the-counter antacids—in her possession while at the school. The principal confronted the student, but she denied the allegation. The principal asked the student if he could search her backpack for the antacids and the student agreed. The search did not uncover any antacids.

The principal believed the reports he had been given were accurate and so he asked the school nurse to search the student's clothing and underwear for the antacids. The nurse took the student into the girls' bathroom and made the student take off her clothes and then pull her underwear from her body to see if the suspected antacids would fall out. No antacids were found in the search.

That night, when the student told her mother about the search, the mother was furious. The following day, the mother consulted a lawyer to determine the legality of the search.

What advice should the lawyer provide?

A. The strip search was reasonable because the student consented to it during her meeting with the principal.

B. The strip search was reasonable because the principal and nurse took adequate steps to protect the student's privacy.

C. The strip search was unreasonable because it was not supported by suspicion that the student was carrying contraband.

D. All strip searches of children without probable cause and a warrant are *per se* unreasonable and unconstitutional.

Other "Reasonableness" Searches

206. A city statute requires hotel owners to collect and maintain basic, biographical information about their hotel guests. The information must be surrendered to police on demand, and failure to comply with an officer's request is a misdemeanor — which can be punished with jail time, a fine, or both.

Believing that a dangerous fugitive might have recently stayed at a certain hotel, police demanded that the hotel manager permit them access to the hotel's registry information from the prior two weeks. The manager refused and was arrested.

Later, the manager challenged the statute under the Fourth Amendment. The state responded, claiming that the Fourth Amendment was inapplicable. What is the most likely ruling from the court?

A. The hotel manager's challenge will fail because he has no expectation of privacy in other people's biographical information.

B. The hotel manager's challenge will fail because the Fourth Amendment provides no protection to commercial businesses.

C. The hotel manager's challenge will succeed because the statute does not properly balance the hotel owner's rights against the police need for the inspection.

D. The hotel manager's challenge will succeed because the statute criminalizes non-criminal conduct and punishes a violation with possible jail time.

207. The county health inspector obtained an administrative warrant to check a local restaurant for health code violations.

The inspector did not suspect that he would find any violations, but requested a warrant based on language in a municipal statute that required annual inspections of all area restaurants. And, according to the county's restaurant inspection schedule, the restaurant was due for its annual inspection.

When the inspector arrived at the restaurant, its owner denied him permission to enter, claiming that the inspection would violate the Fourth Amendment.

Is the restaurant owner's position legally correct?

A. Yes, because the health inspector lacked individualized suspicion of a health code violation.

B. Yes, because the health inspector lacked probable cause to obtain a warrant to search the restaurant.

C. No, because the restaurant owner cannot claim an expectation of privacy in a public restaurant.

D. No, because the administrative warrant is sufficient to permit a search of the restaurant by the health inspector.

208. A woman going on vacation entered the airport and learned that in order to board her flight, she—like all passengers—would have to go through security screening.

The woman objected to the screening, and asked the screener to explain why he suspected her of criminal activity. The screener admitted that he didn't suspect the woman of anything but insisted that the woman would have to be screened in order to get on the plane.

Given the screener's admitted lack of individualized suspicion, can he lawfully require the woman to be screened?

A. Yes, because the government's interest in the screening outweighs the intrusiveness of the screening.

B. Yes, because the woman gave implied consent to the screening when she purchased her airline ticket.

C. No, because the woman did not do anything to give the screener reasonable suspicion of wrongdoing.

D. No, because the screener failed to ask the woman to voluntarily waive her rights prior to screening.

209. One afternoon, two officers stopped at a gun store to conduct a spot inspection of its storeroom. The store's owner told the officers that he would prefer they not inspect the storeroom, but the officers explained that by statute, they were permitted to make annual warrantless inspections of gun stores. The officers also gave the owner a copy of the relevant statute—which was several pages long.

Without reviewing the statute, the owner consented to the inspection. Inside the storeroom, the officers found several prohibited automatic weapons—which they seized. One week later, the owner was charged with weapons violations and he filed a motion to suppress. In the motion, the owner conceded that the officers correctly described the statute to him.

What is the most likely ruling on the motion?

A. The motion will be denied because warrantless searches of closely regulated businesses are permitted under such circumstances.

B. The motion will be denied because the owner voluntarily consented to the search of his storeroom.

C. The motion will be granted because warrantless searches are generally presumed to be unreasonable.

D. The motion will be granted because the owner's consent was based on the officers' show of authority and was involuntary.

210. Based on two months of data demonstrating a rising number of unlicensed and uninsured drivers on state roads, the state police issued a directive to troopers, permitting them to conduct random license and insurance checks. The directive included a statement by the governor, proclaiming the importance of having licensed and insured drivers and giving information about the financial costs associated with uninsured drivers.

The very next day, an officer stopped a driver to find out whether the driver was licensed and insured. During the stop, the officer learned that the driver was not licensed or insured. But the driver also consented to a search of his car during the stop, and the officer found a large bag of methamphetamine in the car's trunk.

The driver was charged with drug trafficking and filed a motion to suppress, claiming that the officer had no authority to stop him. How should the court rule on the motion?

A. The stop was unreasonable because the troopers had unlimited discretion as to which drivers to stop.

B. The stop was unreasonable because the directive was based on data collected over a relatively short period of time.

C. The stop was reasonable because the state has a legitimate interest in ensuring that all drivers are properly licensed and insured.

D. The stop was reasonable as evidenced by the fact that the driver was unlicensed, uninsured, and trafficking drugs.

211. After several dozen opioid-related deaths were reported in a short period of time, police set up several vehicle checkpoints around the city to try to combat the problem. In order to ensure the best process possible, the chief of police created a protocol for the checkpoints, built around several core principles. First, to eliminate possible abuses of discretion, officers would stop every car entering the checkpoint. Second, to minimize inconvenience to drivers, each car would be stopped for no longer than two minutes. Third, to prevent "fishing expeditions," officers would limit their questions to those about opioid use and trafficking.

A driver who was stopped at the checkpoint—in accordance with these principles—admitted to having non-prescription opioids in the trunk of his car. The officer who conducted the stop searched the car and found opioids, cocaine, and methamphetamine inside. The driver was eventually charged with drug crimes.

If the driver files a motion to suppress, what is the most likely ruling on the motion?

A. The motion will be denied because the checkpoint was reasonable and the driver's admission gave the officer probable cause to search his car.

B. The motion will be denied because the police created a reasonable procedure for the checkpoints and the officer followed that procedure in conducting the roadblock.

C. The motion will be granted because despite the best efforts of the chief of police, the primary purpose of the checkpoint was to detect ordinary criminal wrongdoing.

D. The motion will be granted because the "core principles" behind the checkpoint did not provide any direction to officers once they developed probable cause.

212. A driver was traveling down the highway when he noticed a police cruiser parked on the side of the highway with its lights on. The driver slowed down and about a half mile down the road, came across a checkpoint that all cars had to pass through in order to continue on the highway.

The driver stopped at the checkpoint and an officer approached his window. The officer then asked the driver a few questions — if he was having a nice evening, where he was traveling, and whether he had drank alcohol that evening — and the driver answered each question honestly. The officer thanked the driver for his time, explained that he had just been subjected to a sobriety checkpoint, and told him that he was free to go. The driver drove away. The entire stop lasted less than three minutes.

The next day, the driver called his attorney to ask whether the checkpoint was legal. What is the most appropriate response?

A. Checkpoints involve full custodial seizures and so are only permitted if the officer has probable cause to stop a driver.

B. Checkpoints involve *Terry*-type seizures and so are only permitted if the officer has reasonable suspicion to stop a driver.

C. Checkpoints are permitted by the Fourth Amendment but only if they are conducted in a generally reasonable manner.

D. Checkpoints are permitted by the Fourth Amendment but only to the degree allowed by the automobile exception.

213. A law student was driving back to his family home at the end of the term, and was looking forward to taking a break after final exams. After driving for several hours, the student saw signs for a vehicle checkpoint a mile ahead.

When the student entered the checkpoint, he rolled down his window and asked the officer why cars were being stopped. The officer explained that the purpose of the checkpoint was to ensure that all child safety seats were properly installed — assuming a child was traveling in the car. During this brief exchange, the officer smelled marijuana coming from inside the car. The officer directed the student to pull to the side of the road. The student complied, and in a subsequent search of his car, the officer found marijuana and cocaine in the glove box.

The student was charged with possession offenses and filed a motion to suppress. In the motion, the student conceded that the rationale for the checkpoint was proper, but argued for suppression anyway.

How should the court rule on the motion?

A. The motion should be denied because the student's concession about the reasonableness of the checkpoint eliminates any basis for suppression of evidence from the glove box.

B. The motion should be denied because the officer developed probable cause to search the student's car during a lawfully created and reasonably administered checkpoint.

C. The motion should be granted because the officer unreasonably converted an otherwise lawful vehicle checkpoint into a tool for ordinary policing.

D. The motion should be granted because the officer didn't need to speak to the driver for this checkpoint and the suspicion to search the car came from that conversation.

214. A man was driving into the United States from Canada and was stopped at a fixed roadblock at the border. The customs officer asked the man questions about his citizenship and whether he was bringing any prohibited items into the county. The man answered that he was a citizen and that he had nothing illegal in his car.

The agent directed the man to pull his car into an inspection station a few yards away, and to exit his car. The man did as he was told. Working with a mechanic, a second agent placed the car on a lift, removed the gas tank from the car, and discovered several kilos of cocaine secured to the top of the gas tank. The man was arrested and charged with drug crimes.

If the man files a motion to suppress, what sentence most likely appears in the court's ruling on the motion?

A. "Intrusive and non-routine border searches, such as the one here, require at least reasonable suspicion to believe the area searched contains evidence of crime."

B. "Due to the ready mobility in, and the reduced expectation of privacy associated with a car, that car may be searched without a warrant—but the officer must still have probable cause."

C. "The Government may, as here, conduct non-routine searches, but only after a judge determines that the search is substantially related to an important government interest."

D. "The Government's authority to conduct suspicionless inspections at the border includes the authority to remove, disassemble, and reassemble a vehicle's fuel tank."

215. A man lived near the United States border, and was driving home one night after work. A customs officer pulled the man over, and asked him questions about his citizenship. In the course of the conversation, the officer asked the man for consent to search his car. The man hesitated, but he eventually agreed. In the subsequent search, the officer found methamphetamine and weapons in the car's trunk.

The man was charged with drug and weapons charges and filed a motion to suppress. At the hearing on the motion, the prosecutor conceded that the officer did not have individualized suspicion to stop the man.

What is the most likely ruling on the motion?

A. The motion will be denied because the stop can be justified under the border exception, even in the absence of reasonable suspicion for the stop.

B. The motion will be denied because the man voluntarily consented to a search of his car, and the evidence from the trunk was a product of that consent.

C. The motion will be granted because the officer lacked reasonable suspicion for the stop and the evidence from the trunk was a fruit of the unreasonable seizure.

D. The motion will be granted because the officer lacked probable cause for the stop and the evidence from the trunk was a fruit of the unreasonable seizure.

Standing

216. A state trooper saw a car speeding down the highway, and so she pulled the driver and his passenger over. After writing the driver a speeding ticket, the trooper asked him to get out of the car so she could hand him the ticket. The driver stepped out of the car and the trooper frisked him for weapons. She found a loaded pistol in the driver's jacket pocket, which she seized. The trooper then asked the driver for permission to search the car and he consented. In the trunk of the car, the trooper found a bag of cocaine. She arrested both the driver and the passenger and drove them to the police barracks for processing.

The passenger has been charged with possession of cocaine and his attorney has filed a motion to suppress. What is the most likely ruling on the motion?

A. The motion will be granted because the driver's consent was a fruit of an unlawful *Terry* frisk.

B. The motion will be granted because the prosecutor cannot establish that the cocaine belonged to the passenger.

C. The motion will be denied because the driver voluntarily consented to a search of his car.

D. The motion will be denied because the passenger cannot challenge the search of the car.

217. An off-duty police officer was having a drink at his neighborhood bar when a young man carrying a backpack walked inside and ordered a pitcher of beer. After watching the young man for several minutes, the officer became convinced that he was underage. The officer approached the young man and searched the backpack, finding a large bag of drugs inside. The officer seized the drugs and arrested the young man.

Later, the young man was charged with drug possession and his attorney filed a motion to suppress. At a hearing on the motion, the defense attorney argued that the search of the backpack was unreasonable and the drug evidence should be suppressed as a result. In response, the prosecutor urged the judge to deny the motion, because the defense failed to independently establish that the young man had standing to challenge the search of the backpack.

How should the court rule?

A. The motion should be denied because the defense failed to independently establish the young man's standing to challenge the search of the backpack.

B. The motion should be stayed to give the defense an opportunity to independently establish the young man's standing to challenge the search of the backpack.

C. The motion should be granted because, despite the failure of the defense to establish standing, the error is harmless beyond a reasonable doubt.

D. The motion should be granted because the officer had absolutely no authority to search the young man's backpack under these circumstances.

218. After obtaining a search warrant, police searched the home of a woman suspected of being involved in a scheme to steal checks from the mail and forge them for illicit purposes. During the search, police found dozens of stolen checks as well as other pieces of stolen mail. After sifting through the evidence, the prosecutor charged the woman and her alleged accomplice with unlawful possession of stolen mail. The alleged accomplice was the woman's former college roommate, who lived in an apartment on the other side of town.

The accomplice filed a pre-trial motion to suppress. In the motion, the accomplice conceded that she has no expectation of privacy in the house that was searched. But the accomplice also argued that since she has been charged with a "possession" crime, she had automatic standing to challenge the search.

How should the court rule on the accomplice's motion?

A. The accomplice does not have standing because, as she concedes, she does not have an expectation of privacy in the house where the evidence was found.

B. The accomplice does not have standing because "possession" is a legal term of art, and it doesn't really mean that the evidence belongs to the accomplice.

C. The accomplice has automatic standing because due process demands that a defendant charged with a possession crime be permitted to challenge the underlying search.

D. The accomplice has automatic standing because equity demands that a defendant charged with a possession crime be permitted to challenge the underlying search.

219. Agents working for the department of state revenue suspected that a drug dealer and a bank president were involved in a money laundering conspiracy. Working undercover and with a confidential informant ("CI"), one of the agents arranged a meeting between the CI and the bank president to discuss some potential "deals." While the three men were meeting, other agents broke into the bank president's condo, went through his briefcase, and copied a large number of documents. Many of these documents carried the drug dealer's signature, and implicated him in crimes.

Two weeks later, a grand jury indicted the drug dealer for conspiracy. In the indictment, the prosecutor made clear that he intends to use documents from the bank president's briefcase to help establish the case against the drug dealer. One week after the indictment was filed, the bank president died of a heart attack.

Can the drug dealer challenge the introduction of these documents?

A. Yes, because the documents were signed by the drug dealer, so he has an expectation of privacy in them.

B. Yes, because unless the drug dealer is permitted to make the challenge, this egregious government misconduct will go unchecked.

C. No, because the agents did not violate the drug dealer's rights in the process of obtaining the documents.

D. No, because the Fourth Amendment does not protect documents, but only "persons, houses, papers, and effects."

220. A woman was attending a conference out of town and made arrangements to stay at the home of her college roommate. The woman was sleeping in the guest bedroom of the house.

At 2 AM on the first night of her stay, four police officers broke down the front door and entered the roommate's house. After telling the roommate that they had a search warrant, the officers searched the house but they found no evidence—except for a small baggie of marijuana on the bedside table in the guest room where the woman was sleeping. The officers eventually realized that they had misread the address listed on the search warrant which was for the house next door. In spite of this, the prosecutor charged the woman with possession of marijuana.

The woman's attorney has filed a motion to suppress the marijuana. How will the court rule on the motion?

A. The motion will be denied because the woman lacks standing to challenge the search of her friend's home, despite the unreasonableness of the search.

B. The motion will be denied because the woman has no real possessory interest in the home, and so the search did not infringe on her rights.

C. The motion will be granted because despite the woman's lack of standing, the officers' egregious behavior will otherwise go unchecked.

D. The motion will be granted because as an overnight guest, the woman has standing to challenge the unreasonable search within her friend's home.

221. A woman lost her job and needed some cash to pay her rent. After telling a friend about her situation, the friend introduced the woman to her brother, a cocaine dealer. The brother needed a place where he could package drugs and told the woman that he would pay a large fee to use her apartment to package cocaine. The woman agreed to the deal.

Later that week, the brother came to the woman's apartment and gave her a thick envelope of cash. In return, she left the apartment for several hours. After the woman left, the brother got to work at the kitchen table. What the brother didn't realize is that a neighbor across the courtyard was watching him through the kitchen window. Alarmed by what he saw, the neighbor called the police. The police rushed into the apartment, seized the cocaine and paraphernalia, and arrested the brother.

The brother was charged with cocaine possession and filed a motion to suppress the cocaine found in the search. What is the prosecutor's strongest argument in response?

A. The motion should be denied because the brother does not have standing to challenge a search that led to the discovery of cocaine, an illegal drug.

B. The motion should be denied because the police reasonably believed that the cocaine would be removed if not immediately seized.

C. The motion should be denied because a short-term commercial guest does not have standing to challenge the search of a private residence.

D. The motion should be denied because the brother made the conscious choice to package cocaine in front of a window.

222. Police received an anonymous tip that a woman was cooking methamphetamine in the kitchen of her apartment. An officer was assigned to investigate and contacted the landlord to ask for permission to search the woman's apartment. The landlord told the officer that the lease agreement only allowed him to enter the apartment in the event of a flood or a fire but that he didn't care about the lease and he would let the officer into the apartment.

The officer and the landlord met at the apartment building later that day. Using his key, the landlord unlocked the door and let the officer into the apartment. The officer walked into the kitchen, but there was no evidence of methamphetamine production anywhere. However, on the kitchen table, the officer saw a mirror, a straw, and a bag of cocaine. He seized the items and the woman was later arrested and charged with possession of cocaine and paraphernalia.

The woman's attorney has filed a motion to suppress this evidence from her upcoming trial. What is the most likely ruling on the motion?

A. The motion will be granted because the woman has standing to challenge the search and the search was unreasonable.

B. The motion will be granted because the officer unreasonably failed to establish whether the woman was home before entering the apartment.

C. The motion will be denied because only the landlord has standing to challenge the search and he consented to the officer's entry into the apartment.

D. The motion will be denied because the landlord's violation of the lease agreement is a private matter between the woman and the landlord.

223. A state trooper pulled a car over to the side of the road for traveling 25 miles per hour over the posted speed limit; there were two people in the car—the driver and a passenger. The officer asked the driver for consent to search the car and said that he would not write the driver a ticket if he gave consent. The officer added that since the driver had been traveling so fast, the ticket would be "a big one, probably around $300." Reluctantly, the driver agreed to the search.

The officer searched the car and discovered an unregistered handgun in the glove box and a bag of cocaine under the front seat. The officer arrested the driver and the passenger, but the driver insisted that the weapon and drugs belonged to the passenger. The passenger said that this was the first time she'd ever been in the driver's car, and that the weapon and drugs belonged to the driver.

After reviewing the officer's report, the district attorney charged the passenger with possession of cocaine and an unlicensed weapon. If she files a motion to suppress this evidence, how should the court rule on the motion?

A. The motion should be denied because the law presumes that people traveling in a car are in constructive possession of evidence found within the car.

B. The motion should be denied because the passenger can't establish that the search of the car violated her Fourth Amendment rights.

C. The motion should be granted because the driver's consent to search the car was based on coercion and duress, and was therefore involuntary.

D. The motion should be granted because the passenger was unreasonably seized because she was not driving the speeding car; the driver was.

224. A police officer arrested a man and a woman for drunk and disorderly conduct in public. In a subsequent search incident to arrest, the officer found a bottle of powder cocaine inside the woman's purse. When the officer discovered the cocaine, the man said that the cocaine belonged to him and not the woman. Based on the man's statement, the prosecutor charged the man with cocaine possession.

The man's lawyer filed a motion to suppress, arguing that the officer lacked probable cause to arrest the man for drunk and disorderly conduct and that the cocaine should be suppressed as a result. The man's lawyer also alleged that the man and woman were in a long-term relationship, that the man frequently kept small items in the woman's purse when the two were out, and that he often kept watch over the woman's purse when she used the restroom or when they were clothes shopping and she was in the changing room.

If the judge agrees that the arrest was not based on probable cause, should she also suppress the cocaine found in the search incident to arrest?

A. Yes, because the man had sufficient control over the purse to claim a legitimate expectation of privacy in its contents.

B. Yes, because the man claimed ownership of the drugs and that admission is sufficient to confer standing.

C. No, because the drugs were found in the woman's purse and the purse belonged to the woman and not the man.

D. No, because the man's claimed ownership of the drugs has not been established by proof beyond a reasonable doubt.

225. A police officer pulled a car over for speeding and asked the driver for consent to search the car. The driver initially refused but the officer asked a second time and the driver relented and consented to the search. In the trunk, the officer found a blue backpack that had some heroin inside. When the driver saw the backpack, she claimed it wasn't hers but instead belonged to a friend from school, and she gave the officer the friend's name.

Based on the driver's allegation, the friend was later charged with heroin possession. At a pre-trial suppression hearing and in order to establish her standing, the friend testified that the backpack was hers and that she accidentally left it in the driver's car.

May the prosecutor use the friend's suppression hearing testimony — admitting ownership of the blue backpack — at her subsequent trial?

A. Yes, because the friend knowingly, voluntarily, and intelligently waived her Fifth Amendment right to remain silent when she testified at the suppression hearing.

B. Yes, because the defense can always rebut the testimony with evidence that the backpack belonged to the driver, because it was found in her car.

C. No, because even though the suppression hearing and trial are separate events, they are treated as the "same event" under the Fifth Amendment.

D. No, because the friend cannot be put in a position of waiving her Fifth Amendment rights in order to invoke her Fourth Amendment rights.

Fourth Amendment Remedies

226. Two police officers suspected a man of possessing child pornography on his home computer. The officers outlined the details of their investigation to their superior officer, who agreed that there was probable cause to search the computer. The two officers then drove to the man's house and knocked on the door. The man answered and asked the officers what they wanted; the officers did not reply but the first officer handcuffed the man and the second officer conducted a thorough search of the man's house—finding child pornography in the attic, basement, and on the hard drive of the man's laptop. The first officer then arrested the man for possession of child pornography. Later, after the man complained of pain, a medic discovered that the first officer had broken the man's wrist while handcuffing him.

What is the most appropriate remedy for the officers' actions?

A. The man should be given damages to compensate him for his medical expenses associated with his broken wrist.

B. The child pornography evidence should be suppressed from the prosecutor's case-in-chief.

C. The man should be given treble damages because of the flagrant nature of the violation.

D. The child pornography evidence may be admitted at trial, but the judge must allow the man an opportunity to testify about the officers' actions.

227. One morning at 6:15 AM, two police officers executed a search warrant at a private house. According to state law, all warrants are required to be executed during "daytime hours," which is defined as the hours between 7 AM and 10 PM. After searching the house, the officers discovered the items described in the search warrant—as well as some other items in plain view.

When the homeowner learned that state law prohibited such an early morning warrant execution, he urged his lawyer to file a motion to suppress the evidence seized from his house. The lawyer filed the motion, the prosecutor replied, and the judge held a hearing on the motion. Two weeks later, the judge issued her ruling.

If the judge's ruling reflects the current Supreme Court's view toward application of the exclusionary rule, what sentence most likely appears in her opinion?

A. "Suppression of evidence should be our last resort, and not our first impulse."

B. "Where the official action was pursued in complete good faith, however, the deterrence rationale loses much of its force."

C. "All evidence obtained by searches and seizures in violation of the Constitution is, by that same authority, inadmissible in a criminal trial."

D. "Identification of a Fourth Amendment violation is synonymous with application of the exclusionary rule."

228. A police detective suspected a woman had killed her husband and hidden the murder weapon inside the attic of the couple's home. The woman worked as a clerk at the local court and was good friends with several police officers. For these reasons, the detective was worried that the woman might find out if he applied for a search warrant and that she might destroy critical evidence before a warrant could be executed. The detective searched the woman's home without a warrant, and found the murder weapon in the attic—just as he thought he might.

After the woman was charged with her husband's murder, the trial judge refused to suppress the weapon from her trial and she was later convicted and sentenced to life in prison. On appeal, the woman argued that the murder weapon should have been suppressed because it was a fruit of an unreasonable, warrantless search. The appeals court agreed and vacated the woman's conviction based on the trial judge's suppression ruling.

What sentence most likely appears in the court's opinion discussing the suppression issue?

A. "When a judge permits evidence acquired through an unreasonable search to be admitted at trial, he offers tacit support to the officer's misconduct."

B. "When a judge permits evidence acquired through an unreasonable search to be admitted at trial, he violates his judicial oath to uphold the Constitution."

C. "When a judge permits evidence acquired through an unreasonable search to be admitted at trial, the public loses all faith in the judiciary."

D. "When a judge permits evidence acquired through an unreasonable search to be admitted at trial, he makes a mockery of the Supreme Court."

229. A rookie police officer was on patrol one evening when he pulled over a driver for speeding. While interacting with the rookie, the driver was rude, and so the rookie arrested him for disorderly conduct. After placing the handcuffed driver in the back of his patrol car, the rookie searched the driver's car incident to arrest. In the passenger compartment, under the armrest, the rookie found a small amount of marijuana.

The driver was charged with marijuana possession. His attorney filed a motion to suppress, setting forth several different grounds for suppression.

If the judge decides to grant the motion and suppress the evidence, what is the most likely reason?

A. To help complete the training the rookie obviously didn't get at the police academy.

B. To teach the rookie an important lesson he'll never forget.

C. To keep from sending yet another non-violent offender to prison.

D. To deter the rookie and others from making the same mistake in future.

230. Police searched a man's house with a search warrant and discovered a methamphetamine lab in the basement. According to the lead officer, the quantity of drugs seized was the largest in the state's history. After being charged with drug crimes, the man's lawyer filed a motion to suppress, arguing that the warrant did not demonstrate probable cause to search. After a lengthy evidentiary hearing, the judge reluctantly agreed with the defense and ruled that although it was a close case, the affidavit in support of probable cause did not demonstrate probable cause to search.

Does the Constitution require suppression of evidence in this situation?

A. Yes, because the text of the Fourth Amendment mandates that evidence discovered during unreasonable searches be suppressed.

B. Yes, because a police error of this magnitude cannot go unchecked and the police must be appropriately punished.

C. No, because a crime of this magnitude cannot go unchecked and the man must be appropriately punished.

D. No, because the exclusionary rule is a judicially created rule that should only applied when it would have a deterrent effect.

231. A patrol officer pulled a driver over for speeding. While speaking with driver, the officer asked the driver for consent to search the car and—according to the officer—the driver agreed. In the ensuing search, the officer found a rotting corpse in the trunk of the driver's car. The driver was charged with capital murder. In a pre-trial suppression motion, the driver argued that he had refused consent to search the car. After two days of testimony on the issue, the judge found that the driver had consented to the search and denied the motion to suppress. The driver was convicted of murder and sentenced to die.

On appeal to the state supreme court, the driver raised a variety of claims, including one focused on the consent-to-search issue. The court denied all of the driver's claims and affirmed his conviction and sentence. A few months later, the driver filed a federal *habeas corpus* petition, presenting the same claims that he had raised in his appeal to the state supreme court.

What is the most likely ruling from the judge on the Fourth Amendment consent-to-search issue?

A. The claim will be dismissed because the doctrine of collateral estoppel bars the driver from raising the claim in a habeas corpus petition.

B. The claim will be dismissed because the doctrine of *res judicata* bars the driver from raising the claim in a habeas corpus petition.

C. The claim will be dismissed because Fourth Amendment claims are generally not cognizable in *habeas corpus* proceedings.

D. The claim will be dismissed because the doctrine of "law of the case" bars the driver from raising the claim in a *habeas corpus* petition.

232. After an investigation, police developed probable cause to believe that an antiques auctioneer was at the center of an illegal ivory importation scheme. The investigation had spanned several months, and involved the cooperation of several different state agencies. At the conclusion of the investigation, the lead officer presented a detailed warrant application to the magistrate, requesting permission to search the auctioneer's home. The magistrate signed the warrant. Under state law, all searches must be performed within 10 days of the date of the magistrate's signature.

Unfortunately, the officer fell ill the next day and was hospitalized. Given the scope of the investigation, the officer's team was reluctant to conduct the search without him, and so they waited for his recovery. Three weeks later, the officer returned to work and the warrant was executed later that day. The search of the auctioneer's home yielded the very same items identified in the warrant application.

If the auctioneer moves to suppress evidence found in her home, can the officer rely on the good faith exception?

A. No, because an objectively reasonable officer would know that the warrant's probable cause was stale at the time it was executed.

B. No, because it was objectively unreasonable for the officer's team to wait for his recovery.

C. Yes, because an objectively reasonable officer would have executed the warrant as soon as he returned to work.

D. Yes, because the only warrant violation on these facts is a technical violation of state law.

233. An officer presented a search warrant application to a magistrate, requesting permission to search a high school teacher's home for drugs. The magistrate refused to grant the warrant and told the officer he didn't have probable cause for the search.

The officer knew that this particular magistrate had a reputation for being very demanding of police officers and had heard a rumor that the magistrate had been formally reprimanded for his treatment of other officers. Acting in reliance on what he had heard and without conducting any additional investigation, the officer took the warrant application to a second magistrate, who signed it.

The officer then executed the warrant, and found 10 kilos of cocaine at the teacher's home. The teacher was subsequently charged with cocaine possession and distribution. He now seeks to suppress the cocaine, claiming that the warrant does not demonstrate probable cause and that the officer cannot meet the requirements of the good faith exception.

Assuming the state concedes that the warrant lacks probable cause, how should the court rule on the suppression motion?

A. The motion should be granted because the officer failed to show a "special need" for the search, as required for searches involving public school actors.

B. The motion should be granted because the officer cannot demonstrate good faith.

C. The motion should be denied because the officer found the cocaine he was looking for at the teacher's house.

D. The motion should be denied because the officer relied in good faith on the information he had heard about the magistrate's reputation.

234. After a lengthy investigation, a police officer applied for and received a warrant to search the apartment of a college student suspected of selling cocaine. However, on the same day as he applied for the warrant, the officer was in a car accident. The task of searching of the college student's apartment was then assigned to a rookie officer. The rookie executed the warrant and seized two kilos of cocaine, as well as scales, baggies, and other paraphernalia. As he left the apartment, the rookie gave a copy of the one-page search warrant to the college student.

The college student was charged with various crimes and his attorney filed a motion to suppress, attaching the one-page warrant the rookie gave the student. It was a pre-printed form that had been filled in with the college student's name and address, the names and signatures of the officer requesting the warrant and the reviewing magistrate, and a list of items the officer intended to search for. The words, "see attached affidavit," were handwritten on the top of the form. However, there was no attached affidavit.

How should the court rule on the suppression motion?

A. The motion should be granted because the warrant was facially deficient and the rookie could not reasonably assume that it was valid.

B. The motion should be granted because the good faith exception is inapplicable when the officer who obtains a warrant is different from the officer who executes it.

C. The motion should be denied because the rookie demonstrated good faith by doing the best he could under trying circumstances.

D. The motion should be denied because the rookie believed in good faith that the warrant application was complete at the time the magistrate signed it.

235. Under state law, hotel owners are required to collect and maintain certain factual information about their guests—*e.g.*, dates of reservations, duration of stay, method of payment, etc.—and to provide this information on demand to any police officer who requests it. If the owner or his agent refuses, she can be charged with a misdemeanor. Hotel owners challenged the law in federal district court, claiming that it violated their Fourth Amendment expectation of privacy and that they were being forced to disclose records without consent or some mechanism for pre-compliance review.

Three days after the owners filed suit, two officers entered a local hotel and demanded to see the hotel's records. The hotel manager told the officers about the pending lawsuit, but the officers persisted. Afraid of being arrested, the manager gave the officers the records. Ultimately, the statute was found unconstitutional.

However, before the court's ruling, the prosecutor used information from the hotel's records to investigate the hotel owner; he was later charged with money laundering.

If the hotel owner moves to suppress the records, how should the court rule on the motion?

A. The motion should be denied because the hotel manager consented to the search when he gave the records to the officers.

B. The motion should be denied because the officers reasonably relied in good faith on the constitutionality of the statute.

C. The motion should be granted because the officers knew about the pending lawsuit and demanded the records anyway.

D. The motion should be granted because the statute was ultimately found to be unconstitutional.

236. A police officer on routine patrol stopped a driver for speeding. As part of his usual practice, the officer checked to see if there were any outstanding warrants for the driver's arrest. After learning of an active arrest warrant for methamphetamine possession, the officer arrested the driver and searched him incident to arrest. The officer found a small bottle of methamphetamine in the driver's pocket.

The driver was charged with drug possession and his attorney filed a motion to suppress. In the motion, the attorney argued that the arrest was unreasonable because the arrest warrant had been quashed two weeks prior to the traffic stop. At the hearing on the motion, the court clerk explained that the judge had quashed the warrant but that she had forgotten to update the computer system with the judge's order. The clerk also accepted full responsibility for the error and apologized.

What is the most likely ruling from the judge on the suppression motion?

A. The officer acted in good faith and suppression of the evidence on these facts would have no deterrent effect on the police.

B. The officer acted in objectively reasonable good faith because he checked for an outstanding arrest warrant before arresting the driver.

C. The officer arrested the driver for methamphetamine possession and the driver was, in fact, in possession of methamphetamine.

D. The good faith exception doesn't apply here because the court clerk accepted full responsibility for the computer error.

237. A state trooper on patrol stopped a driver for speeding. The officer ran a routine warrant check and discovered an active warrant for the driver's arrest due to failure to pay court-ordered child support. The officer arrested the driver and as she was handcuffing him, called him a "deadbeat dad" and a "loser." The officer then searched the driver incident to arrest and found some crack cocaine in his pocket.

After the driver was charged with drug possession, the driver's lawyer discovered that the arrest warrant had been erroneously issued and that it shouldn't have been in the police computer. The lawyer also learned that in the three weeks prior to the driver's arrest, six other defense attorneys had complained to the police about faulty arrest warrants being issued in ten other cases.

If the driver moves to suppress the crack cocaine found in his pocket, what is his strongest argument in support of suppression?

A. The arrest was unreasonable and the officer lacked good faith because she had personal animus toward the driver.

B. The search was unreasonable and the officer lacked good faith because she converted a routine traffic stop into a search for drugs.

C. The arrest was unreasonable and the officer lacked good faith because the computer error was one of many discovered in the recent past.

D. The search was unreasonable and the officer lacked good faith because she had no reason to believe that the driver had drugs in his pocket.

238. A police officer was on patrol in a residential area when he noticed a driver not wearing her seatbelt. The officer pulled the driver over and gave her a warning about the danger associated with not wearing a seatbelt. At the conclusion of the warning, the officer asked the driver for consent to search her car and the driver agreed. In the search, the officer found a small baggie of cocaine in the trunk of the car. The officer arrested the driver and the local prosecutor charged her with cocaine possession.

The driver later filed a motion to suppress based on the fact that under state law, the officer was only entitled to stop the woman if she was committing some other violation in conjunction with a seatbelt violation. When the officer was asked about this point at the hearing on the suppression motion, he explained that he had recently moved to the state from another jurisdiction where the law permitted traffic stops solely for a seatbelt violation.

Based on these facts, what is the strongest argument in support of the woman's motion?

A. The woman's consent to search the car was not knowing, voluntary, and intelligent.

B. The woman never expressly consented to a search of her car's trunk.

C. The officer's mistake of law was unreasonable under the circumstances.

D. A mistake of law cannot form the basis of an officer's reasonable suspicion.

239. State police developed probable cause to believe that a man was at the head of a conspiracy to distribute cocaine throughout the state and that he delivered the cocaine by car. Through their investigation, the officers learned that the man had a series of drivers—each a suspected co-conspirator—who ferried him around. Every week, the man worked with a different driver and a different car.

One night, a surveillance officer was following the man and his driver when she noticed the driver make an illegal right turn. The officer pulled the car over and asked the driver to get out of the car. Standing out of earshot of the man, the officer asked the driver for consent to search the passenger compartment of the car. The officer also told the driver that he had been under surveillance for some time and that he was about to be charged with conspiracy. Frightened, the driver consented to the search. In the trunk, the officer found several kilos of cocaine.

The prosecutor charged the man and several others with conspiracy to distribute cocaine, and she wants to use the cocaine from the car at the man's upcoming trial. If the man moves to suppress the cocaine, how should the judge rule on his motion?

A. The motion should be denied because the man cannot challenge the search of the car on these facts.

B. The motion should be denied because the officer had probable cause to believe drugs were in the car.

C. The motion should be granted because the driver's consent to search the car was involuntary.

D. The motion should be granted because the officer exceeded the scope of the driver's consent.

240. In order to save money, two law students — one in her first year and the other in his second — commuted to school together from their hometown, 80 miles away. The 2L student drove his car because it had better gas mileage. Because the law school did not provide its students with lockers or other storage, the 2L student gave the 1L student a key to the car so that she could keep her books and other belongings safe during the day while the two were at school.

One evening after a long day at school, the 2L student was driving the car when he was pulled over for speeding. When the 2L student told the officer that he was in law school, the officer explained that he would have to search the car. The officer explained that it "wouldn't look very good" if the Board of Law Examiners were to find out that law students were hiding evidence from police officers. The officer then searched the car and, in the trunk, he found a small bag of marijuana.

The local prosecutor has charged both students with possession of marijuana based on the evidence found in the car. If the 1L student files a motion to suppress, what is the most likely ruling on the motion?

A. The motion will be denied because the 1L student cannot challenge the search of the car on these facts.

B. The motion will be denied because the law of constructive possession dictates that the marijuana belongs to all the occupants of the car.

C. The motion will be granted because the officer searched the 2L student's car without lawful authority.

D. The motion will be granted because the prosecutor cannot demonstrate that the 1L student had any possessory interest in the marijuana.

241. A police officer arrested a man based on a hunch that the man had sold beer to a high school student. The man denied knowing the student, but the officer didn't believe him. As the officer was placing handcuffs on the man, the man said that he would give the officer a lead on a "big-time drug dealer" if the officer would release him. The officer agreed and the man gave the name and address of a woman who — he alleged — was manufacturing methamphetamine in her basement.

The officer relayed the tip to his dispatcher and a second officer was sent to the woman's house. The second officer broke down the front door of the woman's house and went into the basement — and found a methamphetamine lab.

Later investigation revealed that the man had provided the woman with some of her equipment; the prosecutor charged them both with conspiracy to manufacture methamphetamine. If the man moves to suppress the evidence from the woman's house, how should the court rule on the motion?

A. The motion should be denied because the man lacks standing to challenge the warrantless search of the woman's house.

B. The motion should be denied because there are no evidentiary restrictions in conspiracy cases, once the conspiratorial relationship is established.

C. The motion should be granted because the evidence seized from the woman's kitchen is a fruit of the man's unlawful arrest.

D. The motion should be granted because the second officer searched the woman's house with a warrant, exigency, or consent.

242. A police officer on foot patrol saw two men standing on the corner, talking. As the officer approached the men, one of them ran away. Acting on a hunch that the two men were involved in a drug deal, the officer frisked the second man and found a gun and a baggie of methamphetamine in one of his pockets. The officer then told the second man that he would let him go if he would provide the name and address of his methamphetamine source. The second man complied, giving the name and address of a local drug dealer.

After waiting for back-up, the officer raided the drug dealer's house and searched it thoroughly. In the search, the officer found large amounts of methamphetamine, cocaine, and marijuana. The drug dealer was later charged with crimes associated with these drugs and he filed a motion to suppress all of the evidence recovered from his house.

Should the evidence found in the drug dealer's house be suppressed?

A. Yes, because the evidence found in the drug dealer's house is a fruit of the poisonous tree.

B. Yes, because the officer searched the drug dealer's house without a warrant, exigency, or consent.

C. No, because the drug dealer cannot violate the law and, at the same time, seek the law's protection.

D. No, because despite the officer's unreasonable conduct, his hunch was actually correct.

243. A police officer on patrol saw a man standing outside a drug store, smoking a cigarette. Concerned that the man might be about to rob the drug store, the officer frisked the man for weapons and found a crack pipe and a stack of business cards in his jacket pocket. The only information on the business cards was a phone number. The officer arrested the man.

The next day, the officer looked up the number from the cards and learned that it belonged to a woman with a history of drug convictions. The officer placed the woman under surveillance and after several days, developed probable cause to believe that she was selling drugs from her condo. The officer applied for and received a warrant to search the condo; when he executed it, he found large amounts of crack cocaine there. The officer also found a stash of business cards—just like the one he had taken from the man outside the drug store.

The man and the woman were charged with conspiracy to distribute cocaine. Can the evidence from the condo be used against the man from the drug store?

A. Yes, because the evidence from the condo is not directly tied to the officer's unreasonable frisk of the man outside the drug store.

B. Yes, because the business cards taken from the condo establish a conspiracy between the man outside the drug store and the woman from the condo.

C. No, because the evidence from the condo would not have been discovered but for the officer's unreasonable frisk of the man outside the drug store.

D. No, because the business cards taken from the condo can't be considered evidence of a drug crime because they are not, in fact, drugs.

244. One afternoon, a police officer arrested a middle-aged man, mistakenly believing that he was a parole violator. The middle-aged man protested that he did not have a criminal record and claimed that there had to be some mistake. The officer ignored the middle-aged man and drove him to the police station in his cruiser. During the drive, the middle-aged man told the officer that he was willing to exchange information in return for his release and told the officer that his accountant had offered to sell him cocaine the previous week.

Intrigued, the officer decided to investigate the allegation. He placed the accountant under surveillance and with the help of an undercover officer, established probable cause to search the accountant's office for cocaine. The officer obtained a search warrant for the office, executed it, and found 2 kilos of cocaine inside the office safe.

The prosecutor charged the accountant with cocaine possession and the accountant moved to suppress the cocaine from the search of his office. What is the most likely ruling from the court?

A. The motion will be granted because the cocaine from the accountant's office is a fruit of the middle-aged man's unlawful arrest.

B. The motion will be granted to punish the officer for unlawfully arresting the middle-aged man, and to deter the officer from similar errors in future.

C. The motion will be denied because the cocaine evidence was seized pursuant to a lawfully obtained and executed warrant.

D. The motion will be denied because the accountant does not have standing to challenge the middle-aged man's unreasonable arrest.

245. A woman was sitting on a park bench, breastfeeding. An officer walked by and arrested her for public indecency. In a subsequent search incident to arrest, the officer found some marijuana in a diaper bag the woman had with her. The officer took the woman to the police station and she was released several hours later.

Two days after that, the officer called the woman and asked her to come to the police station and give a statement to him about the marijuana. The woman said she'd think about it and hung up the phone. The next day, the woman called the officer and agreed to give a statement. Later that same afternoon the woman drove to the police station and gave a written statement, admitting that she kept marijuana in her baby's diaper bag.

Because breastfeeding in public is not against the law in this jurisdiction, the prosecutor did not charge the woman with public indecency. However, he does want to pursue marijuana possession charges against her. What evidence can the prosecutor permissibly use in his prosecution against the woman?

A. None of the evidence, because both the marijuana and the statement are fruits of the woman's unreasonable arrest for public indecency.

B. The marijuana but not the statement, because the marijuana is the best evidence to show that the woman was in possession of marijuana.

C. The statement but not the marijuana, because there is no direct causal connection between the woman's unreasonable arrest and her statement.

D. Both the marijuana and the statement, because both establish that the woman was in possession of marijuana and also endangered the health of her child.

246. Police received a tip that a man had molested a 10 year-old neighbor at his house. An officer—who also happened to be the child's uncle—drove to the man's house to speak with him. The man answered the officer's knock and when he did, the officer pushed the man aside and barged into the house. The officer yelled at the man and threatened to kill him. The man was terrified.

Just then, a second officer arrived. The second officer ordered the other officer to leave the man's house. Then, in a calm tone of voice, the second officer apologized for the behavior of her colleague. The man accepted the apology. The second officer explained that the man could help clear his name by consenting to a search of his house. The man agreed; in the search, the second officer found child pornography.

The man was charged with possession of child pornography and he filed a motion to suppress the evidence seized from his house. How should the court rule on the motion?

A. The motion should be granted because the child pornography is a fruit of the first officer's warrantless entry and death threat.

B. The motion should be granted because the second officer never told the man that he had a right to refuse the search of his home.

C. The motion should be denied because the second officer's professional conduct removed the taint from the first officer's warrantless entry and threat.

D. The motion should be denied because the man voluntarily consented to a search of his house.

247. A police officer learned that a magistrate had issued a warrant to search his neighbor's house and computers for possession of child pornography. The officer had always been a little suspicious of his neighbor and was concerned that he may have taken unauthorized photographs of her children.

Concerned about her kids and not content to wait for the execution of the warrant, the officer went to the neighbor's house, broke down the door, and searched the house herself. She found a laptop with thousands of pornographic images of children. As the officer was concluding her search, three other officers arrived at the neighbor's house, ready to execute the search warrant.

If the neighbor is charged with possession of child pornography and if he files a motion to suppress the images taken from his laptop, how will the court rule on the motion?

A. The motion will be granted because the officer searched the neighbor's house without a warrant, consent, or exigency.

B. The motion will be granted because the exclusionary rule is designed to deter police misconduct and the officer needs to be deterred.

C. The motion will be denied because the state's interest in catching child pornographers outweighs the neighbor's interest in privacy.

D. The motion will be denied because the police have a lawful, independent source for the discovery of the child pornography.

248. A police officer received a tip that a bar owner was selling cocaine to local teenagers. The officer went to the bar and confronted the owner about the allegations, but the owner denied them. The officer asked the owner for consent to search the bar but the owner refused. The officer searched anyway and found a bag of cocaine in a refrigerator in the kitchen. He then arrested the bar owner.

The D.A. charged the owner with possession of cocaine and the owner's lawyer filed a motion to dismiss. In reply to the motion, the D.A. presented a warrant application that had been completed an hour before the officer went to the bar and searched it. Unbeknownst to the officer, a sheriff's deputy had been investigating the same tip and had hoped to get a warrant to search the bar. Although the warrant had not been signed by a magistrate, the D.A. urged the suppression judge to independently review it and determine whether the sheriff's deputy had demonstrated probable cause to search the bar.

What is the most accurate description of the D.A.'s legal argument?

A. The bag of cocaine from the refrigerator would have been inevitably discovered.

B. The bag of cocaine from the refrigerator was discovered through a lawful, independent source.

C. The sheriff's deputy showed good faith when he attempted to obtain a search warrant for the bar.

D. The good faith of the sheriff's deputy makes up for the bar faith of the officer who searched the bar.

249. A man on trial for murder decided to take the stand and testify in his own defense. The prosecutor's case was a circumstantial one, largely because the judge had ordered that the alleged murder weapon—a large hunting knife with the man's name engraved on the blade, found in the man's house—be suppressed as the fruit of an unreasonable search. According to the judge's suppression ruling, the officers who searched the house exceeded the scope of the search warrant in their discovery of the knife.

On direct exam, the man testified that he didn't know the victim, did not own any knifes beyond those in his silverware drawer, and that those knives were "pretty dull and could barely cut an apple." On cross-examination, the prosecutor presented the man with the previously suppressed hunting knife and asked him if he recognized it. The man's defense attorney moved for a mistrial.

How should the judge rule on the motion?

A. The mistrial motion should be denied because the prosecutor was permitted to use the knife to impeach the man's false testimony.

B. The mistrial motion should be denied because the knife was only was suppressed due to a technical violation of the Fourth Amendment.

C. The mistrial motion should be granted because only a mistrial can correct the manifest injustice created by the prosecutor's questioning.

D. The mistrial motion should be granted because the prosecutor engaged in intentional misconduct by confronting the man with suppressed evidence.

250. A wife was charged with breaking and entering into her ex-husband's house and stealing a valuable painting from him. The painting had been found hanging in the wife's house, but the judge suppressed it from the wife's trial after a police officer admitted to threatening the wife to get consent to search her house.

At her subsequent trial, the wife claimed an alibi but did not testify in her own defense. Instead, she presented testimony from her hairdresser that she had been at the hair salon at the time the crime was alleged to have occurred. The hairdresser also testified that the wife hated the painting and had been annoyed when her husband wanted to hang in their house when they were still married. The prosecutor had the painting brought into the courtroom and asked the hairdresser whether the painting in the courtroom was the same one that the wife allegedly hated and which had been found in the wife's living room. The hairdresser confirmed that it was.

If the defense attorney objects, how should the judge rule on the objection?

A. The objection should be overruled because the prosecutor only used the painting to impeach the hairdresser's testimony and not as substantive evidence of the wife's guilt.

B. The objection should be overruled because the prosecutor's use of the painting was not relevant to the hairdresser's testimony about the wife's alibi.

C. The objection should be sustained because the prosecutor was not permitted to use the painting to impeach defense witnesses other than the wife, had she testified.

D. The objection should be sustained because the prosecutor may only use suppressed evidence to impeach defense witnesses if the defendant herself testifies first.

Fifth Amendment Questions

Privilege Against Self-Incrimination

251. A student enrolled in law school at a large public university submitted a term paper for her final grade in an upper-level seminar. After reviewing the paper, the professor became convinced that the student had plagiarized portions of her paper from a law review article. The professor referred the matter to the dean who, after his own independent review, agreed with the professor's conclusion. According to law school policies, the punishment for plagiarism can include a failing grade, suspension, or expulsion.

The dean met with the student to discuss the paper. At the meeting, the dean confronted the student with her paper and the law review article and demanded an explanation. The student, realizing that she had been caught, replied that she would not answer the dean's questions and that she wanted to invoke her Fifth Amendment privilege to remain silent.

Does the student have a Fifth Amendment right to remain silent in this situation?

A. Yes, because the student's response will show that she plagiarized her paper.

B. Yes, because the student faces expulsion if she responds truthfully.

C. No, because the Fifth Amendment does not apply in this context.

D. No, because if expelled, the student can transfer to another law school.

252. Police charged a man with a bank robbery, and believed that he had been helped by his sister, a bank employee. Police thought that the sister had given her brother critical information about the security guards' work shifts and had unlocked the bank's back doors for him. The brother had escaped from the bank through the back door and into a car parked in the alley.

In order to prove this theory, the prosecutor subpoenaed the sister to testify at her brother's trial, intending to ask her questions about her role in the robbery.

Is the sister being compelled to give testimony under the Fifth Amendment?

A. Yes, because the sister is being forced to give testimony under oath.

B. Yes, because the sister's testimony is necessary to the prosecutor's case.

C. No, because the sister is only a witness here, not the defendant.

D. No, because the sister can always refuse to testify against her brother.

253. A death row prisoner was facing imminent execution and decided to seek clemency from the state's governor. According to a state statute, clemency applicants must be interviewed by members of the state's clemency board. After the interview—at which the prisoner must appear alone—the board members make a non-binding recommendation to the governor as to whether clemency should be granted or not.

The prisoner was concerned about the questions that might be asked of him and whether members of the clemency board would draw negative inferences if he refused to answer their questions. Through his attorney, the prisoner sent a letter to governor, arguing that the clemency process violated his Fifth Amendments rights and requesting some modifications to the interview process. The governor referred the matter to the state attorney general for an opinion.

How should the attorney general best respond to the governor?

A. The prisoner no longer has any Fifth Amendment rights because those rights were forfeited when he was convicted and sentenced to die.

B. The prisoner no longer has Fifth Amendment rights involving the capital crime, which is the focus of the clemency interview.

C. The interview process does not involve Fifth Amendment compulsion because the prisoner's appearance does not involve a subpoena.

D. The interview process does not involve Fifth Amendment compulsion because the prisoner's participation in the interview is voluntary.

254. A man was arrested on suspicion of rape and was brought into an interrogation room for questioning. A detective came into the room and began to question the man about his whereabouts on the night of the crime. For the first half hour, the man refused to make eye contact with the detective and remained silent. But the detective kept on pestering the man with questions and eventually the man confessed to the crime.

After the man was charged with rape, his attorney filed a motion to suppress the statement arguing that the man should have been given *Miranda* warnings at the outset of the interrogation.

What is the attorney's strongest argument for why *Miranda* warnings were required?

A. *Miranda* warnings were required because police procedure requires warnings for custodial interrogations.

B. *Miranda* warnings were required because without warnings it is unclear if the man knew about his privilege against self-incrimination.

C. *Miranda* warnings were required so that the man could make a reasoned choice about invoking or waiving his privilege against self-incrimination.

D. *Miranda* warnings were required because without warnings it is unclear if the man understood his privilege against self-incrimination.

255. An officer on patrol developed reasonable suspicion that a man standing on a street corner was selling drugs. The officer approached the man, explained his suspicions, and asked the man for his name. The man refused to answer and so the officer arrested him for violating a state "stop and identify" statute. The officer searched the man incident to arrest and found a baggie of drugs in the man's pocket.

The man was charged with drug crimes and his attorney filed a motion to suppress. In the motion, the attorney argued that the "stop and identify" statute violates the Fifth Amendment because it forced the man to provide the police with potentially incriminating testimony.

How should the court rule on the motion?

A. The statute compels an incriminating response because the police will check the man's name against arrest records, which may link him to other crimes.

B. The statute compels an incriminating response because as happened here, if a person refuses to respond, he will be arrested and will face a criminal sanction.

C. The statute does not compel an incriminating response because providing a name does not link the man in any way to criminal activity or criminal prosecution.

D. The statute does not compel an incriminating response because a person can avoid arrest and search incident to arrest if he responds to the officer and gives his name.

256. A father was on trial for killing his infant daughter. According to the state's case, the father had been alone with the child for about an hour before she stopped breathing and died, and the father killed her during this period. In contrast, the defense argued that the child's injuries were caused days earlier, most likely by the nanny — who had been the child's primary caregiver since the time of her birth.

At trial, the prosecution subpoenaed the nanny to testify. The nanny's lawyer came to court with her and explained that she did not harm the child in any way and was innocent of any wrongdoing. Still, the lawyer explained that if forced to testify, the nanny would assert her Fifth Amendment right to remain silent.

May the nanny claim a Fifth Amendment privilege against self-incrimination under these circumstances?

A. No, because as long as the nanny is claiming innocence, she doesn't have any credible fear that her trial testimony will link her to a crime.

B. No, because the nanny's refusal to testify under these circumstances interferes with the father's right to confront the witnesses against him.

C. Yes, but the nanny should first be required to establish how her testimony proclaiming her innocence might somehow link her to a crime.

D. Yes, because the nanny has reasonable cause to believe that her testimony might link her to crimes associated with the child's death.

257. An accountant was fired from her job and sued her employer for wrongful discharge and age discrimination. On the first day of trial, the accountant testified about her work and the trauma she felt when she lost her job. On cross-examination, the employer's lawyer asked the accountant whether she had ever embezzled money from the employer. The accountant refused to answer the question, claiming her Fifth Amendment right to remain silent.

Should the judge force the accountant to respond to the question?

A. Yes, because the accountant is being asked the question by a private lawyer, and not by a prosecutor or police officer.

B. Yes, because the accountant may only assert a Fifth Amendment privilege in a criminal case, and this is a civil matter.

C. No, because this is a civil lawsuit and the prosecutor is not present in the courtroom to protect the interests of the state.

D. No, because the accountant has reasonable cause to believe that her testimony might lead to embezzlement charges.

258. After a man was convicted of manslaughter and sentenced to prison, a state police officer swabbed the man's cheek for a DNA sample. The officer told the man that a new state statute authorized collection of DNA profiles of any person convicted of a crime after the effective date of the statute.

Two months after the man's DNA profile was entered into the database, police matched the man to biological evidence collected and preserved from a 10-year-old rape case. The man was charged with rape and a lawyer was appointed to represent him. The lawyer filed a motion to suppress the DNA match, arguing that taking a cheek swab from the man violated his Fifth Amendment rights.

What is the most likely ruling on the motion?

A. Taking a cheek swab did not violate the man's Fifth Amendment rights because it done pursuant to a state statute, which is presumptively constitutional.

B. Taking a cheek swab did not violate the man's Fifth Amendment rights because it did not involve compelling him to provide testimonial evidence.

C. Taking a cheek swab violated the man's Fifth Amendment rights because he was compelled by the officer to give self-incriminating evidence.

D. Taking a cheek swab violated the man's Fifth Amendment rights because he was compelled by the officer to give testimonial evidence.

259. A woman was arrested for her involvement in a demonstration that resulted in the burning of a city-owned building. The arresting officer placed the woman in a line-up with five other women and had the witnesses view the line-up from behind a two-way mirror.

As the officer was leading the woman into the room for the line-up, she said that she was going exercise her Fifth Amendment right to refuse to participate in the line-up. The officer told the woman that she didn't have any right to refuse to participate and told her to get in line.

Who has the correct legal position, the woman or the officer?

A. The woman is correct because she is being compelled to be a witness against herself in a criminal case.

B. The woman is correct because the officer cannot order the woman to forfeit her Fifth Amendment rights.

C. The officer is correct because the woman is not being compelled to give self-incriminating testimony.

D. The officer is correct because the woman has no right to disobey his direct order to participate in the line-up.

260. A man was charged with murder and requested a jury trial. As part of its case, the state planned to present the testimony of a prisoner who had been at the jail with the man and who told police that the man confessed to him. On the second day of trial, the prosecutor called the prisoner to the stand. Before the prosecutor asked any questions, the prisoner announced that he would not testify at all and wanted to assert a blanket Fifth Amendment privilege against self-incrimination.

Can the prisoner properly assert his Fifth Amendment rights in this way?

A. No, because it's unlikely that every one of the prosecutor's questions will lead to some type of incriminating testimony.

B. No, because if he wants to invoke his Fifth Amendment rights he is required to give the prosecutor some advance notice.

C. Yes, because he is being compelled by a state actor to give incriminating testimony that he believes might incriminate him.

D. Yes, because if he is forced to assert his rights in response to specific questions, the jury will reasonably infer his answers are incriminating.

Miranda Custody

261. Police arrested a young woman suspected of burning her neighbor's house to the ground. After transporting the young woman to the police station, the arresting officer placed her in an interrogation room for questioning. The officer removed the handcuffs from the young woman's wrists and gave her a cup of coffee. He then sat down and questioned the woman about the crime without first providing her with *Miranda* warnings. The young woman quickly confessed.

If the young woman is later charged with arson and if she files a pre-trial motion to suppress her statement, how should the court rule on the issue?

A. The young woman was in *Miranda* custody because the officer had placed her under arrest.

B. The young woman was in *Miranda* custody because she was in an interrogation room in a police station.

C. The young woman was not in *Miranda* custody because, although under arrest, she was not handcuffed.

D. The young woman was not in *Miranda* custody because she had not yet been charged with a crime.

262. After a significant amount of money was reported as stolen from a local charity fundraiser, police began to investigate whether the president of the charity had embezzled the money.

Although the police knew they had sufficient probable cause to arrest the charity president, they decided to conduct further investigation before making an arrest. The lead officer called the president and asked her to come to the station to answer some questions. The two arranged a meeting date and time and the president drove to the station and answered questions. The lead officer did not provide the president with *Miranda* warnings at the beginning of the interview, and she admitted to embezzling the money during the interview.

The president has now been charged with embezzlement and seeks to suppress her statements. She claims that she has a life-long fear of police and only agreed to come to the station for the interview because she didn't think she had any other choice.

How should the court rule on the president's motion?

A. The president was not in *Miranda* custody because she was not arrested, despite the fact that the police had probable cause for the arrest.

B. The president was not in *Miranda* custody because a reasonable person would have felt free to leave the interview.

C. The president was in *Miranda* custody because she was scared of the police and only agreed to the interview because she didn't think she had any other choice.

D. The president was in *Miranda* custody because the police had probable cause to arrest her.

263. A ninth grade student was suspected of setting a small fire that led to a larger forest fire. As part of the investigation, a police officer went to the student's school to speak with him. The interview was conducted in a conference room next to the principal's office, with the door closed.

The officer did not give the student *Miranda* warnings prior to questioning him nor did he notify the student's parents in advance of the interview. As a result of the questioning, the student confessed to setting the fire.

Later, as the officer was leaving the school, he mentioned to the principal that the student looked very young for a high school senior and asked whether the student had skipped a grade or two. The principal replied that the student was only in the ninth grade.

The student was later charged with arson and his attorney filed a motion to suppress. At a hearing on the motion, the officer testified that he did not give the student *Miranda* warnings because the interview was informal and non-custodial and because he thought the student was a senior.

If the judge grants the motion to suppress, what is the strongest constitutional reason for doing so?

A. The student's parents were not notified of the meeting with the officer.

B. The officer should have known that he was questioning a ninth grade student prior to beginning the interview.

C. The student's parents were not present during the meeting with the officer.

D. The officer knew of the student's young age when he questioned the student without *Miranda* warnings.

264. Police received a tip that a student teacher was selling marijuana to high school students at the school where he taught. The investigating officer placed the student teacher under surveillance for several days but the officer was unable to corroborate the tip. The officer decided to ask the student teacher to come to the police station for questioning.

After negotiating a meeting time, the student teacher drove to the police station. The officer escorted the student teacher to an interrogation room and closed the door. When the student teacher asked the officer why he closed the door, the officer replied that he was wanted to protect the student teacher's privacy. The officer then questioned the student teacher without first giving him *Miranda* warnings. After twenty minutes of questioning, the student teacher stood up to leave; the officer told him to sit down because the interview was not over. Ten minutes after that, the student teacher confessed to selling marijuana to his students.

The student teacher has now been charged with various drug-related crimes and the prosecutor plans to use the teacher's statement against him at trial. If the student teacher moves to suppress the statement, what is the most likely ruling from the court?

A. The student teacher was not in *Miranda* custody because he drove himself to the police station after negotiating a meeting time.

B. The student teacher was not in *Miranda* custody because the officer only closed the door to protect his privacy.

C. The student teacher was in *Miranda* custody because the officer closed the door to the interrogation room at the start of the interview.

D. The student teacher was in *Miranda* custody because the officer told him that he could not leave the interview room.

265. A prisoner was serving a twenty-year sentence for attempted murder of his wife. Police also suspected that the prisoner had abducted and killed one of his former girlfriends—years before the attempt on his wife's life. Two officers went to the state prison to interview the prisoner about the former girlfriend.

The prisoner was escorted to a conference room to speak to the officers. During the interview, the door to the conference room remained open and the prisoner was not handcuffed. The officers began the interview by telling the prisoner that he did not have to answer their questions and that he could go back to his cell at any time. The officers then asked the prisoner questions about his relationship with his former girlfriend and the circumstances of her disappearance. The prisoner answered the questions and implicated himself in the former girlfriend's death.

The prisoner has now been charged with kidnapping and murder and the prosecutor wants to use his statement against him. If the prisoner files a motion to suppress, what is the most likely ruling from the suppression court?

A. *Miranda* warnings should have been given because the officers knew that they were going to ask about the girlfriend's death.

B. *Miranda* warnings should have given because the prisoner was in *per se* custody since he was incarcerated.

C. *Miranda* warnings did not need to be given because the prisoner was not in custody at the time he was questioned.

D. *Miranda* warnings did not need to be given because convicted prisoners do not have Fifth Amendment rights.

266. A woman was driving home from work one night while texting. An officer saw what she was doing and pulled her over. When the officer approached the woman's car, he asked her, "don't you know how dangerous texting and driving is?" The woman replied that she was an "expert multi-tasker" and offered her opinion that while the law banning texting and driving was a "good idea for ordinary people," it shouldn't be applied to expert texting drivers like her.

The officer gave the woman a ticket and sent her on her way. Later, the woman decided to challenge the ticket. The prosecutor has indicated that at the hearing on the ticket, she will introduce the woman's statement to the officer. The woman claims that her statement is inadmissible because the officer didn't give her *Miranda* warnings.

Is the woman's statement admissible?

A. Yes, because the officer only asked a rhetorical question and the woman volunteered her response.

B. Yes, because the officer was not required to give the woman *Miranda* warnings before asking her questions.

C. No, because the officer placed the woman in *Miranda* custody, so he was required to give her warnings her before asking her questions.

D. No, because the officer seized the woman, so he was required to give her *Miranda* warnings her before asking her questions.

267. One weekend afternoon, a father was driving his 10-year old son to football practice; the father was driving 15 miles per hour over the posted speed limit. An officer saw this and so pulled the father over to the side of the road. After asking the father for his license and registration, the officer directed the father to get out of the car. The officer then handcuffed the father, walked him 20 feet from the car and directed him to sit on the curb. The son stayed in the car and began to cry.

The officer asked the father if he had "anything illegal" in the car, and the father admitted that there was some cocaine in the glove box. The officer returned to the father's car and retrieved the cocaine.

The father has now been charged with possession of cocaine and the prosecutor wants to use the father's statement against him. If the father files a motion to suppress the statement and argues that he should have been given *Miranda* warnings, what is the most likely ruling on the motion?

A. The motion will be granted because the father was in custody at the time he made his statement and should have been given his *Miranda* warnings.

B. The motion will be granted because the officer's act of separating the father from his son violated the father's Fourteenth Amendment Due Process rights.

C. The motion will be denied because traffic stops are never considered to be custodial, and so police don't have to provide *Miranda* warnings.

D. The motion will be denied because police officers have significant discretion in how they conduct traffic stops, in order to protect themselves.

268. Police obtained a warrant to search a private home for drugs. The lead officer rang the doorbell and a woman answered. The lead officer showed the woman the warrant. The woman allowed the officers to enter the house, and she went to the living room, sat down, and turned on the television.

Midway through the search, a rookie officer walked into the living room and asked the woman if she knew why the police were searching her home. The woman replied that she wasn't sure but she thought the search might have something to do with the drugs she stored in her attic. At the conclusion of the search — in which police found a stash of drugs in the woman's attic — the rookie told the lead officer about the woman's statement. The lead officer arrested the woman and the district attorney charged her with drug-related crimes.

The district attorney wants to use the woman's statement at her upcoming trial and the woman's attorney has filed a motion to suppress. How should the court rule on the motion?

A. The woman's statement should be admitted because the woman was not in *Miranda* custody when the rookie asked his question.

B. The woman's statement should be admitted because a person can never be in *Miranda* custody while sitting in her own living room.

C. The woman's statement should be suppressed because the rookie didn't know he was supposed to provide the woman with *Miranda* warnings.

D. The woman's statement should be suppressed because the lead officer failed to tell the rookie to provide the woman with *Miranda* warnings.

269. Police received a report that two men had gotten into a fight outside a particular bar, and that an older man had been badly beaten by a younger man. Afterwards, the younger man left the bar. After questioning several of the bar patrons, the investigating officer learned the identity and address of the younger man. Four officers went to his apartment.

The officers knocked on the door and a woman answered. She said that she was the younger man's roommate and she let the officers inside the apartment and showed them his bedroom; the woman then went back to bed. The four officers crept into the identified bedroom. With their weapons drawn and pointed at the bed, the officers turned on the lights in the bedroom. The younger man, who had been asleep, woke up and asked the officers what they wanted. One of the officers asked the younger man if he had been involved in a bar fight earlier in the evening and gave the name of the bar. The younger man confessed that he had been at that bar and had been in a fight. The officers arrested the younger man.

If the younger man is charged with assault, can his admission be used at his upcoming trial?

A. No, because the younger man was in *Miranda* custody and was not given *Miranda* warnings.

B. No, because the younger man was outnumbered and forced to confess.

C. Yes, because the younger man began the conversation when he asked the police why they were in his apartment.

D. Yes, because the younger man was in familiar surroundings and was not entitled to *Miranda* warnings.

270. A probationer agreed to participate in a group therapy program, successful completion of which would help him earn credit toward an earlier probation release date. As a condition of his participation, the probationer signed an agreement that he would tell the truth in his therapy sessions and that nothing he said in those sessions was confidential. During his third session, the probationer confessed to a rape and murder from twenty years prior. The police had long suspected the probationer of this crime.

Alarmed by the probationer's confession, the therapy session leader contacted the probationer's probation officer. The probation officer called the probationer and asked him to come to her office for a meeting. The two arranged a mutually convenient time and the probationer arrived as scheduled. During the meeting, the probationer repeated his confession to the earlier rape and murder. The probation officer gave this information to the police.

The police re-opened their investigation into this earlier crime and discovered new physical evidence supporting the probationer's confession. The prosecutor then charged the probationer with rape and murder.

Despite the lack of *Miranda* warnings, will the probationer's confession to the probation officer be admitted?

A. Yes, because the probationer knew that nothing he said in the therapy sessions was confidential.

B. Yes, because the probationer was never interrogated by a police officer.

C. Yes, because the probationer was not in custody in the probation officer's office.

D. Yes, because the probationer agreed to tell the truth and did tell the truth.

Miranda Interrogation

271. A police officer arrested a woman suspected of cultivating and selling marijuana. The officer drove the woman to the police station, brought her into an interrogation room, and read her the *Miranda* warnings from a pre-printed card. As he finished, the officer then realized that the portable audio recorder in the room was not working and so he picked it up to check the batteries. While the officer was fiddling with the recorder, the woman said, "I know why I'm here, and I want to tell you why I was growing all of that pot in my backyard."

If the woman is later charged with crimes associated with the marijuana, may the prosecutor use the woman's statement against her?

A. Yes, because the officer tricked the woman into speaking.

B. Yes, because the woman's statement is not a product of interrogation.

C. No, because the woman did not intelligently waive her rights.

D. No, because the woman did not knowingly waive her rights.

272. Two officers were sent to the local mall to investigate a report that a young woman had been robbed in the parking lot. The first officer took a report from the young woman. She gave the officer descriptions of the bright blue purse that had been taken from her and a spider web tattoo on the attacker's left palm. The first officer radioed this information to the second officer, who was driving around the perimeter of the mall.

At the rear of the mall, the second officer spotted a man walking quickly with a bright blue purse in his hand. The second officer stopped his car and the man began to run; the second officer chased after him. After a short distance, the second officer caught up to the man and tackled him to the ground. The second officer then said: "What's on your palm? Show me your palm!" The man showed the second officer his palms; tattooed on the left palm was a spider web with a fly caught in the middle. The second officer arrested the man and he was later charged with robbery.

The prosecutor intends to have the second officer describe the spider web tattoo—which he saw when he tackled the man to the ground. The man's attorney has moved to have this testimony suppressed as a fruit of a *Miranda* violation. Will the suppression motion be successful?

A. Yes, because the man was subjected to unwarned custodial interrogation when the second officer tackled him to the ground and asked an express question.

B. Yes, because the second officer knew when he asked the man to show his palm that it would elicit an incriminating response.

C. No, because although the man was in custody, he was not interrogated because the second officer's question did not compel a testimonial response.

D. No, because although the man was subjected to unwarned custodial interrogation, the second officer's actions were permitted under the public safety exception.

273. A police officer arrested a man suspected of growing marijuana in a greenhouse on his multi-acre property. The officer brought the man into an interrogation room and showed him a recent photo of the greenhouse that had been taken from a police helicopter. The officer then said:

> Look, I've been on the force for thirty years. I've seen it all and every time it's the same thing: you people think you'll get away with it. And I always wonder why. Did you really think you could have something this big on your property and that you wouldn't get caught? Did you think you no one would notice? Did you think you could get away with it?

The man replied, "You're right.... I wasn't thinking. I thought I could hide all of my child pornography in the greenhouse and I'd be fine. But I guess not." The officer was shocked by the man's response because he had no idea that the man was involved in any illegal activity beyond the cultivation of marijuana.

Later, after the man was charged, his attorney filed a motion to suppress the man's statement, arguing that it was the product of unwarned custodial interrogation. How should the judge rule on the motion?

A. The man was interrogated because the officer asked him express questions.

B. The man was interrogated because the officer spoke directly to him.

C. The man wasn't interrogated because the officer only asked rhetorical questions.

D. The man wasn't interrogated because the officer didn't expect the man's response.

274. Early one evening, a police officer arrested a woman for disorderly conduct because she refused to leave a store after being asked to do so by the store manager. At the time she was arrested, the woman didn't have any identification on her.

The officer brought the woman to the police station and asked her to provide some background information, including her name, date of birth, address, and height and weight. The woman answered the officer's questions truthfully. When the officer entered the information into his database, he learned that there was an outstanding warrant for the woman's arrest for murder, issued by a neighboring county.

Two weeks later, the woman was charged with the murder. In a pre-trial hearing, the woman's attorney argued that the arresting officer improperly interrogated the woman without first giving her *Miranda* warnings.

How should the judge respond to this argument?

A. The officer's questions fell within *Miranda* because they were express questions and so the woman should have been warned.

B. The officer's questions fell within *Miranda*, but his failure to provide warnings is harmless beyond a reasonable doubt.

C. The officer's questions didn't fall within *Miranda* because he did not intend his questions to elicit an incriminating response.

D. The officer's questions didn't fall within *Miranda* because they were routine booking questions, normally asked of all arrestees.

275. Two police officers arrested a woman suspected of robbing a bank and drove her to the police station. The officers did not give the woman *Miranda* warnings before starting the drive. About ten minutes from the police station, the first officer remarked to the second officer that the local animal shelter had recently had a very successful fundraiser and that the proceeds had been deposited in the bank the night before the robbery. The second officer asked the first whether the animal shelter would be able to recover the stolen money, and the first officer said that he didn't know. The first officer went on to say that he felt bad for all of the animals that wouldn't receive medical care because the shelter's money had been stolen in the robbery.

The woman, riding in the back seat, overheard this conversation and began to cry. She then said, "It was me! I did it! But I didn't know I'd been hurting all of those cats and dogs!" Two days later, the prosecutor charged the woman with bank robbery. Prior to trial, the woman's attorney filed a motion to suppress, arguing that her statement was a product of unwarned custodial interrogation.

Did the officers interrogate the woman?

A. No, because the officers spoke only to each other and did not address the woman in any way about the bank robbery.

B. No, because there is no reason the officers should have known that their words would prompt the woman to confess.

C. Yes, because the conversation between the officers shows that they wanted the woman to confess to the bank robbery.

D. Yes, because the woman confessed to the bank robbery directly after the officers discussed the crime in her presence.

276. A police officer arrested a teacher suspected of embezzling from her neighborhood association in order to buy classroom supplies for her students. The teacher was well-known in the community for her devotion to students and had won many awards for her teaching. As the officer drove the teacher to the police station, he said to her:

> I want to give you something to think about. I don't want you to respond, but just think about what I'm telling you. Everyone knows that you're a terrific teacher. And you took that money from the neighborhood association for the best of reasons, because you wanted to help the kids. But the neighborhood association is there to help the kids too. That group helps with playgrounds and community events and all kinds of local projects. That money was there for the kids, and you took it away from them.

The teacher's eyes welled up with tears. After a few minutes, she said, "I never thought about it that way. You're right: I took that money right out of my student's hands." The teacher then broke down and began to sob uncontrollably. A week later, the teacher was charged with embezzlement.

If the teacher's attorney files a motion to suppress her statement, how should the court rule on the motion?

A. The teacher was subjected to unwarned custodial interrogation because the officer knew his comments would prompt a response.

B. The teacher was subjected to unwarned custodial interrogation because the officer's comments clearly made her very emotional.

C. The teacher was not subjected to unwarned custodial interrogation because she took some time after his comments to give her response.

D. The teacher was not subjected to unwarned custodial interrogation because the officer directed her not to respond to his comments.

277. Police arrested a man for being an accessory to the murder of a successful businessman. The arresting officer suspected that the man's girlfriend—the businessman's ex-wife—had actually pulled the trigger. After the man was booked at the police station, the arresting officer placed the man in a line-up with five other men. A woman was brought in to view the line-up and after several seconds, she pointed at the man and said to the officer, "he's the one."

The officer then led the man down the hall and into an interrogation room. As the two were walking, the man asked the officer what had just happened. The officer replied, "Something terrible happened to that lady's kid, and she says you're the one who did it." The man replied, "I didn't do anything to anyone's kid. I helped my girlfriend out of a jam with her ex, and that's all." The man didn't know it, but the woman and the other participants in the line-up were all police officers, dressed in street clothes.

The man was later charged with crimes associated with the businessman's death and filed a motion to suppress his statement. What is the most likely ruling on whether the line-up constituted interrogation?

A. The line-up did not constitute interrogation because the officer did not know that the woman's fraudulent identification would prompt an incriminating response.

B. The line-up did not constitute interrogation because despite the police misconduct, the man knew he hadn't committed a crime against a child.

C. The line-up constituted interrogation because the officer should have known the woman's fraudulent identification would prompt an incriminating response.

D. The line-up constituted interrogation because the man was both outnumbered by the officers and outwitted by their shocking and offensive misconduct.

278. A man was arrested for the murder of his son and in response to *Miranda* warnings, he invoked his right to counsel. When the man's wife learned of the arrest, she rushed to the police station and begged to speak with him. The arresting officer reluctantly agreed but told the wife that he would have to be present for the conversation and that he would also record it. The wife agreed and entered the interrogation room with the officer. After the officer turned on a tape recorder and placed it on the table in front of the man, he and his wife had the following conversation:

Wife: What are we going to do?

Man: It'll be okay. Just stop crying.

Wife: I don't think you meant to hurt him.

Man: I didn't mean to hurt him and I didn't want to hurt him.

Wife: I know, I know.

The officer remained silent throughout the entire encounter. Two days later, the man was charged with murder. The man's attorney moved to suppress the man's statement, arguing that he was improperly interrogated after he invoked his right to counsel.

What is the judge's most likely ruling on the issue of interrogation?

A. The man was not interrogated because the arresting officer never spoke when he was in the interrogation room with the man and his wife.

B. The man was not interrogated because the arresting officer merely took prudent and appropriate steps to honor the wife's request.

C. The man was interrogated because even though the arresting officer did not speak, his presence was coercive and prompted the incriminating response.

D. The man was interrogated because allowing his wife to speak to him was coercive and designed to elicit an incriminating response.

279. A man was arrested for a brutal stabbing. At the police station, the arresting officer brought the man into an interrogation room and, without first providing *Miranda* warnings, showed him the bloody knife that had been used to kill the victim. The man began to cry and confessed that he had committed the crime. The man was later charged with murder and a lawyer was appointed to represent him. The lawyer filed a motion to suppress the man's confession, arguing that the officer should have given *Miranda* warnings before showing the man the bloody knife.

At a hearing on the motion, the officer admitted on cross examination that the only reason he showed the man the bloody knife was because he thought it would prompt the man to confess. The defense later argued that the officer's statement established that he had interrogated the man. In response, the prosecutor argued that the officer's subjective intentions were irrelevant to the question of interrogation.

If the judge issues a written opinion ruling on the suppression motion, which quotation most likely appears in the text of the opinion?

A. "The officer's intent is irrelevant to the issue of whether the suspect was interrogated."

B. "Under *Miranda*, we presume illicit police motive until the prosecutor proves otherwise."

C. "The officer's intent is relevant to the issue of whether the suspect was interrogated."

D. "Subjective police intentions play no role in ordinary Fifth Amendment analysis."

280. A police officer arrested a high school junior for cocaine possession. As the officer transported the junior to the police station, she called her dispatcher to notify him of the arrest, saying:

> I've got a kid with me, and I'll be back at the station in about 20 minutes. Drugs. I almost feel bad for him, because I know how this is going to ruin his future. At a minimum, he's never going to get into college, because what college wants a druggie on campus? And he might get expelled from high school as well, and that's going to be tough. What about his parents? If they're anything like the parents I know, he'll get kicked out of the house. Homeless, uneducated, and no future—just to get high. What a waste!

When the officer got off the phone, the junior told the officer that he had purchased the cocaine from his chemistry teacher.

The junior was later charged with cocaine possession, and his attorney filed a motion to suppress his admission in the car due to the officer's failure to provide *Miranda* warnings. In response, the prosecutor argued that the officer never interrogated the junior and so warnings were not required.

How should the judge rule on the motion?

A. The officer did not interrogate the junior because everything the officer said to the dispatcher was factually correct.

B. The officer did not interrogate the junior because she had no reason to known that her words would have any effect on the junior.

C. The officer interrogated the junior because she should have known that her words would elicit an incriminating response.

D. The officer interrogated the junior because
    every high school junior would have been
    upset by what she told the dispatcher.

Miranda Exceptions

281. Police arrested a high school teacher on suspicion that she had been involved in a sexual relationship with one of her students. The teacher had been arrested twice before, and both times she had told police that she wouldn't speak without a lawyer. Each time, the teacher had been released after invoking her right to counsel.

Because the teacher was arrested in the late afternoon, she arrived at the county jail after dinner had been served. As the intake officer led the teacher to her cell, he asked if she wanted a sandwich. The teacher replied that she didn't want anything other than to go home. Two weeks later, the teacher was charged with statutory rape and a public defender was assigned to represent her. The teacher asked the public defender whether the intake officer was allowed to ask her about a sandwich without first administering *Miranda* warnings.

How should the public defender respond?

A. The officer should have given *Miranda* warnings because warnings must be administered every time a police officer poses a question to a suspect in a custodial setting.

B. The officer should have given *Miranda* warnings and his failure to do so necessarily means that the teacher's answer was involuntarily made, regardless of its content.

C. The officer did not have to give *Miranda* warnings because warnings are not required every time a police officer poses a question to a suspect in a custodial setting.

D. The officer did not have to give *Miranda* warnings because the teacher knew her rights from her prior police experience and so warnings would only be a formality.

282. Police arrested a man suspected of being involved in a multi-state drug conspiracy. Police investigation had already identified six houses in two states where they believed drugs were being manufactured and stored.

When the man was brought to the police station, his fingerprints and photograph were taken. After that, he was placed in a chair next to the arresting officer's desk and handcuffed to the desk. Sitting in front of a computer terminal, the arresting officer asked the man for his name, address, height, weight, and hair and eye color. When the man gave his address, the officer knew that he had arrested the right person because the man's address matched the address of one of the drug houses. Two days later, the man was charged with a variety of crimes.

May the prosecutor use the man's statement about his address at the upcoming trial?

A. No; the man's answers are inadmissible because he was placed in custodial interrogation and should have been read *Miranda* warnings.

B. No; the man's answers are inadmissible because the officer discovered key information about the case during the booking process.

C. Yes; the man's answers are admissible because the officer's questions were for administrative and record-keeping purposes only.

D. Yes; the man's answers are admissible because the officer's questions were completely unrelated to the arresting offense.

283. A man was arrested for being drunk in public and was transported to the police station. Once there, the arresting officer handcuffed the man to a chair next to his desk and began to ask the man basic, biographical questions. The man did not answer the officer's questions, instead singing loudly and kicking his legs as if he was in a chorus line. The entire interaction was recorded on video.

The following day, the man was charged with public drunkenness. The prosecutor filed notice that he intended to introduce the video at the man's trial. When the man's attorney objected to the video recording of his client, the prosecutor responded that precinct protocol requires that every arrestee intake be recorded.

What is the correct ruling on the admissibility of the video at the man's trial?

A. The video is admissible under the routine booking question exception.

B. The video is admissible because it is the best evidence of the crime.

C. The video is admissible because it was made according to protocol.

D. The video is admissible because it is not testimonial evidence.

284. Police arrested a fraternity brother suspected of selling cocaine to his friends. As part of the arrest procedure, the arresting officer asked the fraternity brother for his name, height, weight, eye and hair color, and whether he had any existing medical conditions that would require attention during his detention. The fraternity brother replied that he had diabetes and that he required daily insulin injections. Two weeks later, the arresting officer interviewed a young woman who stated that she had recently purchased cocaine from a young man whose name she did not know, but who said that he had diabetes.

The fraternity brother has been charged with drug crimes, and the prosecutor intends to introduce his statement about having diabetes. What is the most likely ruling regarding the statement's admissibility?

A. The statement is inadmissible because it later proved to be incriminating, although not when it was made.

B. The statement is inadmissible because the officer used the information to develop new incriminating information.

C. The statement is admissible because the fraternity brother made it voluntarily and without any hesitation.

D. The statement is admissible because it was made in response to a legitimate and routine booking question.

285. Police at a state university received an anonymous tip that the president of the student government had planted a bomb in the chemistry lab to protest a planned tuition increase. The caller also said that she had heard that were two other bombs planted around campus, but she didn't know if that was true or where the bombs might be. Several officers rushed to the chemistry lab to locate and defuse the bomb; once there, they discovered the president's student ID lying on the floor a few feet from the bomb.

Two other officers went to the president's dormitory and found him outside, smoking a cigarette. The first officer handcuffed the president and the second officer demanded that he disclose the locations of the two other bombs. The president replied that there was only one other bomb and it was at the university library. The bomb at the library was later located and defused, and the president was arrested.

After he was charged, the president filed a motion to suppress his statement made outside the dormitory. Is the statement admissible?

A. The statement is inadmissible because the president was subjected to custodial interrogation without the benefit of *Miranda* warnings.

B. The statement is inadmissible because the officers lacked reasonable suspicion or probable cause to detain the president.

C. The statement is admissible because the need for information about the bomb outweighed the need to comply with the *Miranda* procedure.

D. The statement is admissible because the officers were responding to an exigent circumstance beyond their creation or control.

286. While investigating a shooting at a bar, an eyewitness showed the officer a video she took of the crime on her phone. The eyewitness also gave the officer the suspected shooter's name.

The officer found an address for the suspected shooter and she and four other officers went to his house. They pounded on the door and a woman let them inside and pointed them to the suspected shooter's bedroom door.

With their weapons drawn, the officers broke down the door to the bedroom and found the suspected shooter reading in bed. The first officer asked the suspected shooter if he had been at the bar earlier in the evening and he said yes. The officer then told the suspected shooter that she had seen a video of him shooting another man and asked him where he had hidden the gun. The suspected shooter told the officer that the gun was hidden in the attic of the house. The officer recovered the gun and arrested the suspected shooter.

Later, after he was charged, the suspected shooter's attorney challenged the admissibility of his statements in the bedroom. Are they admissible?

A. The statements are admissible under the public safety exception to *Miranda*.

B. The statements are admissible because the suspected shooter was not in *Miranda* custody.

C. The statements are inadmissible because the officers did not give the suspected shooter his *Miranda* warnings.

D. The statements are inadmissible because police entered the suspected shooter's bedroom without a warrant.

287. Police developed probable cause to believe that a woman had killed her boyfriend by injecting him with poison. An officer obtained an arrest warrant for the woman and went to her house to arrest her. When the officer arrived, the woman was leaving the house and walking toward her car, which was parked in the driveway.

The officer approached the woman and told her that he was going to arrest her. As the officer put handcuffs on the woman, he said, "I'm going to search you before I take you down to the station, but I need to know first if you have anything on you that might hurt me." The woman replied, "I'm clean but I do have a gun in the glove box of the car." The officer requested consent to retrieve the weapon and the woman agreed. Later, at the police station, the woman waived her *Miranda* rights and confessed to killing her boyfriend.

The woman was subsequently charged with murder and filed a motion to suppress the statement she made at her house. What is the prosecutor's strongest argument for the admissibility of the weapon?

A. The statement should be admitted under the routine booking question exception.

B. The statement should be admitted under the public safety exception.

C. The statement should be admitted because it was spontaneously made.

D. The statement should be admitted because it is minimally incriminating.

288. After a man was arrested for cocaine possession, he was placed in a cell for the night. The arresting officer knew that the man had been arrested before, and each time he had been given *Miranda* warnings, he had invoked his right to counsel. In order to prevent that from happening again, the arresting officer decided to place an undercover officer in the man's cell, to see if he could get some information—just in case the man later asked for a lawyer.

Later that evening, an undercover officer was placed in the man's cell. The two struck up a conversation, and over the course of the discussion, the man gave the undercover officer information about a larger drug conspiracy. The man was eventually charged with drug crimes and his attorney filed a motion to suppress the unwarned statements made to the undercover officer.

What is the most likely ruling on the suppression motion?

A. *Miranda* warnings were required because the man was subjected to custodial interrogation.

B. *Miranda* warnings were not required although the man was subjected to custodial interrogation.

C. *Miranda* warnings were not required in this situation because the man was not in *Miranda* custody.

D. *Miranda* warnings were not required in this case because the man was not subjected to interrogation.

289. Late one evening, an animal rights activist broke into a university research lab, and freed all the animals from their cages. The following day, a well-known animal rights group issued a press release, claiming responsibility for the break-in and announcing that there would be similar break-ins at other universities unless all animal experimentation was halted.

Police learned the identity of the activist from a tip, and arrested her. The arresting officer purposefully refrained from giving the activist her *Miranda* warnings and placed her in a holding cell with an undercover officer. The undercover officer was able to get the activist to confide the location of the next planned break-in. The following day the activist was charged with conspiracy and burglary.

The prosecutor wants to use the activist's statement at her trial. If she files a motion to suppress, what is the most likely ruling from the court?

A. The officer's questioning was impermissible because he asked about future crimes rather than the suspected crime.

B. The officer's questioning was impermissible because the officer failed to tell the activist about her rights.

C. The officer's questioning was permissible because the activist didn't know she was speaking to an officer.

D. The officer's questioning was permissible because he only asked about future crimes rather than the suspected crime.

290. A police officer arrested a college sophomore and brought her into an interrogation room for questioning. After hearing the *Miranda* warnings, the sophomore told the officer that she wanted to speak to a lawyer. The officer escorted the sophomore back to the lockup, and told her that he would call the public defender's office and a lawyer would be assigned to her case.

One hour later, the same officer placed a young woman in the same cell as the sophomore. The young woman was really an undercover officer, and she had been assigned the task of getting a confession from the sophomore. The undercover officer began speaking with the sophomore and before too long, the sophomore confided that she had committed the crime for which she had been arrested. Two days later, the sophomore was charged with that crime.

If the sophomore later seeks to suppress her confession, how should the court rule on the motion?

A. The motion should be granted because the officer did not honor the sophomore's invocation of the right to counsel.

B. The motion should be granted because there is no proof that the officer ever called a lawyer, as he promised to do.

C. The motion should be denied because the undercover officer did not coerce the sophomore into making a statement.

D. The motion should be denied because the sophomore's statement is too vague to have any incriminating use at trial.

Miranda Warnings

291. A police officer arrested a man suspected of committing a series of bank robberies. The officer brought the man into an interrogation room; three hours later, the man signed a hand-written confession, admitting that he had committed all of the suspected crimes. Based on the confession, the district attorney charged the man with five counts of bank robbery. Shortly before trial, the man's attorney filed a motion to suppress the confession.

At the suppression hearing, the officer testified that the man confessed "based on his own free will." The officer also explained that he did not threaten the man in any way or use any violence to get him to confess. On cross examination, the officer admitted that the interrogation room did have video recording equipment in it, but that he purposefully did not use it to record the man's interrogation.

How should the judge rule on the motion?

A. The motion should be granted because the officer intentionally failed to record the interrogation session.

B. The motion should be granted because the man was never told of his Fifth Amendment rights at the start of the interrogation session.

C. The motion should be denied because the officer's testimony establishes that the man confessed voluntarily to the crimes.

D. The motion should be denied because the constitution does not demand that interrogations be video recorded.

292. After a woman brought her 2 year-old son to the hospital with several broken bones, police arrested her on suspicion of child abuse. The woman was brought into an interrogation room, and an officer read her the following warnings from a pre-printed sheet:

> You have the right to remain silent and the right to a lawyer to help you protect that right and to help you during interrogation, and if you choose to waive these rights, then the prosecutor may use what you say against you in court. If you lack the financial means to pay for a lawyer, one can be appointed to represent you at no cost.

The woman told the officer that she understood and agreed to waive her rights and speak. She then initialed warnings on the pre-printed sheet, signed the sheet, and gave an incriminating statement. Later, after the woman was charged with child abuse, an attorney was appointed to represent her.

Can the attorney validly claim that the warnings provided to the woman deviated from the requirements of *Miranda v. Arizona*?

A. Yes, because the warnings included a lengthy, run-on sentence.

B. Yes, because the warnings didn't define "financial means."

C. No, because the woman knowingly, voluntarily, and intelligently waived her rights.

D. No, because the warnings conveyed the core information required by *Miranda*.

293. An officer arrested a woman suspected of being a member of a cocaine conspiracy and brought her into an interrogation room for questioning. The woman had a lengthy arrest record. The officer gave the woman the following *Miranda* warnings:

> Before I ask you any questions, you must understand your rights. You have the right to remain silent. Anything you say can be used against you in court. You have a right to talk to a lawyer for advice before we ask you any questions, and to have him with you during questioning. You have this right to the advice and presence of a lawyer even if you cannot afford to hire one. I have no way of giving you a lawyer, but a judge can appoint one to represent you, if you wish, if and when you go to court. If you wish to answer questions now without a lawyer present, you have the right to stop answering questions at any time. You also have the right to stop answering at any time until you've talked to a lawyer.

The woman waived her rights and confessed to being a member of the conspiracy. She was later charged with the crime.

The woman's attorney filed a motion to suppress, arguing that the *Miranda* warnings were inadequate. What is the prosecutor's best argument in response?

A. The warnings were adequate because they reasonably conveyed the information required by *Miranda*.

B. The warnings were adequate even though they included additional information beyond that required by *Miranda*.

C. The warnings may have been inadequate, but the woman knew her rights because of her past experience in the criminal justice system.

D. The warnings may have been inadequate, but the woman's statement is still admissible because it was voluntarily made.

294. Police brought a man into an interrogation room and read him the following *Miranda* warnings from a pre-printed form:

> You have the right to remain silent. If you give up the right to remain silent, anything you say can be used against you in court. You have the right to talk to a lawyer before answering any of our questions. If you cannot afford to hire a lawyer, one will be appointed for you without cost and before any questioning. You have the right to use any of these rights at any time you want during this interview.

In response, the man acknowledged that he understood his rights and confessed to committing several crimes. One week later, the man was charged with several crimes and an attorney was appointed to represent him. In their first meeting, the attorney asked the man why he had waived his rights and the man explained that police told him that he only had a right to have an attorney before questioning, and not during the actual interrogation.

If the attorney files a motion to suppress the man's statement on this basis, how should the court rule?

A. The warnings were adequate because the phrase "before answering any of our questions" referred only to the timing of counsel's appointment.

B. The warnings were adequate because *Miranda* does not include a right to have counsel present during interrogation, but only before the interrogation begins.

C. The warnings were inadequate because the phrase "before answering any of our questions" restricted the man's ability to consult with counsel during the interrogation.

D. The warnings were inadequate because they did not track the exact language from the *Miranda v. Arizona* opinion.

295. Two police officers developed probable cause to believe that a soccer coach was molesting some of the kids on his soccer team. After arresting the coach, the officers brought him into an interrogation room at the police station. The room was small and had a table in the middle. The two officers sat on one side of the table and the coach—wearing handcuffs—sat on the other side. The first officer began the interrogation by telling the coach:

> You don't have to speak to me if you don't want to. That's up to you. If you do decide talk to me, I can tell the prosecutor what you've said, and she might use what you say in court against you. If you want, you can also speak to a lawyer before you and I talk. Also, you should know that I can get you a free lawyer, if that's what you want.

The coach put his head in his hands for about two minutes. He looked up and said to the first officer, "I understand what you're telling me, and I want to tell you what happened." The coach then confessed to molesting some of the kids on his team.

The prosecutor has now charged the coach with several sex crimes, and has indicated that he will have the first officer testify about the coach's confession. The coach's attorney filed a motion to suppress this testimony. What is the attorney's strongest argument in support?

A. Testimony about the confession cannot be presented because the coach was not properly informed of his right to remain silent.

B. Testimony about the confession cannot be presented because the coach never signed a written waiver of his rights.

C. Testimony about the confession cannot be presented because the coach was not properly informed of the consequences of waiving his right to remain silent.

D. Testimony about the confession cannot be presented because the first officer's testimony would be inadmissible hearsay.

296. A police officer was working undercover, investigating a local drug dealer. One day, while having a beer with one of the drug dealer's associates at a local bar, the officer ran into an old high school friend. The high school friend recognized the officer and called him by his true name but the officer pretended not to hear and walked out of the bar.

Concerned that this interaction might be suspicious to the associate, the officer arrested the associate so he could formally interrogate him. Since the officer was working undercover he didn't have his *Miranda* rights card in his wallet, and so he relied on his memory to inform the associate of his rights, stating:

> You have the right to remain silent. If you decide to talk, that'd be up to you. You have the right to an attorney and if you can't afford one, we will get a lawyer for you. You can answer my questions with a lawyer present or without one present, but that'd be up to you.

In response, the associate said, "I don't know ... maybe.... okay, I guess I'll talk to you." The associate then told the officer details of the drug dealer's operation, implicating himself in the process.

The associate has now been charged with conspiracy to distribute drugs and seeks to suppress his statement. If the suppression court decides to grant the motion, what is the best reason for doing so?

A. The waiver was not knowing.

B. The waiver was not intelligent.

C. The waiver was not voluntary.

D. The waiver was not clear and unambiguous.

297. Police obtained an arrest warrant for a high school teacher suspected of selling marijuana to her students. After taking the teacher's photograph and collecting her fingerprints, the arresting officer brought her into an interrogation room. The officer then gave the teacher the following *Miranda* warnings:

> You have the right to remain silent, which means that you don't have to speak to me if you don't want to. If you give up that right, anything you say can and will be used against you in court. Like everyone else charged with a crime, you have a right to counsel, and that's the lawyer who will represent you at trial. If you cannot afford a lawyer, one will be appointed to represent you, even if you decide to plead guilty.

The teacher told the officer that she understood her rights and that she didn't have anything to hide. She then admitted that she sold marijuana to her students, explaining that she believed marijuana use was "perfectly safe" and that she considered its use to be a "victimless crime."

The teacher was later charged with drug charges and several counts of contributing to the delinquency of a minor. If her attorney moves to suppress her confession, what is the most likely ruling from the court?

A. The motion will be granted because the teacher was not properly informed of her Fifth Amendment right to counsel.

B. The motion will be denied because the officer's warnings reasonably conveyed the teacher's rights under *Miranda*.

C. The motion will be granted because the teacher's decision to waive her rights was based on her political beliefs and not her personal interests.

D. The motion will be denied because the teacher knowingly, voluntarily, and intelligently waived her rights.

298. At the conclusion of a lengthy investigation, police obtained an arrest warrant for a prominent politician. The politician had been a venture capitalist before entering politics and was quite wealthy. Two officers arrested the politician at his home and gave him the following *Miranda* warnings:

> You have the right to remain silent. If you give up that right, the prosecutor will be able to use what you say against you at your trial. You also have the right to a lawyer, and that means that you can have your lawyer with you while we question you.

The politician acknowledged that he understood what the officers had told him. He then said to one of the officers, "I can't believe that buying votes is a crime in this state. How else was I supposed to get into office unless I greased the wheels a little?"

The politician was charged with several counts of election fraud and the prosecutor wants to use his statement at the upcoming trial. If the politician files a motion to suppress his statement, what is the most likely ruling from the court?

A. The politician's statement is admissible because informing a wealthy person about the rights of the poor is not constitutionally required.

B. The politician's statement is admissible because it was not made in response to interrogation by the officers.

C. The politician's statement is inadmissible because the officer failed to properly *Mirandize* him.

D. The politician's statement is inadmissible because he never signed a waiver form.

299. A two-year old child was placed in foster care and was thriving in his placement. After several months though, the court ordered the child be returned to his biological mother and assigned a social worker to help the mother with parenting skills.

On the day of the social worker's first scheduled meeting with the mother, the mother told the social worker that the child was not at home but was with one of her friends. The same thing happened on the second and third visits and the social worker never saw the child after he was placed with his mother. Thoroughly suspicious, the social worker arranged for the court to issue an order for the mother to produce the child. When the mother was presented with the order, she refused to comply and so the police arrested her.

At the police station, the arresting officer began to *Mirandize* the mother, but she interrupted him and said, "Don't waste your breath. I watch a lot of TV, so I know my rights." The officer replied, "That's fine. We can get right to it. I need to know where your child is." The mother replied, "I left him in the woods because he cried too much." The officer then asked the woman where in the woods she had left the child, and the woman drew a map to the location. When the police followed the map and found the child, he was dead.

The mother has been charged in her child's death. The prosecutor wants to use her statement and the map at her upcoming trial and the mother has moved to have them suppressed. How should the court rule?

A. The statement will be suppressed as a fruit of a *Miranda* violation, but the map will be admitted because it is non-testimonial, physical evidence.

B. Both the statement and the map will be suppressed as fruits of a *Miranda* violation.

C. Neither the statement nor the map will be suppressed because the mother waived her right to receive full *Miranda* warnings.

D. Neither the statement nor the map will be suppressed because the mother knowingly, voluntarily, and intelligently waived her rights.

300. The chief judge in a rural Midwestern county grew frustrated by the number of defendants who passed through her courtroom who had waived their *Miranda* rights and confessed to crimes during police interrogation. The judge believed that the police were giving proper *Miranda* warnings, but felt that because *Miranda* warnings had become such a regular part of popular culture, suspects just didn't take them as seriously as they should.

With the cooperation of the chief of police, the judge produced a 10-minute video to be shown to suspects who were going to be placed in custodial interrogation. The judge was the sole speaker in the video, and she gave a short but thorough lesson on the Fifth Amendment—including the right to silence and the right to counsel. When the local prosecutor learned of the judge's plan, he filed an emergency petition in the state supreme court seeking to enjoin the police from using the video. One of the claims in the petition asserted that use of the judge's video "would violate the United States constitution because it would effectively eliminate *Miranda* warnings."

What is the most likely ruling from the state supreme court?

A. The prosecutor is correct because the Fifth Amendment demands that *Miranda* warnings be given to suspects in custodial interrogation.

B. The prosecutor is correct because the state judge is attempting to overrule a constitutional decision of the United States Supreme Court.

C. The prosecutor is incorrect because the information in the judge's video provides an equivalent alternative to the *Miranda* warnings.

D. The prosecutor is incorrect because *Miranda* warnings are non-constitutional procedural rules created by an activist court.

Miranda Invocations

301. A man was suspected of leaving his 8 year-old daughter alone in the house without food and was arrested for endangering the welfare of a child. The arresting officer brought the man into an interrogation room and read the man his *Miranda* warnings. The following exchange then occurred:

Man: I want to plead the Fifth.

Officer: What? The fifth? Fifth what? I don't know what that means.

Man: You know, the Fifth. I want to plead the Fifth.

Officer: I have no idea what you're talking about. I never said anything to you about a fifth. A fifth of what? Vodka? Whiskey? Cinnamon schnapps? There's no booze allowed in this interrogation room.

The officer placed a pen and a waiver form in front of the man and left the room, telling him that he'd be back soon. When the officer returned to the room a few minutes later, the man had signed the form. The officer began to interrogate the man and, fifteen minutes later, the man confessed to intentionally starving his child.

The man has now been charged with endangering the welfare of a child and seeks to suppress his confession. How should the court rule on his motion?

A. The confession is inadmissible because the man did not knowingly, voluntarily, and intelligently waive his rights.

B. The confession is inadmissible because the man invoked his Fifth Amendment rights and his invocation was not honored.

C. The confession is admissible because it was unclear whether the man was invoking his right to silence, his right to counsel, or both.

D. The confession is admissible because the officer's confusion demonstrates that it is unclear what the man was actually asking for.

302. A police officer arrested a man after searching the trunk of the man's car and finding several kilos of marijuana inside. That evening, the officer placed the man in an interrogation room and read him *Miranda* warnings. The officer also gave the man a sheet of paper on which the *Miranda* warnings were printed and, after confirming that he understood his rights, the man agreed to speak.

For the first few minutes of the interrogation, the man freely answered the officer's questions. But then the man asked, "You mentioned something before about a free lawyer. Can you tell me some more about how that works?" The officer replied that everything the man needed to know what written on the sheet of paper he had been given earlier. The officer resumed his questioning. Twenty minutes later, the man confessed to being a part of a massive marijuana and cocaine conspiracy.

If the man is later charged with drug crimes and moves to suppress his statement, what is the most likely ruling from the court?

A. The motion will be granted because the officer failed to clarify the man's question about counsel.

B. The motion will be granted because the officer did not honor the man's request for appointed counsel.

C. The motion will be denied because the man waived his rights at the beginning of the interrogation.

D. The motion will be denied because the man never properly invoked his right to counsel and waived his rights.

303. A 15-year old boy was arrested on suspicion that he had vandalized his school by spray-painting the principal's office and pouring syrup on the bleachers in the gym. The arresting officer brought the boy into an interrogation room and read him the *Miranda* warnings. She asked the boy if he understood his rights and the boy said he did, but that he wanted to call his mother. The officer told the boy that he could speak to his mother after the interrogation. The boy sighed and signed a waiver form. After 45 minutes of interrogation, the boy admitted to vandalizing the school.

After the boy was charged with various crimes, his attorney filed a motion to suppress the statement. At the hearing on the motion, the attorney presented the testimony of the boy's mother, who stated that had she been present at the interrogation, she would have advised her son not to speak to the officer.

How should the court rule on the suppression motion?

A. The motion should be denied because the boy never properly invoked his right to counsel and he validly waived his rights.

B. The motion should be denied because the Fifth Amendment applies only to adults in custodial interrogation, not children.

C. The motion should be granted because the mother's testimony establishes that she would have acted as her son's attorney.

D. The motion should be granted because a 15-year old's request for a parent is equivalent to an adult's request for counsel.

304. Police suspected a middle-aged man of killing his neighbor and a warrant was issued for the man's arrest. An officer found the man at a local bar, arrested him, and read him *Miranda* warnings. In response, the man said, "I want a lawyer before I say anything else." The officer took the man to the police station and placed him in a holding cell.

The next day, the officer took the man from the holding cell and placed him in an interrogation room. The officer read the *Miranda* warnings again, but this time, the man signed a *Miranda* waiver form. After signing, the man gave a complete confession to his neighbor's murder. The man was subsequently charged with the crime.

If the man moves to suppress his statement from his upcoming trial, how should the court rule on the motion?

A. The statement will be suppressed because officer did not ask the man if he understood his rights prior to beginning the interrogation.

B. The statement will be suppressed because the officer failed to provide the man with a lawyer after he invoked his right to counsel.

C. The statement will be admitted because the warnings on the day of the arrest were a formality since the officer didn't actually interrogate the man until the next day.

D. The statement will be admitted because the man was given proper *Miranda* warnings and later validly waived his rights.

305. After giving *Miranda* warnings to a woman suspected of killing her toddler, the arresting officer presented the woman with a waiver form and a pen. The following exchange then occurred:

> Woman: I want to make sure I'm doing the right thing here. I need a lawyer to help me get through this. This whole thing is so crazy.

> Officer: It <u>is</u> crazy. That's why I want to talk to you about it.

> Woman: But I didn't do anything wrong.

> Officer: Well, sign that form and tell me what happened. And if you didn't do anything wrong, I'll personally drive you home myself.

> Woman: Okay, if that's what it takes to get back home. I'll sign.

The woman picked up the pen and signed the form. Two hours later, she confessed to killing her toddler by drowning him in the bathtub.

At a subsequent suppression hearing, the prosecutor argued that the confession was admissible because the woman waived her rights. How should the court rule on the motion to suppress?

A. The motion should be granted because the woman clearly and unambiguously invoked her right to counsel and her invocation was not honored.

B. The motion should be granted because the officer tricked the woman into waiving her rights by offering to drive her home from the police station.

C. The motion should be denied because the woman only made a passing reference to a counsel, but she did not clearly and unambiguously request counsel.

D.   The motion should be denied because the woman's decision to waive so soon after mentioning counsel shows that she didn't really want legal help.

306. Police arrested a man suspected of being involved in the disappearance of his business partner. The man was subjected to custodial interrogation and given his *Miranda* warnings. He invoked his right to counsel and was released later that same day. Six months later, when the business partner's corpse was found buried in a shallow grave on the edge of the man's vacation property, the man was rearrested and brought into an interrogation room for renewed questioning. The man was again given his *Miranda* warnings, but this time he waived his rights. He told police that he had killed his business partner the morning of his earlier arrest, and had buried the body after he was released from custody.

The prosecutor charged the man with first-degree capital murder. The man's defense attorney filed a motion to suppress, arguing that the man had invoked his right to counsel at the time of his initial arrest.

What is the prosecutor's strongest argument in opposition to the motion to suppress?

A.   The man's earlier invocation is legally irrelevant because he invoked his right to counsel in an interrogation about kidnapping, and the later interrogation was for a homicide.

B.   The man's right to counsel lasted only while he was in custody for the first arrest, and it expired when he was released from that custody and returned to his normal life.

C.   The man's earlier invocation is legally irrelevant because he knowingly, voluntarily, and intelligently waived his rights when he was placed in custody a second time.

D.   The man's right to counsel lasted for two weeks after he was released from the first arrest and so the police were permitted to place him in renewed *Miranda* custody six months later.

307. An arrestee was brought into an interrogation room and the arresting officer read the man his *Miranda* warnings. The officer told the arrestee that if he wished to waive his rights, he would be required to sign a waiver form, and the officer pointed the arrestee to a sheet of paper on the table in front of him, and to the pen resting beside the form. The officer asked the arrestee if he understood his rights; the arrestee picked up the pen and wrote the word "yes" on a corner of the form. The officer asked the arrestee if he wanted to waive his rights, and the arrestee wrote the word "silent" on another corner of the form.

The officer said to the arrestee, "look, in this room we talk and I want to talk to you about what happened." The officer then began to ask the arrestee questions, but the arrestee remained silent. After 30 minutes of this, the officer asked the arrestee if he was proud of what he'd done. The arrestee replied, "I'm not proud of myself, but if I could do it over again, I'd kill that guy a second time." The arrestee was later charged with murder and his attorney filed a motion to suppress, arguing that the arrestee invoked his right to silence and the officer failed to honor that request.

Did the arrestee invoke his right to silence?

A. The arrestee did not invoke his Fifth Amendment right to silence because he did not verbalize his desire to remain silent.

B. The arrestee did not invoke his Fifth Amendment right to silence because the word "silent" is ambiguous and confusing.

C. The arrestee invoked his Fifth Amendment right to silence because the word "silent" is an unambiguous invocation of the right.

D. The arrestee invoked his Fifth Amendment right to silence because he remained silent for the majority of the interrogation.

308. After a woman was arrested for cocaine possession, the arresting officer decided to interrogate her to see if she would identify the name of her supplier. The officer brought the woman to an interrogation room and read her the *Miranda* warnings. In response, the woman said, "I know my rights and I know what I want. Leave me alone." The officer left the room and arranged for the woman to be placed back in her cell.

Six hours later, the same officer escorted the woman back into the interrogation room. Once the woman was seated, the officer said, "I did what you asked for and I left you alone. Now will you talk to me?" The woman dropped her head and stared at her hands for a few minutes. She then looked up and said, "yeah." The officer asked the woman for the name of her supplier. The woman gave the officer a name. The officer asked the woman how she met the supplier and the woman gave an explanation. The two continued to speak and after an hour, the woman had confessed to being part of a large, multi-state drug conspiracy.

The woman was later charged with conspiracy and other crimes and the prosecutor notified the defense that he planned to use the woman's statement at trial. What is the strongest argument for suppression of the woman's statement?

A. The woman invoked her right to silence and the officer impermissibly re-initiated contact with her six hours later.

B. The officer failed to re-*Mirandize* the woman and obtain a valid waiver when he returned to speak to her.

C. The woman invoked her right to silence and never re-initiated contact with the officer after the invocation.

D. The officer failed to respect the woman's invocation by leaving her alone for at least 24 hours after the invocation.

309. A man suspected of murder was brought to an interrogation room for questioning. After giving the man his *Miranda* warnings, the arresting officer and the man had the following short discussion:

Officer: Do you understand what I told you?

Suspect: You said something about a free lawyer. I want to talk about that.

Officer: A lawyer?

Suspect: Yeah, a lawyer. But it has to be a free lawyer. Before I sign any statement, I want to talk to a free lawyer. Because I want that lawyer to read my statement, to make sure it's right.

Officer: Okay, I can make that happen. I can get you a free lawyer before you sign anything. Is that what you want?

Suspect: That's what I want.

The officer then asked the man if he wanted to waive his rights, and the man said he did. After 15 minutes of questioning, the man confessed to the murder.

After the man was charged with second-degree murder, his attorney filed a motion to suppress the man's statement, arguing that it was obtained in violation of the man's Fifth Amendment right to counsel. How should the court rule on the motion?

A. The statement should be admitted because the man only invoked his right to counsel for a discrete and limited purpose.

B. The statement should be admitted because the man's statement was ambiguous and the officer did not have to honor it.

C. The statement should be suppressed because the man clearly and unambiguously invoked his *Miranda* right to counsel.

D. The statement should be suppressed because the man's limited invocation shows that he didn't understand his rights.

310. A police officer arrested a woman suspected of driving the getaway car used in a bank robbery the previous week. After advising the woman of her *Miranda* rights and asking her if she understood what she'd been told, the officer and the woman had the following exchange:

Woman: I don't know. I just think that maybe I should get a lawyer.

Officer: I asked you if you understood the information I just read to you. Do you understand?

Woman: Yeah. But maybe I should get a lawyer.

Officer: Okay, so you understand. I want to start by talking about where you were last Tuesday afternoon. Do you remember?

Woman: Well, yeah. I do. But I'm just wondering about this lawyer thing.

Officer: So, where were you last Tuesday afternoon? What were you doing?

Woman: Helping my friends at the bank.

The woman eventually gave a full statement, detailing her involvement in the bank robbery and providing the names of the other people involved in the crime. After the woman was charged with bank robbery and conspiracy, she moved to have her statement suppressed.

What is the most likely ruling from the court on the motion to suppress?

A. The motion will be granted because the officer failed to clarify the woman's statement about counsel.

B. The motion will be granted because the officer badgered the woman into confessing to the suspected crime.

C. The motion will be denied because the woman did not invoke her rights and later validly waived them.

D. The motion will be denied because the woman knowingly, voluntarily, and intelligently waived her rights.

Miranda Re-Initiation

311. A police officer arrested a college student for vandalism. As the officer was adjusting the handcuffs on the student, she read him the *Miranda* warnings. The student told the officer that he knew his rights and that he wanted to speak to an attorney. The officer said that she'd make note of the student's request and placed him in the back seat of her patrol car for the drive to the police station. About five minutes into the drive, the student told the officer that he wanted to speak about what he had done.

May the officer speak to the student about the vandalism?

A. Yes, because the student's request to speak with an attorney was not effective since it was made at the time of arrest, before the formal interrogation began.

B. Yes, because although the student invoked his right to counsel in response to the *Miranda* warnings, he reinitiated contact and agreed to further questioning.

C. No, because the short time span between the student's invocation and his change of heart shows that he didn't fully understand the *Miranda* warnings.

D. No, because the student clearly and unambiguously invoked his *Miranda* right to counsel and so he cannot be interrogated until counsel is provided to him.

312. An officer placed an arrestee in an interrogation room and read her the *Miranda* warnings. In response, the arrestee said that she wanted some time alone and didn't want to speak to officer. The officer stepped out of the room for twenty minutes and then returned. He sat down across from the arrestee and began to ask her questions about the crime for which she had been arrested. The arrestee answered the officer's questions; within a short time, she had given a full confession.

Two days later, the arrestee was charged with various crimes and her court-appointed attorney filed a motion to suppress her statement. The prosecutor defended the officer's actions by arguing that he had honored the arrestee's request to be left alone but that the arrestee reinitiated contact with the officer when she responded to his questions.

Is the prosecutor's position correct?

A. No, because the officer here spoke to the arrestee first and the arrestee must speak first for her re-initiation to be valid.

B. No, because the arrestee never independently indicated that she wanted to speak to the officer about the crime or her arrest.

C. Yes, because viewing the facts according to the totality of the circumstances, the arrestee spoke to the officer voluntarily.

D. Yes, because the arrestee clearly knew how to invoke her rights and did not do so when the officer began to question her.

313. A woman was arrested for drunk driving; as part of her arrest, the woman was given *Miranda* warnings. In response, the woman told the arresting officer that she didn't want to speak without a lawyer present. The arresting officer drove the woman to the police station and placed her in a cell.

Two hours later, the woman was fast asleep in the cell when she was woken up by a loud clanging noise. She yelled out for an officer and one arrived about ten minutes later. The woman told the officer that the cell was too noisy and asked what was going on. The officer led the woman from the cell into an interrogation room and asked her how much she had to drink before her arrest. Surprised by the question, the woman blurted out that she'd had seven margaritas before getting in her car and driving home.

The woman was charged with drunk driving and the defense filed a motion to suppress her statement. How should the court rule on the motion?

A. The woman did not re-initiate conversation with the police because the officer saw that she was surprised by his question.

B. The woman did not re-initiate conversation with the police because she only asked about the noise in the cell.

C. The woman re-initiated conversation with the police because she went with the officer into the interrogation room.

D. The woman re-initiated conversation with the police because she yelled out and asked for an officer to come to her cell.

314. A man was arrested and given his *Miranda* warnings; in response, the man asked to be left alone. The officer complied with the man's wishes and placed the man in a cell. The man became bored and thirty minutes later, asked a guard to find the officer. The guard called the officer, who instructed the guard to bring the man to an interrogation room.

Once in the interrogation room, the officer asked the man what he wanted. The man replied that he was bored in the cell and wanted a book or a magazine to read. The officer handed the man a stack of documents — police reports chronicling the status of the investigation and several crime scene photos — and told the man that he'd find them more interesting than a book or a magazine. After reviewing the materials, the man told the officer that he wanted to discuss his case.

Has the man re-initiated conversation about his case?

A. The man has not re-initiated conversation about his case because he never indicated a desire to discuss his case until after he reviewed the documents.

B. The man has not re-initiated conversation about his case because his request that the guard locate the arresting officer was vague and ambiguous.

C. The man re-initiated conversation about his case because by speaking about his boredom, he actually invited the officer to begin a discussion about the case.

D. The man re-initiated conversation about his case because there is no other logical reason why he would have asked the guard to locate the officer.

315. Late one evening, a woman was arrested for the murder of her husband. After being given *Miranda* warnings, the woman said that she had already retained a lawyer and didn't want to speak to police unless the lawyer was present to advise her. The arresting officer told the woman that he would make arrangements for her to consult with the lawyer the following day.

Early the next morning, the woman asked to speak to the arresting officer. He was summoned, and the woman told him that she had given it a lot of thought and wanted to speak about her husband's death. The officer read the *Miranda* warnings for the second time. The woman acknowledged understanding her rights and then signed a waiver form. The officer began to question the woman about her husband's death, and she confessed to poisoning him.

Is the woman's confession admissible?

A. Yes, because the woman knowingly, voluntarily, and intelligently waived her rights.

B. Yes, because the woman reinitiated conversation and then voluntarily confessed to the murder.

C. No, because the officer did not let the woman speak to her lawyer before she reinitiated contact.

D. No, because the officer never bothered to arrange for the woman to consult with her lawyer.

Miranda Waivers

316. Two officers arrested a teenager and brought her into an interrogation room at the police station. One of the officers removed the handcuffs from the teenager's wrists as the second officer read the *Miranda* warnings from a pre-printed form. The teenager was crying uncontrollably but appeared to be listening to what the officer told her. When the officer finished, the teenager took the pen the officer handed her and signed her name at the bottom of the form. The officers then began to ask the teenager questions about a string of neighborhood burglaries that the she was suspected of committing. At first, the teenager said nothing and just kept crying. After about 15 minutes though, she told the police that she had committed the burglaries with the help of her college-aged boyfriend.

After the teenager was charged with conspiracy and several counts of burglary, a public defender was appointed to represent her. The public defender filed a motion to suppress the teenager's statement, arguing that she never validly waived her rights.

What standard should the court use when assessing the validity of the teenager's waiver?

A. Whether the teenager was told of her right to have a parent or guardian present during the interrogation.

B. Whether a reasonable person with the teenager's experience and maturity would have waived her rights.

C. Whether the teenager's waiver was voluntarily made, that is, free from coercion and duress.

D. Whether the teenager's waiver was knowing, voluntary, and intelligent.

317. Two officers arrested a man suspected of being involved in the robbery of a local convenience store. The arrest occurred at a group home for intellectually disabled people where the man lived. At the time of the arrest, the resident assistant who supervised the home told police that the man rarely left the home without her because of the severity of his disability, and she asked if she could come along to the police station. The officers refused.

At the police station, the officers placed the man in an interrogation room, read the *Miranda* warnings, and then put a pre-printed sheet with the *Miranda* warnings in front of him. The man glanced at the sheet and told them that he'd read it. The first officer asked the man if he was willing to waive his rights and the man said he was. The first officer gave the man a pen and told him to sign the sheet; the man drew a circle on the page. The officers then began to interrogate the man and twenty minutes later, he fully confessed to the robbery.

The man was later charged with robbery and his attorney filed a motion to suppress. What is the strongest argument in support of the motion?

A. Because he was intellectually disabled, the man could not knowingly, voluntarily, and intelligently waive his rights.

B. Because he never read the pre-printed form, the man did not knowingly, voluntarily, and intelligently waive his rights.

C. Because he drew a circle on the pre-printed form, the man did not knowingly, voluntarily, and intelligently waive his rights.

D. Because of the totality of the circumstances, the man did not knowingly, voluntarily, and intelligently waive his rights.

318. Several weeks after a local businessman disappeared, police arrested the businessman's secretary on suspicion of murder. At the police station, the secretary was placed in an interrogation room; shortly afterwards, four officers came into the room to conduct the interrogation. The lead officer told the secretary:

> Before we get started, you need to know your rights. You have the right to tell me your side of the story, and you also have the right to refuse to talk to me. That's your choice, to talk to me or not. If you do talk to me, I will relay what you've said to the prosecutor, and she will use what you say against you in court. You also have the right to an attorney and that means that you can talk to a lawyer before we speak and that the lawyer can be with you during the interrogation. And if you can't afford a lawyer, one will be appointed to represent you, at no cost to you.

In response, the secretary then told the lead officer that she understood her rights and that she wanted to "explain what happened." She then fully confessed to killing the businessman after he caught her embezzling from the business.

Based in part on the secretary's confession, the DA charged her with embezzlement and murder. Prior to trial, her attorney filed a motion to suppress her statement. What is the strongest argument in support of the motion?

A. The secretary's waiver of rights was not knowing.

B. The secretary's waiver of rights was not voluntary.

C. The secretary's waiver of rights was not intelligent.

D. The secretary's waiver of rights was not in writing.

319. Police arrested a woman on suspicion that she had killed her teenaged son—one of her three children. The arresting officer brought the woman into an interrogation room at the police station, read the *Miranda* warnings, and placed a waiver of rights form in front of her to sign. The officer then told the woman that if she didn't talk to him, he would arrange for her other two children to be removed from her custody. With tears in her eyes, the woman said that she understood and signed the form. The woman then confessed to murdering her son and dismembering his body.

The woman has been charged with murder and abuse of a corpse and the prosecutor intends to use the woman's statement at trial. What is the strongest argument for suppression of the woman's statement?

A. The woman did not knowingly waive her rights.

B. The woman did not voluntarily waive her rights.

C. The woman did not intelligently waive her rights.

D. The woman did not intentionally waive her rights.

320. A man was brought into an interrogation room for questioning about the murder of his roommate. The arresting officer provided the man with the Miranda warnings, relying on his memory instead of reading the warnings from a pre-printed card. The officer said:

> You have the right to remain silent. You can talk to me if you'd like, but you need to understand that I'm not your lawyer and I'm not your friend and I'm not here to help you. You also have the right to an attorney and if you don't have the money to pay a lawyer, we can get the judge to appoint a lawyer to help you out here.

The officer then asked the man if he understood what he'd been told, and the man said he did. The man agreed to waive his rights and speak to the officer. After ten minutes of interrogation, the man confessed to killing his roommate.

The man has now been charged with murder and seeks to suppress his confession. If the suppression court decides to grant the motion, what is the best reason for doing so?

A. The waiver was not knowing.

B. The waiver was not voluntary.

C. The waiver was not intelligent.

D. The waiver was not clear and unambiguous.

321. A college freshman was arrested for assaulting his roommate after the freshman discovered that the roommate had smoked all of his marijuana. Hoping to learn the name of the freshman's supplier, the arresting officer brought him into an interrogation room and read him the *Miranda* warnings. The freshman agreed to waive his rights and signed a waiver form. The freshman then gave the arresting officer the name and phone number of his supplier and also confessed that he regularly sold cocaine to members of the football team.

What the freshman didn't know what that minutes after he was arrested, his professor—who was also a licensed attorney—called the police station, identified himself as the freshman's attorney, and explained that he did not want the freshman to be interrogated unless he was present. The officer who spoke with the professor agreed to these conditions and reassured the professor that she would relay the message to the interrogating officer—but didn't.

The freshman has now been charged with drug crimes and has moved to suppress his statement. How should the court rule on the motion?

A. The statement is admissible because the freshman knowingly, voluntarily, and intelligently waived his rights.

B. The statement is admissible because the officer's failure to relay the professor's request was an isolated case of negligence.

C. The statement is inadmissible because the professor invoked the freshman's right to counsel for him, and the invocation was not honored.

D. The statement is inadmissible because the officer violated the freshman's due process rights when she lied to his professor.

322. A man who had been twice convicted of domestic abuse of his ex-wife was arrested for assaulting his girlfriend. The arresting officer brought the man into an interrogation room and read the man his *Miranda* warnings; the officer then asked the man if he understood his rights. The man replied that he did and told the officer that he wanted to explain his side of the story. The officer pulled a tape recorder off of a shelf, turned it on, and said to the man, "okay, start talking." The man confessed to the assault, but defended his actions by claiming that his girlfriend had hit him first.

If the man files a motion to suppress and contests the admissibility of his statement, how should the court rule on the motion?

A. The man did not validly waive his rights because his waiver was not in writing.

B. The man did not validly waive his rights because his waiver was not audio recorded.

C. The man knowingly, voluntarily, and intelligently waived his rights before he confessed.

D. The man validly waived his rights because he confessed without any prompting.

323. After his arrest and booking, a man was brought into an interrogation room for questioning. The arresting officer told the man that police were investigating the murder of the man's brother-in-law and that he was the prime suspect in the case. The officer read the man his *Miranda* warnings from a pre-printed sheet of paper. In reply, the man said:

> Okay, what do you want to know? Do you want me to tell you that I killed him? I did kill him, but he was a lousy person and I don't regret what I did. And I threw his body in the river because he treated my sister badly and she didn't deserve what he did to her.

Based on the man's statement, the prosecutor charged the man with murder. At trial, the prosecutor intends to show that the brother-in-law's body was found in the river.

The man's attorney has moved to suppress his statement from the upcoming trial, arguing that he never properly waived his rights. How should the judge rule on the motion?

A. The man gave an implied waiver of his Fifth Amendment rights because he confessed after being informed of his *Miranda* rights.

B. The man gave an implied waiver of his Fifth Amendment rights because he told the police accurate facts after being informed of his *Miranda* rights.

C. The man did not give an implied waiver of his Fifth Amendment rights because there is no proof that he understood his rights.

D. The man did not give an implied waiver of his Fifth Amendment rights because he never signed a *Miranda* rights waiver form.

324. A police officer arrested a suspect for murder and placed him in an interrogation room. The officer read the suspect his *Miranda* warnings from a pre-printed "*Miranda* Rights Form," and then asked the suspect to initial the warnings on the form and sign it at the bottom of the page. The suspect said nothing, did not look at the form, and did not initial or sign it.

The officer then began to ask the suspect questions about the murder; the suspect didn't say anything in response and just stared at the officer. This continued for nearly three hours: the officer asking questions and the suspect remaining completely silent. Finally, the officer grew frustrated and said, "I can't believe that you're not sorry for killing that kid." The suspect started to cry and replied, "I am sorry for what I've done, and you don't know how bad I feel."

The suspect has now been charged with murder and has moved to suppress his statement. How should the court rule on the motion?

A. The statement is inadmissible because the suspect did not initial and sign the pre-printed *Miranda* rights form.

B. The statement is inadmissible because the suspect never properly waived his rights.

C. The statement is admissible because it was voluntarily made.

D. The statement is admissible because the suspect never properly invoked his right to silence.

325. A police officer arrested a woman suspected of five bank robberies during the previous year. As the officer was placing handcuffs on the woman, she asked why she was being arrested. The officer replied, "a bank robbery from last month," but he did not provide the woman with any additional information.

The officer transported the woman to the police station and placed her in an interrogation room. He then read the woman her *Miranda* warnings; she acknowledged that she understood her rights and signed a written waiver form. The officer began the interrogation by asking the woman where she had gotten the idea to rob so many banks. The woman replied that since the first robbery had gone so well and she hadn't been caught, she thought she'd do it a few more times. The woman then told the officer that she wanted to speak to a lawyer so he returned the woman to her cell.

Later, the woman was charged with five counts of bank robbery. Her attorney filed a motion to suppress her statement. How should the court rule on the motion?

A. The woman's waiver was invalid because the officer told her that he wanted to discuss one specific bank robbery when he obviously wanted to discuss all the robberies.

B. The woman's waiver was invalid because the officer tricked her into waiving her rights when he didn't provide complete information about the interrogation.

C. The woman's waiver was valid because her invocation of the right to counsel demonstrates that she understood her rights and how to ask for them.

D. The woman's waiver was valid because the officer properly *Mirandized* her, she acknowledged she understood her rights, and she signed a written waiver form.

Miranda/Fifth Amendment Remedies

326. A man suspected of murdering his wife was brought to the police station for questioning. The officer conducting the interrogation read the man his *Miranda* rights and the man signed a waiver of rights form. The officer then began the interrogation. Two hours later, the man said to the officer, "this is too much and I can't go on. I want you to leave me alone." The officer replied, "I'm on a roll here, and we're not stopping until you confess." The man then confessed to killing his wife.

May the prosecutor use the man's statement at his upcoming trial?

A. Yes, the confession may be used but only to establish the man's guilt.

B. Yes, the confession may be used but only to impeach the man if he testifies.

C. Yes, the confession may be used but only to impeach defense witnesses.

D. Yes, the confession may be used but only *cogito ergo sum*.

327. Armed with an arrest warrant, an officer drove to a private home to make what he believed would be a routine arrest. When the officer knocked on the front door, shots were simultaneously fired at him from two different windows of the house. The officer called for backup and then returned the fire. Several minutes later, the shooting finally stopped. After backup officers arrived, they found a woman inside the house with a gun by her side; the woman was severely wounded. The backup officers were not able to find the other shooter.

The officer accompanied the woman to the hospital and guarded her while she was being treated in the emergency room. The woman was moaning from pain, but the officer told her to "knock it off" and asked her for the name of the other shooter. The woman responded with the name of a man who had recently escaped from prison.

After review, the prosecutor decided not to charge the woman with a crime. But the woman filed a civil rights suit against the officer, claiming that his actions in the emergency room violated her Fifth Amendment privilege against self-incrimination. What is the most likely ruling on the woman's claim?

A. The woman's rights were violated because she was subjected to custodial interrogation in the emergency room without *Miranda* warnings.

B. The woman's rights were not violated because her testimony was not used against her in a criminal case.

C. The woman's rights were not violated because she was not in custody in the emergency room and so she was not entitled to *Miranda* warnings.

D. The woman's rights were not violated because she was not interrogated in the emergency room and so she was not entitled to *Miranda* warnings.

328. Police arrested a man on suspicion that he had killed his neighbor. On the drive to the station, the officer said to the man, "I knew your neighbor, and he was a terrific guy. I don't know how you can live with yourself after what you did to him." The man replied, "I only gave him what he deserved." The man then turned to look out the window and didn't say anything more.

At the police station, the officer took the man through the booking process and then brought him into an interrogation room. The officer gave the man his *Miranda* warnings, and asked the man if he understood them. The man said he did and that he wanted to waive his rights and speak. After signing a waiver form, the man confessed to killing his neighbor. The man was charged with murder the following day.

Prior to trial, the prosecutor conceded that the man's admission during the car ride should be suppressed as a product of unwarned custodial interrogation. But defense counsel argued that the later confession should also be suppressed. What is the most likely response from the judge?

A. The later confession should be suppressed as a fruit of the *Miranda* violation during the car ride.

B. The later confession should be suppressed as a continuing *Miranda* violation from the car ride.

C. The later confession should not be suppressed because the *Miranda* violation during the car ride was only a technical violation of the law.

D. The later confession should not be suppressed because the man was *Mirandized* at the police station and validly waived his rights.

329. An officer brought a man into an interrogation room. The officer had questioned the man the year before and he had invoked his rights. The officer decided not to give the man any *Miranda* warnings, to see if he could get him to confess to a recent robbery before invoking his rights.

After 30 minutes of questioning, the man admitted that he had been present during the robbery but insisted that his friend had been the one to commit the crime. The man then asked the officer why he hadn't been given his *Miranda* warnings and so the officer told the man his rights. The man signed a waiver form. The officer then said:

> Okay, now that that's out of the way, let's get back to what we were discussing before. You were telling me about that robbery, and you were saying that you only watched your friend and that you didn't take anything. I don't believe you, and I want you to tell me what really happened.

The man began to cry and confessed that he had been an equal participant in the robbery.

Later, after the man was charged with conspiracy and robbery, his attorney filed a pre-trial motion to suppress both statements. What is the most likely ruling from the court in response to the motion?

A. The first statement will be suppressed due to the *Miranda* violation; the second statement will be admitted because it was voluntarily made.

B. The first statement will be suppressed due to the *Miranda* violation; the second statement will be admitted because the man waived his rights before speaking.

C. Neither statement will be suppressed because the man knew his rights and he chose to waive them instead of invoking them.

D. Neither statement will be admitted because the man was not warned at the outset and the warnings he was given later were not effective.

330. Police arrested a 17-year-old high school senior; the senior was suspected of killing his great-grandmother because she wouldn't let him use her car. As the arresting officer drove the senior to the police station, the officer told the senior that he was lucky to have known his great-grandmother, and said that she was known around town for being "a good cook and a kind and generous soul." The senior replied, "she wasn't so generous with me and so that's why I took things into my own hands."

Two hours later, the officer brought the senior into an interrogation room and read him his *Miranda* warnings. The officer then re-marked:

> I want you to know that you can choose not to talk to me and you can choose to get a lawyer. But why would you do those things? You've already told me that you killed that poor woman. Why don't you just fill in the details and tell me why you did this horrible crime?

The senior signed a waiver form and gave a detailed confession to the murder. Later, the prosecutor charged the senior with first-degree murder.

What is the senior's strongest argument to suppress the post-warning confession?

A. The *Miranda* warnings were not effective because there was only a two-hour break between the car ride and the interrogation at the police station.

B. The *Miranda* warnings were not effective because the officer treated the second round of interrogation as continuous with the first round.

C. The *Miranda* warnings were not effective because the arresting officer was also the officer who conducted the interrogation at the police station.

D. The *Miranda* warnings were not effective because the high school senior, a juvenile, was incapable of fully understanding his rights.

331. Police executed a search warrant in a woman's home, looking for evidence that she had killed her brother. While the officers were executing the warrant, the woman sat in her living room and was guarded by a rookie police officer. During the search, the rookie asked the woman about her childhood and the woman told him that she and her brother had been at odds their whole lives because their parents favored the brother over her. Police eventually found the brother's body in the basement, buried underneath the water heater. The woman was then charged with murder.

Prior to trial, the judge ruled that the woman's statement to the rookie would be suppressed because of a *Miranda* violation. At trial, the woman testified on her own behalf and denied killing her brother. The woman also explained that she loved her brother dearly, that he had been her best friend, and that there had never been any sibling rivalry between the two of them. On cross-examination, the prosecutor confronted the woman with her statement to the rookie and asked the woman which statement was true. Defense counsel immediately objected.

How should the judge rule on the objection?

A. Sustained, because the statement from the living room was suppressed and the prosecutor's use of it at trial constitutes misconduct.

B. Sustained, because the statement from the living room was an off-hand comment and is not as reliable as a statement made under oath.

C. Overruled, because the statement from the living room can be used to impeach the woman's testimony.

D. Overruled, because the statement from the living room can be used to show the woman's motive to kill her brother.

332. A woman was arrested and charged with breaking into a bar where she used to work, and then stealing money from the cash register and alcohol from the bar. Shortly after the arrest, police interrogated the woman and she admitted the crime. However, because the arresting officer had interrogated the woman without *Miranda* warnings, her statement was suppressed.

At trial, the woman claimed an alibi, and presented the testimony of her roommate in support of the defense. The roommate testified that she and the woman had been out of town on the night in question. On cross-examination, the prosecutor confronted the roommate with the woman's previously suppressed statement, and he asked her whether she realized that she had just committed perjury when she testified about the woman's alibi. The defense objected to the prosecutor's question.

Should the judge sustain the objection?

A. No, because the woman's statement was suppressed from the state's case-in-chief only, and can still be used to impeach.

B. No, because the woman's statement is credible evidence that the roommate committed perjury in her testimony.

C. Yes, because the woman's statement was suppressed and so cannot be used in any way at the woman's trial.

D. Yes, because the woman's statement was suppressed from the state's case-in-chief only, and so may only be used to impeach her if she testifies.

333. A police officer obtained a warrant to arrest a man for possession of child pornography. As the officer arrived at the man's house to execute the warrant, the man was leaving and getting into his car. The officer showed the man the warrant and began to read the man the *Miranda* warnings as she arrested him. Mid-way through the recitation, the man stopped her and said that he knew his rights. The officer said in reply, "Okay, then, let's get right to it. Where do you keep the photos?" The man hesitated for a few seconds and then said, "I'm not sure I should tell you anything about the photos because I don't want you to take them away from me." The officer repeated her question and the man confessed that they were in his kitchen. The man then gave the officer permission to search his kitchen. The officer searched the kitchen and found thousands of pornographic photographs of children, stashed in the kitchen drawers.

If the prosecutor concedes a *Miranda* violation, what evidence should be suppressed?

A. The statement but not the photos, because the photos are non-testimonial evidence and were obtained through a valid consent search.

B. The statement but not the photos, because the photos are the only tangible evidence of the man's guilt for this awful crime.

C. Both the statement and the photos, because the prosecutor concedes the *Miranda* violation and both are fruits of that violation.

D. Neither the statement nor the photos, because the fruit of the poisonous tree doctrine does not apply to *Miranda* violations.

334. The owner of a small chain of grocery stores learned that two of his store managers had been subpoenaed to testify before a grand jury. Concerned that he might be the target of the grand jury's investigation, the owner consulted with his lawyer, but the lawyer said that they would have to wait to see what the grand jury would do. Several weeks after the managers testified, the owner was charged and arrested for food stamp fraud.

At trial, the prosecutor presented evidence showing that the owner had been involved in food stamp fraud for several years and that his fraud activities increased markedly in the weeks right before he was criminally charged. In her closing argument, the prosecutor argued that this was proof of guilt:

> And he knew that he was being investigated, because his managers were speaking to our investigators. But what did he do? Did he come forward? Did he ask to speak to me or to any of people working on the case? Did he come to us and tell us his side of the story? No, he didn't. He just continued to collect profits, even stepped up his game, because he knew he was going to get caught and he wanted to get as much money as he could before we arrested him.

Defense counsel objected, claiming that the prosecutor impermissibly commented on the owner's Fifth Amendment right to remain silent.

How should the judge rule on the objection?

A. Overruled, because the owner never invoked his Fifth Amendment right to remain silent.

B. Overruled, because the owner was acting on the advice of counsel.

C. Sustained, because the prosecutor can't establish the owner's guilt by proving a negative.

D. Sustained, because the prosecutor's comments were inflammatory and prejudicial.

335. A man was arrested for the murder of his wife, and brought into an interrogation room. After receiving his *Miranda* warnings, the man invoked his rights, and was returned to his cell. Shortly afterwards, the man was charged and retained a lawyer to represent him. The state's case at trial was purely circumstantial and was based on the theory that the man killed his wife so he could collect her life insurance money and have a new life with his girlfriend.

At the close of the state's case, the man and his lawyer agreed that there was reasonable doubt as to his guilt, and so the man chose not to testify on his own behalf. During closing arguments, the prosecutor said to the jury:

> Ladies and gentlemen, I've worked so hard during this trial to give you a clear picture of what happened here, and a good reason why you should find the defendant guilty of murdering his wife. You heard testimony about the defendant's affair about how he was the beneficiary of his wife's life insurance policy. But there are some details of the crime we'll never know, because there were really only two witnesses to this crime, and one is dead and the other wouldn't talk when we asked him for an explanation.

Defense counsel immediately objected.

What is the strongest basis of the defense attorney's objection?

A. The prosecutor vouched for his witnesses.

B. The prosecutor commented on the defendant's exercise of his right to remain silent.

C. The prosecutor vouched for his own performance at trial.

D. The prosecutor commented on the verdict he wanted the jury to return.

Non-*Miranda* Challenges to Statements

336. A police officer arrested a man suspected of killing his ex-wife, although her body had not been found. The officer brought the man into an interrogation room and read him the *Miranda* warnings. The man acknowledged that he understood his rights and signed a waiver form.

The officer then pistol-whipped the man with his service revolver, telling the man that he'd better "confess or else." The man—bleeding from the head and whimpering—confessed that he'd killed his wife and buried her body in the basement of their house.

If the man is charged with murder, can his confession be used against him?

A. Yes, because the officer complied with *Miranda* procedure: he told the man about his rights and the man validly waived his rights prior to confessing.

B. Yes, because the man knowingly, voluntarily, and intelligently waived his rights prior to confessing to killing his wife.

C. No, because the man only waived his *Miranda* rights and didn't waive his right to be free from physical brutality at the hands of police.

D. No, because regardless of the officer's compliance with the *Miranda* procedure, the man's confession was involuntarily made.

337. A man was shot by police during a raid on a drug house and transported to the hospital. The man spent several hours in the emergency room before being transferred to the intensive care unit. The man was in tremendous pain and had been given painkillers.

Around midnight, a police officer came to the man's bed and began to question him about the crime. Because the man couldn't speak due to the tube in his throat, the officer told the man to blink twice if he agreed with his—the officer's—statements. The officer then said, "I shot a police officer" and the man blinked twice. The officer said, "I was trying to kill the police officer," and the man blinked once. The officer continued in this vein, and the man blinked his agreement with about half of the officer's statements.

If the man is charged with murder, will the use of his "statement" at trial violate his Fourteenth Amendment rights?

A. No, because the man gave an implied waiver of rights when he blinked in response to the police officer's statements.

B. No, because the man did not blink in agreement to all of the police officer's statements, his "statement" was voluntary.

C. Yes, because under the totality of the circumstances, the man's statement was involuntarily made.

D. Yes, because the man never gave a real statement; instead, he only blinked in response to what the officer said to him.

338. A police officer arrested a woman suspected of running a child pornography ring. The officer brought the woman to an interrogation room and provided her with *Miranda* warnings. The woman verbally acknowledged understanding her rights and then asked, "What is going to happen to me now?" The officer replied that the next step was up to the woman: she could either confess to her crimes or not. But, the officer warned, he couldn't guarantee the woman's physical safety at the jail unless she confessed. He added, "If you want to live through the night I'd suggest you tell me what happened so I can make sure you get put into protective custody in the lock-up." The woman immediately confessed to the suspected crime.

The woman has been charged with a variety of crimes related to child pornography, and seeks to suppress her confession from the trial. What is the correct ruling on the motion?

A. The woman's statement is inadmissible because it was made in response to a threat of physical harm, and so it was involuntarily made.

B. The woman's statement is inadmissible because she did not re-initiate interrogation when she asked, "What is going to happen to me now?"

C. The woman's statement is admissible because she had no way of knowing whether the officer could carry out his threat.

D. The woman's statement is admissible because the officer's threat was too speculative to render her statement involuntary.

339. Police arrested a young man on suspicion that he and his sister had killed their elderly aunt. The arresting officer read the young man the *Miranda* warnings and the man signed a waiver form and agreed to give a statement.

Ten minutes later, the young man admitted to the officer that he had been present when his sister killed his aunt. The young man explained, "I didn't want her to do it and I told her that, but she shot the old lady anyway." The officer replied that the sister had been interrogated earlier in the day and that she had told police that the young man had fired the lethal shot — not her. The young man began to cry, and, then admitted that he had shot his aunt.

The officer was lying: the sister had only just been arrested and her interrogation had not yet started.

If the young man challenges the admissibility of his statement under the Fourteenth Amendment, what is the most likely ruling from the court?

A. The statement is admissible because the young man knowingly, voluntarily, and intelligently waived his rights when he signed the form.

B. The statement is admissible because, under the totality of the circumstances, the young man's will was not overborne by the officer's lie.

C. The statement is inadmissible because the officer lied to the young man to get him to confess to shooting his elderly aunt.

D. The statement is inadmissible because otherwise, the officer will not be penalized and other officers will not be deterred from similar misconduct.

340. Police extracted a confession from a woman by repeatedly threatening to take her children away from her if she didn't confess to killing her stepdaughter. In the confession, the woman described how she'd poisoned the girl over several weeks, and these details matched the forensic findings from the autopsy. After the woman was charged, her attorney filed a motion to suppress and the judge had found that the confession was involuntarily made and inadmissible.

At trial, the woman testified in her own defense. During her direct examination, the woman denied having enough knowledge about chemistry to poison anyone, explaining that she had failed chemistry in high school and generally didn't understand "science stuff." On cross examination, the prosecutor sought to impeach the woman with her previously suppressed confession, but the woman's attorney objected.

May the prosecutor use the woman's statement under these circumstances?

A. No, because involuntary statements cannot be used for any purpose, including to impeach a defendant's testimony.

B. No, because the prosecutor failed to lay a proper foundation before he tried to use the woman's statement to impeach her.

C. Yes, because suppressed statements are admissible to impeach a defendant's testimony, if the defendant testifies.

D. Yes, because regardless of the police conduct associated with the woman's interrogation, her confession is reliable and accurate.

Double Jeopardy

341. A college student was charged with getting into a fight at a bar with another patron. The prosecutor charged the college student with aggravated assault, and the jury acquitted him of the charge. After the jury returned its verdict, the prosecutor spoke with one of the jurors, who explained that the jury thought the college student was guilty of the charged crime, but that he seemed like "such a polite young man" that they didn't want to ruin his future by convicting him of a felony.

Outraged by what the juror had told him, the prosecutor re-charged the college student with aggravated assault. At the second trial, the prosecutor planned to show the jury that the college student was not such a nice guy after all, and that he deserved to be convicted of the felony. Two days before trial, the college student's attorney filed a motion to dismiss the charges, arguing that the renewed charges violated the Double Jeopardy Clause.

How should the court rule on the motion?

A. The motion should be granted because the prosecutor's duty is to "do justice," not to charge people with crimes just because he's angry with the jury.

B. The motion should be granted because the college student cannot be re-prosecuted for a crime after he has already been acquitted of that same crime.

C. The motion should be denied because the prosecutor is permitted to re-charge a defendant with the same charges when the jury nullifies at the first trial.

D. The motion should be denied because a criminal trial is about truth, and the first jury's verdict was obviously against the weight of the evidence.

342. An assistant district attorney charged a man with cocaine distribution and based much of his case on the testimony of the man's ex-girlfriend. Two weeks prior to trial, the ex-girlfriend died in a car accident, and the prosecutor realized that he needed to re-work his case. With the judge's permission, the prosecutor voluntarily dismissed the drug charges without prejudice to re-filing them at a later date.

Several months later, the prosecutor was able to assemble enough evidence to bring the man to trial. The prosecutor re-filed the charges, but the man's attorney filed a motion to dismiss. In the motion, the attorney argued that the Double Jeopardy Clause barred re-filing of the same cocaine distribution charges, and that the prosecutor was harassing the man.

What is the most likely ruling on the motion?

A. The motion will be granted because the Double Jeopardy Clause protects against serial charging of the same crime against the same person.

B. The motion will be granted because the prosecutor cannot re-file criminal charges once they have been voluntarily dismissed.

C. The motion will be denied because jeopardy never attached for the cocaine charges, and so there is no Double Jeopardy Clause violation.

D. The motion will be denied because the prosecutor is blameless in this situation, and the Double Jeopardy Clause is designed to prevent government overreaching.

343. A woman was charged with aggravated battery and attempted murder of her ex-husband. The woman requested a jury trial and a date for the trial was set. On the morning of trial, the prosecutor asked the judge for a continuance, explaining that the ex-husband had been subpoenaed but had failed to appear. The judge granted the request and scheduled the trial for the following month. Over the following year, this sequence of events repeated itself several more times, and each time, the judge granted the prosecutor's motion for a continuance.

At the next trial date, a jury was selected but the ex-husband again failed to appear. The prosecutor asked for another continuance, but the judge instead gave her a choice of either dismissing the charges or beginning with her other witnesses and saving the ex-husband's testimony for the end of her case. The prosecutor refused to dismiss the charges and so the judge administered the oath to the jurors. The prosecutor then told the judge that she would not participate in the trial until all her witnesses appeared. Defense counsel immediately moved for a directed verdict, arguing that since there was no evidence of the woman's guilt, she had to be acquitted. The judge agreed, granted the motion, and dismissed the jurors. Three weeks later, the prosecutor re-filed the charges, arguing that jeopardy had never attached because no evidence had been presented at the trial.

Is the prosecutor's argument correct?

A. Yes, because the woman was never placed in jeopardy since the prosecutor refused to participate in the trial.

B. Yes, because double jeopardy should be assessed based on the totality of the circumstances and not by rigid, mechanical rules.

C. No, because jeopardy attached when the jury was empanelled and sworn, regardless of the prosecutor's participation at the trial.

D. No, because the judge correctly denied the motion for the continuance given the multiple continuances he granted in past.

344. The state's attorney charged a woman with illegal receipt of a firearm, and the judge set a trial date. Two days before the trial was scheduled to start, the woman decided to plead guilty to the charge. Three weeks after the judge sentenced the woman to a year in prison, the state's attorney charged the woman with illegal possession of the same firearm. The woman's attorney filed a motion to dismiss the possession charge, arguing that illegal receipt and illegal possession of the same weapon are the same crime under the Double Jeopardy Clause.

If the trial judge agrees that the two charges are the same, should she grant the motion to dismiss?

A. No, because jeopardy did not terminate for the illegal receipt charge because the woman pleaded guilty and did not go to trial.

B. No, because jeopardy will not terminate for the illegal receipt charge until the woman completes her prison sentence.

C. Yes, because jeopardy attached and terminated for the illegal receipt charge, barring retrial on the illegal possession charge.

D. Yes, because jeopardy for all charges associated with the weapon terminated at the same time jeopardy terminated for the receipt charge.

345. A woman was charged with first degree murder in the killing of one of her co-workers. According to the prosecutor, the woman and the co-worker had been dating for several months, but the co-worker had decided to break up with the woman. The prosecutor alleged that when the woman heard this news, she shot and killed the co-worker. In contrast, the defense claimed that the woman had been the one to break up with the co-worker, and that the co-worker had become violent when he heard the news. According to the defense, the killing was a tragic accident, committed in self-defense.

The jury deliberated for several days, but the foreman told the judge that the jury was deadlocked and unable to reach a verdict. Convinced that further deliberations would be futile, the judge declared a mistrial and dismissed the jury. The following day, the prosecutor recharged the woman with first degree murder. Several days after that, one of the jurors contacted the defense attorney and told her that the jury unanimously believed the woman's self-defense claim, but was confused about how to acquit the woman since she admitted killing the co-worker. The juror then signed an affidavit, explaining what he had told the defense attorney.

The defense attorney filed a motion to dismiss all charges on Double Jeopardy grounds, and attached the juror's affidavit in support of the motion. How should the judge rule on the motion?

A. Double jeopardy bars retrial in this situation because the juror's affidavit established that the jury would have acquitted the woman.

B. Double jeopardy bars retrial in this situation because the jeopardy terminated for the murder charge when the judge dismissed the jury.

C. Double jeopardy does not bar retrial in this situation because jeopardy never terminated for the first degree murder charge.

D. Double jeopardy does not bar retrial in this situation because the defense attorney cannot definitively prove that the jury would have acquitted the woman.

346. A woman set fire to her house one night, hoping to kill her husband—who was sleeping inside. The husband managed to escape from the burning house; he was rushed to the hospital with burns over a significant portion of his body. While the husband lingered in the hospital burn unit, the wife was prosecuted for the arson of the house. At her trial, prosecutors argued that the woman's motive for setting the fire was to kill her husband, although the arson charge did not require proof of motive. The jury returned a guilty verdict for the arson.

Six months after the woman was convicted of arson, the husband died from his injuries sustained in the fire. The prosecutor charged the woman with first-degree intentional murder. The week before trial, the woman's attorney filed a motion to dismiss all charges, arguing that the Double Jeopardy Clause barred a murder prosecution because the prosecutor had argued that the woman had a homicidal motive in the arson trial.

How should the court rule on the motion?

A. The motion should be denied because jeopardy has not yet attached for the homicide.

B. The motion should be denied because arson and murder are different crimes for double jeopardy purposes.

C. The motion should be granted because jeopardy had attached and terminated for the arson charge.

D. The motion should be granted because both crimes arose from the same set of operative facts.

347. A man was convicted at trial of cruelty to animals. According to the proofs at trial, the man was walking his dog when a neighbor's dog broke through the gate surrounding the neighbor's property. The neighbor's dog then attacked the man's dog and killed it. The man returned to his home and retrieved a rope and a knife, tied up the neighbor's dog and then slashed its throat — killing the dog.

At trial, the man asked that the jury be instructed that state law permits a person to kill an animal if the person witnesses the animal attack another animal. The judge refused, telling the man that there is no defense to the killing of an animal. The jury returned a guilty verdict and the man was sentenced to two years of probation. The man appealed, claiming that the trial judge had erred in refusing to give the instruction. The appeals court agreed, and reversed the man's conviction.

Will double jeopardy bar the man's retrial for cruelty to animals?

A. No, because the man has asked for an opportunity to give a defense and has been given that chance, so double jeopardy doesn't bar retrial.

B. No, because jeopardy had attached but is continuing, so the prosecutor is not barred from seeking to retry the man for the same crime.

C. Yes, because jeopardy had attached and terminated for the animal cruelty charge and the prosecutor is seeking to retry the man for the same crime.

D. Yes, because the trial judge committed reversible error when he would not allow the man to present his affirmative defense to the jury.

348. A defendant was charged with capital murder for the killing of two police officers during an escape from the county jail. On the first day of trial, the jury was brought into the courtroom and seated. A minute later, two deputies brought the defendant into the courtroom. The defendant was wearing the street clothes his public defender had provided to him, but he was wearing handcuffs, ankle shackles, and a belly chain. The public defender immediately objected to the restraints, but the judge overruled the objection.

Later that afternoon, after the jury had been on a break, the foreman sent the judge a note on behalf of the entire jury. The note said: "Judge, we want your assurance that we are safe in the courtroom with the defendant. He looks like he's pretty dangerous." The judge shared the note with the prosecutor and public defender, and the public defender requested a mistrial. The judge agreed, granted the motion, and dismissed the jury.

Will the Double Jeopardy clause bar the defendant's retrial on the same charges?

A. No, because double jeopardy would only bar a retrial if the court had *sua sponte* declared a mistrial.

B. No, because jeopardy has attached but not terminated for the capital murder charge, permitting retrial for the same charge.

C. Yes, because jeopardy has attached and terminated for the capital murder charge, barring retrial for the same charge.

D. Yes, because the judge failed to *sua sponte* declare a mistrial when the defendant was initially brought into court.

349. A defendant was charged with possession with the intent to distribute several kilos of cocaine. It wasn't the defendant's first brush with the law; in the previous decade, the defendant had been arrested and charged times for various drugs, and convicted once — serving four years for that conviction. Prior to the start of trial, the judge instructed the prosecutor that she was not permitted to mention the defendant's prior arrests or conviction in front of the jury, unless the man testified to the events himself.

At trial, the prosecutor's case quickly collapsed, as each of her witnesses failed to testify as anticipated. As she was examining her final witness — in an effort to salvage her case — the prosecutor asked the witness if he knew about the defendant's criminal record. Before the witness could answer, the defense objected and the judge sustained the objection. Later in the day, while cross-examining one of the defense witnesses, the prosecutor again asked the witness if he was aware of the defendant's criminal record. Defense counsel immediately moved for a mistrial, which the judge granted. The judge then dismissed the jury.

If the prosecutor re-files the same charges against the defendant, will Double Jeopardy bar retrial?

A. No, because the defense knew of the defendant's criminal record and should have anticipated the questions.

B. No, because the defense moved for the mistrial and is accordingly estopped from arguing against retrial.

C. Yes, because the prosecutor ignored the judge's instructions, so she was in contempt of court.

D. Yes, because the prosecutor intentionally goaded the defense into moving for the mistrial.

350. Police arrested a man for being a felon in possession of a handgun. The county prosecutor charged the man for the crime, and the man elected to go to trial. After deliberating for several hours, the jury acquitted the man. Outraged by the acquittal, the county prosecutor told the local U.S. Attorney about the case, and she charged the man under federal law for being a felon in possession of a handgun. The man's attorney filed a motion to dismiss the charges, arguing that the state and federal charges were identical, and that double jeopardy barred the second prosecution in federal court.

If the federal judge agrees that the charges are the same, does the Double Jeopardy Clause bar the second prosecution?

A. The Double Jeopardy Clause does not bar the second prosecution because it is being pursued by a different sovereign.

B. The Double Jeopardy Clause does not bar the second prosecution because justice will not be served without a conviction.

C. The Double Jeopardy Clause bars the second prosecution because it is a waste of judicial and taxpayer resources.

D. The Double Jeopardy Clause bars the second prosecution because jeopardy has already attached and terminated for the charge.

Grand Jury

351. A grand jury began to investigate whether a police officer had used excessive force against a suspect who had died in his custody. When the officer was subpoenaed to testify, his lawyer sent a complaint letter to the local prosecutor. In the letter, the attorney explained that "the singular role of the grand jury is to determine whether criminal charges should be filed" and asserted that the "the grand jury's investigation of my client's actions violates his constitutional rights and is nothing more than a witch hunt."

Is the attorney's claim legally correct?

A. The attorney's claim is correct; the grand jury has no right to investigate alleged crimes, but may only determine whether or not to issue an indictment.

B. The attorney's claim is correct; the grand jury's right to investigate alleged crimes is limited to those instances where a judge presides over the investigation.

C. The attorney's claim is incorrect; the grand jury is permitted to investigate alleged crimes as well as determine whether or not to issue an indictment.

D. The attorney's claim is incorrect; the grand jury has wide latitude to render assistance to the prosecutor and police in all facets of their work.

352. A plumber developed a plan to make extra money by ripping copper pipe out of his customers' houses and then selling the pipe and pocketing the proceeds. The plumber would replace the copper piping with plastic piping and his customers never noticed the difference. One day on a routine call to fix a toilet, the plumber switched some copper pipe while the homeowner wasn't watching. The homeowner was an assistant district attorney who noticed the switch and asked the police to investigate.

The police investigation showed that the plumber had stolen from dozens of customers and earned about $25,000 from his scam. The assistant district attorney wrote up a criminal complaint and filed it in state court; the complaint charged the plumber with multiple counts of theft by deception.

The plumber's attorney has filed a motion to dismiss the complaint, arguing that the failure to charge the plumber by a grand jury indictment violates the plumber's rights and requires dismissal of all charges.

How should the court rule on the motion?

A. The motion should be denied because the plumber does not have a federal constitutional right to a grand jury indictment in state court.

B. The motion should be denied because the failure to indict the plumber by a grand jury is harmless beyond a reasonable doubt.

C. The motion should be granted because the Sixth Amendment guarantees the right to indictment by grand jury, unless the right is waived.

D. The motion should be granted because the Fifth Amendment guarantees the right to indictment by grand jury, unless the right is waived.

353. A woman was indicted for willfully failing to pay her income taxes over the span of several years. The woman retained an attorney and told him that she was baffled as to why she'd been indicted; the woman claimed that she had accurately reported her income and fully paid her taxes, and she said she'd never received any notice from the government, informing her of a problem.

The attorney performed a diligent pre-trial investigation and was able to determine that the woman had been indicted based solely on the testimony of a government investigator. The attorney filed a motion to dismiss the indictment, arguing that it was based solely on hearsay evidence—which would be inadmissible in at trial.

Should the court dismiss the indictment?

A. Yes, because it is a violation of the woman's Due Process rights to indict her based on evidence that is inadmissible in court.

B. Yes, because it is a violation of the Grand Jury Clause to indict the woman based on evidence that is inadmissible in court.

C. No, because the grand jury is permitted to rely on hearsay evidence when determining whether to indict or not.

D. No, because the woman will have an opportunity at trial to show the jury that the indictment was facially flawed.

354. A grand jury was investigating a man for his involvement in a large drug conspiracy. The evidence that most closely tied the man to the conspiracy was two kilos of cocaine that had been found in the man's car. When the lead police officer first told the prosecutor about the cocaine, she explained that it had been discovered through a lawful consent search of the man's car.

However, on the eve of the officer's grand jury testimony, the officer admitted to the prosecutor that the man had only consented to the search after she threatened to arrest him, even though she didn't have probable cause for the arrest.

May the prosecutor present the cocaine to the grand jury?

A. No, because inadmissible trial evidence cannot be used in grand jury proceedings.

B. No, because a grand jury indictment cannot be based on perjured testimony.

C. Yes, because the exclusionary rule does not apply in grand jury proceedings.

D. Yes, because the cocaine demonstrates the man's involvement in the conspiracy.

355. A prosecutor was presenting a case to the grand jury and was requesting that it indict a man for the rape and murder of a woman in her apartment. According to DNA results from the state police crime lab, the semen from the rape kit did not match the man but instead matched an unknown donor.

The prosecutor sought advice from her supervisor as to whether she would need to provide information about these results to the grand jury. The supervisor replied that the constitution requires the prosecutor to inform the grand jury about any known evidence that is material to the man's guilt or innocence.

Was the supervisor's advice correct?

A. Yes, because the prosecutor's primary role is to ensure that justice is done, and to withhold the evidence would be blatant misconduct.

B. Yes, because the man may be wrongfully convicted if the information is withheld and the grand jury not permitted to consider it.

C. No, because grand jury's role is to decide if there is sufficient evidence to charge, and not to determine the man's guilt or innocence.

D. No, because the grand jury lacks the scientific training to evaluate this sort of highly specialized evidence.

356. One morning, before presenting an eyewitness's testimony to a federal grand jury investigating a murder in a federal park, the prosecutor was smoking a cigarette outside the courthouse when she was joined by the eyewitness. The eyewitness confessed that what she had told the police in their investigation was a lie, and that she actually hadn't seen the crime occur at all. The prosecutor warned the eyewitness not to give this information to the grand jury, but instead told her to testify as to what she had originally told the police.

The eyewitness did as she was told, and testified that she saw the murder, identifying the would-be defendant as the murderer. The grand jury indicted him and his attorney subsequently discovered that the eyewitness had perjured herself.

If the attorney moves to dismiss the indictment claiming that the grand jury's consideration of perjured testimony renders the indictment *per se* unconstitutional, what sentence most likely appears in the court's ruling on the motion?

A. "Despite the broad powers given to a prosecutor in her presentation to the grand jury, justice demands that the indictment be dismissed if it involves perjured testimony."

B. "Since the grand jury functions as an arm of the prosecutor, there are absolutely no limits on the evidence a prosecutor may present for the grand jury's consideration."

C. "Despite the improper use of perjured testimony, an indictment may only be dismissed if that testimony substantially influenced the grand jury's decision to indict."

D. "Because the grand jury functions independently, a court had no power to review the facial validity of an indictment or to dismiss an indictment based on perjured testimony."

357. A woman was subpoenaed to appear before the grand jury. Terrified by the subpoena, the woman met with a lawyer to see if there was any way that she could avoid testifying. At the meeting, the woman told the lawyer that she planned to appear before the grand jury but that she would refuse to answer all questions, citing to the Fifth Amendment privilege against self-incrimination.

What is the proper response to the woman's statement?

A. The lawyer should tell the woman that she has an absolute right to refuse to answer all questions that are asked of her in the grand jury room.

B. The lawyer should tell the woman that she must appear but can refuse to answer all questions that are asked of her in the grand jury room.

C. The lawyer should tell the woman that she does not need to appear if the sole reason for her appearance would be to refuse to testify.

D. The lawyer should tell the woman that she must appear but can refuse to truthfully answer questions if her answers would tend to incriminate her.

358. A woman was subpoenaed to testify before a grand jury that was investigating the theft of a large amount of opiates from a hospital pharmacy. Consistent with office policy, the prosecutor provided the woman with *Miranda* warnings, reciting them from memory. However, because his memory was faulty, the prosecutor forgot to tell the woman that if she could not afford a lawyer, one would be appointed for her at public expense. After acknowledging that she understood her rights, the woman testified in response to the prosecutor's questions.

One month later, the prosecutor charged the woman with perjury, based on her grand jury testimony. In response, the woman's attorney filed a motion to dismiss the charges due to the prosecutor's failure to provide correct *Miranda* warnings at the start of the woman's testimony.

What is the most likely ruling from the court?

A. The charges need not be dismissed because *Miranda* warnings are only required for police questioning.

B. The charges need not be dismissed because *Miranda* warnings are not required for grand jury witnesses.

C. The charges must be dismissed because the prosecutor did not give the woman complete *Miranda* warnings.

D. The charges must be dismissed because the prosecutor violated office policy by not giving complete *Miranda* warnings.

359. After several million dollars went missing from a university endowment, a grand jury began to investigate whether a crime had been committed. The grand jury subpoenaed many witnesses, including the university's president, its chief financial officer, and the accountant who handled most of the university's day-to-day financial matters. In her testimony, the accountant was asked about several checks she had written to herself. She replied by explaining that the president and chief financial officer had directed her to write the checks in recognition for her stellar accounting work.

The grand jury indicted the accountant for embezzlement. After retaining counsel, the accountant filed a motion to dismiss the indictment and to suppress her grand jury testimony from being used at trial, arguing that she had never been warned that she was a target of the grand jury's investigation.

How should the judge rule on the motion?

A. The accountant wasn't a target because she was just one of many witnesses to testify before the grand jury.

B. The accountant had no constitutional right to be told that she was a target of the grand jury's investigation.

C. The prosecutor's failure to inform the accountant that she was a target violates her substantive due process rights.

D. The prosecutor's failure to inform the accountant that she was a target violates her procedural due process rights.

360. A man was subpoenaed to testify before the grand jury about his role in a conspiracy to commit student loan and mortgage fraud. The man had made millions of dollars with this scheme and knew that if charged and convicted, he would face a lengthy prison sentence. For that reason, he hired the best lawyer he could afford to help him prepare his grand jury testimony.

The man and his lawyer appeared at the grand jury room on the appointed date and time. However, the prosecutor told the lawyer that he would not be permitted to enter the grand jury room with the man. Instead, the prosecutor offered the man the opportunity to consult with counsel outside of the grand jury room.

What is the most likely reason for the prosecutor's position?

A. The man is not entitled to counsel because there is no real role for counsel to play until the grand jury indicts the man.

B. The man is not entitled to counsel because he has not yet been indicted, so there is no Sixth Amendment criminal prosecution.

C. The man is not entitled to counsel because he is not being subjected to custodial interrogation in the grand jury room.

D. The man is not entitled to counsel because he has not yet been indicted, so he doesn't need the assistance of counsel.

3

Sixth Amendment Questions

Basic Scope of the Sixth Amendment Right to Counsel

361. A homeless woman attacked a clerk inside a department store and was later arrested for felonious assault. At the time of her arrest, the department store security officer provided police with a store video of the attack. The following day, the woman was brought to court for her arraignment.

The judge explained to the woman that she was being charged with a crime and that if she was found guilty, she faced up to ten years in prison. The judge also told the woman that the constitution guaranteed her a right to counsel and asked her whether she had a lawyer. The woman said that she did not, and said that she had been homeless since losing her job two years before. The judge said that he was sorry to hear about the woman's situation, but he added, "the constitution gives us rights, but that doesn't mean they're free." The judge then told the woman that if she couldn't afford a lawyer, she would have to represent herself at trial. Hearing this news, the woman pled guilty to the charged crime and the judge sentenced her to two years in prison.

On appeal, the woman argued that the trial judge denied her rights by not appointing counsel. What is the most likely ruling from the appeals court?

A. The judge's failure to appoint a lawyer to represent the woman was error because the Sixth Amendment guarantees counsel to all people charged with crimes.

B. The judge's failure to appoint a lawyer to represent the woman was error because the Sixth Amendment guarantees counsel to suspected felons, regardless of income.

C. The judge's failure to appoint a lawyer to represent the woman was harmless error because of the overwhelming proof of the woman's guilt.

D. The judge's failure to appoint a lawyer to represent the woman was harmless error because the judge properly informed the woman of her rights.

362. A mother reported to police that her daughter had been seduced by her history teacher. As proof, the mother offered the daughter's gym shorts, which the mother claimed were stained with the teacher's semen. Police promptly obtained a warrant to take a DNA sample from the teacher. After learning of the warrant, the history teacher retained an attorney. Together, the two appeared at the police station so that police could take a DNA swab the teacher's cheek.

One week later, a police officer went to the teacher's home to interview him. When the teacher met the officer at his front door, he asked the officer what she wanted. The officer explained that the teacher's DNA had been found on the girl's gym shorts and so he wanted to hear the teacher's "side of the story." The teacher confessed that he was in love with the girl and the two had been having sex for the past six months. The officer arrested the teacher. Later that afternoon, at a probable cause hearing, a judge determined that the officer had probable cause for the arrest. Three days after that, a grand jury indicted the teacher for statutory rape.

The prosecutor seeks to use the teacher's statement at his upcoming trial and the teacher seeks to have it suppressed, claiming that the officer should not have spoken to him outside the presence of his attorney. What is the prosecutor's strongest argument in opposition to the suppression motion?

A. The teacher had no Sixth Amendment right to counsel at the time the officer interviewed him at his home.

B. The teacher waived his Sixth Amendment right to counsel when he voluntarily spoke with the police officer.

C. The teacher failed to invoke his Sixth Amendment right to counsel with the officer at the start of the conversation.

D. The teacher's Sixth Amendment right to counsel began only after the post-arrest probable cause hearing.

363. Police received a tip that a man with a felony record was in possession of several handguns. After corroborating the tip, police obtained a warrant to search the man's home. During the subsequent search, police discovered two handguns and a kilo of cocaine hidden in the man's bedroom. The state's attorney charged the man with two counts of being a felon in possession of a firearm.

At the man's arraignment, a public defender was appointed to represent him. Later, the arresting officer transported the man back to the police station and placed him in an interrogation room. The arresting officer began to question the man about the cocaine and to press him for the name of his supplier. Before too long, the man gave the arresting officer the supplier's name and telephone number.

When the man's public defender learned about the man's statement, he filed a motion to have it suppressed under the Fifth and Sixth Amendments. How should the court rule on the Sixth Amendment issue?

A. The officer violated the man's Sixth Amendment right to counsel by questioning him outside the presence of counsel.

B. The officer violated the man's Sixth Amendment right to counsel by not seeking a waiver before beginning to question him.

C. The officer did not violate the man's Sixth Amendment right to counsel because the man had not been charged with possession of cocaine.

D. The officer did not violate the man's Sixth Amendment right to counsel because the man never clearly and unambiguously invoked his right to counsel.

364. A woman charged with cocaine possession agreed to plead guilty in exchange for a recommendation from the prosecutor for a sentence that fell within a reduced range. One month later, the judge held a sentencing hearing. The woman's court-appointed attorney did not appear, and the judge sentenced the woman at the upper end of the sentencing range recommended by the prosecutor. Later, the woman filed a *pro se* appeal, arguing that she was denied the Sixth Amendment right to counsel because her attorney had not appeared at the sentencing hearing.

How should the appeals court rule?

A. The woman's Sixth Amendment rights were violated because she was denied counsel at a critical stage of the criminal proceeding.

C. The woman's Sixth Amendment rights were violated because counsel was ethically bound to appear on the woman's behalf.

B. The woman's Sixth Amendment rights were not violated because judge's sentence fell within the prosecutor's recommended range.

D. The woman's Sixth Amendment rights were not violated because the sentencing hearing did not involve a determination of guilt.

365. A college senior was charged with rape and was represented by retained counsel. The complaining witness was a freshman, and alleged that she knew her attacker because they lived in the same dormitory. Despite this, police arranged for the complaining witness to view the college senior in a line-up, just to be sure. After viewing the line-up, the complaining witness picked the college senior out of the line-up. The college senior's counsel was not notified of the line-up in advance but only learned about it from his client.

Counsel was irate and filed a motion to bar all identification testimony from the college senior's upcoming trial due to an alleged Sixth Amendment violation. How should the court rule on the motion?

A.   There was no Sixth Amendment violation because the college senior was represented by retained, not appointed counsel.

B.   There was no Sixth Amendment violation because it was the lawyer's responsibility to know about important events in his client's case.

C.   There was a Sixth Amendment violation because the college senior's counsel was not informed of the line-up, a critical stage.

D.   There was a Sixth Amendment violation, but the college senior waived any claims when he voluntarily appeared in the line-up.

366. A man was charged with bank robbery and murder. Two days later, the arresting officer called the bank manager and asked her to come to the police station to view several photographs, and to make a possible identification of the defendant.

That afternoon, the bank manager met with the officer and the assistant district attorney assigned to the case. The officer showed the bank manager eight black and white photographs, spread out on a conference table. The officer told the bank manager that he was certain that the man in the 5th photograph—the man charged with the crime—was the bank robber, but he needed the bank manager to confirm the identification. The bank manager agreed with the officer and confirmed that the man in the 5th photograph had robbed the bank.

The prosecutor was upset by the way the officer interacted with the bank manager, and told her supervisor. The supervisor informed the judge, who informed defense counsel. Counsel immediately filed a motion to strike the bank manager's identification testimony, arguing that its admission would violate the man's Sixth Amendment right to counsel.

How should the judge rule on the defense motion?

A.   The man's Sixth Amendment rights were violated because had counsel been present, she could have stopped the officer from his prejudicial conduct.

B.   The man's Sixth Amendment rights were violated because had counsel been present, she could have made a record of the officer's prejudicial conduct.

C.   The man's Sixth Amendment rights were not violated because the display of the photo array to the bank manager was not a critical stage.

D. The man's Sixth Amendment rights were not violated because information of the officer's prejudicial conduct was disclosed to the defense.

367. A woman was convicted of driving while under the influence of alcohol—her third such conviction. At her sentencing, the woman told the judge that she was a single parent of two school-aged children and their sole means of support. She tearfully explained that if she went to jail, her children would have to go into foster care. After careful consideration, the judge decided to place the woman on probation for two years and require her to participate in random drug and alcohol screening. The judge also warned the woman that if she "got into trouble," he would consider sentencing her to jail time. The woman promised that she would not violate the terms of her probation.

Six months later, the woman was arrested for being drunk and disorderly in public, which triggered a hearing to determine revocation of her probation. At the hearing, the woman refused to participate, arguing that she had an absolute right to counsel at the hearing. The judge refused to appoint counsel and eventually revoked the woman's probation and sent her to the county jail.

Was the woman's assertion about her right to counsel correct?

A. Yes, because the Sixth Amendment requires that counsel be appointed to indigent defendants who lose their liberty and are incarcerated.

B. Yes, because the judge failed to inform the woman at sentencing that if she violated her probation, he would deny her counsel at the revocation hearing.

C. No, because the judge told the woman the consequences of a probation violation and she acknowledged that she understood those consequences.

D. No, because a probation revocation hearing is not a critical stage of the proceeding where a probationer has an absolute Sixth Amendment right to counsel.

368. An indigent defendant was convicted of being a felon in possession of a firearm. After the defendant pled guilty and before his scheduled sentencing, the judge ordered him to undergo a routine pre-sentence investigation by a probation officer. The judge explained that the probation officer would write a report for the judge to consider in determining the defendant's sentence. The judge then sent the defendant back to the county jail.

Two weeks later, a probation officer came to the jail and arranged to have the defendant brought to a conference room. The probation officer did not inform the defendant that he could have his attorney present during the interview. The probation officer asked the defendant a series of questions and later submitted his report to the judge. Based on the recommendation in the report, the judge sentenced the defendant to the highest sentence permitted under the state's sentencing guidelines.

If, at the sentencing hearing, the public defender argues that the defendant's sentence is based on a Sixth Amendment violation, what is the prosecutor's strongest argument in response?

A. There was no Sixth Amendment violation because the defendant knew in advance he would be investigated by the probation officer.

B. There was no Sixth Amendment violation because the defendant's rights ended when he pled guilty to the charged crime.

C. There was no Sixth Amendment violation because the defendant voluntarily spoke with the probation officer.

D. There was no Sixth Amendment violation because the meeting with the probation officer was not a critical stage of the proceeding.

369. A young woman was convicted of capital murder for the stabbing death of her former lover. One day prior to the start of the sentencing hearing, the prosecutor arranged for the woman to be evaluated by a state psychiatrist. The prosecutor explained to the psychiatrist that he wanted an opinion as to whether the jurisdiction's "future dangerousness" statutory aggravator could be established, which permits the jury to return a death sentence if it finds that "there is a probability that the defendant poses a continuing threat to society." The prosecutor never told the woman's defense attorney about the evaluation.

The psychiatrist spoke with the woman for several hours, and then appeared in court the following morning to testify. After the prosecutor explained to the judge that the psychiatrist would testify to the woman's future dangerousness, defense counsel moved to bar the psychiatrist's testimony, claiming a Sixth Amendment violation.

How should the judge rule on the defense motion?

A. The woman's Sixth Amendment rights were violated because she was not given a chance to consult with counsel prior to the evaluation.

B. The woman's Sixth Amendment rights were violated because every stage in a capital trial is a critical stage, given the stakes involved.

C. The woman's Sixth Amendment rights were not violated because she waived her right to counsel by voluntarily participating in the evaluation.

D. The woman's Sixth Amendment rights were not violated because she had already been found guilty of capital murder.

370. A college sophomore was charged with being drunk and disorderly in public. If convicted, the sophomore faced a maximum penalty of up to six months of imprisonment, a fine, or both. When the sophomore made his first appearance in court, he explained to the judge that he was living off of student loans, and asked the judge to appoint counsel. The judge refused and instead scheduled a trial date.

On the appointed day, the sophomore appeared in court and pled guilty. After listening to the prosecutor's sentencing recommendation, the judge fined the sophomore $1000 and admonished him to curb his drinking. When the sophomore told his parents about the charge and the fine, they were outraged and hired a lawyer for the appeal.

On appeal, the sophomore's lawyer argued that his conviction should be vacated because the trial judge refused to appoint counsel. What is the most likely ruling from the appeals court?

A. The trial judge's refusal to appoint counsel did not violate the sophomore's Sixth Amendment rights because he was only charged with a petty offense.

B. The trial judge's refusal to appoint counsel did not violate the sophomore's Sixth Amendment rights because he was not sentenced to incarceration.

C. The trial judge's refusal to appoint counsel violated the sophomore's Sixth Amendment rights because his fine would be far less if he had appointed counsel.

D. The trial judge's refusal to appoint counsel violated the sophomore's Sixth Amendment rights because he was charged with a serious, non-petty offense.

371. After watching his favorite football team lose in the playoffs, a man got really drunk at a local bar. As he left the bar, the man was yelling and screaming obscenities and trying to pick fistfights with people walking by him on the street. Police were called and the man was arrested and charged with public intoxication — a misdemeanor in this jurisdiction that can result in a sentence of up to one year in jail. At his initial court appearance the following day, the man told the judge he couldn't afford a lawyer and asked him to appoint counsel. The judge refused.

One week later and without any legal advice, the man pled guilty to public intoxication. He was fined $750 and required to participate in a two-day alcohol awareness program and to attend 12 Alcoholics Anonymous meetings over a six-week period. The day after entering his plea, the man learned that when public intoxication defendants are represented by counsel in this jurisdiction, the lawyers are usually able to negotiate much more lenient sentences than the one the man received.

If the man appeals and argues that he was entitled to the appointment of counsel, how should the appellate court rule?

A. The man's Sixth Amendment rights were violated because he faced the possibility of incarceration if convicted.

B. The man's Sixth Amendment rights were violated because counseled defendants receive more lenient sentences than uncounseled defendants.

C. The man's Sixth Amendment rights were not violated because he knowingly, voluntarily, and intelligently waived his rights when he pled guilty.

D. The man's Sixth Amendment rights were not violated because the judge did not sentence him to a sentence of incarceration.

372. A young man was given a ticket for driving 10 miles over the posted speed limit. The man decided to contest the ticket and asked the judge if she would appoint a lawyer to help him; the judge refused, explaining that "we don't give out free lawyers for this kind of low level nonsense." The man asked the judge to reconsider, but she refused.

The man represented himself as best he could at the subsequent bench trial, but the judge found the man guilty. After rendering her verdict, the judge imposed a one-day suspended jail sentence and two years of reporting probation. Two weeks later, one of the man's friends from high school—now a lawyer— agreed to review his case to determine if there were any grounds for appeal. In particular, the man wanted the lawyer's opinion as to whether the judge should have given him a lawyer for the trial.

What should the lawyer tell the man?

A. The man's Sixth Amendment rights were not violated because he was never actually imprisoned for his conviction.

B. The man's Sixth Amendment rights were not violated because his there was no realistic chance his suspended sentence would be activated.

C. The man's Sixth Amendment rights were violated because he was sentenced to a suspended jail term and denied counsel.

D. The man's Sixth Amendment rights were violated because the harsh terms of the probationary sentence were equivalent to actual incarceration.

373. A middle-aged man was convicted of stealing a car, which is a felony. If this had been a first conviction, the middle-aged man faced up to three years of imprisonment at sentencing. However, under the state's sentencing guidelines, the prosecutor is permitted to request a much longer sentence—up to twenty years of imprisonment—for a current felony conviction if the defendant has at least three prior misdemeanor convictions that meet certain criteria. The middle-aged man had five qualifying misdemeanor convictions on his record.

In four of his prior misdemeanor cases, the middle-aged man was unrepresented by counsel. In each case, the middle-aged man was fined and given a probationary sentence, but he was not sentenced to jail time. In the fifth prior misdemeanor case, the middle-aged man was represented by counsel and was sentenced to spend eight months in jail.

In the pending car theft case, the prosecutor filed notice that she intended to invoke the sentencing enhancement provision of the sentencing guidelines and request that the man be sentenced to twenty years of imprisonment based on the five qualifying misdemeanor convictions.

In determining the sentence for the felony conviction, what part of the middle-aged man's prior record may the sentencing court properly consider?

A. The court may only consider the fifth misdemeanor conviction because the Sixth Amendment requires representation for actual imprisonment.

B. The court may only consider the fifth misdemeanor conviction because the Sixth Amendment requires a more exacting process for such deprivations of liberty.

C. The court may consider all of the prior misdemeanor convictions because the middle-aged man is a recidivist who cannot be rehabilitated.

D. The court may consider all of the prior misdemeanor convictions but may also take into account the fact that the man was unrepresented by counsel in four of the five cases.

374. A defendant was charged with rape and a public defender was appointment to represent him. The public defender did the best he could, but the defendant was convicted and later sentenced to twenty years in prison.

Ten years later, the defendant learned about a new test that could be performed on the biological evidence leftover from his case. He immediately filed a *pro* se motion in the trial court, requesting appointment of counsel to help him prepare his request for testing.

Does the defendant have a Sixth Amendment right to counsel?

A. Yes, because the Sixth Amendment right to counsel continues while the defendant is actually incarcerated for a crime.

B. Yes, because the defendant filed his motion in the same court where the criminal prosecution was initiated and held.

C. No, because the defendant's Sixth Amendment right to counsel ended once he was found guilty of the rape charge.

D. No, because the criminal prosecution has concluded and so the defendant no longer has a Sixth Amendment right to counsel.

375. A woman was charged with murder, and a public defender was appointed to represent the woman at trial. The woman and the public defender disagreed about trial strategy and the woman was eventually convicted. After she was sentenced to life imprisonment, the woman wrote a letter to the trial judge telling him how much she hated the public defender and that she no longer wanted him to work on her case. She also filed a *pro se* notice of appeal for her first appeal of right.

The state appeals court docketed the notice of appeal and the clerk sent the woman a scheduling order. The woman wrote back to the clerk, demanding that a new lawyer be appointed to represent her in the appeal.

How should the clerk properly respond?

A. The clerk should tell the woman that she no longer has a Sixth Amendment right to counsel because the criminal prosecution ended with the appeal.

B. The clerk should tell the woman that she no longer has a Sixth Amendment right to counsel because she fired the public defender—the lawyer she was entitled to.

C. The clerk should tell the woman that she has no right to counsel on appeal and should suggest that she ask the local law school if a law student can provide some help.

D. The clerk should tell the woman that she no longer has a Sixth Amendment right to counsel for her appeal, but she does have a right under the Fourteenth Amendment.

Massiah Doctrine

376. A doctor was charged with Medicare fraud and was subsequently arrested. As the arresting officer was transporting the doctor to the police station, the officer said:

> Explain something to me, will you? You're a doctor and have all the money you need. Why would you go and rip off the government for more? I don't understand why rich people like you do the things you do.

The doctor replied, "You don't know me and you know nothing about my needs. I have three kids in college and a lazy husband, and that's a lot of needs. I had to do what I did just to keep my head above water."

The prosecutor wants to use the doctor's statement at her upcoming trial, and the doctor has moved to have it suppressed. How should the court rule on the motion?

A. The statement should be suppressed because it is a product of non-warned custodial interrogation.

B. The statement should be suppressed because it is a product of uncounseled deliberate elicitation.

C. The statement should be admitted because the doctor was not subjected to express questioning or its functional equivalent.

D. The statement should be admitted because it doesn't really implicate the doctor in the charged crime.

377. A college student was found dead in her dormitory room, and the medical examiner suspected she might have been poisoned. Police began investigate the student's boyfriend— a graduate student in the chemistry department, who had after-hours access to the school's chemistry lab. Police interviewed the boyfriend at his home and he admitted having access to a wide array of chemical agents but denied involvement in the student's death.

Several months later, lab testing confirmed that the student had died from chemical poisoning. The prosecutor charged the boyfriend with murder; he was arrested and brought to the police station for questioning. The boyfriend confessed to using chemicals from the lab to kill the student.

The boyfriend's attorney has filed a motion to suppress both his statements, arguing that each was obtained in violation of the Sixth Amendment right to counsel. Which sentence most likely appears in the judge's opinion?

A. "Because the Sixth Amendment right to counsel attaches when an investigation begins to focus on a suspect, police should have told the defendant about his right to counsel when they questioned him at his home."

B. "Because the Sixth Amendment right to counsel attaches only after a person clearly and unambiguously requests counsel, police were not required to discuss counsel at all until the defendant invoked his rights."

C. "Because the Sixth Amendment right to counsel attaches when a person is placed in custodial interrogation, police were not required to tell the defendant about his right to counsel when they questioned him at his home."

D. "Because the Sixth Amendment right to counsel attaches when a person is charged with a crime, police were only required to tell the defendant about this right to counsel when he was arrested after charges were filed."

378. A man was charged with running a medium-sized heroin conspiracy. At the man's first court appearance, the man told the judge that he had retained a lawyer. With his lawyer's help, the man was released on bond.

Two days later, two officers came to the man's home to question him. The man let the officers inside, invited them to have a seat in his living room, and got them each a cup of coffee. The officers then asked the man whether he had ever produced or sold methamphetamine. The man said he hadn't, but the officers said that they had heard differently. After about fifteen minutes of discussion, the man admitted that he occasionally sold methamphetamine to a dealer on the other side of town. Based on the man's statement and other evidence, the prosecutor charged him with possession and sale of methamphetamine.

If the man's lawyer moves to suppress this statement from the methamphetamine prosecution, how will the court rule on the motion?

A. The motion will be granted because the man never validly waived his Sixth Amendment right to counsel.

B. The motion will be granted because the man had a Sixth Amendment right to counsel for all drug-related crimes.

C. The motion will be denied because the officers never provided the man with *Miranda* warnings before the questioning began.

D. The motion will be denied because the officers did not violate the man's Fifth or Sixth Amendment rights in any way.

379. A judge presiding over a contentious divorce ordered the husband to provide his estranged wife very large monthly payments. The husband was short on cash and so he set fire to his seldom-used beach house with the intent to use the insurance money to pay his estranged wife. The house was burned to the ground and firemen found the estranged wife's dead body in the rubble. The prosecutor asked the medical examiner for an opinion as to whether the estranged wife died in the fire or from unrelated, natural causes.

In the meantime, two days after the fire, the prosecutor charged the husband with arson and police arrested him. On the ride to the police station, the arresting officer asked the husband to rate, on a scale from 1 to 10, how much he hated his estranged wife. The husband replied, "1,000."

The husband's lawyer filed a motion to suppress his statement, arguing that it was made in violation of the husband's Sixth Amendment right to counsel. How should the court rule on the motion?

A. The husband's Sixth Amendment right to counsel was not violated because the husband had only been charged with arson.

B. The husband's Sixth Amendment right to counsel was not violated because police did not yet know how the estranged wife died.

C. The husband's Sixth Amendment right to counsel was violated because the arson and the suspected homicide arose from the same operative facts.

D. The husband's Sixth Amendment right to counsel was violated because the suspected homicide was factually related to the arson.

380. A defendant was being driven to the county jail after his arrest on charges that he had abducted and killed an elderly woman. The defendant had a lawyer and the transport officer had been instructed not to speak to the defendant during the drive. The officer suspected that the defendant had hidden the woman's body in a local park and so, as they drove past the park, the officer said:

> I want you to think about something as we drive past the park coming up on the right. That lady has kids and grand-kids and they want to know what happened to her. They'll want to honor her with a proper funeral, to show respect for what a great lady she was. But they can't do that because we don't know where she is. But you do, only you. You can give them that little bit of comfort. Just think about it: how you might be able to help that poor, grieving family. Don't answer me, just think about it.

The defendant replied that he had only killed the woman "by accident" and directed the transport officer to a shallow grave where he had buried the woman.

The man's defense lawyer subsequently filed a motion to suppress. What is the most likely ruling from the court?

A. The officer did not deliberately elicit information from the defendant because he instructed the defendant not to respond to his statement.

B. The officer did not deliberately elicit information from the defendant because he never asked the defendant any direct or express questions.

C. The officer deliberately elicited information from the defendant because he intentionally tried to get the defendant to speak about the crime.

D. The officer deliberately elicited information from the defendant because he broke the promise to not speak to the defendant during the drive.

381. A young man was charged with planting and detonating a bomb at a state government office and killing three people in the blast. The young man was a member of a group that believed that the size of the government should be drastically reduced and which advocated violence as a means of accomplishing that objective.

The day after the bombing, state police received an anonymous note that said, "we're just getting started" and "there will be more." Deeply concerned about the possibility of additional bombings, the state police arranged for an undercover officer to be placed in the young man's jail cell to see if he would provide additional information of how he committed his crime. At first, the young man ignored the undercover officer. But the undercover officer had been specifically trained in deceptive interrogation techniques, and over a few hours, managed to get the young man to give a full confession. Police used the man's confession to figure out the location of a future bombing site, and they were able to get to the bomb before it detonated, saving many lives.

The young man has filed a motion to suppress his statement from his upcoming trial, claiming that it is the product of uncounseled deliberate elicitation. Is he correct?

A. Yes, because the officer used his training with deceptive interrogation techniques to get the young man to make a statement.

B. Yes, because the officer asked the young man about the charged crime and the young man didn't know he was speaking to a state actor.

C. No, because the imminent threat to public safety permitted the officer to ask questions designed to quell the possible threat.

D. No, because the officer was acting undercover, which is permitted under the covert custodial interrogation exception.

382. A grand jury indicted a man for conspiracy to commit insurance fraud and nine counts of insurance fraud. Six other people were charged as co-conspirators. An officer was given an arrest warrant for the man and was told to arrest him.

The officer went to the man's house and rang the doorbell. When the man answered the door, the officer explained that he wanted to speak to the man about some of his friends who had recently been charged with crimes. The man invited the officer inside, and the officer then went through the list of the indicted co-conspirators, asking the man if he knew them and for details about the last time he had spoken to each one. After the man supplied the officer with the requested information, the officer told the man about the indictment and the arrest warrant, and handcuffed him.

The prosecutor wants to use the man's statement against him at his upcoming trial and the man has filed a motion to suppress, claiming a Sixth Amendment violation. What is the most likely ruling on the motion?

A. The statement will be admitted despite the Sixth Amendment violation because the rule against hearsay is relaxed in trials involving criminal conspiracy.

B. The statement will be admitted despite the Sixth Amendment violation because the man voluntarily spoke with the officer about his co-conspirators.

C. The statement will be suppressed because the man only spoke to the officer because the officer hadn't yet told him about his Sixth Amendment rights.

D. The statement will be suppressed because the officer failed to tell the man about his Sixth Amendment rights and questioned him about the charged crime.

383. Armed with an arrest warrant, an officer went to a private home to arrest a woman on charges of tax evasion. When the woman came to the door, the officer explained to her that she had been charged with a crime and that she would be arrested. The woman burst into tears and asked for a few minutes so that she could calm down. The officer agreed and the two sat down in the kitchen for a cup of coffee.

Still crying, the woman told the officer that she had lost her job a year before. The officer asked the woman how she had been able to pay her mortgage and the woman explained that she had "rigged" her taxes in order to keep the house. Several minutes later, the two left the house and drove to the police station.

What is the woman's strongest argument for suppression of her statement at trial?

A. The statement should be suppressed because the officer's false display of sympathy led the woman to confess to rigging her taxes.

B. The statement should be suppressed because the woman was subjected to custodial interrogation without *Miranda* warnings.

C. The statement should be suppressed because the officer failed to inform the woman of the actual charges filed against her.

D. The statement should be suppressed because the officer deliberately elicited information from the woman in violation of *Massiah*.

384. A woman was charged with being a part of a large cocaine conspiracy. The woman was arrested and taken to the local jail. The woman's retained counsel arranged for her pre-trial release and the woman went home.

The woman was so stressed by the night she'd spent in jail that she made an appointment for a spa day at her favorite spa. Once there, the woman had a few glasses of champagne and began talking about the case with her aesthetician. During her facial, the woman admitted that she was involved in cocaine distribution but insisted that she only sold drugs to people who wanted to have a good time, and not to anyone she believed was an addict. Because of that, the woman insisted that she had only committed a victimless crime, and that the charges should be dropped. The aesthetician contacted the prosecutor and told him about the woman's statement.

Prior to trial, the prosecutor disclosed that the aesthetician was on his witness list and that she would testify to what the woman disclosed to her. Should this testimony be suppressed?

A. Yes, because it is the product of non-counseled deliberate elicitation.

B. Yes, because the woman's intoxication renders her statements suspect and unreliable.

C. No, because the woman spoke to the aesthetician voluntarily and without hesitation.

D. No, because the aesthetician was not acting for the state when she spoke with the woman.

385. The chief financial officer of a national investment firm was charged with embezzling funds. The woman retained counsel and was released on bail prior to trial. Even though the woman had been charged, police continued their investigation, hoping to file additional charges against the woman.

One afternoon, the woman made a date with a friend for a glass of wine. An undercover officer trailed behind the woman, and arranged to be seated at a nearby table so he could listen to what the woman and her friend were saying.

From where he sat, the undercover officer overheard the woman tell her friend that the police hadn't found out about the all of the funds that she'd embezzled. The woman bragged that she held most of these embezzled funds in a large savings account in a bank in another country and that she planned to leave the country and retire in style—just as soon as her trial was over.

The prosecutor wants to use these statements at the woman's upcoming trial, and the woman has moved to have them suppressed. What is the most likely ruling on the motion to suppress?

A. The motion will be denied because the undercover officer engaged in covert custodial interrogation, as permitted by the Fifth Amendment.

B. The motion will be denied because the undercover officer did not engage in deliberate elicitation, as prohibited by the Sixth Amendment.

C. The motion will be granted because the undercover officer engaged in deliberate elicitation, as prohibited by the Sixth Amendment.

D. The motion will be granted because the undercover officer engaged in covert custodial interrogation, as prohibited by the Fifth Amendment.

386. One night while driving home from a dinner date, a woman hit a pedestrian in a crosswalk. Concerned that she might get in trouble for driving while intoxicated, the woman fled the scene and drove home. Several witnesses to the accident reported the car's license plate though, and the woman was arrested and charged with a "hit and run" for leaving the scene of an accident. The woman retained counsel to represent her.

Two days after the accident, the pedestrian died. A prosecutor assigned to review the case asked police to speak to the woman about her state of mind at the time of the accident, so he could better determine whether to charge the woman with negligent homicide or second-degree intentional murder.

May the police lawfully question the woman as instructed without fear of violating her Sixth Amendment rights?

A. Yes, because the woman only has a Sixth Amendment right to counsel for the "hit and run" charge, not for the homicide.

B. Yes, because the prosecutor cannot charge the woman with any form of homicide without first asking her about her *mens rea*.

C. No, because woman's Sixth Amendment right to counsel extends to all crimes that may arise from the same set of operative facts.

D. No, because asking the woman questions about the homicide is designed to elicit information about the "hit and run" charge.

387. An officer arrested a man who had been indicted for conspiracy to commit murder and murder. At the time of the arrest, the officer explained to the man that he had been charged, that he had an absolute right to counsel, and that he could either retain a lawyer or one would be appointed to represent him. The officer then drove the man to the county jail.

During the drive, the man asked the officer what the jail was like. The officer replied truthfully that the jail was "pretty rough" but assured the man that he'd be fine. The man replied, "I think I'll tell everyone that I killed that lady, and then maybe they'll all be scared of me and leave me alone."

After escorting the man into the jail, the officer told the prosecutor about the man's statement. May the prosecutor use the man's statement at his upcoming trial?

A. No, because the officer deliberately elicited the man's statement when he told the man about the "pretty rough" conditions at the jail.

B. No, because the officer clearly knew that the man had an unqualified right to counsel and decided to speak to the man anyway.

C. Yes, because the officer truthfully and accurately answered the man's question about the jail and what he could expect while there.

D. Yes, because the officer did not deliberately elicit the man's statement when he spoke about the "pretty rough" conditions at the jail.

388. A man was charged with possession of child pornography after he downloaded some photos from the internet. After the man's arrest, he met with the lawyer assigned to represent him, who advised that the man keep quiet and not speak to anyone at the jail. The man agreed and was returned to his cell.

After a sleepless night, the man asked to speak to the officer who had arrested him. One hour later, the officer brought the man into an interrogation room; the man said he needed to clear his conscience and explain why he downloaded the photos. The officer presented the man with a waiver form that said that the man had a right to have his lawyer present in the room during questioning and if he waived the right, his statements would be used against him at trial. After reading and signing the form, the man explained to the officer that he had only downloaded the photos because he was doing research on child exploitation, and he wanted to see for himself how bad the problem really was.

May the prosecutor use the man's admission at his trial?

A.   Yes, because it is a statement against penal interest and is therefore admissible.

B.   Yes, because the man knowingly, voluntarily, and intelligently waived his rights.

C.   No, because it was made in the absence of counsel and against counsel's advice.

D.   No, because it only shows the man's motive for the crime, and not his *mens rea*.

389. A woman was indicted for conspiracy to commit murder and was arrested. At the woman's first court appearance, the judge appointed a lawyer to represent her; they spent the next half hour together, discussing her case.

Two days later, the detective on the case arranged for the woman to be brought from the jail cafeteria to an interrogation room adjacent to the warden's office. The detective explained that he knew that she had a lawyer but wanted to know if she wanted to discuss her case without him. After thinking about it for a few minutes, the woman agreed to waive her rights. She then confessed to paying someone to kill her ex-husband.

Should the woman's statement be suppressed?

A.   Yes, because, since the woman's Sixth Amendment rights had attached, her waiver would only be valid if she approached the officer to waive.

B.   Yes, because, since the woman's Sixth Amendment rights had attached and the officer knew that fact, her waiver is presumptively invalid.

C.   No, because even though the woman's Sixth Amendment rights had attached, she preferred to speak to the detective instead of counsel.

D.   No, because even though the woman's Sixth Amendment rights had attached, the officer didn't violate her rights in any way.

390. At a defendant's first appearance in court, the judge informed him that he was being charged with various drug crimes and appointed an attorney to represent him. The judge never asked any direct questions to the defendant, and so he said nothing in response. Two hours later, as the defendant was being transported from the courthouse to the country jail, the transport officer told the defendant that she had been in court earlier. She continued:

> I saw you in court and saw the way the judge spoke to you. I think it's a shame that she never asked you what you want to do, because this is your life and your case. Do you even want that lawyer she gave you?

The defendant replied that he'd had bad experiences with lawyers in past, and that he didn't want to be represented by counsel in his case. He then told the officer that he'd prefer to plead guilty, and admitted to his involvement in the charged crimes.

The defendant later had a change of heart, and decided that he wanted legal assistance. If the lawyer files a motion to suppress the defendant's admission, will it be successful?

A. No, because despite the appointment of counsel by the judge, the officer was allowed to ask the defendant for a waiver.

B. No, because the defendant never spoke in court, and so the officer was allowed to ask him what he wanted to do.

C. Yes, because the officer knew that the judge had appointed counsel, and was not allowed to approach the defendant to request a waiver.

D. Yes, because the officer tricked the defendant into the admission by pretending to care about him and asking him what he wanted to do.

391. A woman was indicted for her role in a drug conspiracy, and she retained a lawyer. At the woman's initial appearance in court, the judge asked the woman whether she wanted him to appoint counsel. The woman replied that she had already retained a lawyer and gave the judge the lawyer's name. The judge called the next case.

Two days later, an officer brought the woman from her cell into an interrogation room. There, the officer explained that he wanted to ask the woman some questions about her case and wanted to know if she would be willing to speak to him. The woman agreed to do so. After an hour of questioning, the woman confessed to being involved in the conspiracy.

When the lawyer learned about the woman's confession, he filed a motion to suppress. What single issue must be decided by the judge in order to rule on the motion?

A. The judge must decide whether the woman knowingly, voluntarily, and intelligently waived her right to counsel.

B. The judge must decide whether the officer knew that the woman's Sixth Amendment rights had already attached.

C. The judge must decide whether the woman's statement was voluntary, given the Sixth Amendment violation here.

D. The judge must decide whether the officer subjectively intended to trick the woman into waiving her right to counsel.

392. A woman was charged with murder and the judge appointed a public defender to represent her. Three days after the appointment, a detective brought the woman into an interrogation room asked her if she would be willing to speak with him about the case. The woman replied that she didn't want to speak without first consulting with the public defender and asked to go back to her cell.

The detective explained that he would honor the woman's request, but he wanted her to give some thought to how public defenders are generally overworked and underpaid. The detective then asked the woman to consider whether the public defender would be able to help her. After a few minutes of silence, the woman told the detective that he was right and that she would probably do better without the public defender. She then signed a waiver form and confessed to the crime.

Is the woman's confession admissible?

A. Yes, because the woman knowingly, voluntarily, and intelligently waived her Sixth Amendment right to counsel.

B. Yes, because the detective did not ask the woman an actual question but instead asked the woman to consider his statement.

C. No, because the woman clearly and unambiguously invoked her right to counsel and the detective did not honor the invocation.

D. No, because the woman did not actually know whether the public defender assigned to her case was overworked and underpaid.

393. A woman was charged with killing her husband. The woman retained counsel and a trial date was set. The woman's lawyer advised her that the police might try to speak to her; the lawyer told the woman that if the police did approach her, she should be sure to ask for her lawyer.

One afternoon, a police officer arranged for the woman to be brought from her cell to an interrogation room. The officer read the woman the *Miranda* warnings and gave her a pre-printed sheet with the warnings on them. He asked the woman if she wanted to talk about her husband's death, and the woman nodded her head in agreement. She then signed and dated the waiver form and handed it back to the officer. Within a half an hour, the woman gave a full confession to killing her husband.

The prosecutor wants to use the woman's confession at her upcoming trial, and the woman wants to have it suppressed. How should the court rule on the motion?

A. The motion should be denied because the woman retained her lawyer, and therefore the Sixth Amendment does not apply to her situation.

B. The motion should be denied because the woman knowingly, voluntarily, and intelligently waived her right to counsel.

C. The motion should be granted because the *Miranda* warnings were inadequate to inform the woman of her Sixth Amendment right to counsel.

D. The motion should be granted because the officer failed to contact counsel and give him advance notice that of the questioning.

394. A man was charged with bank robbery and a local lawyer was appointed to represent him. In their first meeting, the lawyer advised the man not to speak to the police under any circumstances.

Two days after the arraignment, a police officer had the man brought to an interrogation room and the officer gave the man his *Miranda* warnings. The man asked the officer what he wanted to talk about and the officer replied, "I want to talk about a hit and run accident at the mall from six months ago." Disregarding his public defender's advice, the man agreed to speak to the police and signed the waiver form given to him by the officer. Instead of asking about an accident at the mall, the officer began his questioning by asking about the bank robbery. Within a short amount of time, the man gave a full confession to the bank robbery.

Is the man's statement admissible in his upcoming trial?

A. No, because the officer tricked the man into speaking about the bank robbery.

B. No, because the man did not knowingly waive his rights for the bank robbery charge.

C. Yes, because the man validly waived all his rights when he signed the waiver form.

D. Yes, because the man chose to ignore his lawyer's advice and waive his rights.

395. A young woman was arrested for arson. Police attempted to interrogate her, but the young woman refused to speak. A few days later, the young woman was charged with arson and a public defender was appointed to represent her.

Even though the woman had refused to speak at the time of her arrest, the police decided to try a second time to get her to confess. An officer brought the woman into an interrogation room, read the young woman her *Miranda* warnings, and gave her a pre-printed waiver form. The woman read the waiver form and then asked the officer, "this is about that fire, isn't it?" The officer replied that it was, and gave the woman a pen. The officer then left the room for five minutes. When the officer returned to the room, the young woman had signed the waiver form. The officer began to question the young woman about the arson and she eventually confessed to the crime.

The prosecutor wants to use the young woman's confession at her upcoming trial, and the young woman wants to have it suppressed. What is the most likely ruling?

A. The motion will be denied because the officer's failure to witness the young woman's signature constitutes an isolated case of negligence.

B. The motion will be denied because the woman knowingly, voluntarily, and intelligently waived her Sixth Amendment rights.

C. The motion will be granted because the officer's failure to witness the young woman's signature renders her waiver invalid.

D. The motion will be granted because the *Miranda* warnings were insufficient to inform the young woman of her Sixth Amendment rights.

396. A police officer went to a man's house to arrest him on charges of being a felon in possession of a firearm. When the man opened his door, the officer purposefully didn't tell the man that he'd been charged with a crime or that he had a right to counsel. Instead, the officer said only that the man was being arrested for a "gun thing." As the officer was handcuffing the man and searching him incident to arrest, he and the man had the following exchange:

> Officer: Let's talk about the gun.
>
> Man: I don't want to talk about the gun because I'm afraid you'll take it away from me.
>
> Officer: Where is the gun?
>
> Man: Inside the house.
>
> Officer: Where inside?
>
> Man: On the kitchen table.
>
> Officer: Can I go inside and get it?
>
> Man: Yeah, I guess so. Why not? You're already arresting me, how could the gun get me into more trouble?

The officer retrieved the gun and drove the man to the police station.

Prior to trial, the prosecutor conceded that the man's statement should be suppressed because of a Sixth Amendment violation. However, the prosecutor wants to introduce the gun at the man's trial. Is it admissible?

A. The gun is inadmissible because it is a fruit of the poisonous tree (the Sixth Amendment/*Massiah* violation).

B. The gun is inadmissible because the officer searched the man's home without a valid warrant or exigency.

C. The gun is admissible because the fruit of the poisonous tree doctrine doesn't apply to Sixth Amendment violations.

D. The gun is admissible because the man gave valid consent to the warrantless search of his home for the weapon.

397. A grand jury indicted a man for the murder of his 10-year old son and the man was arrested. The child's body had been found in the woods, badly deteriorated, several months after his teachers reported him missing. On the drive to the police station, the arresting officer questioned the man as to how and why he had killed his son; the man confessed that he shot his son and that the murder weapon was hidden in a garden shed in his backyard. The arresting officer radioed this information to his dispatcher and a second officer went out to the house and retrieved the weapon from the shed.

Prior to the man's trial, the defense filed a motion to suppress the man's statement and the gun. In response, the prosecutor filed an affidavit from the man's wife, explaining that she was not at home when the officer retrieved the gun from the shed but that if she had been, she would have given the officer consent to search the shed without a warrant.

What is the prosecutor's argument for admissibility of the gun?

A. The prosecutor's argument is that the gun should not be suppressed because it would have been inevitably discovered through a lawful consent search.

B. The prosecutor's argument is that the gun should not be suppressed because police had a lawful independent source for its admission at the man's trial.

C. The prosecutor's argument is that the wife's would-be consent compensates for the officer's bad faith associated with the Sixth Amendment violation in the car.

D. The prosecutor's argument is that neither the statement nor the gun should be suppressed because the man's wife clearly wanted to help police solve this crime.

398. A woman was charged with manslaughter for the killing of two young kids as they jaywalked across a street on their way to school. At the police station after her arrest, the woman told the arresting officer that she had already retained a lawyer to represent her and that she didn't want to speak unless her lawyer was present in the room. The officer replied that he would abide by the woman's request, but asked her how she would feel if her kids had been killed and the person charged with the crime wouldn't talk to the police. The woman burst into tears and told the officer that she hadn't meant to hurt the kids, but just wanted to "teach them a lesson" about jaywalking.

The next day, the woman was released on bond. Two weeks after that, she returned to the police station with her lawyer in order to be interviewed by the same officer who had originally arrested her. During the interview, the woman admitted to speeding her car up and intentionally hitting the two children.

Are the woman's statements admissible?

A. Both statements are inadmissible; the first is a product of a Sixth Amendment/*Massiah* violation, and the second statement is a direct fruit of that violation.

B. Both statements are admissible; the woman gave an implied waiver of rights when she made the first statement and the second statement was made in the presence of counsel.

C. The first statement is inadmissible because of a Sixth Amendment/*Massiah* violation; the second statement is admissible because it is completely unrelated to the first statement.

D. The first statement is inadmissible because of a Sixth Amendment/*Massiah* violation; the second statement is admissible because it is not a direct fruit of that violation.

399. Police arrested a man charged with shooting a bouncer outside of a bar, but there were no witnesses to the shooting. After the court appointed counsel to the man, police arranged for an informant to be placed in the man's jail cell. The informant was instructed to become friendly with the man and to see if he would admit to the circumstances surrounding the shooting. A couple of days after the informant was placed in the cell, the man told him that he had shot the bouncer "just to watch him die." Prior to trial, the court ruled that this statement was obtained in violation of the man's Sixth Amendment rights, and suppressed it from the upcoming trial.

At trial, the man testified that he had killed the bouncer in self-defense because he believed the bouncer was about to shoot him and thought he had no choice but to shoot the bouncer first. On cross-examination, the prosecutor confronted the man with his statement to the informant, and the defense objected.

How should the judge rule on the objection?

A. The objection should be overruled; the statement is admissible to impeach the man's testimony, but not as evidence of his guilt.

B. The objection should be overruled; admitting the statement will help the jury learn the truth, which is the goal of a criminal trial.

C. The objection should be sustained; the statement is inadmissible because the prosecutor blatantly disobeyed the judge's suppression ruling.

D. The objection should be sustained; the statement is inadmissible due to the Sixth Amendment violation at the jail.

400. A defendant was on trial for possession of heroin. Shortly after his arrest, police had questioned the defendant outside the presence of his lawyer and the defendant had given a statement, admitting to purchasing heroin from an undercover officer. The statement was eventually suppressed due to a Sixth Amendment violation.

At trial, the prosecution presented testimony from the undercover officer, who described the drug sale. In rebuttal, the defense presented the testimony of the defendant's best friend, who explained that the defendant was strongly opposed to all drug use. On cross-examination, the prosecutor attempted to confront the best friend with the defendant's previously suppressed statement and the defense immediately objected.

What is the most likely basis for the defense objection?

A. The prosecutor may only use the defendant's statement to impeach the defendant, if he testifies in contradiction to the statement.

B. The prosecutor may not use the defendant's statement at all, because it was obtained in violation of the defendant's constitutional rights.

C. The prosecutor may only use the defendant's statement after the judge conducts an *in camera* hearing on the statement's impeachment value.

D. The prosecutor may only use the defendant's statement after the judge conducts an *in camera* hearing on how police obtained it in the first place.

Right to Counsel and Identification

401. A defendant charged in state court with rape was placed into a line-up with five other men. The defendant was of average height, was clean-shaven and balding, and was wearing a county jail-issued orange jumpsuit. Each of the five men was also of average height, was clean-shaven and balding, and was wearing a county jail-issued orange jumpsuit. The complaining witness viewed the line-up through a one-way mirror and very quickly identified the defendant as her attacker.

If the defendant later argues that the witness's identification testimony cannot be used at trial, what is the most likely legal basis for his argument?

A. That he was denied the assistance of counsel at a critical stage of the proceeding.

B. That he was not given an opportunity to confront the witness against him.

C. That he was forced to participate in a self-incriminating identification procedure.

D. That he was denied the ability to compel his own witnesses to view the line-up.

402. A man was arrested for robbery of a convenience store. According to an eyewitness, the robber was wearing eyeglasses, a white t-shirt, and loose fitting jeans. The eyewitness also told police that she thought the robber was missing one of the fingers on his left hand.

Shortly afterwards, the arrested man was put into a line-up. The man was wearing eyeglasses, a white t-shirt and loose fitting jeans; he also was missing the ring finger of his left hand. Two other men stood next to him in the line-up: one man was wearing a green t-shirt, the other was wearing a black t-shirt, and neither man was missing any fingers on either hand. After viewing the line-up for less than a minute, the eyewitness identified the arrested man as the same man who had robbed the convenience store.

Later, after he was charged, the arrested man told his lawyer about the line-up. If the lawyer challenges the eyewitness's identification at the line-up, what is the correct ruling from the court?

A. The identification procedure was not flawed because the eyewitness picked the man who best matched her description of the robber.

B. The identification procedure was not a critical stage of the proceeding and so the arrested man had no right to have counsel present.

C. The identification procedure was so flawed that counsel should have been present in order to protect the man's rights.

D. The identification procedure was a critical stage of the proceeding and so the arrested man had a right to have counsel present.

403. One day, a public defender received an envelope in the mail, sent by a local police detective. The envelope contained a cover letter from the detective, explaining that one of the public defender's clients had recently been identified in a line-up. The detective also said that the line-up was uneventful, except for the witness's eventual identification of the public defender's client.

Attached to the letter was a handwritten and detailed summary of what happened at the line-up. The summary included a description of the physical characteristics of all the line-up participants, including a description of the clothing worn and contact information for each participant.

Can the public defender establish that this procedure violates the Constitution?

A. No, because nothing really happened at the line-up, there would have been nothing for the public defender to do had she been present.

B. No, because the police provided the detailed summary, the public defender has the necessary tools for her cross-examination.

C. Yes, but since the police provided the detailed summary, the defendant was not prejudiced by the public defender's absence.

D. Yes, because a post-charging line-up is a critical stage, and criminal defendants have a right to counsel at all critical stages.

404. A college student was arrested and charged with vandalizing a statute on a rival college's campus. A lawyer was appointed to represent the student, and shortly afterward, the police notified the lawyer a line-up had been scheduled for the following week. The lawyer sent a letter to the police officer investigating the case, notifying him that she would object to any line-up procedure that relied on fillers who did not resemble the student or who were not dressed the same as the student. The officer did not respond to the lawyer's letter in any way.

On the day of the line-up, the student and his lawyer appeared at the police station. The fillers in the line-up were all at least ten years older than the student and each was wearing a polo shirt with a police logo on it. The lawyer objected and demanded that new fillers be located before the eyewitness could be allowed to view the line-up.

Is the lawyer permitted to object in this way?

A. Yes, because the Sixth Amendment guarantees the right to counsel at post-charging line-ups, which includes a right for counsel to participate.

B. Yes, because the Sixth Amendment guarantees the right to counsel at post-charging line-ups, which includes a right to lodge objections.

C. No, because a lawyer's objections to the line-up may only be presented in the trial court, to the judge, and as part of the adversarial process.

D. No, because the police officer notified the lawyer of the line-up and so the student's Sixth Amendment right to counsel has been met.

405. A man was charged with robbery of a jewelry store and attempted murder of the store's manager. For several weeks, the manager was in a coma at the hospital. One day, police received a call from the hospital that the manager was waking up from his coma, but that his vital signs were erratic and doctors had placed him in the intensive care unit.

Two officers escorted the man from the county jail to the hospital. For security purposes, the man was in handcuffs, leg irons, and a belly chain. The officers brought the man to the manager's bedside and the first officer asked the manager to blink if the man looked familiar. The manager blinked. The first officer then asked the manager to blink three times if the man was the same person who had robbed the jewelry store. The manager blinked three times and then died. Later that day, the prosecutor withdrew the attempted murder charge and filed a murder charge in its place.

The man's attorney filed a motion to suppress the officers' testimony about the manager's identification. How should the court rule on the motion?

A. The motion should be granted because the man was denied his Sixth Amendment right to counsel at a critical stage.

B. The motion should be granted because it is patently unfair to draw inferences from the blinking of a dying man.

C. The motion should be denied because the state's urgent need for the identification outweighs the man's need for counsel.

D. The motion should be denied because the man was charged with murder only after the show-up at the hospital.

406. Police arrested a man who had been indicted for conspiracy to distribute heroin. Much of the prosecution's case was based on the testimony of the ex-girlfriend of one of the man's alleged co-conspirators, who had been present several times when the two men met. Shortly after the arrest, police arranged for the ex-girlfriend to view the man in a line-up conducted at the police station. The ex-girlfriend was able to identify the man as the person who had met with her ex-boyfriend and as the person she had overheard discussing heroin distribution.

The man's lawyer was never notified of the line-up. When the man notified him that it had occurred, the lawyer filed a motion to suppress testimony related to the identification.

What testimony should be properly suppressed?

A. The ex-girlfriend should not be permitted to testify to her identification of the man at the line-up, but she should be permitted to make an in-court identification of the man at trial.

B. The ex-girlfriend should not be allowed to make an in-court identification of the man at trial, but she should be permitted to testify to her identification of the man at the line-up.

C. The ex-girlfriend should not be allowed to testify to her identification of the man at the line-up, nor should she be allowed to make an in-court identification of the man at trial.

D. The ex-girlfriend should not be allowed to provide any identification testimony, unless the prosecutor can prove that the identification comes from an independent source.

407. A defendant was charged with robbery of a liquor store and a lawyer was appointed to represent him. Once day, while at a lunch at a restaurant near the courthouse, the lawyer ran into the prosecutor and the two began to chat about the case and the upcoming trial. The prosecutor mentioned that he planned to present testimony from a customer who had been in the back of the store at the time of the robbery and who had recently picked the defendant's photo from an array presented to her by the police officer assigned to the case.

The defense attorney was furious that the officer had conducted an identification procedure without his knowledge and outside his presence, and asked the prosecutor what he was going to do about it.

How should the prosecutor properly respond?

A. The prosecutor should reprimand the officer for showing the customer photos and allowing her to identify the defendant outside of the presence of counsel.

B. The prosecutor should speak to the customer to see if he will be able to show at trial that the customer's identification was based on an independent source.

C. The prosecutor should tell the attorney that the identification procedure was not a critical stage and so the defendant had no right to have counsel present.

D. The prosecutor should acknowledge that the identification procedure was a critical stage, and that the officer violated the defendant's rights.

408. An elderly man was charged with manslaughter and hit and run in association with a traffic accident involving the death of a toddler. An attorney was appointed to represent the man, and a line-up was arranged. The attorney was notified of the line-up and was present, although the investigating officer would not allow him to participate in any way or offer suggestions about how to improve the line-up. Instead, the officer instructed the attorney to "sit down, take notes, and go tell the judge if you don't like what you see here."

The elderly man was in his late 70s, was quite frail, and used a cane. The other men in the line-up ranged in age from 50–60 years old and had no mobility issues. The sole eyewitness to the accident viewed the line-up and told the investigating officer that "the old guy with the cane" was the same man that she saw cause the accident and then drive away.

Does the attorney have a legal basis to object to the eyewitness identification procedure used here?

A. Yes, the attorney can move to strike the identification based on the police officer's rude behavior and disrespectful comments.

B. Yes, the attorney can move to strike the identification based on a violation of the elderly man's Fourteenth Amendment due process rights.

C. No, the attorney cannot move to strike the identification because the elderly man made the choice to use his cane at the line-up.

D. No, the attorney cannot move to strike the identification because the elderly man's Sixth Amendment rights have been met.

409. A young man was charged with rape and a public defender was appointed to represent him. According to the initial police report, the complaining witness told police that she did not get a good look at her attacker, but she was certain that she would be able to identify him if given the chance to do so. The following day, the complaining witness picked the young man's photo out of a photo array.

When the public defender subpoenaed the photographs prior to trial, he was provided with eight photos of the same size. Each photo showed a man's head, neck, and shoulders. However, the photo of the defendant was in color and the other seven photos were in black and white.

If the public defender objects to the use of the single color photo, what standard should be applied to evaluate the claim?

A. That the demonstration of a single color photo to the eyewitness is so impermissibly suggestive that it gave rise to a very substantial likelihood of irreparable misidentification.

B. That the demonstration of a single color photo to the eyewitness constitutes a farce and mockery of justice that shocks the conscience and renders the resulting identification *per se* invalid.

C. That the demonstration of a single color photo to the eyewitness is the type of misconduct that so infects the process with unfairness that it makes the resulting identification a denial of due process.

D. That the demonstration of a single color photo to the eyewitness cannot be tolerated unless the prosecutor can establish a compelling government interest in support of the officer's actions.

410. A woman was indicted for embezzling funds from the auto supply store she managed; the woman was free on bond pending trial. According to the indictment, the woman would write checks from the store to herself and then cash the checks at a bank on the other side of town. The prosecutor's witness list included one of the bank's tellers.

Several weeks before trial, the woman was arrested for attacking one of her neighbors and video of the arrest was shown on the local evening news. Two days after the arrest, police investigators met the bank teller in a pre-arranged meeting to help prepare him for trial. During the interview, the bank teller identified the woman from a collection of photos the officers showed him. The bank teller also told the officers that he recognized the woman because he had seen the arrest video on the news. When the defense attorney learned of the identification, he filed a motion to strike it on due process grounds.

How should the court rule on the motion?

A. The motion should be denied because the police were not responsible for the events the defense attorney alleges violated the woman's due process rights.

B. The motion should be denied because any error is harmless due to the fact that the bank likely has video cameras and the woman can be identified that way as well.

C. The motion should be granted because the procedure here was impermissibly suggestive and there is a strong likelihood of irreparable misidentification.

D. The motion should be granted because the police officer intentionally showed the photo array to the bank teller two days after he saw the arrest video on the news.

Ineffective Assistance of Counsel

411. A man was arrested and charged with cocaine possession based on drugs that were found in his car. The man told his court-appointed attorney that he did not consent to the search but the attorney told the man that she wouldn't file a suppression motion because the trial judge never granted them. The man was convicted and sentenced to 10 years of imprisonment.

A new lawyer was appointed to represent the man in his first appeal of right. At their first meeting, the man explained what the trial lawyer told him about filing a motion to suppress and asked the new lawyer for her advice about how to proceed on appeal.

What is the correct response?

A. The new lawyer should tell the man that the Sixth Amendment creates a right to counsel but does not supply a remedy when the right is violated.

B. The new lawyer should tell the man that the Sixth Amendment creates a right to counsel and he is entitled to a new trial if the court finds the right was violated.

C. The new lawyer should tell the man that the Sixth Amendment creates a right to counsel but only permits money damages when a violation is found.

D. The new lawyer should tell the man that the Sixth Amendment creates a right to counsel and he should file a grievance against the lawyer to enforce the right.

412. A man was charged with bank robbery and assault. At his first meeting with his attorney, the man insisted that he was innocent and told the attorney that he had an alibi. The man gave the attorney the names of several alibi witnesses and claimed that each would testify that he was across town at the time the crime was committed, drinking beer and bowling.

At trial, the attorney challenged the testimony of the state's witnesses, suggesting that each had misidentified the man. The attorney never contacted any of the man's proposed alibi witnesses and never presented any alibi evidence to the jury. After deliberating for several hours, the jury found the man guilty as charged. The man retained a new lawyer to represent him on appeal, and the new lawyer filed a brief arguing that the trial lawyer was ineffective.

What standard should the court use to review this claim?

A. Whether the man can prove that the trial was a farce and mockery of justice that shocks the conscience of the reviewing court.

B. Whether the man can prove that the attorney rendered deficient performance and that he was prejudiced as a result.

C. Whether the man can prove his actual innocence of the crimes for which he was charged, tried, and convicted.

D. Whether the man can prove that the attorney departed from constitutionally prescribed standards despite any showing of prejudice.

413. A therapist was charged with stalking one of his patients. According to the patient, she had dated the therapist for two months but then broke up with him. The patient told police that the therapist was unhappy with the break-up and would spend hours in his car, parked outside her house and place of work.

The therapist retained an attorney and told her that he had broken up with the patient—not the other way around—and that after the break-up, the patient sent him flowers several times. The therapist gave the attorney the cards that accompanied the flower deliveries; after reading them, the attorney urged the therapist to go to trial. The attorney told the therapist that she would use the cards to impeach the patient's credibility.

On the day of trial, the attorney confessed to the therapist that she accidentally lost the cards. She counseled the therapist to go to trial anyway and the therapist took the attorney's advice. The jury convicted the therapist of stalking and the judge sentenced him to community service and required him to register as a sex offender.

The therapist retained a new attorney and the new attorney filed a motion for a new trial, alleging ineffective assistance of counsel. Did the attorney render deficient performance?

A. No, because the therapist cannot criticize the trial attorney's performance at the trial he—the therapist—requested.

B. No, because the therapist's conviction did not result in incarceration and so he did not have a right to effective assistance of counsel.

C. Yes, because a reasonably effective attorney would not have advised going to trial without a plausible trial strategy.

D. Yes, because the fact-finder was denied access to critical evidence that would have assisted in the truth-determining process.

414. A man was indicted for murder and a local attorney was appointed to represent him. The attorney was recently licensed and had just opened her own practice after finishing a postgraduate judicial clerkship. The attorney was going through a contentious divorce and was distracted in the weeks before trial. In addition, the attorney's father died one week before trial and she admittedly did not get much work done that week.

At trial, the primary evidence was the testimony of the man's ex-girlfriend, who had pled guilty in return for a sentencing recommendation of 5 to 10 years—instead of life. However, in order to get the favorable sentence, the ex-girlfriend was required to provide truthful testimony against the man. The attorney cross-examined the ex-girlfriend about her plea deal and argued in her closing that the ex-girlfriend was not a credible witness because she had a huge incentive to lie. The jury convicted the man anyway and he was sentenced to life in prison.

On appeal, the man was represented by a new lawyer, who claimed that trial counsel was ineffective. What is the most likely ruling from the court?

A. Counsel's performance was deficient because of the pressures she was facing in her personal life.

B. Counsel's performance was deficient because she was obviously not qualified to handle such a big case.

C. Counsel's performance was not deficient because she didn't let her personal life interfere with her work.

D. Counsel's performance was not deficient because she performed reasonably, given the facts of the case.

415. A defendant was charged with felony murder and an attorney was appointed to represent him at trial. Under the state rules of criminal procedure, the defense in a criminal case may fully waive the right to give an opening statement or it may reserve the right to give the statement at the close of the prosecution's case.

At trial, the attorney decided to reserve his opening statement. When the defendant asked why, that attorney explained that he didn't want to tip the prosecutor off to his theory of the case until the last possible minute. The defendant was eventually convicted and was sentenced to life in prison.

The defendant appealed, alleging ineffective assistance of counsel. What is the most likely ruling on the attorney's performance?

A. Counsel's performance was not deficient because he had a developed a clear strategy based on the facts of this case.

B. Counsel's performance was not deficient because the court rules permitted him to reserve the opening statement.

C. Counsel's performance was deficient because it is *per se* deficient to reserve the opening statement in a criminal case.

D. Counsel's performance was deficient because most trial lawyers wouldn't reserve the opening statement in a criminal case.

416. A man was convicted at trial of shooting and killing a woman outside of a shopping mall. The man was sentenced to life in prison. He appealed his conviction claiming a variety of errors, but his appeals were denied. The man then filed a state post-conviction petition.

In his petition, the man alleged that his attorney was ineffective for failing to fully investigate his case. Had the attorney done so, the man argued, the attorney would have discovered two eyewitnesses to the shooting who gave police a description that exactly matched a different man. The man attached affidavits from each eyewitness to his petition, describing what each saw and stating that each would have testified at trial for the defense, if asked to do so.

Should the court consider the affidavits in assessing the man's ineffectiveness claim?

A. No, because a court may only review an ineffectiveness claim based on the record evidence from the trial.

B. No, because the eyewitnesses did not testify at trial, the man may not expand the record after his conviction.

C. Yes, because the man may challenge counsel's omissions, and the affidavits are offered in support of his claim.

D. Yes, because the eyewitness affidavits represent the best evidence of what those eyewitnesses saw.

417. A man was charged with burglary and attempted statutory rape; according to a police report, the man had gotten out of his own bed in the middle of the night, broken into his neighbor's house, and crawled into bed with the neighbor's teenage son. The man was found sleeping in the son's bed the next morning.

The man insisted to his court appointed attorney that he had no memory of the event and suggested that his memory loss might be due to a prescription medication he had started taking the week before. The man urged the attorney to investigate the medication and its side effects but the attorney declined. She explained to the man that she had practiced for many years before the judge assigned to the case and she knew from experience that the judge "didn't like excuses" and had limited patience for "boring expert testimony." Instead, the attorney explained, her strategy was to argue that the man had only been arrested and charged because the neighbor was angry with him over a property line dispute from the year before.

The jury found the man guilty. On appeal, can the man establish that the trial attorney performed deficiently?

A. Yes, the man can show deficient performance because the trial attorney's strategy ultimately failed.

B. Yes, the man can show deficient performance because the trial attorney didn't really have a strategy.

C. No, the man cannot show deficient performance because the trial attorney's strategy was based on her experience.

D. No, the man cannot show deficient performance because the trial attorney had a trial strategy.

418. A defendant charged with murder insisted to his lawyer that he was innocent and that he had been at his girlfriend's house at the time of the crime. The lawyer asked the defendant for contact information for the girlfriend, but the defendant replied that she would be of no help because she had been sick that day and had spent the entire day in bed, sleeping. The defendant also said that he had already spoken with his girlfriend, and she didn't remember anything from that day.

At trial, the lawyer cross-examined the state's witnesses and argued in his opening and closing that there was reasonable doubt of the defendant's guilt. The jury returned a guilty verdict. Later, in his state post-conviction petition, the defendant alleged that his trial counsel was ineffective for failing to contact the girlfriend and present her alibi testimony. The judge conducted a hearing on the claim and the attorney testified that he did not contact the girlfriend because the defendant led him to believe that the girlfriend would not be able to provide an alibi.

Should this conversation be considered in evaluating whether the attorney rendered deficient performance?

A. No, because the attorney had an obligation to independently investigate all possible defenses, regardless of what the defendant told him.

B. No, because the conversation shows the attorney's state of mind and subjective intentions play no role in Sixth Amendment claims.

C. Yes, because it shows why the attorney reasonably chose not to contact the girlfriend and consider her as a possible defense witness.

D. Yes, because it shows why the attorney failed to do more to protect the defendant from being wrongfully convicted.

419. A politician charged with public corruption retained a lawyer to represent him at trial. Two weeks before the start of the trial, the politician told his lawyer that the judge assigned to his case had a history of taking bribes. The politician then asked the attorney to meet with the judge and to ask him for his "price." The attorney told the politician that he would not bribe the judge and suggested that the politician might be better off with a different lawyer. The politician apologized and said he'd only made the suggestion because he was so anxious about the upcoming trial.

Later, at the trial, the politician was convicted and the judge sentenced him to a lengthy prison term. One month after the sentencing, the judge was arrested for taking bribes from lawyers who appeared in front of him. He was later convicted of taking bribes.

The politician retained a new lawyer to represent him on appeal. If the politician asks the new lawyer to argue that the trial lawyer was ineffective for failing to bribe the judge, how should the new lawyer respond?

A. The attorney's refusal to bribe the judge cannot form the basis of a deficient performance claim under *Strickland*.

B. The attorney's refusal to bribe the judge was reasonable, given that the judge was arrested after the politician's trial.

C. The attorney's refusal to bribe the judge, in light of the judge's arrest and conviction, demonstrates deficient performance.

D. The attorney's refusal to bribe the judge shows that he was not a zealous advocate on the politician's behalf.

420. A man was charged with a shooting on a city street. The only evidence against him at trial was the testimony of a single eyewitness. On cross-examination, the man's lawyer asked the eyewitness where she had been standing at the time of the shooting, and the eyewitness replied that she had been "nearby ... very, very close to the action." The lawyer did not ask any additional questions of the eyewitness and the man was convicted of murder.

Later, the man's family retained a new lawyer to look into his case. The new lawyer filed a motion for a new trial, claiming the trial lawyer had been ineffective for failing to properly cross-examine the eyewitness. Attached to the motion was a police report of a pretrial interview with the eyewitness; the report had been disclosed to the defense two weeks before trial. According to the report, the eyewitness told police she was standing a block away from the shooting and that she "didn't really get a good look" at the shooter.

Can the man prove that his lawyer's deficient performance prejudiced him?

A. No, because the man can't prove which of the eyewitness's two stories are true.

B. No, because the man doesn't know why the lawyer failed to use the report.

C. Yes, because the lawyer's failure to use the report undermined confidence in the verdict.

D. Yes, because the lawyer's failure to use the report affected the jury's verdict.

421. Two lawyers were appointed to represent a defendant charged with capital murder for the shooting of a security guard at an outdoor mall. After conducting an investigation, the lawyers were so convinced of the defendant's innocence they did not spend any time preparing for the penalty phase of the trial.

At trial, the lawyers were surprised when the prosecutor introduced a videotape of the defendant committing the murder; the video was from a security camera at the mall and had been turned over to the defense months before the start of trial. The lawyers argued unsuccessfully against the video's admission, but the defendant was convicted of all charges. Later, at the penalty phase, the lawyers presented no evidence in support of a life sentence and the jury sentenced the defendant to death.

Represented by new counsel, the defendant appealed and claimed ineffective assistance of counsel. In support of his claim, new counsel produced affidavits from twenty witnesses, each of whom would have testified at the penalty phase in support of a life sentence.

Can the defendant establish that he was prejudiced?

A. Yes, because he can show that there is a reasonable probability that he would have been sentenced to life imprisonment, had his attorneys properly defended him at the penalty phase.

B. Yes, because he can show that there is a possibility that he would have been sentenced to life imprisonment, had his attorneys properly defended him at the penalty phase.

C. No, because he cannot show with definitive certainty that he would have been sentenced to life imprisonment, had his attorneys properly defended him at the penalty phase.

D. No, because he has not presented affidavits from the jurors explaining how they would have considered the testimony, had the twenty witnesses testified at the penalty phase.

422. A man was convicted at trial of first-degree murder. The prosecutor's primary evidence was the testimony of the man's girlfriend, who told police that he had not been home on the night of the crime and that he had also bragged about committing the crime. The man's trial lawyer did not cross-examine the girlfriend, telling the man that he was afraid that the girlfriend might say something even more damaging than she had on direct examination.

After the verdict, a new lawyer was appointed to represent the man. When the new lawyer reviewed the trial lawyer's file, she discovered a police report from the only interview with the girlfriend. According to the report, the girlfriend told police that she was out of town on the weekend of the murder and that the man had never mentioned the crime until he was arrested and charged. The new lawyer moved for a new trial, alleging that trial counsel was deficient for failing to cross-examine the girlfriend with the police report from his own file, and that the man was prejudiced as a result.

Should the judge grant a new trial?

A. No, because the man cannot establish that he would have been allowed to introduce the police report at the time of trial.

B. No, because the man cannot establish that he would have been acquitted, had the jury known about the police report.

C. Yes, because the man can establish that the jury would have given great weight to the police report, if it was presented at trial.

D. Yes, because the man can establish that without the jury's consideration of the police report, he did not receive a fair trial.

423. A defendant was charged with murder for the killing of a store clerk during a robbery. In this jurisdiction, first degree murder includes willful, premeditated, and deliberated killings, and second degree murder includes felony murder. If a defendant is convicted of either degree of murder, the sentence is the same: life in prison without the possibility of parole.

At trial, no evidence of premeditation or deliberation was presented. However, the prosecutor did establish the elements for second degree felony murder. The judge instructed the jury on both degrees of murder and the jury found the defendant guilty of first degree murder. The defendant was sentenced to life in prison. Represented by new counsel on appeal, the defendant claimed his trial lawyer was ineffective for failing to object to the judge's instructions on first degree murder or to object to the jury's verdict.

What is the most likely ruling from the appeals court?

A. The defendant cannot show prejudice because the evidence at trial established the elements of second degree felony murder.

B. The defendant cannot show prejudice because his sentence would have been the same if he had been convicted of second degree murder.

C. The defendant can show prejudice because it is clear that he was improperly convicted of first degree murder.

D. The defendant can show prejudice because the judge improperly instructed the jury on both degrees of murder.

424. A man charged with first-degree murder went to trial represented by court appointed counsel. At the close of evidence, the judge gave a reasonable doubt instruction he found in a book of model jury instructions in the courthouse library. The judge didn't realize that the book was over a decade old and its reasonable doubt instruction had been struck by the state supreme court two years after the book was published. Counsel never objected to the instruction and the prosecutor failed to catch the error. The man was convicted and sentenced to life imprisonment.

Represented by new counsel, the man appealed and claimed his trial lawyer was ineffective for failing to object to the faulty instruction. While the man's appeal was pending, the state supreme court issued an opinion in an unrelated case, overturning its own precedent and restoring the same reasonable doubt instruction from the book in the courthouse library—the same one used at the man's trial.

Can the man establish that he was prejudiced by his attorney's failure to object to the reasonable doubt instruction?

A. Yes, because he was convicted based on the use of a faulty reasonable doubt instruction.

B. Yes, because it would be unfair for the court to ignore the magnitude of counsel's error.

C. No, because to find prejudice would give the man relief to which he is not entitled.

D. No, because he cannot actually establish that the jury would have found him not guilty.

425. A woman was charged with murder for killing her boyfriend. In the woman's first meeting with her appointed attorney, she insisted that she had acted in self-defense. When the attorney asked the woman if she had actually seen a gun in the boyfriend's hand, the woman conceded that she hadn't—but quickly noted that he always carried a gun with him.

The night before trial, the attorney was meeting with the woman to discuss strategy. For the first time, the woman told the attorney that she had seen the gun after all; the woman also said that she knew that if she didn't say she saw a gun, the jury would reject the self-defense claim. The attorney explained to the woman that he could not knowingly present perjured testimony and that he might need to withdraw if she insisted on testifying falsely. After a heated discussion, the woman changed her mind. At trial, she testified only that she thought her boyfriend had a gun, and not that she had seen one. The attorney also presented testimony from several other people, each of whom testified that the boyfriend regularly carried a weapon with him. The jury rejected the woman's self-defense claim and convicted her of murder.

If the woman later claims that her attorney was ineffective, will she be able to establish prejudice?

A. Yes, because the attorney had a conflict of interest between his role as a zealous advocate and his duty to adhere to his ethical obligations.

B. Yes, because the attorney's threat to withdraw so close to trial interfered with the woman's constitutional right to testify on her own behalf.

C. No, because the attorney didn't interfere with the woman's right to testify truthfully and the woman's truthful testimony was sufficient for an acquittal.

D. No, because the attorney's threat to withdraw was not communicated to the judge or jury, and so it did not have any impact on the proceedings.

426. A woman was charged with first-degree murder for the killing of her ex-husband and his new wife. In this jurisdiction, a first-degree murder conviction carries a mandatory sentence of life without the possibility of parole.

Because the woman was indigent, a lawyer was appointed to represent her. At their first meeting, the lawyer advised the woman to plead guilty. He explained that the prosecutor assigned to the case had a strong record and rarely lost a case. The attorney also told the woman that the judge was a former prosecutor and was very strict, and that her only chance for a lenient sentence was to admit responsibility and hope the judge would take that into account. The woman accepted her lawyer's advice and pled guilty to two counts of murder. The following day, she was sentenced to two life sentences.

If the woman files a *pro se* motion to withdraw her plea, can she claim her lawyer's ineffectiveness?

A. A defendant who pleads guilty cannot claim ineffective assistance of counsel because the choice to plead guilty is not strategic, and is made by the defendant.

B. A defendant who pleads guilty cannot claim ineffective assistance of counsel because counsel does not serve as an advocate when a defendant pleads guilty.

C. A defendant who pleads guilty may claim ineffective assistance of counsel but because she has admitted guilt, has a higher burden than a defendant who stands trial.

D. A defendant who pleads guilty may claim ineffective assistance of counsel and must demonstrate deficient performance and resulting prejudice.

427. A man agreed to plead guilty to the crime of possession of child pornography, based on images that had been found on his laptop by a computer repair technician. The man insisted that he was innocent and told his lawyer that he suspected his roommate of downloading the images. The lawyer said that the allegations against the roommate weren't credible, and advised the man to plead guilty.

After the man pled and was sent to prison, he filed a *pro se* motion to vacate his guilty plea based on ineffective assistance of counsel. In the motion, the man argued that his attorney never told him that he had a right to testify about his suspicions about his roommate. The judge directed the attorney to respond, and the attorney conceded that he hadn't ever informed the man about the right to testify or even discussed the possibility of going to trial. However, the attorney argued that since the court rule governing pleas required the judge to independently inform the man of his rights during the plea colloquy, the man had not been prejudiced. When the judge independently reviewed the plea colloquy, she verified that she had told the man that by pleading guilty, he was waiving his right to testify in his own defense.

What is the most likely ruling on the man's claim that his attorney was deficient?

A. The attorney's performance was deficient because he failed to inform the man of one of the direct consequences of a guilty plea.

B. The attorney's performance was deficient because he relied on the judge to inform the man of a direct consequence of a guilty plea.

C. The attorney's performance was not deficient because the man's story about the roommate was neither credible nor believable.

D. The attorney's performance was not deficient because the man was actually told that he had a right to testify in his own defense.

428. A woman pled guilty to three counts of felony tax evasion. At sentencing, the woman was placed on one year of probation and was directed to pay her back taxes as well as a large penalty.

Two weeks later, the woman went to vote in a local election. When she got to the polls, she was told that her name had been removed from the voter list due to her felony convictions. The woman was shocked because her lawyer had never told her that by pleading guilty, she might lose her right to vote.

If the woman moves to withdraw her plea based on ineffective assistance of counsel, what is the most likely ruling on deficient performance?

A. The attorney performed deficiently by failing to inform the woman of a direct consequence of a guilty plea.

B. The attorney performed deficiently because he failed to arrange for the woman to maintain her voting rights, despite her plea.

C. The attorney did not perform deficiently because he arranged for the woman to plead to three felonies and stay out of prison.

D. The attorney did not perform deficiently by failing to inform the woman of a collateral consequence of a guilty plea.

429. Police arrested a middle-aged man for transporting marijuana in his truck. The man was not a citizen but was a lawful permanent resident who had lawfully entered the country as a teenager and had never been naturalized. An attorney was appointed to represent the man and the two discussed whether the man should plead guilty. The man told the attorney about his immigration status and said that he was concerned that he would be deported if he didn't go to trial and wasn't acquitted. The attorney told the man not to worry and that he wouldn't be deported because he had lived in the country lawfully for so many years.

Reassured, the man pled guilty. Shortly after his sentencing, the man received a notice that he was about to be deported.

The man filed an emergency motion to stay his deportation and withdraw his plea, alleging counsel's ineffectiveness. If the judge finds the attorney's advice was deficient, what is the most likely reason why?

A. The attorney was deficient because she failed to inform the man of a direct consequence of a guilty plea — possible deportation.

B. The attorney was deficient because she failed to inform the man of a collateral consequence of a guilty plea — possible deportation.

C. The attorney was deficient because she failed to perform basic legal research to answer the man's question about his deportation risk.

D. The attorney was deficient because reasonable counsel must inform her client of the risk of deportation associated with a guilty plea.

430. A woman was charged with sexually abusing her grandchild, a toddler. The woman had absolutely no recollection of the crime; the woman's lawyer told her that she had probably repressed her memory of the crime. The lawyer also told the woman that if she pled guilty and accepted responsibility, she would be eligible for mental health treatment in prison and would eventually become well again.

The woman reluctantly pled guilty. On the day before her sentencing, the woman requested permission to withdraw her plea, citing ineffective assistance of counsel. The woman testified to what the trial lawyer had told her about repressed memories. The trial lawyer conceded that he had no mental health expertise and had read about repressed memories in a magazine at his dentist's office.

If the judge finds the lawyer was deficient, what will the woman have to show to establish prejudice?

A. The woman will have to show that, but for counsel's faulty advice, there is a reasonable probability that she would have insisted on going to trial.

B. The woman will have to show that, but for counsel's faulty advice, there is a reasonable probability she would have insisted on going to trial and would have been acquitted.

C. The woman will have to show that, but for counsel's faulty advice, there is a reasonable probability that she would have considered going to trial.

D. The woman will have to show that, but for counsel's faulty advice, there is a reasonable probability that she would have considered going to trial and would have been acquitted.

431. A defendant was charged with drug crimes after police discovered two kilos of cocaine in his car. At a pre-trial conference, the prosecutor offered the defendant a reduced sentence in return for his guilty plea to the charged crime. The judge asked the defendant if he wanted to accept the offer and the defendant said that he was pretty sure he did, but he wanted a chance to talk it over with his attorney first. Later, the lawyer advised the defendant to reject the offer and go to trial, explaining that the cocaine would have to be suppressed because the police had searched the defendant's car without a search warrant. Based on this advice, the man rejected the plea offer.

The attorney filed a motion to suppress the cocaine and the judge ruled that the search of the car was reasonable under the automobile exception. The defendant was later convicted and sentenced to a prison term far longer than the one in the plea offer. Represented by new counsel, the defendant filed a motion for a new trial based on ineffective assistance of counsel. In the motion, the defendant conceded that he received a fair trial, but argued that he never would have gone to trial but for the attorney's advice.

Can the defendant show that his attorney's deficient performance prejudiced him?

A. Yes, because he can demonstrate that the terms of the plea offer were better than the sentence he actually received.

B. Yes, because there is a reasonable probability that the defendant would have actually pled guilty and received a better sentence.

C. No, because the focus of *Strickland* prejudice is on fairness, and the defendant conceded that he received a fair trial.

D. No, because the Sixth Amendment only applies to pre-trial errors that actually affect the fairness of the trial proceedings.

432. A defendant was charged with first-degree rape and was facing life imprisonment. The judge appointed a lawyer to represent the defendant; the lawyer was the nephew of the judge's golf partner. The lawyer had received his license a few months before and had only just opened his own office, where he specialized in bankruptcy law. The lawyer met with the defendant once before trial, filed no pre-trial motions, and only cursorily reviewed the discovery provided by the prosecutor.

At trial, the prosecutor presented DNA evidence that established the defendant as the source of the biological evidence collected from the complaining witness. The lawyer did not cross-examine the state's expert and conceded in his closing argument that the state's case was "pretty strong." The defendant was convicted. On appeal, and with the help of a new lawyer, the defendant claimed his trial lawyer was ineffective for his inadequate trial preparation and performance. However, the defendant did not challenge the DNA results in any way.

What sentence most likely appears in the appeals court opinion?

A. "*Strickland* does not require us to examine the attorney's performance if the defendant cannot establish prejudice."

B. "*Strickland* mandates that we examine both the attorney's performance and whether the defendant was prejudiced."

C. "*Strickland* requires us to examine the attorney's performance and any resulting prejudice, in that order."

D. "*Strickland* does not set forth any real guidelines for our review, other than determine whether the trial was fair."

433. A man was charged with conspiracy and bank robbery and at his first court appearance, the man asked the judge to appoint counsel. The judge refused, explaining that because of a downturn in the economy, the county was only appointing lawyers in homicide cases. The judge told the man that he'd either have to retain counsel or represent himself.

Relying on a trial advocacy book from the prison library, the man represented himself at trial to the best of his abilities. He gave opening and closing statements, cross-examined the state's witnesses, and made several objections that were sustained. In the end though, the jury returned a guilty verdict. After the judge dismissed the jury, she told the man that he'd done better than many of the lawyers who regularly appeared in her court. Later, the man appealed the judge's ruling denying counsel and requested a new trial.

How should the appeals court assess whether the man was prejudiced?

A. The appeals court should compare the man's performance at trial to the expected performance of a newly licensed public defender.

B. The appeals court should remand the case and ask the trial judge for a detailed report of how the man did at trial.

C. The appeals should look for specific instances where the man's deficient performance undermined confidence in the outcome.

D. The appeals should just presume that the man was prejudiced by the denial of counsel and grant him a new trial.

434. A college student was charged with burglary, conspiracy, and resisting arrest. Because the student had no resources, the judge appointed a lawyer to represent him. On the advice of his lawyer, the student entered a plea of not guilty and requested a jury trial. At the trial, the lawyer vigorously defended the student, but the jury convicted him anyway. The judge excused the jury and dismissed the lawyer. Two weeks later, the judge sentenced the student to six months in the county jail, as required by the state's mandatory sentencing guidelines.

The student's mother hired a lawyer for the appeal. In the appeal, the lawyer argued that the student was denied his right to counsel because the trial lawyer had been dismissed at the end of the trial.

How should the appeals court rule?

A. The student was denied his Sixth Amendment right to counsel, but the mandatory nature of the sentencing guidelines renders any error harmless.

B. The student was denied his Sixth Amendment right to counsel at a critical stage of the proceeding and prejudice at the sentencing should be presumed.

C. The student was not denied his Sixth Amendment right to counsel because his right ended after the jury found him guilty beyond a reasonable doubt.

D. The student cannot claim a denial of his Sixth Amendment right to counsel because he didn't contemporaneously object when the judge dismissed the lawyer.

435. A man was charged with murder and a lawyer was appointed to represent him. The man told the judge that he wanted to represent himself at trial. Because the man had behaved oddly in his various court appearances, the judge ordered a competency evaluation prior to ruling on the man's motion. Three weeks later, a court-appointed psychiatrist evaluated the man and found him competent to waive counsel. In the psychiatrist's written report to the judge, she explained that she based her opinion on police reports given to her by the prosecutor and a lengthy evaluation of the man. The judge granted the motion and the man represented himself at trial, where he was convicted.

On appeal and represented by a new lawyer, the man argued that his conviction should be vacated due to ineffective assistance of counsel. The new lawyer alleged that the man had been hospitalized dozens of times for his mental health problems—including an involuntary commitment the week before the murder—and provided supporting documentation. The new lawyer also attached an affidavit from the previous lawyer, explaining that she did not independently investigate the man's mental health or provide the psychiatrist with any background materials because, in the weeks before the man's competency evaluation, she believed that her appointment as counsel was still pending.

How should the appeals court rule on the Sixth Amendment claim?

A. The claim should be denied because the man cannot establish that there is a reasonability probability that he would have been acquitted if he had been represented by counsel.

B. The claim should be denied because the lawyer's affidavit adequately explains why she did not investigate the man's mental health prior to the competency evaluation.

C. The claim should be granted because the man was constructively denied his right to counsel prior to the competency evaluation and prejudice should be presumed.

D. The claim should be granted because the documents attached to the appeal demonstrate a genuine issue of material fact as to the man's competence to waive counsel.

436. A police officer was arrested and charged with murder for shooting a girl while executing a search warrant at the girl's house. Six officers had been sent to the house to execute the warrant and at the time of the shooting, everyone in the house — except for the girl — was handcuffed and under police control. Video from the officers' body cameras showed that the girl was hiding behind a couch in the living room, and that the officer shot her after she did not respond to his demands that she lie flat on the floor.

The shooting was widely covered by the local and national media. Two months before trial, the officer's appointed lawyer received a death threat and withdrew from the case. A new lawyer was appointed and tried her best to defend the officer, but the jury found him guilty of the girl's murder. After the verdict was read, the lawyer confessed to the officer that she felt like she hadn't done her best work and that she wished she'd had more time to prepare for the trial.

On appeal, the officer alleged that his Sixth Amendment rights were violated. Which argument will give the officer the greatest likelihood of success on his Sixth Amendment claim?

A. Even though the officer was represented at trial, the likelihood that any lawyer, even a fully competent one, could provide effective assistance is quite small.

B. Even though the officer was represented at trial, he was constructively denied the right to counsel as evidenced by the lawyer's admission at the end of the trial.

C. Even though officer was represented at trial, he was actually denied the right to counsel because his first lawyer withdrew the month before the trial.

D. Counsel engaged in specific acts and omissions at the trial and that these acts and omissions had had a prejudicial effect on the outcome of the trial.

437. After a woman was found murdered in her home, police charged a local man with the crime and a lawyer was appointed to represent him. As part of pre-trial discovery, the lawyer received copies of all the police reports on the case. In one report, an officer described his interview with the woman's best friend, who said that the woman had been dating a local businessman at the time of her death and that he was "pretty violent." In a second report, another officer described his interview with the businessman, who admitted to having a volatile relationship with the woman but denied killing her. The second report concluded by noting that the woman had called 911 the week before her death and had claimed that the businessman threw her down the stairs. After making the report, the woman had declined to press charges.

The man chose to go to trial; the lawyer aggressively cross-examined the state's witnesses, but he never argued that the businessman might have committed the crime. The man was convicted and sentenced to life imprisonment. Later, the man discovered that his appointed lawyer had represented the businessman on a real estate matter three months before the murder. The man also learned that after he was convicted, the businessman hired the lawyer to perform all the legal work for his business.

If the man appeals and claims that his lawyer was conflicted at the time of trial, what is the most likely ruling from the court?

A. The man's conviction will be affirmed because he has not provided documentation showing that counsel felt that he was burdened by a conflict.

B. The man's conviction will be affirmed because he has not shown an actual conflict of interest that affected the adequacy of counsel's representation.

C. The man's conviction will be vacated because he has shown that counsel had an actual conflict of interest and so prejudice should be presumed.

D. The man's conviction will be vacated because no reasonable juror would have found the man guilty in light of the damning evidence about the businessman.

438. A woman was on trial for the murder of her husband. At the start of trial, before the jury entered the courtroom, the woman and her attorney were speaking quietly about the upcoming testimony.

The judge directed them both to be quiet and said that in his courtroom, the only people permitted to speak were those who were speaking on the record or directly to the judge. The attorney objected and said that he would need to confer with the woman during the trial, but the judge said that he didn't care. The attorney then asked if it would be okay for he and the woman to write notes back and forth and the judge said no because he wanted the attorney's full attention on the trial.

After a three-day trial at which she was only able to confer with counsel during recesses, the woman was convicted.

What is the woman's strongest argument on appeal?

A. She should receive a new trial because the judge's directive shows that he had an obvious bias against both the woman and her lawyer.

B. She should receive a new trial because the judge's directive interfered with the lawyer's ability to represent her and prejudice should be presumed.

C. She should receive a new trial because the judge did not make any finding that the woman was being disruptive before issuing his directive.

D. She should receive a new trial because the judge's directive was arbitrary, capricious, and a denial of the woman's due process rights.

439. A woman was charged with breaking and entering, and a lawyer was appointed to represent her. The woman asked her lawyer whether he thought she should request a jury trial, and the lawyer explained to the woman that it was her decision, not his. The woman opted for a bench trial.

At trial, the lawyer waived his opening and closing statements and did not cross-examine the state's three witnesses. The judge found the woman guilty and sentenced her to a year in the state prison. The day after sentencing, the woman wrote the attorney a letter, asking him why he hadn't done more to defend her. The attorney replied that he thought the prosecutor's evidence was very weak and that there was no need to challenge it in any way. In the end, the attorney said, he was surprised the judge convicted the woman.

The woman then filed a *pro se* motion for a new trial, alleging a Sixth Amendment violation and requesting a new trial. In support, the woman attached a copy of the attorney's letter to her motion.

Should the judge grant the motion?

A. No, because the judge appointed counsel as required by the Sixth Amendment, and counsel defended the woman based on a legitimate, although losing, strategy.

B. No, because the judge appointed counsel as required by the Sixth Amendment, and the woman failed to contemporaneously object to his performance during the trial.

C. Yes, because the woman was constructively denied her right to counsel since counsel completely failed to subject the state's case to meaningful adversarial testing.

D. Yes, because the woman was actually denied her right to counsel since counsel completely failed to subject the state's case to meaningful adversarial testing.

440. A man was convicted of murder, and his conviction and sentence were affirmed on appeal. The man then filed a *pro se* post-conviction petition, arguing that his trial lawyer was ineffective under the Sixth Amendment. In support of his claim, the man identified eighteen points during the trial where his lawyer failed to object to evidence or testimony, and four instances where the lawyer's cross-examination was allegedly inadequate.

After several months, the judge reviewing the petition issued a lengthy opinion denying relief. In the opinion, the judge first reviewed the man's claim under the standard from *Strickland v. Washington* and then under the standard from *U.S. v. Cronic.*

Did the judge take the correct approach in reviewing the man's Sixth Amendment claim?

A. Yes, because *pro se* pleadings should be liberally construed, and so the judge was just making sure that there was no constitutional violation.

B. Yes, because the judge has absolute freedom to review any claim over which he has jurisdiction, and the man's petition was properly filed.

C. No, because the man's claim properly fell under *Strickland v. Washington,* and so the judge's review under *U.S v. Cronic* was inappropriate.

D. No, because the man's claim properly fell under *U.S. v. Cronic,* and so the judge's review under *Strickland v. Washington* was inappropriate.

Right to Self-Representation

441. A man was charged with murder and the public defender was appointed to represent him. From the start, the man and the public defender did not get along, and the man disagreed with the public defender's planned trial strategy.

One month before trial, on the day of a scheduled status conference, the man asked the judge whether he could "fire" the public defender. The judge asked the man what he meant, and the man replied that he didn't want the public defender working on his case anymore and that he wanted to represent himself at trial.

How should the judge respond?

A. The man has no right to represent himself because the Sixth Amendment requires the appointment of counsel to all indigent defendants charged with crimes.

B. The man has no right to represent himself because the Sixth Amendment requires the appointment of counsel to all indigent defendants charged with felonies.

C. The man may represent himself because the Sixth Amendment includes a right to self-representation by defendants who validly waive their right to counsel.

D. The man may represent himself because the Sixth Amendment includes an individual right to freely determine one's role within a criminal prosecution.

442. A defendant was charged with capital murder and two lawyers were appointed to represent him at his upcoming trial. On the first morning of the trial, before the jury was brought into the courtroom, the defendant stood up and asked the judge for permission to represent himself at trial. The judge asked the defendant for the reasons for his request, but the defendant refused to explain. However, the defendant did tell the judge that he would need ten months to prepare for the trial—the same amount of time that the lawyers had been given to prepare.

Is the judge required to grant the defendant's motion?

A. Yes, because the defendant has an absolute Sixth Amendment right to self-representation.

B. Yes, because the motion was timely since it was made before the first witness was sworn.

C. No, because the defendant's motion is untimely and was made to delay the trial.

D. No, because capital defendants may not waive their Sixth Amendment right to counsel.

443. A defendant charged with robbery requested permission to proceed *pro se*. The judge asked the defendant why he didn't want to be represented by counsel and the defendant replied that he wanted to "plead guilty and move on with his life." The defendant also explained that his appointed lawyer was urging him to go to trial and he didn't want a trial.

The judge then went through the elements of the robbery charge with the defendant, explained that his Sixth Amendment right to counsel meant that he had a right to have the lawyer's assistance during the guilty plea, and described the sentencing range under the state's sentencing guidelines. The defendant acknowledged that he understood but said that he still wanted to waive counsel and plead guilty. The judge dismissed counsel and the defendant then pled guilty.

Two weeks later, after being sentenced, the defendant filed a motion to vacate his plea, claiming that he never properly waived his right to counsel. How should the judge rule on the motion?

A. The motion should be denied because the defendant must attack his guilty plea directly, and cannot do so by attacking the waiver of his Sixth Amendment right to counsel.

B. The motion should be denied because the defendant knowingly, voluntarily, and intelligently waived his Sixth Amendment right to counsel.

C. The motion should be granted because the judge did not tell the defendant that a lawyer would provide an independent assessment of his chance of success at trial.

D. The motion should be granted because the judge never told the defendant that a lawyer could help him with defenses that he might not be aware of.

444. A defendant charged with armed robbery insisted on representing himself at his upcoming jury trial. Despite the defendant's valid waiver of counsel, the presiding judge was concerned that he would be blatantly outmaneuvered by the prosecutor—a seasoned veteran. The judge arranged for a local lawyer to act as "stand-by" counsel to the defendant. Outraged, the defendant filed a motion for reconsideration.

How should the judge rule on the motion?

A. The motion should be denied because the defendant has a right to represent himself at his trial, but that right does not bar the appointment of stand-by counsel.

B. The motion should be denied because by appointing stand-by counsel, the judge is only trying to ensure that the trial doesn't turn into an absolute circus.

C. The motion should be granted because the defendant plainly doesn't want stand-by counsel's help, and the court can save the money for someone who does.

D. The motion should be granted because the appointment of stand-by counsel interferes with the defendant's absolute right to represent himself at his trial.

445. A woman was charged with killing her infant child and the trial judge appointed an attorney to represent the woman. Two months after the appointment, the woman and the attorney had a disagreement about trial strategy and the woman told the judge that she wanted to waive counsel and proceed to trial on her own. The judge tried to discourage the woman from waiving counsel, but she insisted.

Several weeks later, the woman received the prosecutor's discovery and began to realize that she would need help at the trial after all. At the next status conference on the case, the woman asked the judge to appoint stand-by counsel, but he refused, explaining that he would only appoint counsel to fully represent the woman. The woman was adamant that she only wanted stand-by counsel. The woman represented herself at trial and was convicted; she was later sentenced to life in prison without the possibility of parole.

On appeal — and represented by retained counsel — the woman argued that the judge's failure to appoint stand-by counsel violated her Sixth Amendment rights. What is the most likely ruling from the appeals court?

A. The judge's refusal to appoint stand-by counsel did not violate the woman's Sixth Amendment rights because she had no right to stand-by counsel at her murder trial.

B. The judge's refusal to appoint stand-by counsel did not violate the woman's Sixth Amendment rights because the woman validly waived that right to counsel.

C. The judge's refusal to appoint stand-by counsel violated the woman's Sixth Amendment rights, but she was not prejudiced because of the overwhelming evidence of guilt.

D. The judge's refusal to appoint stand-by counsel violated the woman's Sixth Amend-ment rights, given the nature of the charge and the lengthy sentence that the woman faced.

446. A defendant charged with murder waived his right to counsel and was preparing for his upcoming jury trial. The judge appointed stand-by counsel to the defendant and instructed her that she was to answer the defendant's questions about law and procedure. And, while the judge also told stand-by counsel that the defendant was in charge of the defense decisions and presentation, he encouraged her to make objections for the record as necessary to preserve the defendant's rights on appeal.

At trial, the defendant conducted *voir dire*, made opening and closing statements, and led the direct- and cross-examinations of all of the witnesses. Stand-by counsel did as the judge instructed, and lodged objections during the witness testimony. The defendant did not agree with several of these objections, but the judge told him that it was stand-by counsel's job to preserve the record. Eventually, the defendant was convicted and sentenced to life imprisonment.

On appeal, the defendant complained that the participation of stand-by counsel violated his Sixth Amendment rights. What is the most likely ruling on appeal?

A. Stand-by counsel's participation in the case violated the defendant's rights because the defendant has an absolute right to represent himself, without outside help.

B. Stand-by counsel's participation in the case violated the defendant's rights because it destroyed the jury's perception that the defendant was representing himself.

C. Stand-by counsel's participation in the case did not violate the defendant's rights because counsel's objections helped to preserve issues for the defendant's appeal.

D. Stand-by counsel's participation in the case did not violate the defendant's rights because counsel only objected to testimony, and the defendant did everything else.

447. A defendant charged with drunk driving and vehicular manslaughter decided to waive his Sixth Amendment right to counsel. After conducting a lengthy colloquy to ensure that the defendant understood the ramifications of his decision, the judge accepted the defendant's waiver.

Two weeks later, the defendant wrote a letter to the judge, complaining that the warden of the county jail had refused to order the legal materials the defendant specifically requested to help him prepare for his trial. The letter also included information about the books the defendant had requested: a treatise on evidence in criminal cases, a book on trial advocacy, and a manual on how to litigate a drunk driving case. The defendant concluded his letter by asking the judge to "step in and fix this constitutional atrocity."

What is the most likely response to the defendant's letter?

A. The judge should reply that the right to self-representation does not include a right of access to a law library.

B. The judge should reply that the right to self-representation includes access to replacement tools, like law books.

C. The judge should reply that the defendant's treatment within the county prison is beyond her control and jurisdiction.

D. The judge should reply that the defendant's letter provides proof that his waiver of the right to counsel was a bad idea.

448. A college sophomore was arrested and charged with vandalizing several of the buildings on his college campus. At the sophomore's first appearance, the judge appointed a lawyer to represent him. Two weeks later, the lawyer requested — over the sophomore's objection — a competency evaluation. The judge granted the request and an evaluation was conducted by a prison psychiatrist.

The psychiatrist later issued her report, opining that the sophomore was suffering from paranoid schizophrenia and delusions and was incompetent to stand trial. At the very next court appearance, the judge told the sophomore that the psychiatrist thought he was incompetent and that he was going to accept her opinion. The sophomore replied that he didn't trust his lawyer because the lawyer had requested the competency evaluation. Then, the sophomore told the judge that he wanted to waive his right to counsel and represent himself at trial.

May the judge properly allow the sophomore to waive his right to counsel?

A. Yes, because the sophomore's stated distrust for his lawyer will pervade and destroy the attorney-client relationship.

B. Yes, because the sophomore's competency to stand trial is unrelated to his competency to waive his right to counsel.

C. No, because, since the sophomore is incompetent to stand trial, he is also incompetent to waive his right to counsel.

D. No, because the psychiatrist's report only addressed the sophomore's competency to stand trial.

449. A woman was arrested and charged with murder. In the weeks after her arrest, the woman began acting more and more erratically. At the request of her court-appointed counsel, the judge ordered a competency evaluation. The woman was found incompetent to stand trial. One year later, after being involuntarily medicated, the judge determined that the woman had regained her competency and so he set a trial date.

One month before trial, the woman asked the judge for permission to waive her right to counsel. The judge told the woman that she would first have to submit to another competency evaluation. After an evaluation, the psychiatrist opined that the woman was competent to stand trial, but expressed reservations about the woman's ability to represent herself. In particular, the psychiatrist explained that the woman had a delusional belief that evidentiary and court rules did not apply to her and so she believed that the judge would have no authority to restrict her opening or closing statements or her examination of witnesses during the trial. After reviewing the psychiatrist's report, the judge denied the woman's request to waive her right to counsel.

The woman was later convicted and appealed the judge's ruling on the waiver issue. How should the appeals court rule?

A. The woman's right to self-representation was violated because, since the psychiatrist found her competent to stand trial, she has an absolute right to waive her Sixth Amendment right to counsel.

B. The woman's right to self-representation was violated because there was no proof that she couldn't communicate coherently with the court or jury.

C. The woman's right to self-representation was not violated because the trial judge properly determined that she was not competent to conduct the trial by herself.

D. The woman's right to self-representation was not violated because the psychiatrist's opinion shows that she couldn't validly waive her rights.

450. A defendant charged with armed robbery insisted on representing himself at trial, and validly waived his right to counsel. The state's key witness was an eyewitness to the crime, who testified that she had seen the defendant commit the robbery. The defendant tried his best to cross-examine the eyewitness, but was unable to discredit her testimony. The jury found the defendant guilty and the judge sentenced him to jail time.

The defendant retained a lawyer for his appeal and gave his trial file to the lawyer to review. In the file, the lawyer found the prosecutor's discovery, which included information that the eyewitness had twice been charged with filing false police reports and had once been convicted of perjury. The lawyer asked the defendant why he hadn't used this information to impeach the eyewitness, and the defendant admitted that he hadn't really understood the importance of the documents.

If the lawyer claims ineffective assistance of counsel in the defendant's appeal, how will the court rule on the claim?

A. The claim will be granted because despite the fact that the defendant waived his right to counsel, his trial was fundamentally unfair.

B. The claim will be granted because the defendant should have used the impeachment information, and he was prejudiced by the failure to do so.

C. The claim will be denied because a defendant who waives his right to counsel cannot later claim that he ineffectively represented himself.

D. The claim will be denied because a defendant cannot claim ineffective assistance of counsel for failing to use information in his own possession.

4

Answer Key

1.	C	31.	B	61.	C	91.	C
2.	D	32.	B	62.	A	92.	B
3.	D	33.	D	63.	D	93.	C
4.	B	34.	B	64.	D	94.	C
5.	C	35.	C	65.	D	95.	C
6.	B	36.	D	66.	D	96.	C
7.	D	37.	B	67.	C	97.	B
8.	A	38.	A	68.	A	98.	A
9.	B	39.	A	69.	B	99.	B
10.	D	40.	C	70.	B	100.	A
11.	A	41.	B	71.	B	101.	C
12.	B	42.	B	72.	D	102.	C
13.	D	43.	B	73.	A	103.	C
14.	B	44.	B	74.	A	104.	A
15.	D	45.	A	75.	B	105.	D
16.	A	46.	C	76.	B	106.	D
17.	D	47.	A	77.	C	107.	D
18.	B	48.	C	78.	D	108.	C
19.	C	49.	B	79.	D	109.	A
20.	C	50.	D	80.	D	110.	C
21.	A	51.	B	81.	B	111.	A
22.	C	52.	D	82.	C	112.	D
23.	B	53.	D	83.	D	113.	C
24.	D	54.	D	84.	B	114.	D
25.	A	55.	D	85.	A	115.	C
26.	A	56.	A	86.	A	116.	D
27.	C	57.	C	87.	A	117.	A
28.	D	58.	D	88.	D	118.	D
29.	A	59.	C	89.	C	119.	D
30.	C	60.	B	90.	D	120.	C

121.	D	156.	A	191.	D	226.	B
122.	B	157.	C	192.	A	227.	A
123.	C	158.	B	193.	C	228.	A
124.	A	159.	A	194.	C	229.	D
125.	D	160.	D	195.	B	230.	D
126.	B	161.	C	196.	C	231.	C
127.	C	162.	B	197.	C	232.	A
128.	D	163.	D	198.	D	233.	B
129.	B	164.	D	199.	A	234.	A
130.	C	165.	C	200.	C	235.	B
131.	C	166.	D	201.	B	236.	A
132.	C	167.	C	202.	D	237.	C
133.	A	168.	D	203.	C	238.	C
134.	D	169.	D	204.	D	239.	A
135.	B	170.	B	205.	C	240.	C
136.	C	171.	D	206.	C	241.	C
137.	C	172.	A	207.	D	242.	B
138.	A	173.	D	208.	A	243.	A
139.	B	174.	C	209.	A	244.	C
140.	B	175.	D	210.	A	245.	C
141.	A	176.	D	211.	C	246.	A
142.	B	177.	A	212.	C	247.	D
143.	A	178.	C	213.	B	248.	A
144.	A	179.	B	214.	D	249.	A
145.	A	180.	A	215.	C	250.	C
146.	A	181.	D	216.	D	251.	C
147.	A	182.	D	217.	D	252.	A
148.	B	183.	C	218.	A	253.	D
149.	C	184.	C	219.	C	254.	C
150.	D	185.	B	220.	D	255.	C
151.	B	186.	B	221.	C	256.	D
152.	C	187.	D	222.	A	257.	D
153.	D	188.	B	223.	B	258.	B
154.	C	189.	A	224.	A	259.	C
155.	A	190.	A	225.	D	260.	A

261.	A	296.	B	331.	C	366.	C
262.	B	297.	A	332.	D	367.	D
263.	D	298.	C	333.	A	368.	D
264.	D	299.	B	334.	A	369.	A
265.	C	300.	C	335.	B	370.	B
266.	B	301.	B	336.	D	371.	D
267.	A	302.	D	337.	C	372.	C
268.	A	303.	A	338.	A	373.	D
269.	A	304.	B	339.	B	374.	D
270.	C	305.	A	340.	A	375.	D
271.	B	306.	D	341.	B	376.	B
272.	C	307.	C	342.	C	377.	D
273.	A	308.	B	343.	C	378	D
274.	D	309.	A	344.	C	379.	A
275.	B	310.	C	345.	C	380.	C
276.	A	311.	B	346.	B	381.	B
277.	C	312.	B	347.	B	382.	D
278.	B	313.	B	348	B	383.	D
279.	C	314.	A	349.	D	384.	D
280.	C	315.	A	350.	A	385.	B
281.	C	316.	D	351.	C	386.	D
282.	C	317.	D	352.	A	387.	D
283.	D	318.	A	353.	C	388.	B
284.	D	319.	B	354.	C	389.	D
285.	C	320.	C	355.	C	390.	A
286.	C	321.	A	356.	C	391.	A
287.	B	322.	C	357.	D	392.	C
288.	C	323.	C	358.	B	393.	B
289.	C	324.	B	359.	B	394.	B
290.	C	325.	D	360.	B	395.	B
291.	B	326.	B	361.	B	396.	A
292.	D	327.	B	362.	A	397.	A
293.	A	328.	D	363.	C	398.	D
294.	A	329.	D	364.	A	399.	A
295.	A	330.	B	365.	C	400.	A

401.	A		436.	D
402.	B		437.	B
403.	D		438.	B
404.	D		439.	C
405.	A		440.	C
406.	D		441.	C
407.	C		442.	C
408.	B		443.	B
409.	A		444.	A
410.	A		445.	A
411.	B		446.	B
412.	B		447.	A
413.	C		448.	C
414.	D		449.	C
415.	A		450.	C
416.	C			
417.	B			
418.	C			
419.	A			
420.	C			
421.	A			
422.	D			
423.	B			
424.	C			
425.	C			
426.	D			
427.	A			
428.	D			
429.	D			
430.	A			
431.	B			
432.	A			
433.	D			
434.	B			
435.	C			

Fourth Amendment Explanations

Fourth Amendment Searches

1. This question tests on one of two standards for evaluating whether a Fourth Amendment search has occurred: when police interfere with a person's "actual (subjective) expectation of privacy" and when that "expectation [is] one that society is prepared to recognize as reasonable." *Katz v. U.S.*, 389 U.S. 347, 361 (1967) (Harlan, J., concurring). *Katz* distinguishes between the public and private spheres and holds that "[w]hat a person knowingly exposes to the public, even in his own home or office, is not a subject of Fourth Amendment protection." *Id.* at 351.

   C is correct because the woman's unlawful actions occurred in public—where they could have been observed by anyone—and so the Fourth Amendment will not provide her with any protection.

   A is incorrect because—while true—it does not answer the question of whether a search occurs when a government camera photographs a driver's car in a public place. **B is incorrect** because the reasoning is backwards: simply because the woman may have violated the law doesn't mean that the police procedures might not violate the Fourth Amendment. **D is incorrect** because the question asks about a Fourth Amendment violation, not a state law violation.

2. This question tests on two different applications of *Katz*: trespass onto curtilage and use of thermal imagers on a private home. *Katz* protects the home and the home's curtilage. *U.S. v. Dunn*, 480 U.S. 294 (1987). In addition, when police use "sense-enhancing technology" to gather information about "the interior of the home"—information that could not have been obtained without the use of that technology—a search has occurred under *Katz*. *Kyllo v. U.S.*, 533 U.S. 27, 34 (2001).

   D is correct because it addresses both problems here: the officer walked onto the man's front lawn (curtilage) without lawful authority, and he used a thermal imager (sense-enhancing technology) to gather information from inside the home.

   A and C are both incorrect because each suggests that an officer cannot investigate unless certain threshold conditions are met. The officer can always investigate; the Fourth Amendment will only apply when the investigation involves a search or a seizure. **B is incorrect** because the proper focus under the Fourth Amendment is whether objective constitutional requirements are met; the officer's subjective motivations are irrelevant. *Whren v. U.S.*, 517 U.S. 806 (1996).

3. This question tests on whether a person can reasonably claim an expectation of privacy in property he abandons. He cannot. *California v. Greenwood*, 486 U.S. 25 (1988).

    D is correct because it is true that the man cannot claim a legitimate privacy interest—subjective or objective—in abandoned property, and he abandoned the box and its contents when he left it at the woman's house.

    A is incorrect because, mistake or not, the man's note indicates that he abandoned his privacy interest in the contents of the box. **B is incorrect** because the woman's sobriety and state of mind have nothing to do with whether the man has a privacy interest in the box and its contents. **C is incorrect** because it improperly ties the man's Fourth Amendment rights to the break-up; here, the man's Fourth Amendment rights to the box were severed when he abandoned the box and its contents.

4. This question tests on whether dog sniffs performed in a public place are considered searches under *Katz*. They are not. *U.S. v. Place*, 462 U.S. 696 (1983). Instead, dog sniffs are considered *sui generis* because they are "limited both in the manner in which the information is obtained and in the content of the information revealed by the procedure." *Id.* at 707.

    B is correct because it represents the prosecutor's "strongest argument:" if the dog sniff is not a search but if it provided the officer with adequate suspicion to detain the women, then the officer's actions didn't violate the Fourth Amendment.

    A is incorrect because the seizure here—the officer's act of taking the women aside—occurred after the dog sniff, and the prosecutor's "strongest argument" must address the dog sniff. **C is incorrect** because it doesn't respond to question of whether the evidence should be suppressed. **D is incorrect** because—while factually true—the woman's act of handing the officer the heroin came after the dog sniff, and the prosecutor's "strongest argument" is to claim that the officer's actions were lawful from the outset.

5. This question tests on whether aerial surveillance of a private home constitutes a search under *Katz*. Since a person has no reasonable expectation of privacy in public activities, a search does not occur when police view those activities from the air. *Florida v. Riley*, 488 U.S. 445 (1989) (no search where helicopter flew over private house at altitude of 400 feet); *California v. Ciraolo*, 476 U.S. 207 (1986) (no search where fixed wing aircraft flew over private house at altitude of 1,000 feet).

    C is correct because it tracks the holdings of *Riley* and *Ciraolo*: because the officer observed the woman from a public place, and so there was no Fourth Amendment search.

    A is incorrect because it doesn't respond to the Fourth Amendment issues raised in the motion to suppress. **B is incorrect** because the warrant is valid if it demonstrates probable cause, even if the officer intentionally omitted some information from the warrant application. **D is incorrect** because the issue of reasonableness is only relevant if the officer has committed a search, and no Fourth Amendment search occurred in this situation.

6. This question tests on how *Katz* applies in cases of shared privacy. Under *Katz*, an item is either private or it is not; once the item is shared with others, it is public, and the individual cannot claim a reasonable expectation of privacy in that item. *E.g.*, *Smith v. Maryland*, 442 U.S. 735 (1979) (no expectation of privacy under *Katz* in telephone numbers dialed by private individual because numbers are "conveyed" to phone company).

   B is correct because no search occurred here: the officer used the software to detect semi-public and public information and the laptop owner cannot claim an expectation of privacy in anything that is not, in fact, private.

   A is incorrect because it doesn't respond to the question: the laptop owner is complaining about the use of the software on the network files and not about the resulting warrant. **C is incorrect** because the state's "best argument" is that the Fourth Amendment doesn't even apply here, not that it was violated but that the officer acted in good faith. **D is incorrect** because a policy-based argument doesn't respond to suppression issue presented in the question.

7. This question tests on the second standard for a Fourth Amendment search: when "the Government obtains information by physically intruding on a constitutionally protected area." *U.S. v. Jones*, 132 S. Ct. 945, 950 n.3 (2012). In *Jones*, police used a modern GPS device to monitor a private individual's public whereabouts over a four week period. The Supreme Court found that a search occurred because the government "physically occupied private property for the purpose of obtaining information." *Id.* at 949.

   D is correct because it tracks the holding from *Jones*, as applied to identical facts: placement of a GPS device on a suspect's car and the continued monitoring of that device is a Fourth Amendment search. In addition, the spa owner's "strongest argument" would also include a demand that police get a warrant, instead of searching without one. Although the Supreme Court in *Jones* did not decide whether warrants are required for GPS monitoring of cars, requiring a warrant here would strengthen the spa owner's argument.

   A and B are both incorrect because for a search to occur under *Jones*, police must both place and monitor the GPS device — and each answer addresses only one act or the other. **C is incorrect** because it is not the "strongest argument" for suppression: it correctly recognizes that a search occurred, but leaves open the possibility that the search might be reasonable without a warrant.

8. This question tests on application of the *Jones* test using the facts from *Florida v. Jardines*, 133 S. Ct. 1409 (2013). In *Jardines*, the Supreme Court held that use of a drug sniffing dog at the front door of a private house is a search under *Jones* — not because dog sniffs are searches — but because such a practice exceeds

the "implied license" or "customary invitation" that a homeowner grants strangers to enter the curtilage of his home.

A is correct because it re-states the holding from *Jardines*, as applied to identical facts.

B and C are both incorrect because each only addresses the trespass onto the home's curtilage, and not the scope of an "implied license" that the homeowner might grant to a stranger to walk up to his door. **D is incorrect** because it only addresses the homeowner's privacy interests under *Katz*, and this activity is a search under *Jones*.

9.   This question tests on application of the *Jones* test using the facts from *Oliver v. U.S.*, 466 U.S. 170 (1984). In *Oliver*, the Supreme Court held that police entry onto an open field is not a search under *Katz*, even when police ignore the property owner's fences and posted "no trespassing" signs. Although the Supreme Court has not applied the *Jones* test to open fields, it has explained that "the special protection accorded by the Fourth Amendment to the people in their persons, houses, papers and effects[] is not extended to the open fields" and that "the distinction between the [open fields] and the house is as old as the common law." *Hester v. U.S.*, 265 U.S. 57, 59 (1924).

B is correct because it recognizes that trespass onto an open field is not a Fourth Amendment search, even under the test from *Jones*.

A is incorrect because it doesn't address the farmer's challenge to the officers' right to walk onto his property. **C and D are both incorrect** because they each suggest that open fields are protected under the Fourth Amendment and that the court should determine if the farmer granted an implied license for strangers to walk onto his property. However, open fields do not receive Fourth Amendment protection.

10.   This question tests on application of the *Jones* test using the facts from *Bond v. U.S.*, 529 U.S. 334 (2000). In *Bond*, the Court held that "a law enforcement officer's physical manipulation of a bus passenger's carry-on luggage" is a search under *Katz*. *Bond*, 529 U.S. at 335.

D is correct because, since carry-on luggage is a constitutional effect, there is every reason to think that "physical manipulation" of such an effect would be treated as a search under *Jones*.

A is incorrect because the public bus is not what's at issue here; the man's duffel bag — a constitutional effect — is the focus. **B is incorrect** because it focuses on what happened after the officer squeezed the duffel bag, and the issue is the constitutional meaning of the squeeze itself. **C is incorrect** because it focuses on what might make the search reasonable — a warrant versus consent — and the government is arguing that no search occurred on these facts.

Fourth Amendment Seizures

11.   This question tests on one of the basic requirements of a Fourth Amendment seizure: that it requires more than just a casual encounter between an officer and a citizen. *U.S. v. Mendenhall*, 446 U.S. 544, 554 (1980) (noting practical problems associated with classifying all police-citizen encounters as seizures). And, as the Supreme Court has explained, "[i]f there is no detention—no seizure within the meaning of the Fourth Amendment—then no constitutional rights have been infringed." *Florida v. Royer*, 460 U.S. 491, 498 (1983) (plurality opinion).

A **is correct** because it is the only answer that recognizes that the young man was not seized while interacting with the officer.

B, C, and D are all incorrect because each is premised on the idea that the young man was seized—and he wasn't.

12.   This question tests on whether a person is seized just because a police officer asks him a question. A "seizure does not occur simply because a police officer approaches an individual and asks a few questions." *Florida v. Bostick*, 501 U.S. 429, 434 (1991). Instead, "[s]o long as a reasonable person would feel free to disregard the police and go about his business,.... the encounter is consensual" and no seizure has occurred. *Id.*

B is correct because it sets forth the correct standard for a seizure and because a reasonable person in this situation would not have felt compelled to answer the officer's question.

A is incorrect because it suggests that the officer would need to actually stop the man in order to seize him, and a Fourth Amendment seizure can occur without physical contact. **C is incorrect** because for a person to be seized by submission to authority, there must actually be some show of authority. Here, the officer simply asked a question; he did not display any authority to which the man could have submitted. **D is incorrect** because while it sets forth a correct test for a seizure, it reaches the incorrect conclusion on these facts.

13.   This question tests on one of the Supreme Court's definitions for seizures in the context of a drug interdiction on a passenger bus. In this context, a seizure does not occur "[s]o long as a reasonable person would feel free to disregard the police and go about his business." *Bostick*, 501 U.S. at 434. In the bus context, an officer is not required to inform passengers of their right to refuse consent, and the failure to give such information is one of many factors to be considered when assessing what a reasonable person would do in such circumstances. *U.S. v. Drayton*, 536 U.S. 194, 206–207 (2002).

D is correct because it sets forth the correct test for determining whether a person approached by a police officer on a bus is seized within the meaning of the Fourth Amendment.

A is incorrect because *Drayton* expressly holds that the officer does not need to inform a bus passenger of her right to refuse consent. **B is incorrect** because it focuses on the question of whether the alleged seizure was reasonable or not— *i.e.*, whether it was based on reasonable suspicion or probable cause—and the question asks about whether a seizure occurred in the first place. **C is incorrect** because it relies on a definition of seizure that does not apply in this context.

14. This question tests on the definition of a seizure, but focuses on timing: when does a casual encounter with an officer become a Fourth Amendment seizure? The answer to that question can depend on whether the officer exerts physical force over the suspect or whether the suspect submits to the officer's authority. *California v. Hodari D.*, 499 U.S. 621, 626 (1991).

    B is correct because "the quintessential seizure of the person" occurs when the officer uses force to subdue that person. *Id.* at 624.

    A is incorrect because the officer's show of authority to a fleeing suspect is not enough for a seizure; *Hodari D.* expressly rejected that argument and held that, at minimum, the suspect must also submit to the officer's authority. **C is incorrect** because an officer can always "approach" a person, and the Fourth Amendment is only implicated when that "approach" becomes a seizure. **D is incorrect** because it presents an irrelevant issue: the officer's concern doesn't address the question of whether or not the young man was seized.

15. Like the previous question, this question also tests on the definition of seizure from *Hodari D.*: application of physical force or submission to the officer's authority. *Id.* at 626.

    D is correct because it properly recognizes that the driver pulled over because the lights were distracting him, not because he recognized and submitted to the officer's authority.

    A is incorrect because it misstates the facts: the driver here submitted, but not to the officer's authority. Because the driver didn't know that he was being followed by an officer and pulled over only because the lights were distracting, the "submission to the officer's authority" test has not been met. **B and C are both incorrect** because each focuses on whether a search occurred. Here, the driver's only possible argument for suppression is that the pipe was discovered as a result of an unreasonable seizure.

16. This question tests on whether a police officer's use of deadly force constitutes a Fourth Amendment seizure using the relevant facts from *Tennessee v. Garner*, 471 U.S. 1 (1985). "[T]here can be no question that apprehension by the use of deadly force is a seizure subject to the reasonableness requirement of the Fourth Amendment." Id. at 7.

    A is correct because the officer shot the prowler, which *Garner* holds is a Fourth Amendment seizure.

    B is incorrect because it misstates the rule from *Garner*, and illogically suggests that the issue of whether the prowler was seized depends on his ability—or not—to walk away after being shot. **C and D are both incorrect** because each states that the prowler was not seized, and he clearly was.

17. This question tests on whether a seizure occurs when there's no physical contact between the officer and suspect and when the suspect doesn't intentionally submit to the officer's authority. A seizure may still occur on these facts "when there is a governmental termination of freedom of movement through means intentionally applied." *Brower v. County of Inyo*, 489 U.S. 593, 597 (1989).

    D is correct because it acknowledges that the intentional use of the spike strip to stop the suspect's car was a seizure, and that the state's "best argument" would be to concede the seizure and focus on reasonability.

    A is incorrect because there can be no forfeiture of rights without a finding of wrongdoing, and the suspect here had not been found guilty of any crime at the time he ran from police. **B is incorrect** because a seizure can occur even if the officer doesn't actually touch the suspect. *E.g.*, *Hodari D.*, 499 U.S. at 626 (seizure can occur where suspect submits to officer's authority). **C is incorrect** because there are other tests for when a seizure occurs, aside from *Hodari D.*'s "submission to authority" test.

18. This question tests on whether a seizure occurs when a person does not feel "free to leave," and demonstrates how that test can lead to problematic results, depending on the context. Although the Supreme Court has used the "free to leave" test, *Mendenhall*, 446 U.S. at 554, it has also observed that a person may not be free to leave a particular situation for reasons having nothing to do with the police. *E.g.*, *INS v. Delgado*, 466 U.S. 210, 218 (1984) (factory workforce was not "free to leave" because of "voluntary obligations to [the] employer[]," and not because of actions of INS agents); *Bostick*, 501 U.S. at 436 (bus passenger not "free to leave" because he had not yet reached his destination, not because of coercive acts by police).

    B is correct because the officer did not mandate the teenager's attendance at the presentation, the school did. As such, to the extent the teenager felt like he had to stay at the presentation, it was because of the restrictions on him placed by the school and not by the officer.

    A is incorrect because it doesn't respond to the question and because it's untrue: "special needs" searches are governed by the Fourth Amendment. **C is incorrect** because it is too broadly worded: the Fourth Amendment might have limited application in a private school, but "absolutely no application" goes too far. **D is incorrect** because it does not respond to the teenager's argument that he was unreasonably seized.

19. This question tests on the issue of whether and when a car passenger is seized if the driver of that car is pulled over by the police. When a driver is seized, his passengers are seized also. *Brendlin v. California*, 551 U.S. 249 (2007). In the car passenger context, the passenger is seized when he manifests his "submission to authority:" when the car stops and when the passenger signals his submission by reasonably staying seated. *Id.* at 258.

C **is correct** because it recognizes both that the officer's seizure of the passenger began when the car was stopped—not later, when the officer arrested him—and that the officer plainly lacked authority for the stop.

A is incorrect because it fails to recognize that both the driver and passenger were seized. **B is incorrect** because the focus on the legality of the search incident to arrest doesn't address the question of whether the passenger was lawfully seized at the time of the stop. **D is incorrect** because it focuses on the lawfulness of the arrest, and the passenger's argument focuses on the seizure, which occurred earlier in time.

20. This question tests on the minimum level of suspicion required for a seizure: reasonable articulable suspicion. *Terry v. Ohio*, 392 U.S. 1 (1969). Reasonable suspicion "is a less demanding standard than probable cause and requires a showing considerably less than preponderance of the evidence." *Illinois v. Wardlow*, 528 U.S. 119, 123 (2000). Still, reasonable suspicion "requires at least a minimal level of objective justification" for the officer's action. *Id.*

C **is correct** because it sets forth the correct legal standard for the traffic stop— reasonable suspicion—and recognizes that the standard was met here.

A is incorrect because it suggests that an officer can only seize a person based on probable cause, and *Terry* holds that reasonable suspicion is sufficient for some types of seizures. **B is incorrect** for two reasons: it suggests that the officer's concern did not equate to reasonable suspicion, and that reasonable suspicion is not enough to support the traffic stop. **D is incorrect** because traffic stops—even those brief in duration—are seizures under the Fourth Amendment.

Probable Cause and Reasonable Suspicion

21. This question tests on probable cause to search, defined as a "fair probability that contraband or evidence of a crime will be found in a particular place." *Illinois v. Gates*, 462 U.S. 213, 239 (1983); *see also Safford v. Redding*, 557 U.S. 364, 371 (2009) ("fair probability or substantial chance of discovering evidence of criminal activity"). Probable cause is required for automobile exception searches. *California v. Acevedo*, 500 U.S. 565 (1991).

A is correct because there is no probable cause to search on these facts: there is only an unverified allegation of criminal activity and an observation that two people have met for breakfast for three consecutive weeks.

B is incorrect because an officer does not need to corroborate every aspect of a tip; the officer only needs to establish probable cause to search or seize. **C is incorrect** because the thoroughness of the officer's investigation is irrelevant if the investigation doesn't lead to probable cause. **D is incorrect** because the officer never saw a drug sale between the woman and the bartender.

22. This question tests on probable cause to arrest (seize), using the relevant facts from *Maryland v. Pringle*, 540 U.S. 366 (2003). Probable cause to arrest turns on "whether, at that moment, the facts and circumstances within [the officers'] knowledge and of which they had reasonably trustworthy information were sufficient to warrant a prudent man in believing that the [suspect] had committed or was committing an offense." *Beck v. Ohio*, 379 U.S. 89, 91 (1964).

    C is correct because it is an "entirely reasonable inference from these facts that any or all three of the occupants had knowledge of, and exercised dominion and control over, the cocaine." *Pringle*, 540 U.S. at 372.

    A and B are both incorrect because each suggests that the officer only had probable cause to arrest one of the three men, and the officer's probable cause extended to all three. **D is incorrect** because it focuses on voluntariness of the front seat passenger's statement, and his only plausible argument for suppression is that the statement is a fruit of an unlawful seizure.

23. This question tests on how probable cause is assessed: according to the totality of the circumstances. *Gates*, 462 U.S. at 230.

    B is correct because it refers to the correct legal standard—totality of the circumstances—and reaches the correct conclusion on these facts.

    A and C are both incorrect because each addresses only some of the facts of the case and the prosecutor's "strongest argument" is that all of the circumstances together establish probable cause here. **D is incorrect** because the driver is not challenging the dog's other alerts; instead, she is challenging the dog's overall reliability.

24. This question tests on how information from anonymous third parties should be assessed when evaluating probable cause. For a period of time, such information was reviewed according to a two-pronged test that examined the tipster's "basis of knowledge" and "veracity." *Gates*, 462 U.S. at 229 (describing the "*Aguilar-Spinelli*" test). *Gates* abandoned this approach, however, in favor of a totality of the circumstances test. *Id.* at 238.

    D is correct because the teacher's "strongest argument" is that there was no probable cause to arrest him, and because it refers to all of the facts known to the officer, *i.e.*, the totality of the circumstances.

    A, B, and C are all incorrect because each focuses on deficiencies in the officer's investigation of the anonymous caller and not on the totality of the circumstances.

25. This question tests on how a court should determine whether a drug dog's alert is sufficient to form probable cause to search, using facts derived from *Florida v. Harris*, 133 S. Ct. 1050 (2013). Because probable cause is a fluid concept and is to be assessed according to the totality of the circumstances, "evidence of a dog's satisfactory performance in a certification or training program can itself provide sufficient reason to trust his alert." *Id.* at 1057.

A is correct because it presents the "strongest argument:" that the evidence presented at the suppression hearing is sufficient to demonstrate the dog's reliability.

B and C are both incorrect because, by referring to what will "always" be established, each is too broadly worded. **D is incorrect** because it doesn't respond to the question and so doesn't present the prosecutor's "strongest argument."

26. This question tests on the definition of reasonable articulable suspicion, which is the minimum level of suspicion required to search or seize. Reasonable articulable suspicion "is considerably less than proof of wrongdoing by a preponderance of the evidence" and is "obviously less" than probable cause. *U.S. v. Sokolow*, 490 U.S. 1, 7 (1989). It has also been described as a "moderate chance of finding evidence of wrongdoing." *Safford*, 557 U.S. at 371 (2009).

    A is correct because the woman's actions—drinking from a paper-wrapped bottle in public—gave the officer the minimal suspicion he needed to seize her.

    B is incorrect because it addresses the duration of the stop, and the question asks about the right to stop. **C is incorrect** because it suggests that because the officer was wrong about what the woman was drinking, his suspicion is negated. Since reasonable suspicion and probable cause are far less than absolute certainty, an officer's suspicion can be both legitimate and wrong. **D is incorrect** because it suggests that police need more than reasonable suspicion for a *Terry* stop, and that is all that is needed.

27. This question tests on whether an officer's hunch is sufficient to form reasonable articulable suspicion to frisk a person for weapons. It is not; instead, the officer "must be able to articulate something more than an inchoate and unparticularized suspicion or hunch." *Sokolow*, 490 U.S. at 7.

    C is correct because there is no concrete reason here—other than a coincidence— for the officer to suspect that the driver was armed and dangerous. In other words, the officer's suspicion is based only on a hunch, which is not enough for a frisk.

    A is incorrect because the officer's hunch is not enough for reasonable suspicion. **B and D are both incorrect** because the driver did nothing suspicious during the stop, and each answer states that he did.

28. This question tests on what should be considered in the reasonable articulable suspicion assessment. When evaluating whether that standard has been met, a court should not assess facts in isolation; instead, a court "must look at the totality of the circumstances of each case to see whether the detaining officer has a particularized and objective basis for suspecting legal wrongdoing." *U.S. v. Arvizu*, 534 U.S. 266, 273 (2001).

    D is correct because it provides the correct standard for assessing reasonable articulable suspicion: the totality of the circumstances.

    A, B, and C are all incorrect because each addresses only one fact in isolation, and not according to the totality of the circumstances standard.

29. This question tests on reasonable articulable suspicion—the requirement to frisk a suspect—using the relevant facts from *Florida v. J.L.*, 529 U.S. 266 (2000). "An accurate description of a subject's readily observable location and appearance is of course reliable in this limited sense: It will help the police correctly identify the person whom the tipster means to accuse. Such a tip, however, does not show that the tipster has knowledge of concealed criminal activity." *Id.* at 272.

A is correct because the officer lacked reasonable suspicion to believe the man was armed and dangerous. Instead, the caller alleged that he was and nothing in the officer's investigation proved or disproved that allegation.

B is incorrect because it suggests that the possibility of a shooting justifies the frisk, but the frisk requires reasonable suspicion. (While the Supreme Court in *J.L.* suggested that there might be some extraordinary situations where the need for reliability might be relaxed, a report of a person with a firearm is not one of those situations. *Id.* at 273–274.) C is incorrect because it suggests that the officer had reasonable suspicion on these facts, and per *J.L.*, he didn't. D is incorrect because the fact that the police found the weapon can't be used to retroactively justify the frisk.

30. This question tests on reasonable suspicion to seize, using the facts of *Alabama v. White*, 496 U.S. 325 (1990). Although the Supreme Court considered *White* to be a "close case," it concluded that "under the totality of the circumstances[,] the anonymous tip, as corroborated, exhibited sufficient indicia of reliability to justify the investigatory stop of [the] car." *Id.* at 332.

C is correct because it is the best of the available answers: the tip gave some predictive information about future events—which the officers were able to corroborate—and so they had reasonable suspicion for the stop.

A and B are both incorrect because each suggests that police cannot seize unless they verify every detail in a tip. "[B]ecause an informant is shown to be right about some things, he is probably right about other facts that he has alleged, including the claim that the object of the tip is engaged in criminal activity." *Id.* D is incorrect because it suggests that the officers needed probable cause to stop the woman, and reasonable suspicion will suffice for a traffic stop.

Warrants

31. This question tests on the constitutionally required components of a warrant. The Warrant Clause of the Fourth Amendment sets forth three core requirements for a warrant: that it be "based on probable cause," that it be "supported by oath or affirmation," and that it "particularly describe[] the place to be searched, and the persons or things to be seized." U.S. CONST. AMEND. IV. In addition, the warrant application must be reviewed by a "neutral and detached magistrate" or judicial officer. *Johnson v. U.S.*, 333 U.S. 10, 13–14 (1948). Although local law or practice may require more, the Federal Constitution does not.

B is correct because the warrant here met the requirements of the Warrant Clause, despite the officer's intentional failure to comply with state law.

A, C, and D are all incorrect because each focuses on the state law violation and possible remedies. However, the question asks about suppression under the Fourth Amendment, and a state law violation is irrelevant to the federal issue. *E.g.*, *Virginia v. Moore*, 553 U.S. 164 (2008) (officer's state law violation in making arrest does not provide a suppression remedy as arrest of suspect was based on probable cause).

32. This question also tests on the constitutionally required components of a warrant.

    B is correct because the warrant meets constitutional requirements: it is based probable cause, based on a sworn statement; it describes with particularity the items to be seized; and was reviewed by a neutral and detached magistrate.

    A is incorrect because the length of a police officer's investigation has no bearing on whether the resulting warrant is valid or not. **C is incorrect** because the good faith exception is only relevant when the warrant is somehow deficient—and the warrant here is not. **D is incorrect** because the officer's omission of his badge number is irrelevant to the federal constitutional issue presented in the question.

33. This question tests on the standard for assessing probable cause, which is required for all warrants. Probable cause is established when, according to the totality of the circumstances, there is a "fair probability" that the police have enough suspicion to either search or seize. *Illinois v. Gates*, 462 U.S. 213 (1983). Probable cause is a "fluid concept" and is to be assessed based on the totality of the circumstances. *Id.* at 232.

    D is correct because it provides the correct standard from *Gates* for assessing probable cause: the totality of the circumstances.

    A, B, and C are all incorrect because each addresses only a component of the officer's investigation in this case and not the results of the investigation in their entirety.

34. This question tests on probable cause to search: a "fair probability that contraband or evidence of a crime will be found in a particular place." *Id.* at 239; *see also Safford v. Redding*, 557 U.S. 364, 371 (2009) ("fair probability or substantial chance of discovering evidence of criminal activity").

    B is correct because the officer didn't have probable cause to search the man's home: the girl alleged that she had been sexually assaulted in her own home and nothing in the facts suggests that the officer might find evidence in the man's home.

    A is incorrect because it suggests that the officer had probable cause to search the home but that the application failed to mention the laptop. Instead, there was no probable cause to search the home at all. **C is incorrect** because it a policy-based answer to a legal question and so doesn't represent the "most likely" ruling from the court. **D is incorrect** because it doesn't address the question; the officer had probable cause to believe the man had committed a crime, but that doesn't equate to probable cause to search the man's home for photographs—especially when none of the girl's allegations involved the man's home or photographs.

35. This question tests on probable cause to arrest (seize): "whether, at that moment, the facts and circumstances within [the officers'] knowledge and of which they had reasonably trustworthy information were sufficient to warrant a prudent man in believing that the [suspect] had committed or was committing an offense." *Beck v. Ohio*, 379 U.S. 89, 91 (1964).

    C is correct because the officer had a hunch the waitress knew about the cocaine, but not probable cause to believe that she was involved with the bartender in the cocaine scheme.

    A is incorrect because it refers to the fruits of the search incident to arrest, not whether the arrest was lawful in the first place—which is the focus of the question. **B is incorrect** because, although the officer may have profiled the waitress as a drug dealer, it doesn't respond to the question of whether she had probable cause to arrest her. **D is incorrect** because warrantless arrests are permitted in many situations, assuming the officer has probable cause to make the arrest.

36. This question tests on how tips and other third-party information should be considered in the probable cause equation. For many years, the Supreme Court required that such information be assessed according to a strict, two-prong test; the test was known as the *Aguilar-Spinelli* test and required examination of the basis of the tipster's knowledge and his record for providing truthful information. *Spinelli v. U.S.*, 393 U.S. 410 (1969); *Aguilar v. Texas*, 378 U.S. 108 (1964). However, in 1983, the Supreme Court supplanted the *Aguilar-Spinelli* test with the more flexible "totality of the circumstances" test. *Gates*, 462 U.S. at 230.

    D is correct because the officer didn't have probable cause: the tip provided a lot of innocent detail and the officer's investigation did not add anything. The only slightly suspicious thing about the man was that he paid for his lunch from a large roll of bills, but that fact alone does not provide probable cause to arrest.

    A and B are both incorrect because each refers back to the strict requirements of the *Aguilar-Spinelli* test and implies that an arrest warrant cannot be issued unless each prong is established. *Gates* clearly rejects that approach. **C is incorrect** for two reasons. First, it states that *Aguilar-Spinelli* is the proper test for evaluating hearsay and other third-party information. Second, it incorrectly ties issuance of the warrant only to the anonymous letter, instead of to the totality of the circumstances.

37. This question tests on the proper role of a magistrate and what it means to be "neutral and detached." If the magistrate steps out of his judicial role and helps

the police in their investigation, he becomes a member of the executive and loses his ability to be "neutral and detached." *Lo-Ji Sales v. N.Y.,* 442 U.S. 319 (1979) (town justice who participated in search was not neutral and detached).

B is correct because it is the principal's "strongest argument:" the magistrate provided substantive assistance to the officer in her investigation and in so doing, abandoned her judicial role.

A is incorrect because it's irrelevant whether the officer understood the financial documents or not; instead, the issue is whether the constitutional requirements for a warrant have been met. **C and D are both incorrect** because neither provides the principal with a suppression remedy. As such, neither answer represents the principal's "strongest" argument for suppression.

38. This question tests on the qualifications to be a magistrate. "[A]n issuing magistrate must meet two tests. He must be neutral and detached, and he must be capable of determining whether probable cause exists for the requested arrest or search." *Shadwick v. City of Tampa,* 407 U.S. 345, 350 (1972). In *Shadwick,* the Court expressly "reject[ed] … any per se invalidation of a state or local warrant system on the ground that the issuing magistrate is not a lawyer or judge." *Id.* at 352.

    A is correct because it correctly states the law and directly responds to the defense attorney's challenge.

    B is incorrect because if it were true, there would be no need for magistrates—ever. **C is incorrect** because it does not address the magistrate's objective ability to make the probable cause determination, which is the basis of the defense attorney's challenge. **D is incorrect** because it doesn't respond to the question, and because it's untrue. Presumably, if the magistrate was unable to make the probable cause assessment, that would be a legitimate concern for a defense attorney.

39. This question tests on proper warrant procedure. Ideally, if a magistrate tells a police officer that his affidavit does not demonstrate probable cause, the officer should conduct additional investigation instead of just looking for another magistrate to issue the warrant. However, ultimately, the warrant must demonstrate probable cause.

    A is correct because, even if the officer should have followed the first magistrate's directions, the warrant is still valid if it demonstrates probable cause.

    B is incorrect because the fruits of the search can't make up for a deficiency in the warrant. **C and D are both incorrect** because neither addresses the core requirement that a search warrant must be based on probable cause.

40. This question tests on whether a magistrate who works on a contingency basis can be neutral and detached. A magistrate "who has a direct, personal, substantial, pecuniary interest in his conclusion to issue or to deny the warrant" is neither neutral nor detached. *Connally v. Georgia,* 429 U.S. 245, 249 (1977) (*per curiam*).

    C is correct because the magistrate was not neutral and detached because his compensation was directly tied to the warrants she signed.

A, B, and D are all incorrect because none address the issue of whether contingency payments affect the magistrate's ability to fairly and neutrally assess warrant applications.

41. This question tests on the requirement that the warrant actually demonstrate the officer's probable cause, instead of merely alleging that probable cause exists. *E.g., Nathanson v. U.S.*, 290 U.S. 41, 47 (1933) ("[m]ere affirmance of belief or suspicion" insufficient to establish probable cause).

    B is correct because while the officer may have had probable cause to arrest the teacher, the warrant didn't set forth any details about the officer's investigation and so it didn't demonstrate probable cause.

    A is incorrect because it does not respond to the question and instead addresses an irrelevant consideration—the child's consent. **C is incorrect** because—while perhaps true—it doesn't respond to the question of whether probable cause has been established or not. **D is incorrect** because probable cause requires more than just the officer's word; instead, probable cause is something that has to be demonstrated with specific facts.

42. This question tests on what an officer must include in a warrant to demonstrate probable cause.

    B is correct because the information supplied in the warrant application was too brief and conclusory to demonstrate probable cause.

    A, C, and D are all incorrect because each addresses a possible deficiency in the officer's investigation. However, the focus here is not on the quality of the officer's investigation, but instead on whether the warrant application itself demonstrates probable cause.

43. This question tests on the particularity requirement, which requires that the warrant itself "particularly describ[e] the place to be searched, and the persons or things to be seized." U.S. CONST. AMEND. IV. "[T]he purpose of the particularity requirement is not limited to the prevention of general searches.... [a] particular warrant also assures the individual whose property is searched or seized of the lawful authority of the executing officer, his need to search, and the limits of his power to search." *Groh v. Ramirez*, 540 U.S. 551, 561 (2003).

    B is correct because the warrant here was deficient: it did not describe what the officer was looking for and the officer did not otherwise connect the warrant to the affidavit.

    A is incorrect because it suggests that the particularity clause requires that police state only where in the house they want to search; however, the particularity clause also requires the police to state what they're looking for. **C is incorrect** because there's nothing in the facts to suggest that the warrant referred back to or otherwise incorporated the affidavit. **D is incorrect** because regardless of the government's interest, the warrant still has to comply with the Constitution.

44. This question tests on the "knock and announce" rule, using the relevant facts from *Hudson v. Michigan*, 547 U.S. 586 (2006). The rule dictates that officers properly announce their presence before executing a warrant inside a private home and "forms a part of the reasonableness inquiry under the Fourth Amendment." *Wilson v. Arkansas*, 514 U.S. 927, 929 (1995). "What the knock-and-announce rule has never protected ... is one's interest in preventing the government from seeing or taking evidence described in a [lawfully obtained] warrant." *Hudson*, 547 U.S. at 594. As such, when police violate the knock and announce rule, "the exclusionary rule is inapplicable." *Id.*

   B is correct because it represents the practical effect of the holding in *Hudson* and is the prosecutor's "best argument" against suppression.

   A is incorrect because it addresses the degree of the violation, not the appropriate remedy. **C is incorrect** for two reasons: knock and announce doesn't depend on the homeowner being at home and the answer doesn't address the question of the homeowner's remedies. **D is incorrect** because there is nothing in these facts that suggests that the homeowner was destroying evidence.

45. This question tests on what time of day a warrant should be executed within a private home. Time of day is arguably relevant to the Fourth Amendment reasonableness inquiry, just like the knock and announce requirement. Many states have statutes in place that mandate daytime execution, unless some exception is met. *See* Wayne R. LaFave, et al., 2 *Criminal Procedure* § 3.4(g) (3d. Ed. 2007 & 2014 Supp.). However, because the reasons for daytime execution of warrants serve different interests from those requiring warrants in the first instance, nighttime execution of an otherwise-valid search warrant will likely not result in suppression of evidence. *See e.g., Hudson*, 547 U.S. at 594.

   A is correct because it is the answer that most closely tracks the reasoning of *Hudson*: a valid warrant will authorize the officers' actions, regardless of the knock and announce or time of day violation.

   B is incorrect because evidence is suppressed when it is obtained unreasonably, not because the person it is obtained from might have been injured along the way. **C is incorrect** because it refers to an absolute, and there are other ways to deter misconduct short of suppression. **D is incorrect** because "[s]ubjective intentions play no role in ordinary ... Fourth Amendment analysis." *Whren v. U.S.*, 517 U.S. 806, 813 (1996).

46. This question tests on the appropriate remedy for when an officer exceeds the scope of a search warrant. The officer's search is restricted by the particularity clause, *i.e.*, the specific description of things he wishes to search for. *Harris v. U.S.*, 331 U.S. 145, 190 (1947) ("a search warrant ... is limited in scope by the Fourth Amendment to those articles set forth with particularity in the warrant ...").

C is correct because it addresses the scope problem presented by these facts: how, when searching for "live marijuana plants," could the officer justify searching inside kitchen drawers and a toilet tank?

A is incorrect because there are no facts given to indicate that the officer lied to the magistrate. **B is incorrect** because the officer's failure to find the items he thought he might find — marijuana plants — does not mean that he didn't have probable cause to begin with. **D is incorrect** because the officer is permitted to seize items that aren't mentioned in the warrant, as long as he does not violate the scope of the warrant.

47. This question tests on whether probable cause can grow "stale" due to the passage of time. Given that probable cause to search relates to a "presently existing condition," what an officer believes to be true on the day she obtains the warrant may be significantly different at some point in the future. *See* Wayne R. LaFave, et al., 2 *Criminal Procedure* § 3.3(g) (3d. Ed. 2007 & 2014 Supp.).

    A is correct because the probable cause in this case — which focused on evidence which could be easily moved — had very likely gone stale in the six weeks between when the police obtained the warrant and when they executed it.

    B and C are both incorrect because neither addresses the staleness question. **D is incorrect** because it suggests that police wouldn't have probable cause unless they definitively knew where the cocaine was hidden. Probable cause requires far less than that level of certainty; all that is required is a "fair probability" that certain facts are true.

48. This question tests on what a reasonable officer should do when he realizes a problem with his search warrant before he executes it.

    C is correct because a reasonable officer, upon learning of a serious flaw in a search warrant, would not execute that warrant.

    A is incorrect because it places fault with the officer's reliance on the confidential informant, but the issue is what the officer should do once he learns that a key part of his probable cause may be untrue. **B is incorrect** because the woman's information doesn't affect the facial validity of the warrant; the woman's information instead undercuts the validity of the probable cause itself. **D is incorrect** because the woman's "strongest argument" is not that the police exceeded the scope of the warrant, but that her house shouldn't have been searched in the first place.

49. This question tests on the right of an officer, armed with an arrest warrant, to enter a private home to make a lawful arrest. "[F]or Fourth Amendment purposes, an arrest warrant founded on probable cause implicitly carries with it the limited authority to enter a dwelling in which the suspect lives when there is reason to believe the suspect is within." *Payton v. New York*, 445 U.S. 573, 603 (1980).

    B is correct because the arrest warrant gave the arresting officer the right to enter the bank president's home, and the weapon was in plain view.

A is incorrect because the shotgun really wasn't in a location where "anyone" could have seen it. Instead, it was in a location where people entering the bank president's home could see it. **C is incorrect** because the officer doesn't need a search warrant to enter the home, as long as he has a lawful arrest warrant. **D is incorrect** because the officer doesn't require an invitation to enter; the arrest warrant gives him the authority to enter.

50. This question tests on warrant-based arrests within a third party's home, using the relevant facts from *Steagald v. U.S.*, 451 U.S. 204 (1981). "[J]udicially untested determinations are not reliable enough to justify an entry into a person's home to arrest him without a warrant, or a search of a home for objects in the absence of a search warrant." *Id.* at 213.

    D is correct because it accurately describes what happened in this situation: police searched a private home with a warrant, exigency, or consent.

    A, B, and C are all incorrect because they do not address the right of the officers to search the girlfriend's home for the young man.

Warrantless Arrests

51. This question tests on the common law rules for warrantless arrests. At common law, "a peace officer was permitted to arrest without a warrant for a misdemeanor or felony committed in his presence as well as for a felony not committed in his presence if there was reasonable ground for making the arrest." *U.S. v. Watson*, 423 U.S. 411, 418 (1976).

    B is correct because it recognizes that the common law would have permitted the woman's arrest since the officer had probable cause to believe she committed a felony.

    A is incorrect because it is too broadly worded, and suggests that the common law would have permitted the arrest even without probable cause. **C is incorrect** because it fails to recognize that the officer had probable cause for the arrest. **D is incorrect** because it is untrue: the common law did permit warrantless arrests under some circumstances.

52. This question tests on the "modern" rules for warrantless arrests, which largely mirror the common law rules. "The balance struck by the common law ... has survived substantially intact ... in the form of express statutory authorization" for warrantless, public arrests. *Watson*, 423 U.S. at 421.

    D is correct because the arrest was based on a statute that tracks the common law rule.

    A is incorrect because by referring to "all non-violent arrests," it misconstrues the common law rule for warrantless arrests. **B and C are both incorrect** because the rules for warrantless arrests distinguish between felonies and misdemeanors, not the underlying elements of the crime or whether the arrestee posed a danger to the arresting officer.

53. This question tests on post-arrest probable cause determinations. "Whatever procedure a State may adopt, it must provide a fair and reliable determination of probable cause as a condition for any significant pretrial restraint of liberty, and this determination must be made by a judicial officer either before or promptly after arrest." *Gerstein v. Pugh*, 420 U.S. 103, 124–125 (1975).

    D is correct because it recognizes the deficiency here: that the arraignment judge never made a determination of whether the officer had probable cause to arrest the man in the first place.

    A is incorrect because a court appearance and a chance to enter a plea is not the same as a determination that there was probable cause to arrest. **B is incorrect** because the "prosecutor's responsibility to law enforcement is inconsistent with the constitutional role of a neutral and detached magistrate." *Id.* at 117. **C is incorrect** because it doesn't respond to the question; instead, it presents a reason why there may not be probable cause on these facts.

54. This question tests on the requirements for a "prompt" post-arrest probable cause hearing. "[A] jurisdiction that provides judicial determinations of probable cause within 48 hours of arrest will, as a general matter, comply with the promptness requirement of *Gerstein*." *County of Riverside v. McGlaughlin*, 500 U.S. 44, 56 (1991).

    D is correct because the student's probable cause hearing occurred on a Monday, and he was arrested the previous Thursday evening — well outside of the 48-hour window required by *McGlaughlin*.

    A and C are both incorrect because, by failing to address the delayed probable cause hearing, neither represents the "most likely" ruling. There are also no facts to support the allegations in C. **B is incorrect** because it is not the "most likely" ruling; although there is some "flexibility" in the 48-hour rule, "intervening weekends" are not the sort of "extraordinary circumstance[s]" that will relieve a state of its obligation to conduct a timely probable cause hearing. *Id.* at 57.

55. This question tests on the substantive requirements for a post-arrest probable cause hearing — also called a "*Gerstein* hearing." "[A]dversary safeguards are not essential for the probable cause determination required by the Fourth Amendment [because t]he sole issue is whether there is probable cause for detaining the arrested person pending further proceedings." *Gerstein*, 420 U.S. at 120.

    D is correct because the purpose of the *Gerstein* hearing is to determine whether there was probable cause for the arrest, not whether the defendant is guilty or not.

    A and B are both incorrect because the woman was not yet charged with a crime when she appeared before the magistrate, and Sixth Amendment rights do not begin until charging. *E.g.*, *Rothergy v. Gillespie County*, 554 U.S. 191 (2008). **C is incorrect** because it doesn't address the reason for the woman's complaint — that she believed she was entitled to an adversarial hearing to determine probable cause for her arrest.

56. This question tests on whether the arresting officer has to have probable cause to believe the arrestee has committed the arresting offense, or whether probable cause to believe that he has committed any offense will suffice. "[A]n arresting officer's state of mind (except for the facts that he knows) is irrelevant to the existence of probable cause.... That is to say, his subjective reason for making the arrest need not be the criminal offense as to which the known facts provide probable cause." *Devenpeck v. Alford*, 543 U.S. 146, 153 (2004).

    A is correct because the officer had probable cause to believe the student had committed a crime—just not the crime the student was actually arrested for—and so the arrest was reasonable under the Fourth Amendment.

    B is incorrect because the Supreme Court in *Devenpeck* expressly rejected a requirement that the arresting offense be "closely related" to the actual committed offense, explaining that imposing such a requirement would lead to "arbitrary consequences." *Id.* at 155. **C is incorrect** because *Devenpeck* holds that if the officer has probable cause for the arrest, it doesn't matter that the arrestee was arrested for the wrong crime. **D is incorrect** because it doesn't respond to the question: the issue here is whether there was probable cause for the student's arrest.

57. This question tests on the constitutional reasonableness of an arrest that violates state law. "When officers have probable cause to believe that a person has committed a crime in their presence, the Fourth Amendment permits them to make an arrest"—even if that arrest violates state law. *Virginia v. Moore*, 553 U.S. 164, 178 (2008). And if the arrest is "constitutionally permissible," police may then search the arrestee incident to arrest. *Id.* at 177–178.

    C is correct because it recognizes that the issue of suppression under the Fourth Amendment is separate from the issue of whether an arrest violates state law.

    A is incorrect because it suggests that there should be a Fourth Amendment remedy, even when the Fourth Amendment isn't violated. **B and D are both incorrect** because "[s]ubjective intentions play no role in ordinary ... Fourth Amendment analysis." *Whren v. U.S.*, 517 U.S. 806, 813 (1996).

58. This question tests on the location of a warrantless arrest, using a statute similar to the one found unconstitutional in *Payton v. New York*, 445 U.S. 573 (1980). "[F]or Fourth Amendment purposes, an arrest warrant founded on probable cause implicitly carries with it the limited authority to enter a dwelling in which the suspect lives when there is reason to believe the suspect is within." *Id.* at 603. However, at the same time, because "physical entry of the home is the chief evil against which the wording of the Fourth Amendment is directed," "searches and seizures inside a home without a warrant are presumptively unreasonable." *Id.* at 585–586.

    D is correct because the only plausible basis for the officer's warrantless entry into the home is the statute; no other exception applies. If the statute is unconstitutional—and *Payton* holds that it is—then the warrantless entry and arrest are both unreasonable.

A, B, and C are each incorrect because none address the core issue presented by these facts: the officer entered a private home without a warrant, exigency, or consent.

59. This question tests on the reasonability of warrantless arrests for low-level offenses. "If an officer has probable cause to believe that an individual has committed even a very minor criminal offense in his presence, he may, without violating the Fourth Amendment, arrest the offender." *Atwater v. City of Lago Vista*, 532 U.S. 318, 354 (1991).

C is correct because the officer here witnessed the public littering and so had probable cause and statutory authority to make the arrest.

A, B, and D are all incorrect because each suggests that there are additional limits on an officer's ability to make such an arrest—beyond those set forth in *Atwater*.

60. This question tests on whether the manner of conducting an otherwise lawful warrantless arrest can render that arrest unreasonable. If the arrest is conducted in an "extraordinary manner"—the arrest may be deemed unreasonable. *Id.* at 354.

B is correct because it represents the "strongest argument:" that an officer who intentionally uses his car to hit a helmetless moped rider—just so he can arrest the moped rider—is conducting an unreasonable arrest.

A is incorrect because misdemeanor arrests don't always require a warrant. **C is incorrect** because it is not the "strongest argument:" maybe the officer should have given the moped rider more of a warning, but the fact that he intentionally hit him is the critical issue here. **D is incorrect** because it focuses on what happened after the arrest, not the events leading up to the arrest.

Exigent Circumstances

61. This question tests on the basic concept of exigent circumstances: an "emergency or dangerous situation" that justifies an officer acting without a warrant—where one would ordinarily be required. *Payton v. New York*, 445 U.S. 573, 583 (1979).

C is correct because the prosecutor's "strongest argument" is that the officer could have gotten a warrant because he had probable cause, but was prevented from doing so by the exigency.

A is incorrect because it refers generally to the bartender's "workplace," and the police searched the bartender's locker, which was reserved for his "personal property." **B is incorrect** because it refers only to probable cause and not exigent circumstances. **D is incorrect** because the bartender's expectation of privacy in the locker doesn't depend on the evidence recovered in the search.

62. This question tests on the standard required to act on a possible exigency—probable cause—using the relevant facts from *Kirk v. Louisiana*, 536 U.S. 635 (2002). In the context of an entry into a home, "police officers need either a warrant or probable cause plus exigent circumstances in order to make a lawful entry…." *Id.* at 638.

     A is correct because there were no exigent circumstances here. At most, the officer had a "concern" that the evidence would be destroyed, but his concern was unsupported by the facts.

     B is incorrect because the officer did have probable cause for the arrest because the third buyer verified the drug purchase. **C and D are both incorrect** because neither addresses the exigency and the warrantless entry into the man's house.

63. Like the previous question, this question also tests on the requirement that the officers have probable cause to act on a possible exigency.

     D is correct because it refers to both probable cause and the exigency.

     A and B are both incorrect because each says that the police have to take some additional action or make some additional finding before acting on the exigency. All that is required is an exigency and probable cause. **C is incorrect** because it suggests that the entry wasn't authorized because the police eventually discovered that no one was in peril. The correct analysis focuses on what the police knew at the time of the entry, and not what they discovered afterwards.

64. This question tests on how a court should assess a claim of exigent circumstances. "To determine whether a law enforcement officer faced an emergency that justified acting without a warrant, this Court looks to the totality of circumstances." *Missouri v. McKneely*, 133 S. Ct. 1552, 1559 (2013).

     D is correct because it provides the correct standard for determining the existence of an exigency: the totality of the circumstances.

     A, B, and C are all incorrect because each addresses only one fact in isolation, not all the facts together.

65. This case tests on categorical or *per se* exigencies, using the relevant facts from *McKneely*. "While the natural dissipation of alcohol in the blood may support a finding of exigency in a specific case, … it does not do so categorically. Whether a warrantless blood test of a drunk-driving suspect is reasonable must be determined case by case …" *Id.*, 133 S. Ct. at 1563.

     D is correct because it recognizes the Supreme Court's general preference for non-categorical rules in the Fourth Amendment context. *U.S. v. Drayton*, 536 U.S. 194, 201 (2002) ("for the most part[,] *per se* rules are inappropriate in the Fourth Amendment context").

     A is incorrect because it expresses a preference for categorical rules, which is the opposite of the Supreme Court's general approach under the Fourth Amendment. **B is incorrect** because it doesn't respond to the prosecutor's argument about *per se* exigencies, but instead addresses the issue of whether there was an exigency in this case. **C is incorrect** because it doesn't make any sense: if the warrant is superfluous, the suppression motion should be denied, not granted.

66. This question tests on the automobile exception, which is one of a "limited class of traditional exceptions to the warrant requirement that apply categorically and [does] not require an assessment of whether the policy justifications underlying the exception ... are implicated in a particular case." *McKneely*, 133 S. Ct. at 1559 n.3. Under the automobile exception, "police may search an automobile and the containers within it where they have probable cause to believe contraband or evidence is contained." *California v. Acevedo*, 500 U.S. 565, 580 (1991).

    D is correct because it states the correct requirement for the automobile exception—probable cause—and recognizes that no independent showing of exigency is required to search a car under that exception.

    A and B are both incorrect because each refers to why there was inadequate proof of an exigency, and the automobile exception does not require that. Instead, the officer must only have probable cause to search. **C is incorrect** because the facts provide no way of knowing state law regarding implied consent for drivers with probationary licenses.

67. This question tests on the "police-created exigency" doctrine, using the facts from *Kentucky v. King*, 131 S. Ct. 1849 (2011). "Police may not rely on the need to prevent destruction of evidence when that exigency was 'created' or 'manufactured' by [their own conduct]." *Id.* at 1857. As long as police "do not gain entry to premises by means of an actual or threatened violation of the Fourth Amendment," they are not responsible for creating the exigency. *Id.* at 1862.

    C is correct because it accurately describes what happened here: police knocked, the young man chose not to answer the door, and the officer heard sounds that gave her probable cause to believe that evidence was being destroyed.

    A and B are both incorrect because neither focuses on the fact that all the officer did here was knock on the door. *i.e.*, the police here did "no more than any private citizen might do." *Id.* **D is incorrect** because there was no consent to enter on these facts, tacit or otherwise.

68. This question tests on the "police-created exigency" doctrine and provides an example where police did "gain entry to [the] premises by means of an actual or threatened violation of the Fourth Amendment." *King*, 131 S. Ct. at 1862.

    A is correct because it directly and properly responds to the woman's claim that the officer created the exigency.

    B is incorrect because the officer is allowed to "approach" the woman's door; the issue here is with the officer's forced entry into the woman's house. **C and**

D are both incorrect because neither presents the woman's "strongest argument," which should address the fact that the officer created the exigency.

69. This question tests on the scope of the exigency exception. In general, the right to rely on the exigency lasts as long as the exigency lasts; when the exigency is over, police must either get a warrant or rely on some other exception to support their actions. *E.g., Mincey v. Arizona*, 437 U.S. 385 (1978) (four day search of apartment not justifiable under exigency exception when all injured people had received medical aid and had been removed from the apartment).

    B is correct because the officers lawfully entered the home in response to the gunshots and restricted the scope of their search to the area associated with the exigency.

    A is incorrect because the entry into the house wasn't unlawful and because inevitable discovery doesn't apply to these facts. **C is incorrect** because the question asks about the admissibility of the cocaine and not its evidentiary value. **D is incorrect** because the police can always respond to a situation that presents itself to them; they just can't manipulate the situation to avoid complying with the warrant requirement.

70. This question also tests on the scope of the exigency exception, using facts derived from *Mincey v. Arizona*.

    B is correct because it specifically addresses the problem here, *i.e.*, that the backup officers had absolutely no authority to search the apartment after the exigency concluded and without a warrant.

    A is incorrect because the presumption against warrantless activity in the home can be overcome through consent or an exigency, and this answer doesn't address those two possibilities. **C is incorrect** because there was no Fourth Amendment forfeiture; "it suffices here to say that this reasoning would impermissibly convict the suspect even before the evidence against him was gathered." *Id.* at 391. **D is incorrect** because there is no "homicide scene" exception to the Fourth Amendment. *Id.* at 393 ("If the warrantless search of a homicide scene is reasonable, why not the warrantless search of the scene of a rape, a robbery, or a burglary?").

71. This question tests on the "emergency aid" exigent circumstance, which permits police to "enter a home without a warrant to render emergency assistance to an injured occupant or to protect an occupant from imminent injury." *Brigham City, Utah v. Stuart*, 547 U.S. 398, 403 (2006).

    B is correct because the facts suggested that the aunt needed help: the middle-aged woman had expressed concern for the aunt's well-being, police saw a motionless person (presumably the aunt) lying on the couch, and no one answered the doorbell.

    A is incorrect because the implied consent argument is quite weak on these facts, and B provides a better and more "accurate" response. **C is incorrect** because police didn't know if the aunt was alive or dead. **D is incorrect** because the police weren't required to corroborate the middle-aged woman's claims; they were instead required to act on probable cause.

72. This question tests on the "destruction of evidence" exigent circumstance, "an emergency, in which the delay necessary to obtain a warrant, under the circumstances, threatened the destruction of evidence." *Schmerber v. California*, 384 U.S. 757, 770 (1966).

D is correct because the only exigency here is a remote and hypothetical one.

A and B are both incorrect because each states the officer's actions were reasonable because of the remote possibility of an exigency, and police must have probable cause of an actual exigency in order to rely on the exception. C is incorrect because while harvesting the plants would destroy them, the problem here is that the officer had no reason to believe that they were about to be harvested.

73. This question tests on the "burning building" exigent circumstance, using the relevant facts from *Michigan v. Tyler*, 436 U.S. 499 (1978). "[A]n entry to fight a fire requires no warrant, and once in the building, officials may remain there for a reasonable time to investigate the cause of the blaze. Thereafter, additional entries to investigate the cause of the fire must be made pursuant to the warrant procedures governing administrative searches." *Id.* at 511.

A is correct because even though the fire marshal didn't need a warrant to enter the building initially, the fire had been extinguished—and the exigency had ended—by the time the he returned to take the photographs.

B is incorrect because the fire marshal was permitted to seize the container due to the exigency. C is incorrect because it is too broadly worded: the fire marshal's initial entry was valid because it was based on a legitimate exigency, so the gasoline container is admissible. D is incorrect because it is "impossible to justify a warrantless search on the ground of abandonment by arson when that arson has not yet been proved, and a conviction cannot be used *ex post facto* to validate the introduction of evidence used to secure that same conviction." *Id.* at 505–506.

74. This question tests on the "hot pursuit" exigent circumstance, using facts from *U.S. v. Santana*, 427 U.S. 39 (1976). "[H]ot pursuit means some sort of a chase, but it need not be an extended hue and cry in and about [the] public streets." *Id.* at 43. "[A] suspect may not defeat an arrest which has been set in motion in a public place... by the expedient of escaping to a private place." *Id.*

A is correct because the warrantless arrest began in a public area and the partner's pursuit of the dealer into her home was justified by a legitimate fear that she would destroy evidence of her crimes.

B is incorrect because the prosecutor's "strongest response" must justify the warrantless entry into the house; a legitimate exigency will clearly provide that justification, but the need to make an arrest might not. C is incorrect because the partner didn't order the dealer to do anything; instead, he identified himself and informed her that she was under arrest. **D is incorrect** because it presents a factual explanation—*i.e.*, that the partner needed to recover the cash—for a legal issue, and is therefore not the "strongest" argument for the prosecutor to make.

75. This question also tests on the "hot pursuit" exigent circumstance, using the facts from *Minnesota v. Olson*, 495 U.S. 91 (1990).

    B is correct it represents the suspect's "strongest argument:" that there was no exigency because the officers had the building surrounded and would have been able to arrest the suspect when he eventually left.

    A is incorrect because it's untrue: the caller's report and the suspect's statement— "tell them I left"—provided the police with probable cause to believe the suspect was in the apartment. **C is incorrect** because the officer did corroborate the tip when he called the apartment and heard the suspect speaking in the background. **D is incorrect** because it's not the suspect's "strongest argument."

76. This question tests on application of the plain view exception in the context of an exigency. "[T]he police may seize any evidence that is in plain view during the course of their legitimate emergency activities." *Mincey*, 437 U.S. at 393. And, under the plain view exception, police may seize evidence if (1) the officer is in a lawful vantage point to view the evidence; (2) he does not engage in additional search activity to get to access the evidence; and (3) he has probable cause to suspect that the evidence is linked to a crime. *E.g.*, *Horton v. California*, 496 U.S. 128, 136–137 (1990).

    B is correct because all the requirements of plain view have been met here: the officer was lawfully in the house responding to an exigency; he did not need to search to gain access to the handgun; and he had probable cause to believe that the handgun had been used in a recent shooting.

    A and D are both incorrect because the "most likely" ruling from the court will focus on the exigency, not on consent. **C is incorrect** because, while handgun possession can be legal, the officers here had probable cause to believe the handgun had been used in the shooting.

77. Like the previous question, this question also tests on plain view in the context of an exigency.

    C is correct because the officers were permitted to enter the fraternity house, but had no reason to look on the second floor or in the closet.

    A is incorrect because the Fourth Amendment rights are not tied to the age of the person asserting them. **B is incorrect** because the officer did not view the evidence from a lawful vantage point; here, the officers were permitted to enter the home, but not to search the house as they did. **D is incorrect** because the exigency exception does not require proof of that the exigency be severe, just that an exigency actually exist.

78. This question tests on exigency and police intent, using the relevant facts from *Brigham City, Utah v. Stuart*. "An action is 'reasonable' under the Fourth Amendment, regardless of the individual officer's state of mind, as long as the circumstances, viewed objectively, justify [the] action." *Id.*, 547 U.S. at 404. In other words, "[t]he officer's subjective motivation is irrelevant." *Id.* at 398.

    D is correct because it accurately describes what happened here: the officers acted reasonably and in response to a legitimate exigency.

    A is incorrect because it refers to the officers' subjective motivations, and "[s]ubjective intentions play no role in ordinary ... Fourth Amendment analysis." *Whren v. U.S.*, 517 U.S. 806, 813 (1996). **B is incorrect** because it suggests that police need to witness violence over a minimum threshold before they can act under the exigency exception. "The role of a peace officer includes preventing violence and restoring order, not simply rendering first aid to casualties; an officer is not like a boxing (or hockey) referee, poised to stop a bout only if it becomes too one-sided." *Brigham City, Utah*, 547 U.S. at 406. **C is incorrect** because it makes no sense: the people inside the house didn't forfeit their rights, they just didn't hear the officers' knock.

79. This question tests on whether police must suspect crime over a certain threshold severity in order to act under the exigency exception, using the relevant facts from *Michigan v. Fisher*, 558 U.S. 45 (2009) (*per curiam*). "Officers do not need ironclad proof of a likely serious, life-threatening injury to invoke the emergency aid exception." *Id.* at 49.

    D is correct because it accurately summarizes the facts known to the officer at the time he entered the house.

    A is incorrect because the officer reasonably suspected that the man had done more than simply cut his hand. **B is incorrect** for two reasons: it speaks in absolute language, and it ignores the other facts known to the officers at the scene. **C is incorrect** because it refers to only to past events—the smashed car and downed fence posts—and doesn't address the bloody towel covering the man's hand or his yelling.

80. This question tests on a possible exigency situation, using the relevant facts from *Welsh v. Wisconsin*, 466 U.S. 740 (1984). "In *Welsh*, the only potential emergency confronting the officers was the need to preserve evidence of the suspect's blood-alcohol level, an exigency the Court held insufficient under the circumstances to justify a warrantless entry into the suspect's home." *Brigham City, Utah*, 547 U.S. at 399.

    D is correct because it accurately recognizes that the only exigency here was a minimal one, at best.

    A is incorrect for two reasons: it refers to the reasonable suspicion standard (instead of probable cause) and fails to recognize the fact that the woman was suspected of committing a civil infraction, not a crime. **B is incorrect** because, while it correctly refers to probable cause, *Welsh* holds that collection of evidence for a civil infraction is not sufficiently serious to permit a warrantless entry into a private home. **C is incorrect** because the woman's ability to walk home is only one factor that the police should consider as part of the totality of the circumstances.

Plain View

81. This question tests on the plain view exception, which permits an officer to seize evidence if he: (1) is in a lawful vantage point to view the evidence; (2) doesn't engage in additional search activity to get to access the evidence; and (3) has probable cause to suspect that the evidence is linked to a crime. *E.g., Horton v. California*, 496 U.S. 128, 136–137 (1990).

    B is correct because all three requirements of the plain view exception are met here: the officer observed the bong while responding to an emergency call, he did not have to search to view it, and he had probable cause to believe it was evidence of crime. As such, the officer would have been authorized to seize the bong.

    A is incorrect because the exigency here only supports the officer's entry into the home, and plain view has two additional requirements. **C is incorrect** because the facts indicate that the officer was legitimately responding to an exigency, so consent wouldn't necessarily be required. **D is incorrect** because application of plain view doesn't depend on the reason for the officer's presence. Instead, the first requirement of plain view simply requires that the officer be lawfully present when he views the evidence.

82. This question tests on a key aspect of the plain view doctrine: that it doesn't apply to what an officer sees but doesn't otherwise have lawful access to. *Texas v. Brown*, 460 U.S. 730, 738 n.4 (1983). In other words, "plain view" is different from "plain sight."

    C is correct because by standing on the sidewalk and viewing a private home, the officer here neither searched nor seized, which are threshold requirements for the Fourth Amendment to apply.

    A is incorrect because by referring to the "requirements" of the plain view doctrine, the answer pre-supposes that the doctrine applies. **B is incorrect** because it conflates "plain view" and "plain sight," and the two are distinct. **D is incorrect** because the plain view doctrine doesn't exist to restrict the police.

83. This question tests on the first requirement for plain view. "It is, of course, an essential predicate to any [claim of plain view] that the officer did not violate the Fourth Amendment in arriving at the place from which the evidence could be plainly viewed." *Horton*, 496 U.S. at 136.

D is correct because it represents the prosecutor's "strongest argument:" due to the caller's consent, the officer was lawfully inside the home and so he viewed the evidence from a "lawful vantage point."

A is incorrect because the caller only consented to the officer's entry into her house, not to the discovery of the marijuana. **B and C are both incorrect** because each claims that the caller lacks standing, and she clearly has standing in her own home.

84. This question also tests on the first requirement under the plain view exception.

B is correct because the warrant only permitted the officer to look for certain items, none of which could fit inside the "small jewelry box." As such, when the officer found the cocaine, he did not view it from a lawful vantage point.

A is incorrect because it is too narrowly worded: the warrant restricted the officers' search within the home, but the warrant would not restrict seizure of evidence found in plain view, assuming the requirements of plain view had been met. **C is incorrect** because, while the warrant authorized the officer to look inside the drawer, the evidence was found in a closed jewelry box inside the drawer. **D is incorrect** because the homeowner's failure to adequately hide the cocaine has nothing to do with the legal requirements of the plain view doctrine.

85. This question tests on the second requirement for plain view, using facts similar to those from *Arizona v. Hicks*, 480 U.S. 321 (1987). That second requirement mandates that the officer not engage in any type of Fourth Amendment "search" to access the evidence. *Id.* at 325 (finding a search occurred where officer moved stereo component to get access to its serial number).

A is correct because it's true: by reaching into the pile to pull out and identify the canvas bags, the officers were engaging in a Fourth Amendment search, *i.e.*, they were interfering with the homeowner's reasonable expectation of privacy (*Katz*) and they were physically intruding on a constitutionally protected area for the purpose of collecting information (*Jones*).

B and C are both incorrect because they are untrue: the officers' entry into the apartment would've been permitted under the exigency exception and the facts indicate that the officers saw the pile of cloth as they were leaving the apartment, and that they didn't postpone their stay. **D is incorrect** because it suggests that officers are bound by the initial report that got them involved in the first place, and real-life is much more dynamic than that.

86. This question also tests on the second requirement for plain view exception.

A is correct because the officer was authorized to conduct a protective sweep of the house, given the woman's threatening statement. *Maryland v. Buie*, 494 U.S. 325 (1990). The lawful protective sweep gave the officer right of access to the kitchen, which is where he found the crack pipe.

B is incorrect because while the woman did threaten the officers, the threat alone does not make the crack pipe admissible. Instead, the threat provides authority for the protective sweep, and the crack pipe is admissible because it was found during a lawful sweep. **C is incorrect** because the presumption against warrantless activity was defeated by the woman's threat, which gave the officer a right to conduct a sweep. **D is incorrect** because the warrantless search was conducted because of the woman's threats, not because of the sleeping dog.

87. This question tests on the second requirement for plain view, using facts similar to those from *Texas v. Brown*, 460 U.S. 730 (1983).

    A is correct because "[i]t is … beyond dispute that [the officer's] action in shining his flashlight to illuminate the interior of [the driver's] car trenched upon no right secured to the latter by the Fourth Amendment." *Id.* at 739–740.

    B is incorrect because the focus of the driver's argument is that the flashlight exposed the shotgun, not that it exposed anything personal about him. **C is incorrect** because it assumes that the search issue is relevant only if it reveals illegal information. However, if the officer had engaged in a Fourth Amendment search to access the shotgun, it wouldn't have been discovered in plain view. **D is incorrect** because the issue of threats to the officer's safety is unrelated to the question of whether the officer found the shotgun in plain view.

88. This question tests on the third requirement for plain view, using facts similar to those in *Stanley v. Georgia*, 394 U.S. 557 (1969). That third requirement dictates that evidence can be seized in plain view only if the officer has probable cause to believe that it is evidence of a crime, *i.e.*, a "fair probability" that certain evidence is evidence of crime. *Illinois v. Gates*, 462 U.S. 213, 239 (1983)

    D is correct because the officer did not have probable cause to believe that the negatives contained impermissible images until he held the negatives up to the light, and plain view requires that the officer have probable cause at the outset.

    A is incorrect because an officer can exceed the scope of a warrant and seize evidence not mentioned in the warrant, assuming the requirements of the plain view exception are met. **B is incorrect** because it would actually hurt the homeowner's suppression claims: by arguing that the evidence belongs to someone else, the homeowner is also tacitly conceding that he doesn't have standing to challenge its seizure. **C is incorrect** because it addresses the weight of the evidence, and the homeowner is challenging the admissibility of the evidence.

89. This question also tests on the third requirement for plain view.

    C is correct because all three requirements of plain view are met here: the officer observed the evidence while conducting a lawful stop, he did not have to search to view it, and he arguably had probable cause to believe the pill bottle contained cocaine.

    A is incorrect for two reasons. First, it misstates the facts: the officer did ask the driver to identify the contents of the bottle, but that doesn't mean that he couldn't identify the contents himself. Second, it suggests that the officer has to know for certain what's in the bottle to seize it, and plain view only requires probable cause. **B is incorrect** because it suggests that the officer was somehow manipulating the evidence to evaluate it, when he was just picking up something that had fallen to the ground. **D is incorrect** because it focuses only on the first requirement for plain view (the officer's lawful vantage point) and the question asks for the court's ruling on the overall suppression issue.

90. This question tests on whether the plain view exception requires that the officer's discovery of evidence be inadvertent, using facts similar to those from *Horton v. California*, 496 U.S. 128 (1990). "[E]ven though inadvertence is a characteristic of most legitimate plain view seizures, it is not a necessary condition." *Id.* at 130.

   D is correct because it properly recognizes that the officer doesn't have to be surprised by the discovery of the evidence for the plain view exception to apply.

   A and B are both incorrect because each suggests that inadvertent discovery is a requirement for plain view, which is wrong. **C is incorrect** for two reasons: the tenant didn't leave the lottery tickets where anyone could see them, and the answer focuses on the *Katz* test for a search when the focus should really be on plain view.

91. This question tests on application of the plain view exception in the context of a typical *Terry* stop and frisk. *See Terry v. Ohio*, 392 U.S. 1 (1969). If, while conducting a proper *Terry* frisk, the officer develops probable cause to believe that he feels a weapon or contraband, the same principles that underlie the plain view exception authorize the officer to retrieve the evidence from the suspect. Otherwise, "resort to a neutral magistrate under such circumstances would often be impracticable and would do little to promote the objectives of the Fourth Amendment." *Minnesota v. Dickerson*, 508 U.S. 366, 375 (1993).

   C is correct because it correctly states the rule from *Terry*, giving appropriate acknowledgement to the plain view principles that apply to a *Terry* stop and frisk.

   A and B are both incorrect because neither accurately recognizes that during the frisk, the officer developed probable cause to believe the man had weapons in his pocket. **D is incorrect** because the man did nothing to indicate that he was a specific threat to the police officer; instead, the man's actions gave the officer reasonable suspicion to believe that he was going to commit a robbery of the jewelry store.

92. This question also tests on the plain view exception in the context of a *Terry* stop and frisk.

   B is correct because the officer knew that there wasn't a weapon in the man's pocket and he also did not have probable cause to believe the cylinder contained contraband until he pulled it out and inspected it. As such, under *Terry*, the officer was not permitted to retrieve the item. *Dickerson*, 508 U.S. at 376 ("[T]he Fourth Amendment's requirement that the officer have probable cause to believe that the item is contraband before seizing it ensures against excessively speculative seizures").

   A is incorrect because the officer did have the requisite suspicion to believe the driver was armed and dangerous; the man's statement — "maybe yes and maybe no"—provided that suspicion. **C is incorrect** because an officer is permitted to order the driver and passengers out of the car during a routine traffic stop, even in the absence of probable cause or reasonable suspicion. *Pennsylvania v. Mimms*, 434 U.S. 106 (1977). **D is incorrect** because *Terry* doesn't require probable cause to frisk; it requires reasonable suspicion.

93. This question tests on extension of the plain view exception to other senses, such as smell. "[I]t has been held that it is no search for a lawfully positioned officer 'with inquisitive nostrils' to detect incriminating odors." Wayne R. LaFave, et al., 2 *Criminal Procedure* §3.2(b) (3d. Ed. 2007 & 2014 Supp.) (plain view doctrine applies to "smell, hearing, and touch").

    C is correct because the all of the requirements for plain view/smell have been met: the officers observed the evidence from a lawful vantage point (a lawful sweep of the house conducted during a warrant-based search); the officers did not search the bags to develop their probable cause (the bags were already emitting an odor of marijuana); and, due to the smell, the officers had probable cause to believe the bags contained marijuana.

    A is incorrect because it states that the plain view doctrine applies only to what an officer sees, and plain view principles also apply to other senses, such as the sense of smell. **B is incorrect** because the officers didn't need to know with absolute certainty what was in the duffel bags, but instead needed probable cause—which they had. **D is incorrect** because the officers did not exceed the scope of the warrant; if the evidence falls within plain view or smell, then the officers can seize it regardless of the warrant.

94. This question tests on the plain view exception in the context of an automobile exception search. Under the automobile exception, police may "search an automobile and the containers within it where they have probable cause to believe contraband or evidence is contained." *California v. Acevedo*, 500 U.S. 565, 580 (1991).

    C is correct because the officer smelled the marijuana smoke in "plain smell," and that smell—together with the woman's reaction to his question—gave him probable cause to search the car for drugs.

    A is incorrect because an officer conducting a traffic stop is not restricted by the reason for the stop, if the situation naturally develops into a different type of inquiry. **B is incorrect** because the officer had probable cause to believe that there were drugs in the car and so was permitted so search the car under the automobile exception. **D is incorrect** because the officer had to search for the evidence found in the car, so it was not discovered in plain view.

95. This question tests on the plain view exception in the context of a search incident to arrest exception. Searches incident to arrest require: (1) a constitutionally lawful arrest; (2) a search conducted relatively contemporaneously with the arrest; and (3) a search limited in scope to the arrestee and areas within her immediate reach. *U.S. v. Robinson*, 414 U.S. 218 (1973); *Chimel v. California*, 395

U.S. 752 (1969). In the context of a search of a car incident to arrest, police may search only when the arrestee is a "recent occupant" of the car, and when the "arrestee is within reaching distance of the vehicle or it is reasonable to believe the vehicle contains evidence of the offense of arrest." *Arizona v. Gant*, 556 U.S. 332, 351 (2009).

C is correct because the officer was permitted to search the car incident to the driver's arrest and he found the weapon in plain view.

A is incorrect because it suggests that the search is unlawful because the expected evidence wasn't found. However, a search is reasonable if it is "justified at its inception, and ... reasonably related in scope to the circumstances which justified the interference in the first place," *Terry*, 392 U.S. at 20—and not whether the "right" evidence was found along the way. **B is incorrect** because the issue is not whether the ownership of the car was discovered in plain view; instead, the issue is whether the weapon was. **D is incorrect** because it is untrue; while some people may have a reduced or non-existent expectation of privacy in certain areas because of their incarceration or the terms of their release, the driver's status as a convicted felon doesn't completely eliminate his expectation of privacy in his car.

Searches Incident to Arrest

96. This question tests on the basic requirements for a search incident to arrest: (1) a constitutionally lawful arrest; (2) a search performed relatively contemporaneously with the arrest; and (3) a search limited in scope to the arrestee and areas within her immediate reach. *E.g., U.S. v. Robinson*, 414 U.S. 218 (1973); *Chimel v. California*, 395 U.S. 752 (1969).

C is correct because it is a correct statement of the search incident to arrest rule.

A is incorrect because, in the non-automobile context, police are not required to have any suspicion in order to conduct a search incident to arrest; instead, the right to search incident to arrest is tied to the right to arrest. **B is incorrect** because there is generally no connection between the right to search and the arresting offense. Instead, in the non-automobile context, courts will look to see whether the three core requirements have been met. **D is incorrect** because it refers to the right to seize evidence, and the question asks about the right to search for that evidence in the first instance.

97. This question tests on the first of the two rationales for searches incident to arrest: officer safety. *E.g., Arizona v. Gant*, 556 U.S. 332, 338 (2009); *Robinson*, 414 U.S. at 234; *Chimel*, 395 U.S. at 763.

B is correct because it provides the "best reason" to allow the search incident to arrest: without a search of the backpack to secure possible weapons, the officer may have been in jeopardy.

A, C, and D are all incorrect. Each presents a true statement: searching the backpack may have yielded all kinds of helpful evidence. But the question asks for the "best reason" for the court to deny the suppression motion, and a reason directly tied to the search incident to arrest exception—which permits the search of the backpack—provides the strongest support for the court's ruling.

98. This question tests on the second of the two rationales for searches incident to arrest: preservation of evidence related to the arresting offense. *E.g., Gant,* 556 U.S. at 338; *Robinson,* 414 U.S. at 234; *Chimel,* 395 U.S. at 763.

   A is correct because it directly refers to one of the rationales for a search incident to arrest and so it will be the "most likely" basis for the court's ruling.

   B is incorrect because "a search is not to be made legal by what it turns up." *U.S. v. Di Re,* 332 U.S. 581, 595 (1948). Instead, "[i]n law [a search] is good or bad when it starts and does not change character from its success." *Id.* **C is incorrect** for two reasons. First, nothing in the facts indicates what the officer "knew" about whether the arrestee had a weapon or not. Second, even if the officer did know that the arrestee was unarmed, a search incident to arrest is more thorough than a frisk conducted pursuant to *Terry v. Ohio,* 392 U.S. 1 (1968). **D is incorrect** because the right to search incident to arrest depends on the exception's requirements being met; outside of the automobile context, there is no connection between the right to search and the nature of the arresting offense.

99. This question tests on the first requirement for a search incident to arrest: a lawful arrest. "When officers have probable cause to believe that a person has committed a crime in their presence, the Fourth Amendment permits them to make an arrest," even if that arrest violates state law. *Virginia v. Moore,* 553 U.S. 164, 178 (2008).

   B is correct because the officer had probable cause to believe the driver had committed a crime, regardless of the fact that state law did not permit the arrest.

   A is incorrect because the good faith exception only applies, if at all, when there has been an unreasonable search or seizure. Here, despite the fact that the arrest was made in violation of state law, it was still based on probable cause and so was a reasonable Fourth Amendment seizure. **C is incorrect** because it doesn't address the issue of whether the evidence should be suppressed or not, and the question asks about suppression. **D is incorrect** because the officer's subjective motivation for the arrest is irrelevant; instead, a court confronted with Fourth Amendment issues should focus solely on objective criteria. *Whren v. U.S.,* 517 U.S. 806, 813 (1996).

100. This question also tests on the first requirement for a search incident to arrest: the requirement that police actually make the arrest. When police issue a citation in lieu of arrest, "the concern for officer safety is not present to the same extent and the concern for destruction or loss of evidence is not present at all." *Knowles v. Iowa,* 525 U.S. 113, 119 (1998). Thus, police may not "search incident to citation." *Id.* at 118.

A is correct because it properly recognizes that the officer was not permitted to search without an arrest.

B is incorrect because it improperly ties an officer's right to search to his belief that he will find evidence during the search, and the issue here is the absence of an arrest. **C is incorrect** because it likewise fails to focus on the issue here: the absence of an arrest. **D is incorrect** because it makes no sense; the right to conduct a search incident to arrest doesn't depend on the health of the person being searched.

101. This question tests on the second requirement for a search incident to arrest: that it be conducted close in time to the arrest. "Searches and seizures that could be made on the spot at the time of arrest may legally be conducted later when the accused arrives at the place of detention." *U.S. v. Edwards*, 415 U.S. 800, 803 (1974).

    C is correct because it focuses on the question of whether the officer acted reasonably under the circumstances. In other words, it is the "most likely" ruling from the court.

    A is incorrect because it refers to suppression on a *per se* basis and "for the most part, *per se* rules are inappropriate in the Fourth Amendment context." *U.S. v. Drayton*, 536 U.S. 194, 201 (2002). **B is incorrect** because it doesn't address the reason for the delay, which is the key to determining whether the delayed search is reasonable or not. **D is incorrect** because the weight of the evidence isn't relevant to the suppression issue; instead, the court should consider whether the seizure of that evidence violated the Fourth Amendment or not.

102. This question tests on the temporal requirement for searches incident to arrest, where there is a delayed search attributable to the police.

    C is correct because it addresses the delay and so represents the "most likely" ruling. Given that the "touchstone of the Fourth Amendment is reasonableness," *Florida v. Jimeno*, 500 U.S. 248, 250 (1991), the prosecutor would have a difficult time defending the officers' actions here as reasonable, when they appear to be negligent instead.

    A and D are both incorrect because each refers to the rationales for searches incident to arrest, and neither addresses the reason for the delay. **B is incorrect** because it improperly suggests that a search incident to arrest will always be reasonable, no matter how long the search is delayed or the reason for the delay.

103. This question tests on a delayed search incident to arrest, but where the delay is attributable to the arrestee.

    C is correct because it acknowledges the delay and provides an explanation for the delay, which would provide the prosecutor with the "strongest argument."

    A and B are both incorrect because each incorrectly links the right to search incident to arrest to suspicion and neither addresses the delay issue presented by the facts. **D is incorrect** because the facts don't indicate that the officer was trying to help the doctor, and because trying to assist with a medical issue isn't the "strongest" legal argument on these facts.

104. This question also tests on a delayed search incident to arrest, but where no one is really at fault for the delay.

A is correct because it provides the "most likely" ruling: that the second search incident to arrest was conducted be a female officer in order to best respect the driver's privacy. In other words, the search was conducted as reasonably as possible.

B is incorrect because it's not the "most likely" ruling as it doesn't address the steps taken by the officer to respect the driver's privacy. Instead, the answer says that the search was reasonable because it was reasonable. **C is incorrect** because the Supreme Court has never imposed such a restriction in the search incident to arrest context. **D is incorrect** because it places an improper limit on the proper scope of a search incident to arrest.

105. This question tests on the third requirement for a search incident to arrest: that the scope of the search be limited to the areas where an arrestee "might reach." *Cupp v. Murphy*, 412 U.S. 291, 295 (1973). This assessment requires a careful review of the facts of the case, with recognition that "the scope of a warrantless search must be commensurate with the rationale that excepts the search from the warrant requirement" in the first place. *Id.*

D is correct because the facts indicate that the man was close to his backpack at the time of the search. As such, it's possible that he could have lunged for a weapon hidden inside.

A is incorrect because the backpack was within the man's reaching area at the time of the search and so the search of the backpack didn't exceed the scope of a proper search incident to arrest. **C and D are both incorrect** because abandonment of property and consent to search are both irrelevant to the scope of a proper search incident to arrest.

106. This question tests on the right to search the passenger compartment of an arrestee's car incident to arrest. Police may conduct such searches, but only when the arrestee is a "recent occupant" of the car, and when the "arrestee is within reaching distance of the vehicle or it is reasonable to believe the vehicle contains evidence of the offense of arrest." *Gant*, 556 U.S. at 351. "[A]n arrestee's status as a 'recent occupant' may turn on his temporal or spatial relationship to the car at the time of the arrest and search … it certainly does not turn on whether he was inside or outside the car at the moment that the officer first initiated contact with him." *Thornton v. U.S.*, 541 U.S. 615, 622 (2004).

D is correct because it accurately identifies the arrestee's legal status as a "recent occupant" of the car.

A is incorrect because it doesn't address the driver's legal status as a "recent occupant"—the focus of the question. The driver was arrested two blocks away from his car, but he also had just left the car. **B is incorrect** because it addresses the weight of the evidence, and not its admissibility. **C is incorrect** because it does not address the Fourth Amendment issues presented by these facts.

107. This question tests on the "recent occupant" requirement from *Gant*. Although the Supreme Court has not fully defined what a "recent occupant" is, the phrase implies that the arrestee has had some level of occupancy in the car shortly before the arrest.

    D is correct because there are no facts here that the arrestee had occupied her car (recently or otherwise); instead the facts indicate that the arrestee was approaching the car so that she could occupy it in future.

    A and C are both incorrect because each pre-supposes that the search was lawful, which assumes that the woman was a recent occupant of her car—and she wasn't. **B is incorrect** because it refers to the weight of the evidence found in the car, and not its admissibility.

108. This question tests on the two rationales for searches incident to arrest—officer safety and preservation of evidence of crime—as they apply in the context of car searches. One of these rationales must be present when an officer searches the car of a "recent occupant" incident to arrest. *Gant*, 556 U.S. at 351.

    C is correct because it recognizes that neither rationale for a search incident to arrest is present on these facts.

    A and B are both incorrect because each refers to only one of the rationales for a search incident to arrest, and so neither provides the "most likely" reason for the judge's ruling. Instead, the "most likely" reason would be one that speaks to both rationales. **D is incorrect** because it doesn't respond to the question, and fails to recognize that the arrest was supported by probable cause.

109. This question tests on the scope of a search of a car incident to arrest. "When a policeman has made a lawful custodial arrest of the occupant of an automobile, he may ... search the passenger compartment of that automobile.... [and] examine the contents of any containers found within the passenger compartment...." *New York v. Belton*, 453 U.S. 454, 460 (1981).

    A is correct because searches of cars incident to arrest are restricted to the passenger compartment of the car, and—unless some other exception applies—cannot be extended to the trunk.

    B, C, and D are all incorrect because the problem here is that the search exceeded the proper scope of a search incident to arrest—not that the drug dealer acted in a way that would have permitted a search of the trunk, or that the officer needed suspicion to search the trunk.

110. This question tests on the right to search the passenger compartment of an arrestee's car incident to arrest. Police may conduct such searches, but only when the arrestee is a "recent occupant" of the car and when the "arrestee is within

reaching distance of the vehicle or it is reasonable to believe the vehicle contains evidence of the offense of arrest." *Gant*, 556 U.S. at 351.

C is correct because while the woman was a recent occupant of her car, neither of *Gant's* two conditions are met: she could not access her car from the back of the locked police cruiser, and the officer didn't have any reason to believe that evidence of the arresting offense would be in the car.

A, B, and D are all incorrect because none presents the "strongest defense argument."

111. This question also tests on the right to search the passenger compartment of an arrestee's car incident to arrest.

A is correct because it provides the "strongest argument" for the prosecutor: the ex-husband was a "recent occupant" of his car and could have reached for the gun in his car.

B and D are each incorrect because there is nothing in the fact pattern to indicate the ex-husband had either threatened the officers or was about to do so. Moreover, an actual threat is not required under *Gant*. **C is incorrect** because it ties the right to search incident to arrest to the commission of a particular type of offense. While police must make a lawful arrest in order to a search incident to arrest, the arrest doesn't have to be for any particular type of crime.

112. Like the previous two questions, this question tests on the right to search the passenger compartment of an arrestee's car incident to arrest.

D is correct because *Gant* permits searches incident to arrest when "it is reasonable to believe the vehicle contains evidence of the offense of arrest." *Id.*, 556 U.S. at 351. Here, the officer witnessed the drug dealer selling drugs from the van and then arrested him. Together, these facts support a "reasonable belief" that the officer would find additional drugs in the van.

A is incorrect because it's untrue: the officer witnessed a drug sale from the van and so he has reason to believe additional drugs would be found in the van. **B is incorrect** because the officer's failure to arrest the buyer has no bearing on the right to search the van incident to arrest. **C is incorrect** because *Gant* ties the right to search to the arresting offense, and not just what an officer witnesses.

113. This question tests on *Gant's* "reasonable to believe" standard. *Id.* at 351. Although the *Gant* Court never defined "reasonable to believe," that standard necessarily has to be less than probable cause; otherwise, *Gant* searches would become automobile exception searches. *E.g., U.S. v. Vinton*, 594 F.3d 14, 25 (D.C. Cir. 2010).

C is correct because it is the "strongest defense argument in support of suppression:" if the officer has no suspicion that evidence of the arresting offense (forgery) could be found in the car, the car can't be searched incident to arrest.

A is incorrect because it equates "reasonable to believe" with probable cause. **B is incorrect** because it equates the right to search incident to arrest with an actual threat. **D is incorrect** because the arrestee was under control at the time of the search, so if the search is permissible, it will have to be because it was reasonable to believe that evidence of the arresting offense could be found in the car.

114. Like the previous question, this question tests on the meaning of *Gant's* phrase, "reasonable to believe."

    D is correct because it equates "reasonable to believe" with "reasonable suspicion."

    A, B, and C are all incorrect because each provides an implausible definition for "reasonable to believe:" a correct guess, no suspicion, and probable cause, respectively.

115. This question tests on the proper scope of a search of a car incident to arrest. Such searches, even after *Gant,* are limited to the passenger compartment of the car and the closed containers located therein. *Id.* at 351.

    C is correct because if *Gant's* requirements are met and the officer is permitted to search the passenger compartment of the car, he may also search closed containers in the passenger compartment.

    A is incorrect because is artificially divides searches into permissible "brief glimpses" and impermissible "extensive searches" — something the Supreme Court has not done. *E.g., Arizona v. Hicks,* 480 U.S. 321, 325 (1987) ("[a] search is a search. . . ."). **B is incorrect** because the question asks about the right to search and not the evidence that was eventually discovered. **D is incorrect** because it is too broadly worded; assuming an officer may search a car incident to arrest, the search is restricted to the passenger compartment of the car.

Terry Stop and Frisk

116. The question tests on the core requirements of a *Terry* stop and frisk. *Terry v. Ohio,* 392 U.S. 1 (1968). Under *Terry,* police may briefly "stop" (seize) a person if they have reasonable suspicion that the person is involved in criminal activity. *Terry* also permits a "frisk" (search) of the exterior of the suspect's clothes for weapons, assuming the officer has reasonable suspicion that the person is "armed and presently dangerous." *Id.* at 24.

    D is correct because it best states the rule from *Terry,* as applied to these facts: the officer saw the man acting suspiciously and in a way that is consistent with someone who is about to rob a bank. The officer's observations provided him with reasonable suspicion to investigate further, which he did.

    A and C are both incorrect because *Terry* requires reasonable suspicion and both answers refer to probable cause. **B is incorrect** because *Terry* does not require the officer to know when a future crime might occur, only that he have reasonable suspicion "in light of his experience that criminal activity may be afoot." *Id.* at 30.

117. This question tests on the level of suspicion required to stop and/or frisk: reasonable suspicion. Reasonable suspicion "is considerably less than proof of wrongdoing by a preponderance of the evidence," and is "obviously less" than probable cause. *U.S. v. Sokolow*, 490 U.S. 1, 7 (1989). At the same time however, the officer "must be able to articulate something more than an "inchoate and unparticularized suspicion or hunch." *Id.* at 15.

    A is correct because the officer's inability to articulate the reasons why he found the man suspicious shows that he only had a hunch that the man was involved in criminal activity.

    B is incorrect for two reasons. First, the facts show that the officer's actions were based on more than dislike for the man; the problem is that the officer could not adequately articulate those reasons. Second, "[s]ubjective intentions play no role in ordinary, probable cause Fourth Amendment analysis." *Whren v. U.S.*, 517 U.S. 806, 813 (1996). **C and D are both incorrect** because "not fitting in" and "seeming strange" do not add up to reasonable suspicion unless the officer can articulate objective reasons for his concern.

118. This question tests on what should be considered in the reasonable suspicion assessment. When evaluating whether that standard has been met, a court should not assess facts in isolation; instead, a court "must look at the totality of the circumstances of each case to see whether the detaining officer has a particularized and objective basis for suspecting legal wrongdoing." *U.S. v. Arvizu*, 534 U.S. 266, 273 (2001).

    D is correct because it provides the correct standard for assessing reasonable suspicion: the totality of the circumstances.

    A, B, and C are all incorrect because each addresses only one fact in isolation, not all the facts together.

119. This question tests on reasonable suspicion using the facts of *Illinois v. Wardlow*, 528 U.S. 119 (1999). In that case, the Supreme Court held that "headlong flight" from police in a "high crime neighborhood" forms reasonable suspicion for a *Terry* stop.

    D is correct because it re-states the holding from *Wardlow* on materially indistinguishable facts.

    A is incorrect because it is incomplete: while the *Wardlow* Court acknowledged that mere presence in a "high crime area" isn't enough to form reasonable suspicion, *id.* at 124, the suspect here also acknowledged the police presence and then ran. According to *Wardlow*, that additional fact is essential. **B is incorrect** because it doesn't answer the question: running might be a "sensible choice," but that doesn't mean the officer wouldn't have reasonable suspicion. **C s incorrect** because there's nothing in the facts to suggest why the men were huddled together—maybe they were huddled together against the wind and cold, or maybe they were just talking. Without additional facts and reasonable inferences from those facts, the officers would not have reasonable suspicion.

120. This question tests on reasonable suspicion, using the relevant facts of *Sibron v. New York*, 392 U.S. 40 (1967), the companion case to *Terry*. In *Sibron*, the Supreme Court held that speaking with known drug users—without more—does not equate to reasonable suspicion: "[t]he inference that persons who talk to narcotics addicts are engaged in the criminal traffic in narcotics is simply not the sort of reasonable inference required to support an intrusion by the police upon an individual's personal security." *Id.* at 62.

     C is correct because the officer here only observed the CI speaking to known heroin addicts—nothing more. The officer didn't see the CI exchange or use drugs or do anything to remotely suggest that he was presently involved in any sort of criminal activity.

     A is incorrect because it focuses on the right to frisk and the CI's "strongest argument" is that the officer didn't have the right to stop him in the first place. B and D are both incorrect because each answer pre-supposes that the officer had the right to stop the CI, and he didn't. *Id.* at 268.

121. This question tests on reasonable suspicion, using facts derived from of *Florida v. J.L.*, 529 U.S. 266 (2000). In *J.L.*, the Supreme Court held that "an anonymous tip that a person is carrying a gun…, without more" is insufficient for reasonable suspicion.

     D is correct because the officer lacked reasonable suspicion to believe the woman was involved in any criminal activity. Most of the information from the tip could've been observed by anyone at the coffee shop and the allegation that the woman had an illegal weapon—without more—is not enough to establish reasonable suspicion.

     A is incorrect because it's untrue: the officer was able to corroborate the tip, at least in the sense that he found a woman who matched the physical description provided by the tipster. B is incorrect because it pre-supposes that the officer had the right to stop the woman in the first place, and he didn't. C is incorrect because the officer doesn't need to identify the anonymous tipster for a *Terry* stop; instead, he only needs reasonable suspicion.

122. The question tests on the basic right to stop (seize) a person under *Terry*, which is distinct from the right to frisk (search) the person. *Terry* permits a brief seizure, short of arrest, when the officer has reasonable suspicion to believe that "criminal activity may be afoot." *Id.*, 392 U.S. at 30.

     B is correct because it the threshold legal requirement for a *Terry* stop—reasonable suspicion—was not present on these facts. Instead, the officer only saw two men exchanging something that he admittedly could not identify.

     A, C, and D are all incorrect because each provides a factual reason why the officer may have lacked reasonable suspicion, *i.e.*, that the officer didn't witness a drug sale or drug use. While these factual reasons are relevant in determining whether the officer had the right to stop, the question asks for the "strongest legal argument."

123. This question tests on the proper duration of a *Terry* stop. Although there is no set time limit, a *Terry* stop is supposed to be brief—just long enough to "confirm or dispel" the officer's suspicion. *U.S. v. Sharpe*, 470 U.S. 675, 686 (1985).

C **is correct** because the stop here lasted as long as was necessary for the officers to become convinced that the woman was safe and that a crime hadn't been committed.

A **is incorrect** because it doesn't respond to the question: the father is complaining about the duration of the stop and not the right to stop in the first instance. **B and D are both incorrect** because each addresses fault for the duration of the stop. Although relative fault can be relevant when addressing extended stops, this 10-minute stop did not last so long that fault might become an issue.

124. This question tests on the proper duration of a *Terry* stop and when such a stop becomes a *de facto* arrest. The answer requires an examination of the facts to determine whether the restraints placed on the suspect's liberty were the equivalent of those associated with a formal arrest, whether the suspect was moved from a public to a private area, or whether the police diligently pursued their investigation. *Dunaway v. New York*, 442 U.S. 200 (1979) (suspect transported to police station); *Florida v. Royer*, 460 U.S. 491 (1983) (suspect moved from public area to private room); *U.S. v. Sharpe*, 470 U.S. 675 (1985) (officers acted diligently despite prolonged stop).

A **is correct** because it accurately describes why the traffic stop was extended: because the suspect wouldn't get off the phone and not because the officer wasn't diligent in his efforts.

B **is incorrect** because the Supreme Court has never set a presumptive time limit on a *Terry* stop. C **is incorrect** because it's non-legal and the question asks for the prosecutor's "best argument" in response to the driver's legal argument. D **is incorrect** because it overstates the officer's legal authority under *Terry*.

125. This question also tests on the proper duration of a *Terry* stop, using facts derived from *Rodriguez v. U.S.*, 135 S. Ct. 1609 (2015). In this question, the duration of the stop is extended by the officer, and not the suspect. Under *Terry*, the stop is supposed to last long enough "confirm or dispel" the officer's suspicion. *Sharpe*, 470 U.S. at 686. In the context of a traffic stop, that means that the officer's authority to detain the driver ends when the purpose of the stop—issuance of a warning or traffic ticket—has been accomplished. *Rodriguez*, 135 S. Ct. at 1609.

D **is correct** because it is the woman's "strongest argument:" that the officer impermissibly prolonged the *Terry* stop by making her wait for the dog, and the cocaine is a fruit of that unlawful seizure.

A, B, and C are all incorrect because each addresses—in a different way—the right to search the trunk after the K-9 unit arrived at the scene. However, the question asks for the young woman's "strongest argument," which is that the officer extended the stop without proper authority, and that she should have been permitted to leave ten minutes earlier.

126. This question tests on the proper limits of a *Terry* stop and whether an officer's movement of a suspect from a public area to a secluded area will convert the stop into a *de facto* arrest. In at least one case, the Supreme Court has noted that such movement will be a factor in assessing whether the *Terry* stop has become an arrest. *Florida v. Royer*, 460 U.S. 491 (1983).

B is correct because it recognizes that the nature of the woman's seizure changed when she was moved from the bar (a public area) to the manager's officer (a private area) and kept there for 20 minutes.

A is incorrect because it improperly ties the *Terry* stop to the amount of noise in the bar area. **C and D are both incorrect** because each speaks to the officer's motivations for moving the young woman. However, an officer's subjective motivations are irrelevant in the Fourth Amendment context; courts should examine objective criteria only. *E.g., Whren v. U.S.*, 517 U.S. 806, 813 (1996).

127. This question tests on the proper scope of questioning during a *Terry* stop. The Supreme Court has not directly addressed this issue, but has cautioned that *Terry* stops are to be brief in duration, *i.e.*, long enough to "confirm or dispel" the officer's suspicion. *Sharpe*, 470 U.S. at 686. With that said, human interactions are dynamic and not static, and so—as long as *Terry's* other requirements are met—an officer's questioning may reasonably deviate from the initial reason from the stop.

C is correct because the officer here complied with *Terry's* requirements and so there's no basis for suppression.

A is incorrect because an officer can legitimately ask about an issue unrelated to the stop, assuming the initial stop was valid. **B is incorrect** because we expect the officer's questions be designed to get the information he needs; that's why he's asking the questions in the first place. **D is incorrect** because it only addresses the reason for the initial stop, and the man is challenging the events that occurred after he was stopped.

128. This question tests on whether *Miranda* warnings are required for routine *Terry* stops. "The comparatively nonthreatening character of [Terry stops] explains the absence of any suggestion in our opinions that *Terry* stops are subject to the dictates of *Miranda*." *Berkemer v. McCarty*, 468 U.S. 420, 440 (1984).

D is correct because, as a correct statement of law, it is the prosecutor's "strongest argument" in response to the motion to suppress.

A is incorrect because it's untrue: *Miranda* warnings can be required for "preliminary, investigative questions," assuming the suspect is subjected to custodial interrogation. *Miranda v. Arizona*, 384 U.S. 436 (1966). **B and C are both incorrect** because each sets forth a faulty basis for when *Miranda* warnings are required—the status of the suspect as a juvenile or the number of suspects the officer is questioning, respectively.

129. This question tests on when an officer may frisk a suspect. Frisks may only be performed when the officer has reasonable suspicion that the suspect is "armed and presently dangerous." *Terry*, 392 U.S. at 24.

B is correct because the officer admitted that he lacked reasonable suspicion that the man was armed and presently dangerous; instead, the officer's testimony explains that he just made an assumption.

A is incorrect because the officer's classification of the man as a "drug dealer" doesn't address the right to frisk the man. **B is incorrect** because *Terry* does not permit "automatic" searches, but only those based on the appropriate suspicion. **D is incorrect** because the reasoning is backwards: it assumes that since the officer found a weapon, the search was valid. But "a search is not to be made legal by what it turns up. In law it is good or bad when it starts and does not change character from its success." *U.S. v. Di Re*, 322 U.S. 581, 595 (1948).

130. This question also tests on when an officer may frisk a suspect.

C is correct because the officer only had reasonable suspicion to believe the teenager was engaged in underage drinking, not that he was armed and dangerous.

A is incorrect because it speaks to the right to "approach" the teenager, and an officer can always approach a person on the street. It's only when the officer's actions are classified as a "search" or "seizure" that the Fourth Amendment is at issue. **B is incorrect** because it doesn't address the frisk, which is the issue here. **D is incorrect** because the right to frisk depends on suspicion of weapons, and not necessarily on the type of crime suspected.

131. Like the previous two questions, this question also tests on when an officer may frisk a suspect.

C is correct because it states the correct rule for frisks under *Terry*.

A and B are both incorrect because each refers to the probable cause standard and *Terry* frisks only require reasonable suspicion. **D is incorrect** because *Terry* only permits a frisk if the officer believes that the suspect is armed and dangerous, and not just that he is about to commit a crime.

132. This question tests on the proper scope of a *Terry* frisk. Under *Terry*, if an officer has reasonable suspicion to believe that a suspect is armed and dangerous, he may "conduct a patdown search to determine whether the person is in fact carrying a weapon." *Terry*, 392 U.S. at 24. "The purpose of this limited search is not to discover evidence of crime, but to allow the officer to pursue his investigation without fear of violence...." *Adams v. Williams*, 407 U.S. 143, 146 (1972). Despite this limitation, an officer conducting an otherwise lawful *Terry* frisk may seize evidence that he legitimately discovers along the way. *Minnesota v. Dickerson*, 508 U.S. 366, 375 (1993).

C is correct because it recognizes the officer's right to seize evidence he legitimately discovers while conducting a lawful *Terry* frisk.

A is incorrect because it doesn't address the facts of what happened here: that, during a lawful frisk, the officer "recognized" that the suspect had other evidence of crime. **B is incorrect** because the officer discovered the ammunition before he discovered the weapon; nothing in *Terry* requires that the officer stop the frisk with the first piece of evidence he discovers. **D is incorrect** because a *Terry* frisk is lawful only if the officer has reasonable suspicion at the outset, not if he develops that suspicion while in the middle of the frisk.

133. This question also tests on the proper scope of a *Terry* frisk and whether an officer may manipulate an item he feels during an otherwise lawful frisk, in order to identify that item. If the incriminating nature of the item is not readily apparent to the officer, he may not engage in further search activity—beyond the *Terry* frisk—to develop his suspicion. *Dickerson*, 508 U.S. at 379.

     A is correct because the officer "used her fingers to slide the lumps back and forth"—*i.e.*, to manipulate what she felt to develop her probable cause—and *Terry* only permits an open-handed frisk for weapons.

     B is incorrect because it doesn't fully address what happened here: the officer "felt" the lumps during the frisk, but she also manipulated the lumps because she didn't know what they were. **C and D are both incorrect** because *Terry* frisks are for weapons and not for other forms of evidence. If an officer suspects a person is carrying something other than a weapon, then she must rely on other Fourth Amendment exceptions to discover and seize that other evidence.

134. This question tests on the extension of *Terry* frisks to cars. Such frisks are permitted if the officer has reasonable suspicion to believe that "the suspect is dangerous and the suspect may gain immediate control of weapons" within the passenger compartment of a car. *Michigan v. Long*, 463 U.S. 1032, 1048–1049 (1983).

     D is correct because it refers to the correct legal standard required for the frisk: reasonable suspicion.

     A is incorrect because it is an incorrect statement of law: *Long* permits frisks of cars under certain circumstances. **B is incorrect** because the officer is not required to be certain, but is instead required to have reasonable suspicion. **C is incorrect** because it overstates the officer's authority by referring to what the officer can "always" do.

135. This question tests on the proper scope of a *Terry* frisk of a car. Such a frisk is restricted to the "passenger compartment of an automobile, limited to those areas in which a weapon may be placed or hidden ..." *Long*, 463 U.S. at 1049.

     B is correct because it properly recognizes that the scope of a car frisk is restricted to the car's passenger compartment.

A, B, and D are all incorrect because each suggests that an officer can conduct a *Terry* frisk of the trunk of a car, and he cannot. Instead, the frisk is restricted to the passenger compartment.

Protective Sweeps

136. This question tests on *Buie* protective sweeps, which are limited warrantless searches for dangerous individuals, present at the scene of an in-home arrest. *Maryland v. Buie*, 494 U.S. 325 (1990). To conduct a protective sweep, "there must be articulable facts which, taken together with the rational inferences from those facts, would warrant a reasonably prudent officer in believing that the area to be swept harbors an individual posing a danger to those on the arrest scene." *Id.* at 327.

    C is correct because it presents the "strongest argument" for the sweep: the officer thought someone inside the house posed a danger.

    A and B are both incorrect because each exclusively ties the right to conduct a protective sweep to past events, *i.e.*, fraternity hazing and the arresting offense. To the extent that past events have relevance, it is because they inform the officer's present concern that someone inside the house poses a present danger to those at the scene. **D is incorrect** because there are no facts that indicate that anyone in the fraternity house was acting "rowdy" at the time of the arrest.

137. This question tests on the level of suspicion required for a *Buie* sweep: reasonable articulable suspicion, which is the same level of suspicion required to conduct a stop and frisk under *Terry v. Ohio*, 392 U.S. 1 (1969). *Buie*, 494 U.S. at 327.

    C is correct because it refers to the proper level of suspicion for a *Buie* sweep: reasonable articulable suspicion.

    A is incorrect because it incorrectly ties the right to conduct the sweep to the arresting offense; *Buie* sweeps are permitted when the officer has reasonable suspicion that someone poses a danger to those on the arrest scene—regardless of the arresting offense. **B is incorrect** because it refers to the probable cause standard, and a *Buie* sweep requires reasonable suspicion. **D is incorrect** because protective sweeps are permitted when officers face a threat from third parties, not the arrestee.

138. This question also tests on the level of suspicion required for a *Buie* sweep.

    A is correct because nothing in the facts remotely suggests that the officers faced a threat from a third party—or even that there was anyone else in the house aside from the officers and the arrestee.

    B and D are both incorrect because each places the focus on threats from the arrestee, and *Buie* sweeps are to protect from danger from third parties. **C is incorrect** because the sweep is permitted if the facts suggest a present danger from third parties, and the man's criminal record—alone—did not.

139. This question tests on the proper scope of a *Buie* sweep. *Buie* sweeps are not searches for evidence, they are searches for people: "individuals posing a danger to those on the arrest scene." *Id.* at 327.

    B is correct because the sweep was unreasonable for two reasons: the officers had no suspicion of a threat from third parties and the officers searched for evidence, and not people.

    A and D are both incorrect because each pre-supposes that the sweep would have been reasonable if the man had threatened the officers. But, even if the man had made a threat to the officers, *Buie* only permits a search for third parties who pose a threat. **C is incorrect** because it improperly suggests that the officer had a valid reason to search and that the only problem with the sweep was with its scope.

140. Like the previous question, this question also tests on the proper scope of a *Buie* protective sweep.

    B is correct because the officer exceeded the proper scope of the sweep when he looked in a place—the kitchen drawers—where a person cannot reasonably hide.

    A is incorrect because, under these circumstances, the officer had the authority to conduct the protective sweep: the officers heard strange noises coming from inside the house and the arrestee's statement gave the officers reasonable suspicion to believe the noises were coming from a person who posed a threat to them. **C is incorrect** because it doesn't address where in the kitchen the officer searched. **D is incorrect** because the officers only had a warrant for the man's arrest, and not a search warrant for his house.

141. This questions tests on the application of the plain view doctrine within the scope of a *Buie* sweep. There is "no dispute" that if officers are conducting a lawful *Buie* sweep they may seize evidence that they find in plain view. *Id.*, 494 U.S. at 330.

    A is correct because it represents the "most likely" ruling from the court: that since the officer had the authority to enter the garage under *Buie*, he was in a "lawful vantage point" to view the cocaine-related evidence.

    B is incorrect because it suggests that the officers needed—and had—probable cause to search the garage. **C and D are both incorrect** because each ignores the plain view issue and suggests scope problems where there are none.

142. This question tests on some of the differences between *Buie* sweeps, searches incident to arrest, and *Terry* frisks.

    B is correct because the officers had the right to search the woman incident to arrest, but did not have any suspicion that a dangerous person was hiding in her home and so were not permitted to expand the scope of their search to include a *Buie* sweep.

    A is incorrect because it suggests that the scope of a *Buie* sweep—like the scope of a search incident to arrest—is tied to the "reach" of the arrestee. It is not; instead, the scope of a *Buie* sweep is restricted to areas where a dangerous person at the arrest scene might be hiding. **C is incorrect** because, regardless of the arresting offense, the officers had the right—at the very least—to search the woman incident to arrest. **D is incorrect** because it confuses the right to search incident to arrest with the right to conduct a *Terry* frisk.

143. This question tests on extension of *Buie* sweeps into non-residential settings. Although the *Buie* Court never expressly restricted its holding to residential arrests, much of the Court's reasoning depends on a residential arrest. Still, to apply *Buie*'s holding to non-residential settings, police would need some suspicion that the "area to be swept harbors an individual posing a danger to those on the arrest scene." *Buie*, 494 U.S. at 327.

    A is correct because *Buie* arguably doesn't apply in non-residential settings and even if it did, the officer had no reasonable concern of danger. Instead, all he heard was "loud music."

    B is incorrect because it doesn't respond to the question, which asks about the right to conduct a protective sweep. **C and D are both incorrect** because, even if *Buie* sweeps are permitted in non-residential settings, the officer had no reason to fear third parties. Instead, all he heard was "loud music."

144. This question tests on extension of *Buie* into situations where an arrest occurs directly outside the house. Although the Supreme Court has not yet considered this question, "virtually all" of the circuit courts of appeal "have recognized that the *Buie* protective sweep doctrine applies to an arrest occurring just outside a residence." *U.S. v. Jones*, 667 F.3d 477, 485 n.10 (4th Cir. 2012) (collecting cases).

    A is correct because it gives the "strongest argument" for extending *Buie*, especially relative to the other answers: two distraught women had already come out of the house and the officers had to work to restrain them. Arguably, this gave the officers reasonable suspicion to believe that more equally angry people might come out of the house.

    B is incorrect because the curtilage of the home, while protected under the Fourth Amendment, is still not the same as the home. **C is incorrect** because the plain view exception only applies if the officer is lawfully inside the house. **D is incorrect** because it makes no sense.

145. This question also tests on the extension of *Buie* to a situation where the officers are legitimately on the premises—but not to arrest—when the other requirements of *Buie* have been met. The Supreme Court has not addressed this situation, but at least seven circuit courts of appeal "have refused to confine the protective sweep doctrine to contexts in which officers execute arrest warrants." *U.S. v. Miller*, 430 F.3d 93, 99 (2nd Cir. 2005) (citing cases). "Although an arrest may be highly relevant to the determination of whether officers possess reasonable suspicion of danger..., the effectuation of an arrest, regardless of whether pursuant to a warrant, is not the *sine qua non* of a permissible protective sweep." *Id.*

A is correct because—as the answer most closely aligned with the requirements of *Buie*—it represents the prosecutor's "best argument."

B is incorrect because it doesn't address the officer's suspicion that the husband was about to grab a weapon; if *Buie* is to be extended to non-warrant situations, it's most likely that a court would still require the officer to have suspicion that the area swept harbors a dangerous person. **C is incorrect** because the wife did not give consent—express or implied—for a full search of the house. At most, she consented to the officers' entry into the house. **D is incorrect** because the handgun was found before the arrest and not as part of a search incident to arrest.

Automobile Exception Searches

146. This question tests on the automobile exception, under which police may "search an automobile and the containers within it where they have probable cause to believe contraband or evidence is contained." *California v. Acevedo*, 500 U.S. 565, 580 (1991).

     A is correct because, as a basic restatement of the automobile exception rule, it is the "most likely" ruling from the court.

     B and D are both incorrect because each suggests that the officer can only search if there is probable cause and some additional exigency. Instead, all that is required is probable cause. **C is incorrect** because an officer's ability to obtain a search warrant is irrelevant; the automobile exception instead focuses on whether or not there is probable cause to support the search.

147. This question tests on the original rationale for the automobile exception: the ready mobility of automobiles. "[T]he circumstances that furnish probable cause to search a particular auto for particular articles are most often unforeseeable; moreover, the opportunity to search is fleeting since a car is readily movable." *Chambers v. Maroney*, 399 U.S. 42, 50–51 (1970).

     A is correct because it directly addresses the mobility rationale.

     B, C, and D are all incorrect because each asserts a specific reason why, in this case, the officer did not have to get a search warrant. The automobile exception authorizes warrantless searches of automobiles without delving into case-specific facts.

148. This question tests on a second, later-articulated rationale for the automobile exception: the reduced expectation of privacy in cars. "One has a lesser expectation of privacy in a motor vehicle because its function is transportation and it seldom serves as one's residence or as the repository of personal effects. A car has little capacity for escaping public scrutiny. It travels public thoroughfares where its occupants and its contents are in plain view." *Cardwell v. Lewis*, 417 U.S. 583, 590 (1974) (plurality opinion).

B is correct because it directly addresses the expectation of privacy rationale.

A is incorrect because drivers have some expectation of privacy in their cars, just less than they do in their homes. **C is incorrect** because the Supreme Court treats all cars equally, and does not consider case-by-case arguments about individual circumstances. **D is incorrect** because the relevant expectation of privacy here is the between the driver and his automobile, not the driver and his drugs.

149. This question tests on the definition of an "automobile," using the facts from *California v. Carney*, 471 U.S. 386 (1985). "[A]pplication of the vehicle exception has never turned on the other uses to which a vehicle might be put. The exception has historically turned on the ready mobility of the vehicle, and on the presence of the vehicle in a setting that objectively indicates that the vehicle is being used for transportation." *Id.* at 394.

     C is correct because it properly recognizes that a motor home is considered an automobile under the Fourth Amendment, not a home.

     A is incorrect because it ignores the fact that the motor home was capable of being driven away. **B is incorrect** because even though it was parked, the motor home was "obviously readily mobile by the turn of an ignition key." *Id.* at 393. **D is incorrect** because it is policy-based, and so does not represent the "most likely" ruling—especially if there is a better answer to select.

150. This question tests on level of suspicion required for an automobile exception search. Assuming an officer has probable cause, he may search the "automobile and the containers within it where they have probable cause to believe contraband or evidence is contained." *Acevedo*, 500 U.S. at 580.

     D is correct because nothing in these facts suggests that the officer would find evidence in the car. Instead, the officer believed that the woman had lied to him about how much wine she had consumed, and the only evidence to support that was the receipt—which the woman had already given him.

     A and B are both incorrect for the same reason: the woman's lie gave the officer suspicion that she had consumed more alcohol than she originally claimed, not that there would be evidence within the car. **C is incorrect** because it states the wrong standard for an automobile exception search. Such searches are permitted if the officer has probable cause, not reasonable suspicion.

151. This question tests on the scope of an automobile exception search, which is restricted only by the officer's probable cause. *Acevedo*, 500 U.S. at 580.

     B is correct because the driver's "strongest argument" is that the officer exceeded the scope of his probable cause when he searched the trunk, because his probable cause was limited to the glove box.

     A is incorrect because the driver's admissions gave the officer probable cause to believe that the car contained an unlicensed weapon. **C is incorrect** because the officer doesn't need consent to search a car if he has probable cause. **D is**

incorrect because automobile exception searches do not require proof of danger; they require probable cause.

152. This question also tests on the scope of an automobile exception search. In this question, the officer's probable cause is directed toward the car generally—and is not restricted to one specific area of the car—which means that he is permitted to search the entire car. *Acevedo*, 500 U.S. at 580.

    C is correct because it correctly recognizes that the scope of a permissible automobile exception is tied to the officer's probable cause.

    A is incorrect because it improperly focuses on the evidence that was seized, and not the area that was searched. **B is incorrect** since the officer's probable cause extended to the area under the driver's seat because the young man sat in that seat before and after making drug sales. **D is incorrect** because the officer's reliance on the anonymous tip is irrelevant as long as the search is supported by probable cause and is properly restricted in scope.

153. This question tests on how the automobile exception treats closed containers within cars. While at one time the Supreme Court required police to get a warrant to search a closed container within a car—assuming the officer's probable cause was limited to the closed container—that rule has been eliminated. Now, "police may search an automobile and the containers within it where they have probable cause to believe contraband or evidence is contained." *Acevedo*, 500 U.S. at 580.

    D is correct because it is a correct statement of the law: the officer had probable cause to search the suitcase, the suitcase was in the car, and so the officer was permitted to search the suitcase.

    A is incorrect because "[t]he officer's subjective motivation is irrelevant" under the Fourth Amendment, "as long as the circumstances, viewed objectively, justify [the] action." *Brigham City, Utah v. Stuart*, 547 U.S. 398, 404 (2006). **B is incorrect** because the automobile exception does not require police to establish that they couldn't get a warrant; instead, police must establish probable cause. **C is incorrect** because the reasonableness of the search depends on probable cause, not the evidence recovered in the search.

154. This question tests on whether an officer may search closed containers belonging to a car passenger. "[P]olice officers with probable cause to search a car may inspect passengers' belongings found in the car that are capable of concealing the object of the search." *Wyoming v. Houghton*, 526 U.S. 295, 307 (1999).

    C is correct because it represents the prosecutor's "strongest argument:" the driver's admission provided probable cause for the search of the car and the baggie of cocaine provided probable cause for the search of the passenger's purse.

    A is incorrect because it's not the prosecutor's "strongest argument." The driver's admission suggests that the passenger might also be involved in cocaine use, but it doesn't "necessarily" mean that she was. **B is incorrect** because the passenger's laughter is odd, but didn't provide the officer with probable cause to believe that she had been smoking marijuana. **D is incorrect** because it is too broadly worded to be a valid argument.

155. This question tests whether the automobile exception requires separate proof of exigent circumstances. That extra proof is not required, because the automobile exception is one of "a limited class of traditional exceptions to the warrant requirement that apply categorically and thus do[es] not require an assessment of whether the policy justifications underlying the exception ... are implicated in a particular case." *Missouri v. McNeely*, 133 S. Ct. 1552, 1559 n.3 (2013).

A is correct because it states the correct rule for the automobile exception: police may search an automobile consistent with their probable cause that evidence is located within the automobile.

B, C, and D are all incorrect because each improperly suggests that the police must have an additional reason for the warrantless search — *i.e.*, a reason beyond probable cause — in order for the automobile exception to apply.

156. This question tests on whether an automobile exception search is considered reasonable after the car is in police control, *i.e.*, after it has lost its quality of being "readily mobile" and one of the exception's rationales is no longer applicable. "[T]he justification to conduct [an automobile exception search] does not vanish once the car has been immobilized; nor does it depend upon a reviewing court's assessment of the likelihood in each particular case that the car would have been driven away, or that its contents would have been tampered with, during the period required for the police to obtain a warrant." *Michigan v. Thomas*, 458 U.S. 259, 261 (1982) (*per curiam*).

A is correct because the suspect's admission gave the police probable cause to search the car for the weapon.

B and D are both incorrect because each speaks in terms of absolutes — the suspect losing "all expectation of privacy" and police "always" being required to get warrants, respectively. Given that "[t]he touchstone of the Fourth Amendment is reasonableness," *Florida v. Jimenez*, 500 U.S. 248, 250 (1991), answers containing absolutes will rarely offer the "strongest argument." **C is incorrect** because the automobile exception does not require separate proof of exigency; it requires proof of probable cause.

157. This question tests on whether an automobile exception search is still considered reasonable if the driver is not available to drive the car away. "If a car is readily mobile and probable cause exists to believe it contains contraband, the Fourth Amendment thus permits police to search the vehicle without more." *Pennsylvania v. Labron*, 518 U.S. 938, 940 (1996) (*per curiam*) (authorizing searches where suspects had been arrested before searches began).

C is correct because the police had probable cause to search the minivan, which is all that is needed for an automobile exception search.

A and D are both incorrect because the facts don't give sufficient information to conclude that the minivan had been "abandoned." **B is incorrect** because—by providing a rationale for a warrantless entry into a house—it's not the "strongest argument."

158. This question tests on the interaction between the automobile and plain view exceptions. Assuming the requirements of the plain view exception are met—(1) the officer is in a lawful vantage point to view the evidence; (2) he does not engage in additional search activity to access the evidence; and (3) he has probable cause to suspect that he is viewing evidence of crime—the officer may seize that evidence. *E.g., Horton v. California*, 496 U.S. 128, 136–137 (1990).

     B is correct because the requirements of plain view were met on these facts: the officer had probable cause to search the car for drug evidence and came across the child pornography while legitimately conducting that search.

     A is incorrect because, as a non-legal, policy-based argument, it is not the "most likely" ruling from the court. **C is incorrect** because it's untrue: the officer in this situation simply responded to the situation as he found it. **D is incorrect** because while the officer only had probable cause to search for marijuana, he found the child pornography during his search for marijuana—and the "most likely" ruling would address the evidence that was found.

159. This question tests on the differences between the various types of car searches: automobile exception searches, searches incident to arrest, inventory searches, and *Terry* frisks of cars. Each type of search has its own requirements and scope limits.

     A is correct because the officer's discovery of cocaine in the woman's pocket—during a lawful search incident to arrest—gave him probable cause to believe there would be additional drugs in the car. Under the automobile exception, if the officer has probable cause, the scope of the search is limited only by that probable cause.

     B is incorrect because a search of a car incident to arrest is restricted to the car's passenger compartment. *New York v. Belton*, 453 U.S. 454, 460 (1981). **C is incorrect** because it is not the "strongest argument;" while the jurisdiction's inventory code may permit a search of a car trunk, the scope of an inventory search is limited by the inventory code itself. Here, there is no information given about the inventory code. **D is incorrect** because a *Terry* frisk of a car for weapons is restricted in scope to the car's passenger compartment. *Michigan v. Long*, 463 U.S. 1032, 1051 (1983).

160. This question also tests on the differences between the most common types of car searches.

     D is correct because it provides the prosecutor's "best argument," relative to the other answers.

     A is incorrect because it's not the "best argument:" discovering an unlicensed weapon on the driver doesn't give the officer probable cause to believe that more weapons will be found in the car. **B and C are both incorrect** because the officer searched the car before arresting the driver, and an inventory search and search incident to arrest would each require an arrest before conducting a search.

161. Like the previous two questions, this question also tests on different types of car searches.

     C is correct because the most plausible justification for the search is that the officer was following the municipality's inventory code in searching the car.

     A is incorrect because the officer's actions can't be defended as a search incident to arrest: the woman was unable to access the car and the officer had no reason to believe that evidence of the arresting office could be found in the car. *Arizona v. Gant*, 556 U.S. 332 (2009). **B is incorrect** because the officer lacked probable cause to search the car and so the automobile exception wouldn't authorize the search. *Acevedo*, 500 U.S. at 580. **D is incorrect** because the officer did not have any suspicion that the car contained a weapon, and because the driver wouldn't have been able to access the car anyway.

162. This question tests on the extension of the automobile exception to other vehicles such as motorcycles. Although the Supreme Court has never ruled on this issue, motorcycles—like automobiles—are readily mobile and heavily regulated by the state. As such, there is every reason to believe that they fall within the automobile exception.

     B is correct because it recognizes that the automobile exception likely permits warrantless searches of motorcycles and addresses the fact that there was no probable cause to search the saddlebags.

     A is incorrect because it fails to recognize that the common features between the two types of vehicles. **C is incorrect** because an inventory search would only be permitted here if the officer was arresting the motorcyclist or impounding his motorcycle, and neither happened here. **D is incorrect** because while it recognizes the extension of the automobile exception to motorcycles, it doesn't address the lack of probable cause for the search.

163. This question also tests on the extension of the automobile exception—this time to motor boats.

     D is correct because it is the answer that most accurately applies the automobile exception to these facts: drinking and boating is prohibited, the officer saw the man drinking on his boat, and the officer also saw a cooler on the deck of the boat.

     A is incorrect because the rules of boating etiquette don't govern Fourth Amendment reasonableness. **B is incorrect** because the facts state that the officer saw the man drinking a beer, and don't leave that issue up for debate. **C is incorrect** because presumably, some suspicion would be required for a state actor to board the boat and search it.

164. This question tests on one of the anomalies associated with the automobile exception: that it permits probable cause-based searches of containers found inside a car, but does not permit those same containers to be searched if they are not inside the car when the officer encounters them. The officer may have the authority to search that container under another Fourth Amendment exception, but not under the automobile exception.

D is correct because it responds to the prosecutor's argument and recognizes that the exception does not permit automobile searches outside of the vehicle.

A is incorrect because the scope of a proper automobile exception search is the vehicle itself, and not areas outside of the vehicle. **B is incorrect** because it's an incorrect statement of law and the reference to "recent occupants" is tied to the search incident to arrest exception. **C is incorrect** because it's untrue: the officer had probable cause to search the passenger's jacket but he wasn't authorized to search under the automobile exception.

165. This question also tests on the same issue as in the previous question, but adds a twist where the officer deliberately uses the automobile exception to search an item that he would otherwise need a warrant to search. Regardless, "[s]ubjective intentions play no role in ordinary ... Fourth Amendment analysis." *Whren v. U.S.*, 517 U.S. 806, 813 (1996).

C is correct because the facts state that the officer had probable cause to believe that there were drugs in the green backpack and the green backpack was inside the car.

A and B are both incorrect because the officer had probable cause to search the green backpack, so his subjective motivations are irrelevant. **D is incorrect** because — even if true — it doesn't provide a proper basis for the search.

Consent Searches

166. This question tests on consent searches. "In situations where the police have some evidence of illicit activity, but lack probable cause to arrest or search, a search authorized by a valid consent may be the only means of obtaining important and reliable evidence." *Schneckloth v. Bustamonte*, 412 U.S. 218, 227 (1973).

D is correct because the driver voluntarily consented to a search of the trunk of her car.

A is incorrect because consent searches don't require any pre-existing suspicion; they only require valid consent. **B is incorrect** because "[s]ubjective intentions play no role in ordinary, probable cause Fourth Amendment analysis." *Whren v. U.S.*, 517 U.S. 806, 813 (1996). **C is incorrect** because the driver unlocked her car trunk only after she gave verbal consent to the search, and so her act of unlocking the trunk isn't relevant to the question of whether or not she gave consent.

167. This question tests on the standard for consenting to a search. Although waivers of other types of constitutional rights must be knowing, voluntary, and intelligent, all that is required for valid consent to search is that the consent be voluntary, *i.e.*, free from coercion and duress. *Bustamonte*, 412 U.S. at 229.

    C is correct because the consent here was valid: the police didn't coerce the man in any way, and there's no suggestion that his consent is a product of duress.

    A and D are both incorrect because each focuses on a "knowing" waiver — *i.e.*, what the person knows — and consent to search only requires voluntariness. **B is incorrect** because the man's alleged unequal treatment doesn't have anything to do with a voluntary waiver.

168. This question also tests on valid consent, and what a court should consider when assessing whether consent was voluntarily given. "Voluntariness is a question of fact to be determined from all the circumstances...." *Bustamonte*, 412 U.S. at 248–249.

    D is correct because it refers to the proper test for assessing voluntary consent: the totality of the circumstances.

    A and B are both incorrect because each presents a legal standard for assessing consent, and the question asks about what facts the court should consider. **C is incorrect** because it implies that Fourth Amendment consent requires a knowing waiver, when all that is required is that the consent be voluntary.

169. Like the previous question, this question also tests on voluntary consent.

    D is correct because it refers to all of the relevant facts from the fact pattern, *i.e.*, the totality of the circumstances.

    A, B, and C are all incorrect because each answer refers only to some of the facts in the fact pattern, and not all the relevant facts.

170. This question tests on voluntary consent in the context of a traffic stop, using the facts of *Ohio v. Robinette*, 519 U.S. 33 (1996). In *Robinette*, the Supreme Court held that it would be "unrealistic to require police officers to always inform detainees that they are free to go before consent to search may be deemed voluntary." *Id.* at 40.

    B is correct because it's true: the consent was voluntary and the officer did not prolong the stop in any way that might suggest an unreasonable seizure.

    A is incorrect because it doesn't make any sense: there's nothing about driving fast that suggests that the driver might also be transporting drugs. **C is incorrect** because it contradicts the holding from *Robinette*. **D is incorrect** because requesting consent to search does not change the nature of the encounter if the traffic stop is "lawful at its inception," conducted reasonably, and otherwise doesn't infringe on any other constitutional rights. *E.g.*, *Illinois v. Caballes*, 543 U.S. 405 (2005).

171. This question tests on voluntary consent, using facts similar to those of *Bumper v. North Carolina*, 391 U.S. 543 (1967). "When a law enforcement officer claims

authority to search a home under a warrant, he announces in effect that the occupant has no right to resist the search." *Id.* at 550. In such a situation, the homeowner's consent is not voluntary because it is coerced. *Id.*

D is correct because it properly addresses the connection between the officer's show of authority and the aunt's invitation to enter the house.

A and B are both incorrect because each ignores the connection between the officer's show of authority and the aunt's invitation to enter the house—which is the critical issue on these facts. **C is incorrect** because the aunt's invitation to enter the house was plainly premised on her understanding that the officers had a warrant and that the warrant gave them a right to come inside.

172. This question also tests on voluntary consent.

A is correct because the mother only gave consent after the officer threatened that if she refused, a judge might "take[] her kids away." Because the consent was based on a threat, it is involuntary.

B is incorrect because the officer is not required to corroborate a tip if he has valid consent to search. **C is incorrect** because the speculative nature of the officer's threat doesn't change the fact that it was still a threat, and that the woman only gave consent after the officer referred to a judge removing her kids from the home. Finally, **D is incorrect** because blaming the woman for giving consent doesn't address the legal question of whether her consent was voluntary.

173. This question tests on implied consent. Police may search if they have valid consent, no matter if the consent is express or—as here—implied.

D is correct because, when the woman "opened the door wide and stepped to one side," she impliedly consented to the officer's entry, and once he was inside he saw the pipe in plain view.

A and C are both incorrect because each focuses on the officer's suspicion prior to coming to the woman's house. An officer doesn't need to have any suspicion to search if he has valid consent for that search. *Bustamonte*, 412 U.S. at 227. **B is incorrect** because consent to search does not need to be verbalized, it just needs to be voluntary.

174. This question tests on how to evaluate the scope of consent. "The standard for measuring the scope of a suspect's consent under the Fourth Amendment is that of objective reasonableness—what would the typical reasonable person have understood by the exchange between the officer and the suspect?" *Florida v. Jimeno*, 500 U.S. 248, 251 (1991).

C is correct because it evaluates the facts according to the reasonable person standard.

A, B, and D are all incorrect because each refers to a particular type of reasonable person—business owner, baker, and bakery customer—and *Jimeno* holds that the scope of consent should be assessed according to the "typical" reasonable person.

175. This question tests on scope of consent, using the facts from *Florida v. Jimeno*. In *Jimeno*, the Supreme Court explained that "[t]he scope of a search is generally defined by its expressed object," *id.* at 251, and upheld a consent-based search of a closed container in a car where the officer had told the driver that he suspected drugs were in the car before requesting consent for the search.

D is correct because, following *Jimeno*, "it was objectively reasonable for the police to conclude that the general consent to search [the] car included consent to search containers within that car which might bear drugs," *id.*, especially because the officer told the driver that he suspected drugs were in the car.

A is incorrect because it doesn't address the question of whether the driver's consent extended to the closed container in the car (the paper bag). **B is incorrect** because this question is focused on the scope of the search, and not whether the officer had pre-existing suspicion. **C is incorrect** because, by generically referring to "a driver" and "all closed containers," it is too broadly worded. Certainly, there are instances where consent to search a car might not extend to a closed container.

176. This question tests on limitations placed on a consent search. If a "typical reasonable person" would have understood that the scope of consent was limited, then the scope of the officer's search will be so limited. *Jimeno*, 500 U.S. at 251.

D is correct because it addresses the driver's consent and her time limit, and because it correctly recognizes that the officer honored those limits.

A is incorrect because it doesn't represent the "most likely" ruling. Although the driver didn't affirmatively agree to the officer's unlocking of the trunk, she did agree to the search—with some limitations. As such, the "most likely" ruling will address those limitations and whether they were honored. **B is incorrect** because it's untrue: nothing in the facts suggests that the search of the trunk took longer than the five minutes permitted by the driver. **C is incorrect** because it doesn't address the driver's limitations on the duration of the search.

177. This question tests on revocation of consent. Consent can be revoked or withdrawn; again, the question turns on how a "typical reasonable person" would assess the situation. *E.g., Jimeno*, 500 U.S. at 251.

A is correct because, by hanging onto her backpack (after first giving consent) and walking away, a reasonable person would understand that the protester was withdrawing her consent to search.

B and C are both incorrect because both refer to the First Amendment and the reasonability of searches is governed by the Fourth Amendment. **D is incorrect** because it improperly suggests that once consent is given it can't be revoked.

178. This question tests on whether a police officer may draw an adverse inference against a person who refuses consent to search, *i.e.*, for the exercise of a constitutional right. The Supreme Court has "consistently held that a refusal to cooperate, without more, does not furnish the minimal level of objective

justification needed for a detention or seizure." *Florida v. Bostick*, 501 U.S. 429, 437 (1991).

C is correct because the officer's testimony makes clear that his suspicion was based solely on the man's refusal to consent to the frisk.

A is incorrect because it's untrue: the man exercised his rights in a calm and clear manner, and there's nothing objectively suspicious about that. **B is incorrect** because the officer's improper frisk of the man can't be buttressed after-the-fact by the evidence found in the man's pockets. Instead, the frisk needs to be "justified at its inception." *Terry v. Ohio*, 392 U.S. 1, 20 (1968). **D is incorrect** because it doesn't address the consent issue.

179. This question tests on whether an officer can draw an adverse inference against a person from the manner in which consent is refused—but not from the fact of refusing. There is a fine line to be drawn here, because "[p]ermitting the police to rely on the atmospherics of the refusal or withdrawal of consent to supply the reasonable suspicion necessary to objectively justify an otherwise unlawful search or detention strips the legal right of withdrawal of all practical value." *U.S. v. Carter*, 985 F.2d 1095, 1100 (D.C. Cir.) (Wald, C.J., dissenting).

B is correct because the driver's conduct—beyond his refusal to consent to the search of his car—likely only provided the officer with reasonable suspicion, not probable cause.

A is incorrect because—ignoring all facts associated with the driver's refusal to give consent, and just considering the driver's nervousness, stammering, and reaching for the item on the passenger's seat—the officer didn't have probable cause to believe the car contained a weapon. **C and D are both incorrect** because each refers to the officer's suspicion coming from the refusal to give consent, which is impermissible.

180. This question tests on common authority: "mutual use of the property by persons generally having joint access or control for most purposes." *U.S. v. Matlock*, 415 U.S. 164, 171 n.7 (1974). If the consenting party has common authority over the area at issue, "it is reasonable to recognize that any of the co-inhabitants has the right to permit the inspection in his own right and that the others have assumed the risk that one of their number might permit the common area to be searched." *Id.*

A is correct because a kitchen is a commonly shared space between housemates and, absent any facts to the contrary, the officer reasonably believed the male student had common authority over the kitchen.

B and D are both incorrect because each misstates the rule about common authority and consent searches. **C is incorrect** because the officer could reasonably assume that the male student had common authority over the kitchen. And, while there may be situations where the officer should inquire further before assuming that an individual has common authority over an area, the facts here don't suggest that this is one of those situations.

181. This question tests on common authority, using the facts from *Frazier v. Cupp*, 394 U.S. 731 (1969). In *Frazier*, the Supreme Court explained that it would not "engage in ... metaphysical subtleties" by addressing a claim that one person had common authority over just a small portion of a duffel bag lent to him by another, and not the entire bag. *Id.* at 740.

    D is correct because a court would "most likely" find that the teenager had common authority over the entire duffel bag, despite the cousin's claim. To hold otherwise would require a court to divide the bag into separate zones—each potentially inches apart—and determine who had actual control over each.

    A is incorrect because it's not the "most likely" ruling; even assuming that the cousin's claim was true and that he had restricted the teenager's use of the bag to the zippered compartment, *Frazier* holds that a court shouldn't do what the cousin is asking it to. **B is incorrect** because the teenager didn't—and can't—waive his cousin's rights when he consented to a search of the bag. **C is incorrect** because waiver isn't really applicable here. The most that could be said on these facts is that, when he lent the bag to the teenager, the cousin "assumed the risk" that the teenager might let someone look inside. *Id.* at 740.

182. This question tests on "apparent authority" to consent, *i.e.*, consent given by a person who does not have actual authority to consent, but who appears to have actual authority. The standard for assessing consent in this context is objective: whether "the facts available to the officer at the moment [would] warrant a man of reasonable caution in the belief that the consenting party had authority over the premises." *Illinois v. Rodriguez*, 497 U.S. 177, 188 (1990).

    D is correct because the officer's interactions with the woman gave him an objective basis to believe that she had actual authority over the area her husband's home office: the office was located in the house where she lived and she was cleaning the office when she discovered the cocaine.

    A is incorrect because it addresses the woman's actual authority to consent to a search of the room, and not her apparent authority. **B is incorrect** because it wrongly implies that consent can only come from those with actual authority and *Rodriguez* permits consent from others as well. **C is incorrect** for several reasons, not least of which is that it doesn't respond to the question.

183. Like the previous question, this question tests on apparent authority to consent.

    C is correct because it uses the objective standard from *Rodriguez*, and it reaches the correct conclusion on these facts: the teenager was sitting in the passenger seat and his statement gave a strong indication that someone else owned the car. Given these facts, a reasonable police officer would have inquired further to ascertain whether the teenager had authority to consent to the search of the car.

    A is incorrect because it's not the "strongest argument." Although the teenager did use conditional language—he said, "I guess it'll be okay"—a stronger argument would be that he lacked the authority to consent in the first place. **B is incorrect** because the issue of constructive possession assumes that the evidence has been admitted, and the friend is arguing that the evidence should be suppressed. **D is incorrect** because the officer's off-duty status is an issue of state law, and the question asks about suppression under the federal constitution.

184. This question tests on "dueling consent," relying on facts similar to those in *Georgia v. Randolph*, 547 U.S. 103 (2006). Dueling consent occurs where two people — both present at the scene and each with common authority over the area at issue — give police conflicting answers about consent to search the area. In such a situation, "a physically present inhabitant's express refusal of consent to a police search is dispositive as to him, regardless of the consent of a fellow occupant." *Id.* at 122–123.

   C is correct because it properly recognizes that the officer must honor the husband's refusal to consent, even though the wife gave her consent.

   A and B are both incorrect because each contradicts the holding from *Randolph*. What would be the point of the husband's refusal if the officer could search anyway, based on the wife's consent? **D is incorrect** for two reasons. First, common authority "under the Fourth Amendment may … be broader than the rights accorded by property law." *Id.* at 110. Second, on these facts, it was reasonable for the officer to assume that wife had common authority over the house.

185. This question tests on a variation on dueling consent, relying on the facts of *Fernandez v. California*, 134 S. Ct. 1126 (2014). In *Fernandez*, the Supreme Court held that "an occupant who is absent due to a lawful detention or arrest stands in the same shoes as an occupant who is absent for any other reason." *Id.* at 1134. In other words, if police lawfully remove the objecting party from the premises they may then rely on the consenting party's voluntary consent to search.

   B is correct because it recognizes why the officers here acted reasonably: because they were permitted to arrest the man and they didn't coerce the woman into giving consent.

   A is incorrect because — by not addressing both the arrest and the consent — it doesn't represent the "most likely" ruling. **C is incorrect** because it's untrue: the facts indicate that police had probable cause for the man's arrest, making his removal from the apartment "objectively reasonable." *Id.* at 1134. **D is incorrect** because the *Fernandez* Court expressly rejected this argument, explaining that it runs contrary to "widely shared social expectations" and would create a "plethora of practical problems" in application. *Id.* at 1135.

Inventory Searches

186. This question tests on the inventory exception. "Examining all the items removed from the arrestee's person or possession and listing or inventorying them is an

entirely reasonable administrative procedure. It is immaterial whether the police actually fear any particular package or container; the need to protect against such risks arises independent of a particular officer's subjective concerns." *Illinois v. Lafayette*, 462 U.S. 640, 646 (1983).

B is correct because it is the "most likely justification" for the officer's actions here: he inventoried the bag as part of an "incidental administrative step following arrest and preceding incarceration." *Id.* at 644.

A is incorrect because the contents of the bag are not in the officer's plain view; instead, because the officer "went through" the bag—*i.e.*, he searched it—the plain view exception doesn't apply. **C is incorrect** because it pre-supposes the woman is going to have a trial. **D is incorrect** because a search incident to arrest is not the "most likely justification" for the officer's search of the bag; such a search would only be permitted if it was within the woman's reach at the time of arrest—a fact not provided in the fact pattern.

187. This question also tests on the inventory exception and whether the search must be spatially and temporally related to the arrest. In general, an inventory search is reasonable if it is "conducted according to standardized criteria," *Colorado v. Bertine*, 479 U.S. 367, 374 n.6 (1987), and not whether the area searched was temporally or spatially related to the arrestee.

D is correct because it is the "most likely" ruling: the officer followed the code in conducting the search and so the search was reasonable under the inventory exception.

A and B are both incorrect because each focuses on irrelevant criteria—the timing of the search and the location of the search relative to the place of arrest—and not whether the officer adhered to the jurisdiction's inventory code. **C is incorrect** because an inventory search conducted for the "sole purpose of investigation" is no longer a proper inventory search—meaning the resulting search would be unreasonable. *Id.* at 372.

188. This question tests on the rationales for inventory searches. There are three: "the protection of the owner's property while it remains in police custody . . . ; the protection [of] the police against claims or disputes over lost or stolen property . . .; "and the protection of the police from potential danger." *South Dakota v. Opperman*, 428 U.S. 364, 369 (1976).

B is correct because it ties the reasonability for the inventory search to one of the recognized rationales.

A, C, and D are all incorrect, although each presents a true statement. But the question asks for the "most likely" reason why the court will deny the suppression motion, and a reason directly tied to Supreme Court precedent provides the strongest support for the court's ruling.

189. This question also tests on the rationales for inventory searches, and whether one, two, or three of these rationales must be present for the inventory search

to be reasonable. The Supreme Court has never imposed that requirement, instead focusing on whether the search was conducted according to established criteria.

A is correct because, by all appearances, the inventory search here was reasonable and lawful—despite the fact that the rationales for an inventory search might not have been present.

B and C are both incorrect because each suggests that an inventory search is unreasonable unless one of the rationales is present, which is untrue. **D is incorrect** because its language—referring to "evidence of the arresting offense"—refers to part of the standard for searching a car incident to arrest, *Arizona v. Gant*, 556 U.S. 332 (2009), and such a search is different from an inventory search.

190. This question tests on how to assess the proper scope—and accordingly, the reasonableness—of an inventory search. The "view that standardized criteria or established routine must regulate the opening of containers found during inventory searches is based on the principle that an inventory search must not be a ruse for a general rummaging in order to discover incriminating evidence." *Florida v. Wells*, 495 U.S. 1, 4 (1990). As such, if the inventory code permits the opening and search of a closed container, the officer may open that container. In the absence of an inventory procedure, "opening all containers or ... opening no containers" would be "unquestionably permissible," as would "the opening of closed containers whose contents officers determine they are unable to ascertain from examining the containers' exteriors." *Id.*

A is correct because the officer did not follow any set procedure in searching the car; instead, the officer's testimony established that he created his own procedure and that the procedure didn't have a principled way to account for closed containers found inside the car.

B is incorrect because the right to conduct the inventory search, or the scope of the search, doesn't depend on the nature of the arresting offense. **C is incorrect** because it's untrue: the officer's testimony showed that he didn't have an "established procedure" for searching closed containers. **D is incorrect** because the question asks about suppression of evidence, not fault for the omission of an inventory procedure.

191. This question tests on the reasonability of an inventory search, using the relevant facts from *Colorado v. Bertine*, 479 U.S. 367 (1987).

D is correct because it accurately describes the inventory code: the inventory code gives the officer some discretion in conducting inventory searches, but it also gives guidance for the exercise of that discretion.

A is incorrect because it fails to recognize that the inventory code places limits on the officer's exercise of discretion. **B is incorrect** because the issue here is the officer's exercise of discretion, not the documentation of his decision. **C is incorrect** because the search would be unreasonable if the "sole purpose" for the inventory search was investigation. *Id.* at 372. In that sense, the officer's subjective motivation would be relevant.

192. This question tests on whether an officer's impermissible motivation to arrest and conduct an inventory search affects the reasonableness of the search. If the officer's "sole purpose" for the search is to conduct an investigation, then the inventory search is unreasonable. *Colorado v. Bertine*, 479 U.S. 367, 372 (1987). However, if the arrest is supported by objective criteria — even if the officer has an impermissible motive in making the arrest — the resulting inventory search will not be found unreasonable on that basis. *Arkansas v. Sullivan*, 532 U.S. 7691 (2001) (*per curiam*).

A is correct because the arrest was lawful and the officer followed the inventory code.

B is incorrect because the automobile exception requires probable cause that evidence can be found in the car and the officer here only had a hunch that the woman was a drug trafficker. C is incorrect because the officer had probable cause to believe that the woman had committed an arrestable offense: driving without a seat belt. D is incorrect because the officer's relevant act — the arrest — was based on probable cause.

193. This question tests on inventory searches of locked parts of a car during an inventory search. This issue has not been finally decided by the Supreme Court, although lower courts have "frequently" upheld such searches. LaFave, et al., 3 *Search and Seizure* § 7.4(a) n.93 (5th ed. 2012).

C is correct because it is the "best" response: the Supreme Court has repeatedly upheld inventory searches conducted with limited discretion and according to the jurisdiction's inventory code.

A is incorrect because the glove box was locked. B is incorrect because even though there is a reduced expectation of privacy in cars, the driver still can claim some expectation of privacy. D is incorrect because — by focusing on a hypothetical — it's not the "best" answer.

194. This question tests on the interaction between the inventory and plain view exceptions. Assuming the requirements of the plain view exception are met — (1) the officer is in a lawful vantage point to view the evidence; (2) he does not engage in additional search activity to access the evidence; and (3) he has probable cause to suspect that he is viewing evidence of crime — the officer may seize that evidence. *E.g., Horton v. California*, 496 U.S. 128, 136–137 (1990).

C is correct because all three requirements of the plain view exception are met on these facts: the inventory code permitted the officer to search the baskets so he viewed the cocaine from a lawful vantage point; he did not search — other than what was permitted by the inventory code — to access the bag of cocaine; and he had probable cause to believe the bag contained cocaine.

A is incorrect because it completely misses the point of the plain view exception: officers may seize evidence they legitimately find while looking for something else. **B is incorrect** because the officer's search of the baskets was permitted under the jurisdiction's inventory code. **D is incorrect** because there is no inadvertency requirement—either that the discovery of evidence be inadvertent or not—for the plain view exception.

195. This question tests on the interaction between the inventory and automobile exceptions. Under the automobile exception, "police may search an automobile and the containers within it where they have probable cause to believe contraband or evidence is contained." *California v. Acevedo*, 500 U.S. 565, 580 (1991).

   B is correct because the officer developed probable cause for an expanded search after he found the cocaine under the seat. As such, his search is lawful under the automobile exception.

   A is incorrect because the facts don't suggest that the officer believed the bag contained a gun. **C and D are both incorrect** because neither addresses the probable cause the officer developed when he found the cocaine under the seat.

Special Needs Searches

196. This question tests on the "special needs" exception, using facts derived from *National Treasury Employees Union v. Von Raab*, 489 U.S. 656 (1989). To evaluate a special needs search, a court must first determine whether a special need actually exists: an "exceptional circumstance[] in which special needs, beyond the normal need for law enforcement, make the warrant and probable-cause requirement impracticable." *New Jersey v. T.L.O.*, 469 U.S. 325, 351 (1985) (Blackmun, J., concurring). Next, once a legitimate special need has been found, a court must weigh "the intrusion on the individual's interest in privacy against the special needs that supported the program." *Ferguson v. Charleston*, 532 U.S. 67 (2001).

   C is correct because it correctly describes the two-step analysis required for evaluating a purported special needs search: identification of a legitimate special need and balancing the interests of the individual against those of the state.

   A is incorrect because suspicionless searches are permitted in a variety of situations, *e.g.*, inventory searches don't require any particularized suspicion. **B and D are both incorrect** because each refers to a standard for judicial review, which is irrelevant here.

197. This question tests on an example of a special needs search, using facts derived from *Griffin v. Wisconsin*, 483 U.S. 868 (1987). "A State's operation of a probation system, like its operation of a school, government office or prison, or its supervision of a regulated industry, likewise presents special needs beyond normal law enforcement that may justify departures from the usual warrant and probable cause requirements." *Id.* at 873–874.

   C is correct because it is the "most likely" ruling: the state has offered a legitimate special need, and by requiring proof of reasonable suspicion before conducting the search of the probationer's home, it has balanced the interests of the probationer against those of the state.

A is incorrect because the evidence should be suppressed if the search itself is unreasonable, not because of the type of evidence that was recovered during the search. **B is incorrect** because a presumptively unreasonable search may still be reasonable if a valid reason — here, that the search is permitted under the special needs exception — is offered to rebut the presumption. **D is incorrect** because application of the special needs exception doesn't "void" the probationer's rights; instead, because the state can articulate a legitimate special need, the probationer's rights are balanced against the intrusiveness of the search.

198. This question also tests on a possible special needs search — where the asserted "special need" is the desire to have sober elected officials — using facts derived from *Chandler v. Miller*, 520 U.S. 305 (1997).

   D is correct because the preamble to the bill sets forth political reasons for drug testing but nothing "important enough to override the individual's acknowledged privacy interest, sufficiently vital to suppress the Fourth Amendment's normal requirement of individualized suspicion." *Id.* at 318.

   A is incorrect because suspicionless searches are sometimes permitted under the Fourth Amendment. **B is incorrect** because the constitutionality of the statute — which mandates suspicionless governmental searches — will primarily turn on the Fourth Amendment, not the Tenth Amendment. **C is incorrect** because the "best" response is that the entire premise behind the law is flawed, not that the law would be constitutional if it was slightly modified.

199. This question also tests on a possible special needs search, using facts derived from *Ferguson v. Charleston*, 532 U.S. 67 (2001). Because the special needs exception allows searches and seizures that might otherwise be restricted by the Fourth Amendment — *e.g.*, suspicionless or warrantless drug testing — a court should "not simply accept the State's invocation of a special need." *Id.* at 81. Instead, a court should "consider all the available evidence in order to determine the relevant primary purpose" for the program. *Id.*

   A is correct because the policy is not supported by an appropriate special need: "the central and indispensable feature of the policy from its inception was the use of law enforcement to coerce the patients into substance abuse treatment." *Id.* at 80.

   B, C, and D are all incorrect because none address the fact that the "the immediate objective of the searches was to generate evidence for law enforcement purposes." *Id.* at 83.

200. This question tests on the balancing that is permitted after a special need has been found: weighing "the intrusion on the individual's interest in privacy against the special needs that supported the program." *Ferguson v. Charleston*, 532 U.S. 67 (2001); *see also New Jersey v. T.L.O.*, 469 U.S. 325, 351 (1985) (Blackmun, J., concurring) ("Only in those exceptional circumstances in which special

needs, beyond the normal need for law enforcement, make the warrant and probable-cause requirement impracticable, is a court entitled to substitute its balancing of interests for that of the Framers.").

C is correct because it weighs the intrusion on the officers from the testing against the needs of the state.

A is incorrect because the officer retains his expectation of privacy in his body, regardless of whether he is on-duty or not. **B and D are both incorrect** because—by addressing only one interest or the other, and not the balance of interests—they are not the "most likely" answer.

201. This question also tests on the balancing required to evaluate a special needs search.

    B is correct because it addresses the necessary balancing and points out the critical flaws in the protocol: it permits warrantless searches of private homes and opens the door to criminal prosecutions for any evidence found in plain view during the search.

    A is incorrect because it is uses absolute terms, and the question asks about balancing. **C is incorrect** because it doesn't really address balancing but instead blames the drug user. **D is incorrect** because, while it does address the balancing of needs, it does so for non-legal reasons.

202. This question tests on a special needs search in the context of a public school. "[W]hile children assuredly do not shed their constitutional rights ... at the schoolhouse gate ... Fourth Amendment rights, no less than First and Fourteenth Amendment rights, are different in public schools than elsewhere; the 'reasonableness' inquiry cannot disregard the schools' custodial and tutelary responsibility for children." *Vernonia School District 47J v. Acton*, 515 U.S. 646, 656 (1995).

    D is correct because it refers to the two requirements necessary to evaluate a special needs search: the existence of a legitimate special need and a balancing of the rights of the individual against the needs of the state.

    A is incorrect because it improperly suggests that the special needs exception has no application in the public schools. **B is incorrect** because it suggests that the only danger associated with underage drinking involves drunk driving, and there are other dangers as well. **C is incorrect** because, by referring to exigency, it ignores the special needs exception.

203. This question tests on the balancing required for school searches. Public school searches conducted under the special needs exception generally require reasonable suspicion, not probable cause. *New Jersey v. T.L.O.*, 469 U.S. 325, 341 (1985). From there, "first, one must consider whether the ... action was justified at its inception; second, one must determine whether the search as actually conducted was reasonably related in scope to the circumstances which justified the interference in the first place...." *Id*.

C is correct because it addresses the actual operation of the policy, and describes the steps taken to limit the scope of these warrantless locker searches.

A and B are both incorrect because each sets forth a weak rationale for the policy, which is not the "best defense." **D is incorrect** because "a search is not to be made legal by what it turns up." Instead, "[i]n law [a search] is good or bad when it starts and does not change character from its success." *U.S. v. Di Re*, 332 U.S. 581, 595 (1948).

204. This question tests on suspicionless drug testing in the public schools, using the facts from *Vernonia School District 47J v. Acton*, 515 U.S. 646 (1995). Although the Court has approved of reasonable suspicion-based special needs searches, "the Fourth Amendment imposes no irreducible requirement of such suspicion" and suspicionless special needs searches are also sometimes permissible. *Id.* at 653.

D is correct because it is the only answer that correctly refers to the necessary balancing that the court must conduct.

A is incorrect because the Court has approved of suspicionless special needs searches, in both the school and non-school contexts. *Id.* (suspicionless testing of student athletes); *Board of Education of Independent School District No. 92 v. Earls*, 536 U.S. 822 (2002) (suspicionless testing of students participating in extra-curricular activities); *National Treasury Employees Union v. Von Raab*, 489 U.S. 656 (1989) (suspicionless testing of customs employees); *Skinner v. Railway Labor Executives' Ass'n*, 489 U.S. 602 (1989) (suspicionless testing of certain railway employees). **B is incorrect** because it doesn't make any sense: students who are selected for testing are not determined to be drug users until after their urine is tested. **C is incorrect** because the students clearly have standing to challenge the policy.

205. This question tests on strip searches of school children under the special needs exception, using the relevant facts from *Safford Unified School Dist. No. 1 v. Redding*, 557 U.S. 364 (2009). "The indignity of the search does not, of course, outlaw it, but it does implicate the rule of reasonableness ... that the search as actually conducted [be] reasonably related in scope to the circumstances which justified the interference in the first place.... The scope will be permissible, that is, when it is not excessively intrusive in light of the age and sex of the student and the nature of the infraction." *Id.* at 385.

C is correct because the principal had absolutely no reason to suspect that the student had antacids hidden in her clothes or underwear—especially after he searched the backpack and didn't find anything.

A is incorrect because the student only consented to a search of her backpack, not the strip search. **B is incorrect** because, even if accurate, the strip search itself was not "reasonably related in scope to the circumstances which justified the interference in the first place...." *New Jersey v. T.L.O.*, 469 U.S. 325, 341 (1985). **D is incorrect** because *Safford* did not categorically prohibit strip searches in the absence of a warrant; instead, it held that such a search must be supported by reasonable suspicion of danger or reasonable suspicion that the contraband is in hidden in the student's underwear. *Id.* at 377.

Other "Reasonableness" Searches

206. This question tests on administrative searches, using the facts from *Los Angeles v. Patel*, 135 S. Ct. 2443 (2015). "Official entry upon commercial property is a technique commonly adopted by administrative agencies at all levels of government to enforce a variety of regulatory laws; thus, entry may permit inspection of the structure in which a business is housed, ... or inspection of business products, or a perusal of financial books and records." *See v. City of Seattle*, 387 U.S. 541, 543–544 (1967). In order to evaluate the reasonableness of such inspections, courts must "balance[e] the need to search against the invasion which the search entails." *Camara v. Municipal Court of City and County of San Francisco*, 387 U.S. 523, 537 (1967).

C is correct because it is the "most likely" ruling: on balance, the hotel manger's interests against spot inspections and without judicial oversight outweigh the state's need to inspect the hotel registry under such circumstances.

A is incorrect because the hotel owner is not claiming an expectation of privacy in "in other people's biographical information;" instead, he is claiming an expectation of privacy in his own business records. **B is incorrect** because the Fourth Amendment does provide some protection to businesses. However, in the administrative search context, that protection is balanced against the need for the information requested and the intrusion of the search. **D is incorrect** because it makes no sense: conduct is criminal if it is defined as such.

207. This question tests on the warrant requirement for administrative searches. "[A]dministrative entry, without consent, upon the portions of commercial premises which are not open to the public may only be compelled through prosecution or physical force within the framework of a warrant procedure." *See*, 387 U.S. at 545. However, "[p]robable cause in the criminal law sense is not required" to obtain an administrative warrant. *Marshall v. Barlow's, Inc.*, 436 U.S. 307, 320 (1978). Instead, probable cause for an administrative search—which then becomes the reason to issue the warrant—is based on "a showing that reasonable legislative or administrative standards for conducting an ... inspection are satisfied with respect to a particular establishment." *Id.*

D is correct because it is the only answer that recognizes that the warrant was issued based on the inspection timetable set forth in the municipal statute.

A and B are both incorrect because the health inspector doesn't need individualized suspicion or traditional probable cause to obtain an administrative warrant. **C is incorrect** because, if true, the Fourth Amendment would have no application outside of a private home. But "[t]he businessman, like the occupant of a residence, has a constitutional right to go about his business free from unreasonable official entries upon his private commercial property. The business-man, too, has that right placed in jeopardy if the decision to enter and inspect for violation of regulatory laws can be made and enforced by the inspector in the field without official authority evidenced by warrant." *See*, 387 U.S. at 543.

208. This question tests on another type of balancing-type reasonableness searches and seizures: security screening at airports. Although the Supreme Court has not ruled directly on post-9/11 airport screenings, it has observed that the balancing associated with administrative searches is "well illustrated" by airport screenings, and that "the lower courts that have considered the question have consistently concluded that such searches are reasonable [as] Fourth Amendment" administrative searches. *National Treasury Employees Union v. Von Raab*, 489 U.S. 656, 675 n.3 (1989).

A is correct because it is the only answer that refers to a balancing of rights, which is the proper focus for an administrative search.

B is incorrect because the implied consent theory is significantly attenuated on these facts: "[t]he point is not that one has consented or impliedly consented to the search by virtue of deciding to be an airline passenger; rather, it is a matter ... of narrowing the search to the need...." *See* Wayne R. LaFave, et al., 2 *Criminal Procedure* § 3.9(h) (3d. Ed. 2007 & 2015 Supp.). **C and D are both incorrect** because the screener doesn't need individualized suspicion or consent under the administrative search exception.

209. This question tests on an administrative search of a "closely regulated business," using facts derived from *U.S. v. Biswell*, 406 U.S. 311 (1972). "Certain industries have such a history of government oversight that no reasonable expectation of privacy ... could exist for a proprietor over the stock of such an enterprise.... [W]hen an entrepreneur embarks upon such a business, he has voluntarily chosen to subject himself to a full arsenal of governmental regulation." *Barlow's*, 436 U.S. at 313. Only four industries have been found to fall within the "closely regulated business" category: liquor sales, firearm dealing, mining, and automobile junkyard operations. *Patel*, 135 S. Ct. at 2454–2455. However, in order to conduct a warrantless search of a closely regulated business, three criteria must be met: (1) there must be a "substantial government interest" underlying the regulatory scheme; (2) warrantless searches must be "necessary to further the regulatory scheme;" and (3) the inspection program must provide "a constitutionally adequate substitute for a warrant" by providing notice to the business owner and limiting the discretion of the individual conducting the search. *New York v. Burger*, 482 U.S. 691, 702–703 (1987).

A is correct because weapons dealing is considered a "closely regulated business" and so the spot inspection of the business without a warrant is most likely reasonable.

B is incorrect because the owner's consent is irrelevant if officers are allowed to search under the administrative search exception. **C is incorrect** because it doesn't recognize the fact that the gun shop is a "closely regulated business," and so the warrant requirement might be somewhat relaxed. **D is incorrect** because if the officers are permitted to search, the owner's consent is not involuntary.

210. This question tests on suspicionless stops of cars for legitimate non-law-enforcement reasons, using facts derived from *Delaware v. Prouse*, 440 U.S. 648 (1979). As with administrative searches, "the permissibility of [this] law enforcement practice is judged by balancing its intrusion on the individual's Fourth Amendment interests against its promotion of legitimate governmental interests." *Id.* at 654.

    A is correct because on balance, the trooper's unlimited discretion intrudes too much on the driver's right to be free from unreasonable searches and seizures. Put another way, if police want to stop random drivers for what might be a legitimate non-police need, they must have either reasonable suspicion or probable cause.

    B and C are both incorrect because the state's interest is not at issue here; instead, the issue is whether the method used to promote that interest—suspicionless, discretionary stops—strikes the proper balance. **D is incorrect** because the reasonability of a stop is not assessed by the evidence it uncovers.

211. This question tests on vehicle checkpoints, using facts derived from *City of Indianapolis v. Edmond*, 531 U.S. 32 (2000). In a vehicle checkpoint, police stop every car, or stop cars according to a regular and pre-determined schedule. However, even if the checkpoint limits an officer's discretion as to which cars to stop, the Supreme Court has "never approved a checkpoint program whose primary purpose was to detect evidence of ordinary criminal wrongdoing." *Id.* at 41. Instead, police wishing to find evidence of "ordinary criminal wrongdoing" must rely on warrants and traditional warrant exceptions to support their actions.

    C is correct because it accurately describes the problem with this checkpoint: however well-intentioned, it is unconstitutional because it impermissibly allows police to circumvent the Fourth Amendment. "Without drawing the line at [checkpoints] designed primarily to serve the general interest in crime control, the Fourth Amendment would do little to prevent such intrusions from becoming a routine part of American life." *Id.* at 454.

    A and B are both incorrect because the checkpoint here was unreasonable. **D is incorrect** because it doesn't address the proper issue, *i.e.*, whether police have the right to make the stop in the first place.

212. This question also tests on vehicle checkpoints, using facts derived from *Michigan State Police v. Sitz*, 496 U.S. 444 (1990).

    C is correct because it is a correct statement of law: if the checkpoint sufficiently limits the officer's discretion (to avoid abuses) and if the "primary purpose" of the checkpoint is not to "detect evidence of ordinary criminal wrongdoing," then the balance of interests will weigh in favor of the government.

A and B are both incorrect because both refer to a requirement of individualized suspicion for a stop. However, if the checkpoint is designed correctly, no individualized suspicion is necessary. **D is incorrect** because the automobile exception focuses on probable cause to search a vehicle, and this question deals with the right to stop the vehicle in the first place.

213. This question tests on whether a vehicle checkpoint—*i.e.*, a brief seizure justified for non-law-enforcement reasons—becomes unreasonable when it results in the discovery of criminal evidence. A "claim that particular exercise of discretion in locating or operating a checkpoint is unreasonable is subject to post-stop judicial review." *U.S. v. Martinez-Fuerte*, 428 U.S. 543, 559 (1976). However, if the officer conducting the checkpoint otherwise follows the Fourth Amendment, the checkpoint won't be defeated because it uncovered evidence.

    B is correct because it best describes what happened here: the checkpoint was lawful, the student opened his window, the officer smelled marijuana, and the officer then developed probable cause to search the car for marijuana.

    A is incorrect because the student's concession only addresses the right to seize in the first place. What if the checkpoint had been conducted at gunpoint? The student's concession wouldn't eliminate a claim that the seizure was conducted unreasonably. **C is incorrect** because it misstates the facts: the officer didn't use the checkpoint as a ruse to look for evidence. Instead, the officer developed probable cause to search during the course of a lawful vehicle checkpoint. **D is incorrect** because it also misstates the facts: the student rolled down his window to speak to the officer, which is how the officer smelled the marijuana. While the checkpoint arguably only required visual inspection of cars—to look for a child and a car seat—the officer can't be faulted for responding to what the student put in front of him.

214. This question tests on border searches, using the relevant facts from *U.S. v. Flores-Montano*, 541 U.S. 149 (2004). "[S]earches made at the border, pursuant to the long-standing right of the sovereign to protect itself by stopping and examining persons and property crossing into this country, are reasonable simply by virtue of the fact that they occur at the border...." *U.S. v. Ramsay*, 431 U.S. 606, 616 (1977).

    D is correct because it reflects the balance that is struck in border searches and recognizes that they are generally permissible, even in the absence of individualized suspicion. (D is a near-verbatim quotation from *Flores-Montano*. *Id.* at 155.)

    A is incorrect because the Supreme Court has rejected the routine/non-routine distinction for searches of property at the border. *Id.* at 152. **B is incorrect** because, as a restatement of the automobile exception rule and that rule's requirement of probable cause, it fails to recognize that the "Government's interest in preventing the entry of unwanted persons and effects is at its zenith at the international border," *id.*, and so suspicionless searches of property are the rule, rather than the exception. **C is incorrect** because it refers to a level of scrutiny for judicial review—which is irrelevant here.

215. This question tests on searches and seizures near the border conducted by "roving patrols," *i.e.*, officers who stop drivers as they drive down the road and not as part of a fixed checkpoint. Such searches and seizures are different than those conducted at a fixed checkpoint. "[T]hose lawfully within the country, entitled to use the public highways, have a right to free passage without interruption or search unless there is known to a competent official, authorized to search, probable cause for believing that their vehicles are carrying contraband or illegal merchandise." *Almeida-Sanchez v. U.S.*, 413 U.S. 266, 274–275 (1973).

C **is correct** because the stop would only be reasonable if the officer had reasonable suspicion, and the prosecutor conceded that he did not.

A **is incorrect** because it's untrue: *Almeida-Sanchez* holds that border searches are only permissible at actual or constructive borders. **B is incorrect** because it doesn't respond to the man's argument that his consent is a product of his unreasonable seizure. **D is incorrect** because seizures can be justified with reasonable suspicion, and they don't always require probable cause. However, the issue here is that the officer didn't even have reasonable suspicion.

Standing

216. This question tests on standing, which is the right of a party to make a claim—here, a claim that a search is unreasonable, and the fruits of that search should be suppressed. "Fourth Amendment rights are personal rights which, like some other constitutional rights, may not be vicariously asserted." *Rakas v. Illinois*, 439 U.S. 128, 133–134 (1978). Thus, a person has standing to raise a Fourth Amendment claim when he can establish a "legitimate expectation of privacy" in the area searched or the item seized. *Id.* at 143.

D **is correct** because the passenger has no standing in this situation: she has no expectation of privacy in either the driver's body or the trunk of the driver's car.

A **is incorrect** because the passenger cannot challenge the *Terry* frisk of the driver, despite the fact that it was unreasonable because it wasn't based on adequate suspicion. Instead, only the driver would be able to make this argument. **B is incorrect** because it addresses the weight to be given to the cocaine, not its admissibility. **C is incorrect** because only the drive is able to challenge his ability to voluntarily consent to a search of his car.

217. This question tests on how Fourth Amendment standing should be analyzed: "the better analysis forthrightly focuses on the extent of a particular defendant's rights under the Fourth Amendment, rather than on any theoretically separate, but invariably intertwined concept of standing." *Rakas*, 439 U.S. at 139.

D is correct because the officer had no reasonable suspicion to stop the young man under *Terry*, or to frisk him or search his belongings. But notice that the correct ruling in this situation does not require the court to first address standing and then address whether a search occurred; instead, the two inquiries are collapsed into one.

A, B, and C are all incorrect because each is premised on the idea that standing requires a separate, threshold analysis, and it does not.

218. This question tests on "automatic standing," using facts derived from *U.S. v. Salvucci*, 448 U.S. 83 (1980). There is no such thing as "automatic standing," even when the defendant is charged with a possession crime. *Id.*

    A is correct because it uses the test from *Rakas* and reaches the correct conclusion about the accomplice's standing, based on her concession that she had no expectation of privacy in the house.

    B is incorrect for two reasons: it makes no sense and it also conflates standing with the question of whether the elements of the crime are met on these facts. **C and D are both incorrect** because each focuses on a legal principle—equity and due process—that isn't part of the standing analysis.

219. This question tests on how the standing requirement can sometimes lead to disturbing results, using facts derived from *U.S. v. Payner*, 447 U.S. 727 (1980). *Payner* addresses the authority of the lower federal courts to invoke the supervisory powers. U.S. Const. Art. III § 1. Still, as to the standing issue, the Court explained that its "Fourth Amendment decisions have established beyond any doubt that the interest in deterring illegal searches does not justify the exclusion of tainted evidence at the instance of a party who was not the victim of the challenged practices." *Payner*, 447 U.S. at 735.

    C is correct because the drug dealer does not have an expectation of privacy in the bank president's condo or briefcase, and so doesn't have standing to challenge the search.

    A is incorrect because the issue here is about the standing of the drug dealer to challenge the search of the area where the papers were found, and not whether he signed the papers. **B is incorrect** because Fourth Amendment standing does not depend on the inability of someone else to make the challenge; instead, standing turns on the question of whether the person claiming standing can demonstrate that his personal rights were violated. **D is incorrect** because the documents are "papers," and fall within the Fourth Amendment.

220. This question tests on the "absolute limit of what text and tradition permit" in terms of standing: whether an overnight guest has standing to challenge a search of a private residence. *Minnesota v. Carter*, 525 U.S. 83, 96 (1998) (Scalia, J., concurring). "We will all be hosts and we will all be guests many times in our lives. From either perspective, we think that society recognizes that a houseguest has a legitimate expectation of privacy in his host's home." *Minnesota v. Olson*, 495 U.S. 91, 98 (1990).

D is correct because the woman is an overnight guest and so has standing to challenge the unreasonable entry into the house that led to the discovery of the marijuana on her bedside table.

A, B, and C are all incorrect because each states that the woman does not have standing in her friend's house and, as an overnight guest, she does.

221. This question tests on whether a short-term commercial guest of a private home has standing to challenge a search of that home, using facts derived from *Minnesota v. Carter*. He does not. *Id.*

    C is correct because it accurately describes the brother's limited ties to the woman's apartment and recognizes that an expectation of privacy can't be established under these circumstances.

    A is incorrect because it suggests that a defendant's standing is tied to the evidence recovered in a search, and standing instead depends on having an expectation of privacy in the area searched. **B is incorrect** for two reasons. First, it suggests that the brother has standing to challenge the search, and he doesn't. Second, there are no facts that support the assertion that the officers believed — reasonably or otherwise — that the evidence would soon be moved. **D is incorrect** for two reasons: it provides a factual response to a legal question, and it does not address the issue of standing.

222. This question tests on whether an apartment tenant has standing to challenge a search of the apartment, using facts derived from *Chapman v. U.S.*, 365 U.S. 610 (1961). She does.

    A is correct because an apartment tenant does have standing to challenge the search of her apartment, even though she may not be the owner of the property. *Id.* And, because the officer searched the apartment without a warrant, consent, or exigency, the search was unreasonable.

    B is incorrect because the officer's failure to establish the woman's presence is not what makes the search here unreasonable; instead, the search was unreasonable because it was performed without a warrant, consent, or exigency. **C is incorrect** because it fails to recognize that the woman has an expectation of privacy in her own apartment. **D is incorrect** because it does not respond to the motion to suppress and so does not represent the "most likely" ruling from the court.

223. This question tests on whether a "mere passenger" in a car has standing to challenge a search of that car. *Rakas*, 439 U.S. at 133–134. She does not.

    B is correct because the passenger, who admittedly has no ties to the car, cannot establish an expectation of privacy in the car.

    A is incorrect because it doesn't respond to the question of whether or not the evidence should be suppressed. **C is incorrect** because the passenger doesn't have standing to challenge the driver's consent to search; only the driver can challenge the legitimacy of his consent. **D is incorrect** because the seizure of a car's passenger—when the driver of the car is reasonably seized—is not unreasonable. *Brendlin v. California*, 551 U.S. 249 (2007).

224. This question tests on standing based on claimed ownership, using facts derived from *Rawlings v. Kentucky*, 448 U.S. 98 (1980). "While [claimed] ownership of the drugs is undoubtedly one fact to be considered[,] ... *Rakas* emphatically rejected the notion that arcane concepts of property law ought to control the ability to claim the protections of the Fourth Amendment ... After *Rakas*, the [proper inquiry is] whether governmental officials violated any legitimate expectation of privacy held by [the defendant]." *Rawlings*, 448 U.S. at 105.

A is correct because the man's control over the woman's purse is sufficient for him to have an expectation of privacy—and standing—in the purse, despite the fact that he did not own it.

B is incorrect because claimed ownership—alone—is insufficient for standing; instead, *Rawlings* and *Rakas* dictate that the person claiming standing must have a legitimate expectation of privacy in the area searched. **C is incorrect** because its focus on actual ownership undercuts the *Rakas* inquiry. **D is incorrect** because it conflates the proof necessary to establish guilt at trial with standing and suppression.

225. This question tests on the use of the defendant's testimony about standing (given at a suppression hearing) at her later trial. "We find it intolerable that one constitutional right should have to be surrendered in order to assert another.... [and hold that] when a defendant testifies in support of a motion to suppress evidence on Fourth Amendment grounds, his testimony may not thereafter be admitted against him at trial on the issue of guilt unless he makes no objection." *Simmons v. U.S.*, 390 U.S. 377, 394 (1968).

D is correct because it recognizes that the friend's suppression hearing testimony cannot be used to establish her guilt of the charged crime.

A is incorrect because it doesn't recognize the difficult choice faced by a defendant who needs to testify to assert standing, but who also wants to preserve his Fifth Amendment privilege against self-incrimination. **B is incorrect** because it doesn't answer the question: the issue is whether the friend's testimony is admissible, not how the defense attorney should rebut the testimony if it is admitted. **C is incorrect** because it doesn't make sense.

Fourth Amendment Remedies

226. This question tests on the exclusionary rule, which dictates that "evidence obtained by searches and seizures in violation of the Constitution is, by that same authority, inadmissible in a state court." *Mapp v. Ohio*, 367 U.S. 643, 655 (1961).

B is correct because it recognizes that the "most appropriate" remedy for an unreasonable search is suppression of evidence from the state's case-in-chief.

A and C are both incorrect because money damages are not the "most appropriate" remedy for an unreasonable search. **D is incorrect** because it doesn't actually describe a remedy: the man already has a right to testify in his own defense. *Rock v. Arkansas*, 483 U.S. 44 (1987).

227. This question tests on the current Court's view of the exclusionary rule. While "[e]xpansive dicta in *Mapp* ... suggested wide scope for the exclusionary rule," the Court has "long since rejected that approach." *Hudson v. Michigan*, 547 U.S. 586, 591 (2006).

    A is correct because it recognizes that the current Supreme Court is reluctant to broadly apply the exclusionary rule. (A is a near-verbatim quotation from *Hudson*. *Id.* at 591.)

    B is incorrect because the officers here—who presumably knew the time and the statutory definition of "daytime"—did not act in good faith. (B is a verbatim quotation from *Michigan v. Tucker*, 417 U.S. 433, 447 (1974)). **C and D are both incorrect** because each is too broadly worded to reflect the current Supreme Court's view toward application of the exclusionary rule. (C is a verbatim quotation from *Mapp*, 367 U.S. at 655, and D is a near-verbatim quotation from *Arizona v. Evans*, 514 U.S. 1, 13 (1995)).

228. This question tests on the first of the two original rationales offered for the exclusionary rule: judicial integrity. "Nothing can destroy a government more quickly than its failure to observe its own laws, or worse, its disregard of the charter of its own existence." *Mapp v. Ohio*, 367 U.S. 643, 659 (1961).

    A is correct because it refers to a recognized rationale for the exclusionary rule and so is the "most likely" answer—especially in light of the other choices.

    B is incorrect because it is untrue: a judge who permits unreasonably obtained evidence to be used at trial may well be following the Constitution. *E.g., U.S. v. Leon*, 468 U.S. 897 (1984) (outlining good faith exception to the Fourth Amendment exclusionary rule). **C and D are both incorrect** because each uses hyperbole and so neither represents the "most likely" answer.

229. This question tests on the second of the two original rationales offered for the exclusionary rule: deterrence of police misconduct. "[S]uppression is not an automatic consequence of a Fourth Amendment violation. Instead, the question [of suppression] turns on the culpability of the police and the potential of exclusion to deter wrongful police conduct." *Herring v. U.S.*, 555 U.S. 135, 137 (2009). More recently, the Court has stated that the exclusionary rule's "sole purpose" is to deter future police misconduct. *Davis v. U.S.*, 131 S. Ct. 2419, 2426 (2011).

    D is correct because it refers to a recognized rationale for the exclusionary rule and so is the "most likely" answer—especially in light of the other choices.

A, B, and C are all incorrect because none refers to a recognized rationale for the exclusionary rule.

230. This question tests on whether the exclusionary rule is constitutionally mandated. Although the exclusionary rule was originally considered to be constitutionally required, that view has changed. The Court now explains that the exclusionary rule "is a judicially created remedy designed to safeguard Fourth Amendment rights generally through its deterrent effect, rather than a personal constitutional right of the party aggrieved." *U.S. v. Calandra*, 414 U.S. 338, 348 (1978).

    D is correct because it properly describes the status of the exclusionary rule and concludes that there would be little deterrent effect on these facts.

    A is incorrect because the text of the Fourth Amendment doesn't "mandate" that unreasonably seized evidence be suppressed; instead, the Fourth Amendment protects against unreasonable searches and seizures. Whatever the exclusionary rule is—a remedial measure or a constitutional imperative—it is not part of the text of the Fourth Amendment. **B is incorrect** because suppression is an unlikely remedy where the police obtained a warrant and where probable cause is found wanting in a "close case." **C is incorrect** because application of the exclusionary rule shouldn't depend on the nature of the alleged offense.

231. This question tests on the practical effect of characterizing of the exclusionary rule as a "judicially created remedy." Because the rule is "prudential rather than constitutionally mandated," it "does not proscribe the introduction of illegally seized evidence in all proceedings or against all persons, but applies only in contexts where its remedial objectives are thought most efficaciously served." *Pennsylvania Bd. of Probation and Parole v. Scott*, 524 U.S. 357, 363 (1998). Accordingly, the Court has found numerous contexts where the rule does not apply. *E.g.*, *id.* (exclusionary rule not required for state parole revocation hearings); *U.S. v. Leon*, 468 U.S. 897 (1984) (exclusionary rule does not apply where officer shows objectively reasonable good faith reliance on magistrate's signature on the warrant); *Calandra*, 414 U.S. at 348 (1978) (exclusionary rule does not apply in grand jury proceedings); *Stone v. Powell*, 428 U.S. 465 (1976) (exclusionary rule does not apply in *habeas corpus* proceedings where prisoner had full and fair opportunity to litigate the claim in the state courts).

    C is correct because it recognizes that the exclusionary rule is not cognizable in every type of proceeding—especially where a litigant was given a full and fair opportunity to litigate his Fourth Amendment claim in other proceedings.

    A, B, and D are all incorrect because each refers to a different finality of judgment doctrine that has nothing to do with the exclusionary rule.

232. This question tests on the good faith exception, which permits use of warrant-based evidence where later examination of the warrant reveals that it was somehow defective or flawed. *U.S. v. Leon*, 468 U.S. at 920. For the good faith exception to apply, the officer's reliance on the magistrate's signature must be "objectively reasonable." *Id.* at 922.

A is correct because an objectively reasonable officer would know that waiting three weeks after issuance of a warrant—especially in light of state law requiring execution of a warrant within 10 days of its issuance—renders the warrant's probable cause stale and unreliable.

B is incorrect because *Leon's* objective reasonableness standard applies to the officer's reliance on the magistrate's signature, not his deference to a co-worker. **C is incorrect** because it doesn't address the delay in executing the warrant and whether that delay was objectively reasonable. **D is incorrect** because despite the state law violation, the probable cause to search was likely stale by the time the officer recovered and executed the warrant—which is more than a "technical violation."

233. This question also tests on the good faith exception, and the requirement that the officer's reliance be "objectively reasonable." *Leon*, 468 U.S. at 922. That standard is not met when the warrant is "based on an affidavit so lacking in indicia of probable cause as to render official belief in its existence entirely unreasonable." *Id.*

    B is correct because there's no good faith here: the officer was told that his application didn't demonstrate probable cause and then relied on rumors and innuendo to reject the magistrate's concern. In addition, the fact that the prosecutor now concedes the point undercuts any argument that the officer acted in an "objectively reasonable" way, as required for the good faith exception to apply.

    A is incorrect because the "special needs" exception has no application in the search of a private home, even if the home belongs to a public school teacher. **C is incorrect** because the fact that the officer eventually discovered the cocaine doesn't address deficiencies in the warrant procedure. **D is incorrect** because—if true—there would be no point in having a good faith exception.

234. This question also tests on the good faith exception, and presents another circumstance where an officer cannot claim good faith: when the warrant itself is "so facially deficient—*i.e.,* in failing to particularize the place to be searched or the things to be seized—that the executing officer[ ] cannot reasonably presume it to be valid." *Leon*, 468 U.S. at 922.

    A is correct because it recognizes that there was no good faith here: even though the executing officer was a rookie, he should have recognized that a warrant that doesn't include a showing of probable cause is facially defective.

    B is incorrect because it's untrue: different officers can be involved in obtaining the warrant and executing it, but the warrant itself must still be valid. **C is incorrect** because the officer's good faith is tied to the warrant's sufficiency and not the officer's overall work ethic. **D is incorrect** because the warrant must be valid at the time it is executed, not just at the time it is obtained.

235. This question tests on an extension of the good faith exception, based on a statute similar to the one found unconstitutional in *Los Angeles v. Patel*, 135 S.

Ct. 2443 (2015). "Unless a statute is clearly unconstitutional, an officer cannot be expected to question the judgment of the legislature that passed the law. *Illinois v. Krull*, 480 U.S. 340, 349–350 (1987). For that reason, when officers act in objectively reasonable reliance upon a statute authorizing [their actions], but where the statute is ultimately found to violate the Fourth Amendment," the resulting evidence will not be suppressed. *Id.* at 343.

B is correct because there was no indication that the statute was "clearly unconstitutional"—the Supreme Court's decision in *Patel* was 5–4—and so the officers had no other real choice but to rely on its constitutionality.

A is incorrect because the hotel manager didn't consent to the search; he gave the police the records because he was "afraid" of being charged with a crime. **C is incorrect** because knowledge of the just-filed lawsuit doesn't defeat the officers' objectively reasonable reliance on the constitutionality of the statute. **D is incorrect** because the question focuses on the officers' good faith at the time of the search, and not what happened later in time.

236. This question tests another extension of the good faith exception, based on facts similar to those from *Arizona v. Evans*, 514 U.S. 1 (1995). "The exclusionary rule was historically designed as a means of deterring police misconduct, not mistakes by court employees." *Id.* at 14. However, like an officer's ability to rely in good faith on the constitutionality of a state statute, an officer may in most instances also rely in good faith on the work of court employees.

A is correct because the officer's reliance on what he was told by the court clerk was objectively reasonable. Although the court clerk admitted to making a mistake, *Krull* holds that a mere mistake is not enough to suppress evidence under these circumstances.

B is incorrect because the officer's "good faith" is related to his reliance on the court clerk, not his act of checking for a warrant. **C is incorrect** because it doesn't respond to the issue presented by the facts. **D is incorrect** because the clerk's acceptance of responsibility is why the good faith exception applies—not why it doesn't.

237. This question tests on an extension of the good faith exception: where the officer relies on a mistake made by another employee of the police department. "The extent to which the exclusionary rule is justified by ... deterrence principles varies with the culpability of the law enforcement conduct." *Herring*, 555. U.S. at 143. Accordingly, "when police mistakes are the result of negligence ... rather than systemic error or reckless disregard of constitutional requirements, any marginal deterrence [of the exclusionary rule] does not pay its way." *Id.* at 147–148.

C is correct because it is the driver's strongest argument: that the computer error was not an isolated one, but instead was part of a more systemic problem.

A is incorrect because the officer's subjective motivations are irrelevant in the Fourth Amendment context; instead, courts should examine objective criteria only. *E.g., Whren v. U.S.*, 517 U.S. 806, 813 (1996). **B is incorrect** because the driver claims that his arrest was unlawful, and the discovery of the drugs came as a result of the arrest. **D is incorrect** because the drugs were found in a search incident to arrest; such searches require the authority to arrest, and don't require individualized suspicion that evidence will be found in the arrestee's pockets.

238. This question tests on whether an officer's mistake of law—where that mistake leads to the discovery of evidence—will result in suppression. If the officer's mistake is "objectively reasonable," then suppression is not required. *Heien v. North Carolina*, 135 S. Ct. 530 (2014). If the mistake is unreasonable, then suppression is the appropriate remedy. *Id.*

C is correct because it recognizes that a mistake of law can form the basis of an officer's reasonable suspicion, but it also acknowledges that the mistake here was unreasonable because the officer admittedly didn't know the law.

A is incorrect because it sets forth the incorrect standard for a valid consent search. *Schneckloth v. Bustamonte*, 412 U.S. 218, 229 (1973) (consent to search must only be voluntary). **B is incorrect** because the woman's "strongest argument" is that the officer had no right to stop her, not that he exceeded the scope of her consent. **D is incorrect** because it contradicts the holding of *Heien*.

239. This question tests on standing, which is the right of a party to claim a violation of law. "Fourth Amendment rights are personal rights which, like some other constitutional rights, may not be vicariously asserted." *Rakas v. Illinois*, 439 U.S. 128, 133–134 (1978). To claim standing, a person must demonstrate a "legitimate expectation of privacy" in the area searched. *Id.* at 143.

A is correct because the man lacks standing to challenge a search of the car: the facts state that he is only a passenger and that he changes cars weekly—so, even as a passenger, he most likely doesn't develop any "expectation of privacy" in the cars.

B, C, and D and all incorrect because each focuses on the actual search of the car, which the man doesn't have standing to challenge.

240. This question also tests on standing, but in a situation where the passenger can readily claim an "expectation of privacy" in someone else's car.

C is correct because the 1L student has standing to challenge the search and because the officer did not have a legitimate reason to search the car.

A is incorrect because the passenger here likely has standing: she regularly rides in the car, she has a key to the car, and she keeps her belongings in the car. **B and D are both incorrect** because each focuses on the weight of the marijuana evidence and the question asks about its admissibility.

241. This question tests on the fruit of the poisonous tree doctrine. "[T]the exclusionary rule reaches not only primary evidence obtained as a direct result of an illegal search or seizure, but also evidence later discovered and found to be derivative of an illegality or fruit of the poisonous tree." *Segura v. U.S.*, 468 U.S. 796, 804 (1984).

C is correct because the evidence in the woman's house was only discovered because of the man's statement, and the man's statement was only made because he was illegally arrested.

A is incorrect because it doesn't respond to the man's suppression argument. The man here doesn't have standing in the woman's house, but he does have standing to challenge his own unlawful detention—the "poisonous tree." And, since the evidence from the woman's house was discovered as a direct result of that poisonous tree, the man's lack of standing in the woman's house is irrelevant. **B is incorrect** for two reasons. First, it is too broadly worded. Second, a conspiratorial relationship between the man and woman has not yet been established, but has only been alleged. **D is incorrect** because the court's ruling should address the connection between the man's arrest and his statement, and the subsequent search of the woman's house.

242. This question tests on the fruit of the poisonous tree doctrine, and when a person may properly invoke its protections.

    B is correct because the drug dealer doesn't need to invoke the fruit of the poisonous tree doctrine to have the evidence from his house suppressed. Instead, because he has standing in his house, he can make the more direct argument that evidence from the house must be suppressed because the search of the house was plainly unreasonable.

    A is incorrect because the fruit of the poisonous tree doctrine—which is used to suppress secondary and derivative evidence—isn't the appropriate vehicle for the drug dealer to request suppression. Instead, the drug dealer should argue that the drugs (primary evidence) should be suppressed as a direct violation of his rights (the unreasonable search of his house). **C is incorrect** because it doesn't make any sense. **D is incorrect** because even though the officer's hunch was correct, his actions must still comply with the Fourth Amendment.

243. This question also tests on the fruit of the poisonous tree doctrine.

    A is correct because the officer searched the woman's condo with a warrant that was only partially based on the information he received as a result of the unreasonable frisk of the man. While the two are connected, the connection is not a "direct" one—as the answer describes.

    B is incorrect because it addresses guilt for the crime, and the question asks about admissibility of the evidence. **C is incorrect** because it disregards the officer's surveillance of the woman and the probable cause he developed as a result of that surveillance. **D is incorrect** because the question asks about admissibility of the evidence, not its weight.

244. This question also tests on the fruit of the poisonous tree doctrine, and how it interacts with standing. To claim a Fourth Amendment violation, a person must have standing in the "poisonous tree;" however, she does not also have to demonstrate standing in the fruits that are discovered from that poisonous tree.

C is correct because it is the "most likely" ruling: evidence seized pursuant to a legitimate search warrant is admissible.

A and B are both incorrect because the accountant doesn't have standing to challenge the middle-aged man's unlawful arrest; instead, the accountant only has standing to allege a violation of his own rights. **D is incorrect** because, although it properly states the rule about standing and reaches the correct conclusion, it is not the "most likely" ruling because it doesn't address the suppression issue presented by the question.

245. This question tests on the first of three exceptions to the fruit of the poisonous tree doctrine: attenuation. "The notion of the 'dissipation of the taint' attempts to mark the point at which the detrimental consequences of illegal police action become so attenuated that the deterrent effect of the exclusionary rule no longer justifies its cost." *Brown v. Illinois*, 422 U.S. 590, 609 (1975) (Powell, J., concurring). Attenuation is assessed by looking to the "temporal proximity of the arrest" to its fruits, "the presence of intervening circumstances," and "the purpose and flagrancy of the official misconduct." *Id.* at 603–604.

    C is correct because it recognizes that the taint of the unlawful arrest was gone by the time the woman made her voluntary statement several days after her arrest.

    A and D are both incorrect because each places the voluntary statement, made days after the arrest, on the same level as the evidence found in the search incident to the unlawful arrest. **B is incorrect** because it addressed the weight of the evidence and not its admissibility, and the question asks about the latter.

246. This question also tests on attenuation.

    A is correct because there is no attenuation here: even though the second officer's professional conduct might be described as an intervening circumstance, it was too close in time to the first officer's death threat for the exception to apply.

    B is incorrect because the officer is not required to tell the man he has a right to refuse consent. **C is incorrect** because the threat was made right before the man gave consent, so the consent is most likely a product of the threat. **D is incorrect** because the man gave his consent moments after the first officer threatened to kill him, so his consent is likely involuntary.

247. This question tests on the second exception to the fruit of the poisonous tree doctrine: independent source. "The independent source doctrine teaches us that the interest of society in deterring unlawful police conduct and the public interest in having juries receive all probative evidence of a crime are properly balanced by putting the police in the same, not a worse, position that they would have been in if no police error or misconduct had occurred." *Nix v. Williams*, 467 U.S. 431, 443 (1984).

    D is correct because it correctly describes the search warrant as a "lawful, independent source," and it also recognizes that suppression in this case in inappropriate because it would both punish the officer who conducted the warrantless search as well as those who went to the trouble of obtaining a warrant for the very same evidence.

A is incorrect because it doesn't address the lawfully obtained warrant. **B is incorrect** because it doesn't address the effect suppression would have on the officers who obtained the warrant—who did everything right and don't need to be deterred. **C is incorrect** because it is a policy-based answer to a legal question.

248. This question tests on the third exception to the fruit of the poisonous tree doctrine: inevitable discovery. "If the prosecution can establish by a preponderance of the evidence that the information ultimately or inevitably would have been discovered by lawful means ... then the deterrence rationale has so little basis that the evidence should be received. Anything less would reject logic, experience, and common sense." *Nix.* 467 U.S. 444.

A is correct because if the suppression judge agrees that the warrant demonstrates probable cause, then the D.A.'s argument is that the warrant would have been signed and executed and the cocaine would have been found anyway.

B is incorrect because the warrant hadn't been signed, and so the D.A. can't offer an actual independent source for the cocaine. **C is incorrect** because the good faith exception does not apply to the sheriff's deputy: he did nothing wrong, and so doesn't have to explain his actions by claiming good faith. **D is incorrect** because it's not an "accurate description" of the D.A.'s argument as it doesn't correspond to any recognized legal exception.

249. This question tests on the impeachment exception to the Fourth Amendment exclusionary rule. "It is one thing to say that the Government cannot make an affirmative use of evidence unlawfully obtained. It is quite another to say that the defendant can turn the illegal method by which evidence in the Government's possession was obtained to his own advantage, and provide himself with a shield against contradiction of his untruths. Such an extension of the [exclusionary rule] would be a perversion of the Fourth Amendment." *Walder v. U.S.,* 347 U.S. 62, 65 (1954). Thus, the prosecutor may use suppressed evidence to impeach regardless of whether the questionable statements are made on direct examination, *id.,* or cross-examination. *U.S. v. Havens,* 466 U.S. 620, 626 (1980).

A is correct because the man committed perjury when denied owning any knives beyond the dull knives in his silverware drawer, and so the prosecutor was permitted to impeach that testimony.

B is incorrect because it doesn't respond to the question and because, if true, there'd be no point to suppressing evidence ever. **C and D are both incorrect** because the prosecutor didn't engage in misconduct and there was no manifest injustice; instead, the defendant committed perjury and the prosecutor called him on it.

250. This question also tests on the impeachment exception and whether it applies to witnesses other than the defendant. It does not: "expanding the impeachment exception to encompass the testimony of all defense witnesses likely would chill some defendants from presenting their best defense and sometimes any defense at all—through the testimony of others. *James v. Illinois*, 493 U.S. 307, 314–315 (1990).

C is correct because it properly states the scope of the Fourth Amendment impeachment exception.

A, B, and D are all incorrect because each suggests that the prosecutor can use the suppressed evidence in some way to impeach any defense witness, and he cannot.

Fifth Amendment Explanations

Privilege Against Self-Incrimination

251. This question tests on the scope of the Fifth Amendment privilege against self-incrimination, which states that "[n]o person ... shall be compelled in any criminal case to be a witness against himself...." U.S. Const. amend. V. The Self-Incrimination Clause does not protect a person from responding to any question asked of her, but instead only applies when the person is being "compelled" by a state actor to provide a "self-incriminating" and "testimonial" response. *E.g., U.S. v. Hubbell*, 530 U.S. 27, 34–38 (2000); *Fisher v. U.S.*, 425 U.S. 391 (1975).

   C is correct because the student is not being "compelled" to give an "incriminating" response, at least as those words are defined in the context of the Fifth Amendment. While the student's answer will likely get her in trouble with the law school, that is not enough to trigger the protections of the Fifth Amendment.

   A is incorrect because, even assuming that the dean of this public university law school is a state actor, the student does not face "compulsion" and is not being asked to give an "incriminating" response. **B and D are both incorrect** because being sanctioned for plagiarism in law school is not a criminal sanction.

252. This question tests on "compulsion," which must be present for a person to claim a Fifth Amendment privilege against testifying. Compulsion requires being forced to respond in such a way that the individual faces the "the cruel trilemma of self-accusation, perjury or contempt." *Murphy v. Waterfront Commissioner of New York Harbor*, 378 U.S. 52, 55 (1964).

   A is correct because the sister is being compelled to make the type of choice that the Fifth Amendment protects against: to admit criminal responsibility, to lie, or to be held in contempt for refusing to testify.

   B is incorrect because the value of the sister's testimony to the prosecutor's case doesn't dictate whether she is being "compelled" to respond. **C is incorrect** because the Fifth Amendment protects anyone from being compelled to give incriminating testimony, not just a person charged with a crime. **D is incorrect** because it doesn't respond to the question: the sister may refuse to testify, but the question asks whether she is being compelled to testify.

253. This question tests on compulsion, using the relevant facts from *Ohio Adult Parole Authority v. Woodward*, 523 U.S. 272 (1998). "It is difficult to see how a

voluntary interview could 'compel' respondent to speak. He merely faces a choice quite similar to the sorts of choices that a criminal defendant must make in the course of criminal proceedings, none of which has ever been held to violate the Fifth Amendment." *Id.* at 286.

D is correct because the prisoner is not being compelled—forced—to participate in the clemency interview. Instead, because the prisoner can choose to participate in the clemency process (or choose not to), compulsion is not present.

A and B are both incorrect because each suggests that the Fifth Amendment would apply in these circumstances, but for the prisoner's conviction. However, the best response to the prisoner's claim is that the Fifth Amendment doesn't apply at all—to anyone—because the clemency interview process doesn't involve compulsion. **C is incorrect** because a person may face compulsion without a subpoena.

254. This question also tests on the scope of the Fifth Amendment privilege against self-incrimination. Because "compulsion [is] inherent in custodial surroundings," "no statement obtained from the defendant [in such situations] can truly be the product of his free choice." *Miranda v. Arizona*, 384 U.S. 436, 458 (1966).

C is correct because it's the man's "strongest argument:" that he was being compelled to provide self-incriminating and testimonial information, and so he needed to be given *Miranda* warnings, *i.e.*, told about his Fifth Amendment rights.

A is incorrect because it doesn't offer a reason why the warnings would be required; instead, it states that the warnings are required because they're required. **B and D are both incorrect** because each focuses on elements of a proper waiver of *Miranda* rights and the question asks why the warnings should be given in the first place.

255. This question tests on "incrimination," using facts derived from *Hiibel v. Sixth Judicial District Court of Nevada, Humboldt County, et al.*, 542 U.S. 177 (2004). "The privilege … extends to answers that would in themselves support a conviction under a … criminal statute but likewise embraces those which would furnish a link in the chain of evidence needed to prosecute the claimant for a … crime." *Hoffman v. U.S.*, 341 U.S. 479, 486 (1951).

C is correct because there's nothing in these facts that suggests that the man's name—by itself—is incriminating; his name neither ties him directly to a crime nor supplies a "link in the chain of evidence" to tie him to a crime.

A is incorrect because the concern described here—what might happen if the police check the man's name against arrest records—is too speculative to be considered incriminating. Instead, "[a]nswering a request to disclose a name is likely to be so insignificant as to be incriminating only in unusual circumstances." *Hiibel*, 542 U.S. at 191. **B is incorrect** because the fear of arrest can't convert a non-incriminating response into an incriminating one. **D is incorrect**

because it doesn't respond to the question of whether the man's response would be incriminating.

256. This question also tests on incrimination, using facts derived from *Ohio v. Reiner*, 532 U.S. 17 (2001) (*per curiam*).

D is correct because the nanny was the child's primary caregiver and the father is trying to blame her for the child's death. As such, her testimony may well "incriminate her."

A is incorrect because it suggests that the Fifth Amendment only protects the guilty, and it protects the innocent as well. *Id.* at 21. **B is incorrect** because the nanny's right to claim a Fifth Amendment privilege depends on the requirements of the privilege being met, not on a balance between her rights balanced against the father's. **C is incorrect** because forcing the nanny to make such a showing would, in fact, force her to incriminate herself.

257. This question also tests on incrimination and the standard for assessing whether a response links the speaker to criminal activity. The Fifth Amendment privilege is "confined to instances where the witness has 'reasonable cause' to apprehend danger from a direct answer." *Hoffman*, 341 U.S. at 486.

D is correct because an admission under oath to criminal activity is the sort of "reasonable cause" that will allow a person to claim the privilege.

A is incorrect because it doesn't respond to the question: a private lawyer asked the question about embezzlement, but the judge would be the one to force the accountant to respond. **B is incorrect** because the Fifth Amendment can be asserted in any proceeding—civil or criminal—assuming the person has reasonable cause to believe that her response will be later used in a criminal proceeding. **C is incorrect** because it makes no sense: the accountant's right to assert her Fifth Amendment rights does not depend on a prosecutor being present in the courtroom.

258. This question tests on the definition of testimony. "[T]o be testimonial, a ... communication must itself, explicitly or implicitly, relate a factual assertion or disclose information." *Doe* v. *U.S.*, 487 U.S. 201, 210 (1988).

B is correct because while the man was compelled to give a cheek swab and the results of the swab were incriminating, the swab itself is not testimonial.

A is incorrect because it doesn't respond to the man's argument, or the question. **C and D are both incorrect** because neither includes all three components of a Fifth Amendment claim—compulsion, incrimination, and testimony. However, even if all the components were present in the answer, the cheek swab is non-testimonial because it does not communicate anything beyond the man's physical characteristics.

259. This question also tests on the definition of testimony. "[C]ompelling the accused merely to exhibit his person for observation by a prosecution witness prior to trial involves no compulsion of the accused to give evidence having testimonial significance. [Such a practice] is compulsion of the accused to exhibit his physical

characteristics, not compulsion to disclose any knowledge he might have." *U.S. v. Wade*, 388 U.S. 218, 222 (1967).

C is correct because the woman is not being compelled to give a testimonial response; instead, she is being compelled to participate in a line-up and display her "physical characteristics."

A is incorrect because it is a misstatement of law. **B is incorrect** because the woman can't invoke a Fifth Amendment privilege in this situation, so the officer is not ordering her to forfeit that privilege. **D is incorrect** because it does not respond to the legal issue presented by the question.

260. This question also tests on the definition of Fifth Amendment testimony.

A is correct because presumably the prosecutor would ask the prisoner at least a few preliminary questions—*e.g.*, for his name—that don't require an incriminating testimonial response.

B is incorrect because the Fifth Amendment right applies when a person is forced to give incriminating testimony, and not to any other timing issue. **C is incorrect** because the prosecutor has not asked the prisoner any questions, and so his assertion of rights is premature. Instead, the prosecutor must first ask the question so that the judge can determine whether the witness has "reasonable cause to apprehend danger from a direct answer." *Hoffman*, 341 U.S. at 486. **D is incorrect** because the Fifth Amendment allows a person to remain silent, but does not protect against every consequence associated with that choice.

Miranda Custody

261. This question tests on the first requirement for the receipt of *Miranda* warnings: that the suspect be in "custody." A suspect is considered to be in *Miranda* custody when he "has been taken into custody or otherwise deprived of his freedom of action in any significant way." *Miranda v. Arizona*, 384 U.S. 436, 444 (1966).

A is correct because the young woman was under arrest at the time of the interrogation, and her arrest plainly meets the "taken into custody" definition from *Miranda*.

B is incorrect because *Miranda* custody does not depend on being in a particular location or not; instead, the focus should be on the degree to which the suspect's freedom is restricted. **C is incorrect** because *Miranda* custody does not depend on the use of handcuffs or not. **D is incorrect** because the *Miranda* custody analysis is completely separate from the issue of whether a person is charged with a crime.

262. This question tests on the issue of what should be considered in the *Miranda* custody analysis. *Miranda* custody turns on objective criteria, and not the subjective views of the officer or suspect. *Yarbrough v. Alvarado*, 541 U.S. 652, 662 (2004).

B is correct because objectively, the president was not in *Miranda* custody: she had arranged a convenient time to meet with the officer and had driven herself to the police station—and was presumably going to drive herself back home again. Under these circumstances, a reasonable person in this situation would not feel like her freedom of action was limited in a "significant" way.

A is incorrect because it limits *Miranda* custody to formal arrest situations, which applies *Miranda* too narrowly: a person is in *Miranda* custody if he is arrested, but *Miranda* custody can also occur under circumstances short of formal arrest. **C is incorrect** because it focuses on subjective criteria and *Miranda* custody turns on objective criteria. **D is incorrect** because the issue is not whether police could have arrested the president, but is instead whether she was in *Miranda* custody or not.

263. This question tests on whether an officer's knowledge of the suspect's age is relevant in the objective *Miranda* custody analysis. The suspect's age can be considered, assuming "age was known to the officer at the time of the interview, or would have been objectively apparent to a reasonable officer." *J.D.B. v. North Carolina*, 131 S. Ct. 2394, 2404 (2011).

D is correct because it presents a constitutional argument and recognizes that the officer knew that the student was relatively young—despite being confused about what grade the student was enrolled in.

A and C are both incorrect because neither responds to the "constitutional argument" requested by the question. And, while a jurisdiction may limit or prohibit the questioning of child suspects without a parent or guardian, nothing in the U.S. Constitution does. **B is incorrect** because it focuses on the student's grade and not his age—which is the relevant criteria for the custody analysis.

264. This questions tests on a situation that doesn't begin with *Miranda* custody but evolves into *Miranda* custody.

D is correct because no reasonable person would feel free to leave the interview after the officer told him that he could not leave, so that point marks the beginning of *Miranda* custody. And, even though the student teacher was not formally arrested, he was "deprived of his freedom of action in [a] significant way," *Miranda*, 384 U.S. at 444, so he should have been given his *Miranda* warnings at that point.

A is incorrect because it suggests that the encounter between police and suspect can't ever change from non-custodial to custodial. While the fact that the student teacher drove himself to the police station is relevant to the *Miranda* custody inquiry, so too are the events that occurred after the student teacher arrived at the station. **B and C are both incorrect** because the door could be closed—with the goal of preserving the student teacher's privacy—without the student teacher being placed in *Miranda* custody.

265. This question tests on what types of situations—short of custodial arrest—are considered categorical, or *per se*, custody. Under *Miranda*, the "custody" inquiry

is an objective one, and involves asking whether "was there a formal arrest or restraint on freedom of movement of the degree associated with a formal arrest." *Thompson v. Keohane*, 516 U.S. 99, 112 (1995). Because the custody inquiry depends on all the facts and circumstances, there is no categorical *Miranda* custody beyond custodial arrest—even when the suspect is incarcerated. *Howes v. Fields*, 132 S. Ct. 1181 (2012) (prisoners who are questioned within a prison are not *per se* in custody).

C is correct because it represents the "most likely" ruling: although incarcerated, the prisoner's freedom of movement was not restricted to the point where he was in *Miranda* custody.

A is incorrect because *Miranda* custody does not depend on the questions asked in the interview; instead, *Miranda* custody depends on restrictions on the suspect's freedom. **B is incorrect** because short of custodial arrest, there is no *per se Miranda* custody; instead, a court should examine the totality of the circumstances to assess whether a suspect is in custody or not. *Fields*, 132 S. Ct. at 1189. **D is incorrect** because it is untrue: prisoners still have a privilege against self-incrimination.

266. This question tests on whether routine traffic stops are considered custodial under *Miranda*. The general rule is that they are not, which means that officers are not required to provide *Miranda* warnings to most stopped motorists. *Berkemer v. McCarty*, 468 U.S. 420 (1984). There are two reasons for this rule. First, a routine traffic stop is necessarily brief in duration and so it does not present the same issues as in a prolonged interrogation—where the suspect will usually believe that the interrogation will continue until he confesses. *Id.* at 437–438. Second, a routine traffic stop is semi-public, so is different from a stationhouse interrogation—where the suspect will necessarily be separated from everyone but his interrogator. *Id.* at 438–439.

B is correct because it recognizes that the woman was not in *Miranda* custody because her freedom of action was not restricted in a "significant" way—as *Miranda* requires for custody.

A is incorrect because it doesn't respond to the custody issue. **C is incorrect** because it provides an incorrect statement of law: *McCarty* holds that routine traffic stops are not custodial under *Miranda*. **D is incorrect** because it equates Fourth Amendment seizures with *Miranda* custody. While there is significant overlap between the two, *McCarty* dictates that the overlap is not complete.

267. This question also tests on whether *Miranda* warnings need to be given in a traffic stop, but within the context of a far-from-routine traffic stop. While *McCarty* holds that *Miranda* warnings don't need to be given in routine situations, *McCarty* is inapplicable on these facts because this traffic stop was not routine.

A is correct because the father was in custody when he made the statement, since there was "restraint on [his] freedom of movement of the degree associated with a formal arrest." *Thompson*, 516 U.S. at 112.

B is incorrect because it doesn't respond to the question; even if this could be considered a Fourteenth Amendment violation, the father is arguing a *Miranda/* Fifth Amendment violation. **C is incorrect** because it overstates the holding in *McCarty*: *McCarty* holds only that routine traffic stops are not custodial, not that traffic stops can never be custodial. **D is incorrect** because, while true, it does not respond to the question of whether the father was in *Miranda* custody.

268. This question tests on another variation of *Miranda* custody: whether a person detained during the execution of a lawful search warrant is in *Miranda* custody. While such detention is a Fourth Amendment seizure, absent additional facts, the detention is not equivalent to *Miranda* custody. *Michigan v. Summers*, 452 U.S. 692, 702 n.15 (1981).

    A is correct: the woman was not under arrest, her liberty had not been restrained in any way, and it appears that the only reason she stayed in the house while the search was underway was because she wanted to watch television—not because the police detained her in any way.

    B is incorrect because a person can be in *Miranda* custody while sitting in her living room, assuming the facts also demonstrate she "has been taken into custody or otherwise deprived of [her] freedom of action in any significant way." *Miranda*, 384 U.S. at 444. Those facts just aren't present here. **C and D are both incorrect** because each presupposes that the woman should have been given *Miranda* warnings, and she was not in *Miranda* custody.

269. This question tests on whether a person can be in *Miranda* custody when in his own home, using facts derived from *Orozco v. Texas*, 394 U.S. 324 (1969). As with all *Miranda* custody issues, the answer does not depend on the person's location but instead turns on a review of the objective criteria.

    A is correct because the suspect here was in *Miranda* custody: he was woken from sleep by four police officers who were pointing their weapons at him, and so he was "deprived of his freedom of action in [a] significant way." *Miranda*, 384 U.S. at 444.

    B is incorrect because it focuses on the number of officers and not on the *Miranda* custody issue. **C is incorrect** because the *Miranda* custody determination doesn't turn on who began the conversation. Instead, *Miranda* custody turns on the degree to which the suspect's freedom is restrained. **D is incorrect** because it ignores the fact that the police officers woke the man up and held him at gunpoint.

270. This question tests on yet another variation of *Miranda* custody, using the relevant facts of *Minnesota v. Murphy*, 465 U.S. 420 (1984).

    C is correct because it recognizes that the probationer was not in custody when he arranged a "mutually convenient time" to meet with his probation officer in the presumably familiar setting of his probation officer's office.

    A and D are incorrect because neither responds to the question: the probationer did waive confidentiality and did agree to tell the truth, but the question asks about the failure to provide *Miranda* warnings—a completely different issue. **B is incorrect** because questioning by a police officer is not a prerequisite for the issuance of *Miranda* warnings. *E.g., Estelle v. Smith*, 451 U.S. 454 (1981) (*Miranda* warnings required prior to examination by state psychiatrist for use in capital sentencing).

Miranda Interrogation

271. This question tests on the second requirement for the receipt of *Miranda* warnings: the suspect be subjected to "interrogation." *Miranda v. Arizona*, 384 U.S. 436, 444 (1966). "Volunteered statements of any kind are not barred by the Fifth Amendment and their admissibility is not affected" by the *Miranda* decision. *Id.* at 478.

     B is correct because the woman's statement is not a product of the officer's words or actions. Instead, the woman's statement is best described as a spontaneous admission.

     A is incorrect because the officer was legitimately trying to fix the audio recorder and didn't trick the woman at all. **C and D are both incorrect** because they each refer to waiver, and waiver would only be an issue if the officer had interrogated the woman—and he didn't.

272. This question tests on a key assumption underlying all interrogations: that the interaction between the state actor and suspect produce "testimony." "[T]o be testimonial, a ... communication must itself, explicitly or implicitly, relate a factual assertion or disclose information." *Doe* v. *U.S.*, 487 U.S. 201, 210 (1988).

     C is correct because the tattoo on the man's hand is not testimonial evidence: it doesn't disclose anything except for the pattern of the tattoo.

     A is incorrect because, while the man was in custody and asked a question, the evidence obtained—information about the spider web tattoo—is not testimonial. **B is incorrect** because the question focuses on the failure to give *Miranda* warnings, which are required when a suspect is subjected to custodial interrogation. So, even if the officer was absolutely certain that the man had a tattoo on his palm, asking him to show the tattoo does not implicate *Miranda* because the tattoo is not testimonial. **D is incorrect** because the public safety exception is an exception to the requirement that *Miranda* warnings be given in the first instance. Here, because there was no interrogation, there was no need to give warnings.

273. This question tests on the first type of conduct that will meet the definition of interrogation: express questioning. *Rhode Island v. Innis*, 446 U.S. 291, 301 (1980).

     A is correct because the officer here asked the man three separate express questions about the investigation: "Did you really think you could have something this big on your property and that you wouldn't get caught? Did you think you no one would notice? Did you think you could get away with it?"

B is incorrect because it is possible for an officer to speak directly to a suspect — *e.g.*, by speaking about issues "normally attendant to arrest and custody," *id.* — and not "interrogate" him. **C is incorrect** because *Innis* doesn't distinguish between rhetorical and non-rhetorical questions; instead, *Innis* distinguishes between interrogation and non-interrogation. **D is incorrect** because "police surely cannot be held accountable for the unforeseeable results of their words or actions." *Id.* at 301–302.

274. This question tests on a certain type of questions: those "normally attendant to arrest and custody." *Innis*, 446 U.S. at 301. Such questions — even though they may be express — fall within the "routine booking exception" to *Miranda*, and warnings are not required before police ask such questions. *Pennsylvania v. Muniz*, 496 U.S. 582 (1990) (plurality opinion).

D is correct because it recognizes that the officer asked the woman questions but that the questions don't meet the test for interrogation.

A is incorrect because it fails to recognize that the officer's express questions were focused on "arrest and custody" and not in any way associated with the investigation. **B is incorrect** because harmless error analysis is inapplicable if, as here, there is no error in the first place. Here, because the officer didn't need to provide *Miranda* warnings, there was no error. **C is incorrect** because it cites to the incorrect standard for interrogation; the issue is not what the officer actually intended but instead what the officer should know.

275. This question tests on the second type of conduct will meet the definition of interrogation, using facts derived from *Rhode Island v. Innis*. "[T]he term interrogation under *Miranda* refers not only to express questioning, but also to [its functional equivalent:] any words or actions on the part of the police (other than those normally attendant to arrest and custody) that the police should know are reasonably likely to elicit an incriminating response...." *Id.*, 446 U.S. at 301.

B is correct because the officers here had no reason to know that the woman would be "peculiarly susceptible to an appeal to [her] conscience" about cats and dogs. *Id.* at 302. As such, their comments are not considered interrogation under the "functional equivalent" test from *Innis*.

A, C, and D are all incorrect because — while each states a fact that can be relevant to the issue of interrogation — the core of the "functional equivalent" test "focuses primarily upon the perceptions of the suspect" and whether the officers "should have known that their conversation was reasonably likely to elicit an incriminating response." *Id.* at 301, 302. Since nothing in the facts shows that the woman had a known weakness for animals, the officers' comments did not constitute interrogation.

276. This question also tests on the "functional equivalent" to police interrogation, using facts derived from *Brewer v. Williams*, 430 U.S. 387 (1977).

A is correct because the officer here took advantage of what he knew about the teacher—her perception of herself as a devoted teacher—to elicit an incriminating response.

B is incorrect because the effect of the officer's words is not the key to determining whether the "functional equivalent" test has been met or not. Instead, the focus is properly on the "perceptions of the suspect." *Innis*, 446 U.S. at 301. **C is incorrect** because the fact that the teacher took a few minutes to respond doesn't negate that the officer "should have known" that his comments were "reasonably likely to elicit an incriminating response." *Id.* at 301, 302. **D is incorrect** because directing the teacher to not respond is not dispositive of the issue of whether she was interrogated or not. *Williams*, 430 U.S. at 399 n.6 (concession by counsel at oral argument that "Christian burial speech"—which included directive that suspect think about officer's words and not respond—was *Miranda* interrogation).

277. This question also tests on the "functional equivalent" to police interrogation. In *Innis*, the Court specifically noted that a "reverse line-up"—"in which a defendant would be identified by coached witnesses as the perpetrator of a fictitious crime, with the object of inducing him to confess to the actual crime of which he was suspected in order to escape the false prosecution," *id.*, 446 U.S. at 299—could be considered interrogation.

C is correct because it recognizes that the predictable effect of the reverse line-up and the officer's statement about the false identification is that the man would confess.

A is incorrect because *Innis* directs that the standard is whether the officer "should have known," not whether he actually did know. Presumably, an officer should know that falsely accusing someone of a serious crime will prompt an incriminating response, even if the officer has no knowledge of whether the person has a susceptibility of being falsely accused. **B is incorrect** because it doesn't address the effect of the reverse line-up on the man, and assumes that the line-up wouldn't have any effect because the man knew he was innocent. **D is incorrect** because it's not the "most likely" ruling: it doesn't address the effect of reverse line-up or cite to the standard from *Innis*.

278. This question also tests on the "functional equivalent" to police interrogation, using the facts from *Arizona v. Mauro*, 481 U.S. 520 (1987).

B is correct because it's the "most likely" ruling: "[p]olice departments need not adopt inflexible rules barring suspects from speaking with their spouses, nor must they ignore legitimate security concerns by allowing spouses to meet in private." *Id.* at 530.

A is incorrect because it's too narrowly worded: the officer's silence is certainly important, but so is the wife's insistence that she speak to her husband and the fact that the police did nothing to manipulate the conversation between the two. **C is incorrect** because the officer's mere presence in this situation isn't enough for interrogation: there could be "a number of legitimate reasons—not related to securing incriminating statements—for having a police officer present." *Id.* at 528. **D is incorrect** because it's not the "most likely" ruling, given that the husband was aware of the officer's presence and that he knew the conversation was being recorded.

279. This question tests on the role of police intent in determining whether a particular police practice equates to interrogation. Police intent is not completely irrelevant, because intent "may well have a bearing on whether the police should have known that their words or actions were reasonably likely to evoke an incriminating response." *Innis*, 446 U.S. at 301 n.7. At the same time, the interrogation inquiry should "focus[] primarily upon the perceptions of the suspect, rather than the intent of the police." *Id.*

C is correct because, by recognizing that the officer's intentions are relevant—but not dispositive—to the issue of interrogation, it best tracks the reasoning of *Innis*.

A and D are both incorrect because each speaks in absolute terms and suggests that the officer's intentions play no role whatsoever—which defies common sense. B is incorrect because it is worded both too broadly (by referring generically to all *Miranda* situations) and too strongly (by referring to the presumption).

280. This question tests on the importance of the "perceptions of the suspect" in evaluating whether interrogation has occurred. *Innis*, 446 U.S. at 301. While the focus is properly on the suspect and his perceptions, "[a] practice that the police should know is reasonably likely to evoke an incriminating response from a suspect thus amounts to interrogation." *Id.*

C is correct because an officer should know that telling a teenager that he'll likely be homeless, uneducated, and have no future is the kind of statement that is likely to elicit an incriminating response.

A is incorrect because interrogation doesn't depend on the officer telling the truth or not; instead, the focus should properly be on the effect of the officer's words. B and D are both incorrect because each is too broadly worded.

Miranda Exceptions

281. This question tests on the basic idea that *Miranda* warnings are not required in every situation that involves custodial interrogation. Instead, there are three exceptions to *Miranda*, or situations where police are not required to give warnings: when police ask routine booking questions, when they ask questions about public safety, and when they place a suspect in covert custodial interrogation.

C is correct because it recognizes that the officer's question in this situation was so banal that warnings were not required—even though the suspect was in *Miranda* custody and the officer asked her an express question.

A is incorrect because it is too broadly worded, and would require *Miranda* warnings for a whole range of questions—like the one here, about a sandwich. **C is incorrect** because the teacher asked her lawyer about a possible *Miranda* violation and the reference to voluntariness improperly ties the failure to warn to a 14th Amendment violation. **D is incorrect** because if *Miranda* warnings are required, they must be given regardless of the suspect's prior knowledge or contacts with the criminal justice system. *E.g.*, *U.S. v. Patane*, 542 U.S. 630 (2004) (suppressing statement where complete warnings were not given after suspect assured police that he knew his rights).

282. This questions on the first exception to *Miranda*: the routine booking exception. *Pennsylvania v. Muniz*, 496 U.S. 582 (1990) (plurality opinion). This exception "exempts from *Miranda*'s coverage questions to secure the biographical data necessary to complete booking or pretrial services." *Id.* at 601.

    C is correct because it accurately describes the officer's questions here and the scope of the routine booking question exception.

    A is incorrect because warnings are not required under the routine booking exception, despite the fact that the suspect is in *Miranda* custody and is being asked an express question. *Id.* at 601. **B and D are both incorrect** because the exception does not look at the suspect's answers or the relationship between the question and the arresting offense to determine whether the questions are "routine" or not. Instead, the question itself must be examined to determine whether it is routine.

283. This question tests on the routine booking question exception using facts derived from *Pennsylvania v. Muniz*. Because *Miranda* warnings are designed to inform a suspect of his Fifth Amendment privilege against self-incrimination—a testimonial privilege—the routine booking question exception only applies to the suspect's testimonial answers to routine booking questions. If the suspect's responses are non-testimonial, then the exception is inapplicable because *Miranda* is inapplicable. *Muniz*, 496 U.S. at 590–593 (distinguishing between "delivery" of suspect's words and "content" of those words; only content is testimonial).

    D is correct because the recording—which shows the delivery of the man's responses—does not reveal testimonial evidence.

    A is incorrect because the routine booking exception will only apply when testimonial evidence is at issue. **B is incorrect** because the best evidence rule is irrelevant in this context. **C is incorrect** because application of the exception turns on whether the questions are routine and whether the answers are testimonial, not whether the officer followed police protocol in recording the intake.

284. This question tests on whether post-questioning events can retroactively change a routine booking question's characterization as "routine."

    D is correct because it's the "most likely" ruling: police genuinely need information about the medical needs of detainees, and the officer's question appears to be routine because at the time it was asked, the officer had no idea that the answer would have any significance at all to the crime under investigation.

A is incorrect because it's not the "most likely" ruling. If a question's classification as a "routine booking question" depends on whether its answer ever has any evidentiary use, then the words "routine" and "booking" have no meaning at all. **B is incorrect** because it misstates the facts: the officer here didn't use the fraternity brother's answer to "develop" new information, but instead used the information to link him to the young woman. In any event, nothing in the routine booking question exception bars an officer from conducting additional investigation. **C is incorrect** because the question is about whether *Miranda* warnings were required or not, and not whether the statement is admissible under the 14th Amendment.

285. This question tests on the second exception to *Miranda*: the public safety exception. According to this "narrow exception," police do not need to give Miranda warnings where "the need for answers to questions in a situation posing a threat to the public safety outweighs the need for the prophylactic rule protecting the Fifth Amendment's privilege against self-incrimination." *New York v. Quarles*, 467 U.S. 649, 657–658 (1984).

    C is correct because the possibility that there were additional bombs on campus presented an imminent threat and so the police were permitted to ask the student government president limited questions to resolve that threat.

    A is incorrect because it doesn't recognize the public safety exception at all, or that it might apply on these facts. **B is incorrect** because the officers did have adequate suspicion to seize the president, given the tip and the fact that the president's student ID was found next to the bomb in the chemistry lab. **D is incorrect** because—by focusing solely on the Fourth Amendment's exigent circumstances exception—it fails to respond to the question.

286. This question tests on the difference between investigatory questions and public safety questions, using the relevant facts from *Orozco v. Texas*, 394 U.S. 324 (1969).

    C is correct because the public safety question doesn't apply here since there was no threat to public safety. "[T]he questions about the gun were clearly investigatory; they did not in any way relate to an objectively reasonable need to protect the police or the public from any immediate danger associated with the weapon. In short there was no exigency requiring immediate action by the officers beyond the normal need expeditiously to solve a serious crime." *Quarles*, 467 U.S. at 659 n.8 (explaining why the public safety exception didn't apply in *Orozco*).

    A is incorrect because there is no threat to public safety on these facts. **B is incorrect** because the suspected shooter was in *Miranda* custody: he was in his bedroom and facing five officers with drawn weapons. **D is incorrect** because it's not the best answer: for the suspected shooter's statements to be considered a fruit of the officers' warrantless entry into his home, more facts would be required about the woman's apparent authority to give consent for the entry into the house and bedroom.

287. This question tests on the public safety exception in the context of a search incident to arrest.

B is correct because it's the prosecutor's strongest argument: the officer had probable cause to believe the woman had committed a homicide using a syringe and so needed to determine if she had a similar weapon with her at the time of the arrest.

A is incorrect because the woman wasn't being booked when she made the statement—she was being arrested. **C is incorrect** because it's untrue: the woman didn't speak spontaneously, but in response to the officer's question. **D is incorrect** because the question asks about admissibility of the statement, not its evidentiary value.

288. This question tests on the third exception to *Miranda*: the covert custodial interrogation exception. This exception "reject[s] the argument that *Miranda* warnings are required whenever a suspect is in custody in a technical sense and converses with someone who happens to be a government agent." *Illinois v. Perkins*, 496 U.S. 292, 297 (1990).

C is correct because it recognizes that the man was in a custodial setting—a jail cell—but not in *Miranda* custody. As such, warnings were not required.

A is incorrect because it suggests that *Miranda* warnings are required every time a suspect is questioned in a custodial setting, and *Perkins* dictates otherwise. Instead, the custody required must be *Miranda* custody. **B is incorrect** because while the suspect here was in custody "in the technical sense," *Perkins*, 496 U.S. at 297, this technical custody is different from *Miranda* custody. **D is incorrect** because the undercover officer's conduct met the definition of *Miranda* interrogation. *Rhode Island v. Innis*, 446 U.S. 291, 301 (1980) (defining interrogation as "express questioning or its functional equivalent").

289. This question tests on the core rationale for the covert custodial interrogation exception. "Conversations between suspects and undercover agents do not implicate the concerns underlying *Miranda*. The essential ingredients of a police-dominated atmosphere and compulsion are not present when an incarcerated person speaks freely to someone whom he believes to be a fellow inmate." *Perkins*, 496 U.S. at 296.

C is correct because it recognizes that the compulsion associated with custodial interrogation is not present when the suspect doesn't know she's speaking to a state actor.

A and D are both incorrect because each focuses on the subject matter of the questioning by the undercover officer, not on the officer's ability to conduct the unwarned questioning in the first place. **B is incorrect** because it suggests that warnings were required here, which contradicts the holding of *Perkins*.

290. This question also tests on covert custodial interrogation and the difference be-tween coercion and deception. "*Miranda* forbids coercion, not mere strategic deception by taking advantage of a suspect's misplaced trust in one he supposes to be a fellow prisoner.... *Miranda* was not meant to protect suspects from boasting about their criminal activities in front of persons whom they believe to be their cellmates." *Perkins*, 496 U.S. at 297, 298.

C **is correct** because the undercover officer did not coerce the sophomore into making a statement. Instead, the undercover officer deceived the sophomore.

A **is incorrect** because an invocation of the right to counsel protects the soph-omore from police coercion, but doesn't protect the sophomore from her own stupidity. And, although Justice Brennan suggested in his *Perkins* concurrence that covert custodial interrogation should not be permitted in the post-invocation context, *id.* at 300 n.* (Brennan, J., concurring), "that contention is inconsistent with the analysis of the *Perkins* majority." *See* Wayne R. LaFave, et al., 2 *Criminal Procedure* § 6.7(c) & n.142 (3d. Ed. 2007 & 2014 Supp.) (col-lecting cases). B **is incorrect** because the question asks about the events in the jail cell, not what happened outside of the sophomore's knowledge. D **is in-correct** because the question asks about the admissibility of the statement, not its weight.

Miranda Warnings

291. This question tests on the core requirement of *Miranda v. Arizona*: suspects subjected to custodial interrogation must be given information about their Fifth Amendment privilege against self-incrimination so that they can make a reasoned decision whether to exercise or waive that right. *Miranda v. Arizona*, 384 U.S. 436 (1966).

B **is correct** because *Miranda* requires warnings be given to suspects who are subjected to custodial interrogation, and the suspect here was in custodial in-terrogation but was never given the *Miranda* warnings.

A **is incorrect** because the man is requesting suppression of his statement, which is a remedy available for *Miranda* violations, not recording violations. C **is in-correct** because it refers to the Fourteenth Amendment's voluntariness test, and the issue here is the lack of *Miranda* warnings. D **is incorrect** because it doesn't address the lack of warnings, only the failure to record.

292. This question tests on the basic content of *Miranda* warnings. "Prior to any questioning, the person must be warned that he has a right to remain silent, that any statement he does make may be used as evidence against him, and that he has a right to the presence of an attorney, either retained or appointed." *Mi-randa*, 384 U.S. at 444. The Supreme Court "has never indicated that the 'rigidity' of *Miranda* extends to the precise formulation of the warnings given a criminal defendant." *California v. Prysock*, 453 U.S. 355, 359 (1981). Instead, the warnings

must "reasonably convey" the information required by the *Miranda* decision. *Duckworth v. Eagan*, 492 U.S. 195, 203 (1989).

D is correct because the warnings here addressed the core requirements from *Miranda*: the right to remain silent, the cost of waiving that right, the right to counsel, and that counsel will be appointed if the suspect can't afford counsel.

A is incorrect because *Miranda* requires information about constitutional rights, not grammatically correct sentence structure. **B is incorrect** because the reference to "financial means" does "reasonably convey" what *Miranda* requires: if the suspect "is indigent, a lawyer will be appointed to represent him." *Miranda,* 384 U.S. at 473. **C is incorrect** because the question asks about adequacy of the warnings, not about waiver.

293. This question tests on the adequacy of *Miranda* warnings, using the warnings from *Duckworth v. Eagan*.

A is correct because it is the prosecutor's "best argument:" despite the reference that an attorney would be provided "if and when" the woman went to court, the warnings "reasonably conveyed" the information required by *Miranda*. (In *Eagan,* the court found that the "if and when" language was not problematic because it "accurately described the procedure for the appointment of counsel in Indiana" and because *Miranda* does not require an attorney to be available round-the-clock at the police station. *Eagan,* 492 U.S. at 204–205.)

B is incorrect because it suggests that inclusion of "additional information" — without regard to what that additional information says — is enough to render adequate warnings inadequate. Instead, inclusion of "additional information" will only be an issue if that additional information somehow distorts the information required by *Miranda*. **C is incorrect** because police must always provide adequate warnings regardless of the suspect's prior knowledge of, or experience with, the criminal justice system. *E.g., U.S. v. Patane,* 542 U.S. 630 (2004) (suppressing statement where complete warnings were not given after suspect assured police that he knew his rights). **D is incorrect** because the prosecutor's "best argument" would address the claim that the warnings were inadequate, and would not tacitly concede that they weren't by arguing that the statement was still admissible under the Fourteenth Amendment.

294. This question tests on the adequacy of *Miranda* warnings, using the warnings from *Florida v. Powell,* 559 U.S. 50 (2010). At issue in *Powell* was the meaning of the phrase, "before answering any of our questions." "To reach the ... conclusion ... that the attorney would not be present throughout the interrogation, the suspect would have to imagine an unlikely scenario: To consult counsel, he would be obliged to exit and reenter the interrogation room between each query." *Id.* at 62.

A is correct because it is the "most likely" ruling from the court: the warnings reasonably conveyed what *Miranda* requires and the man's interpretation of the warnings was pretty convoluted.

B is incorrect because it is an incorrect statement of law; the Fifth Amendment right includes "not merely a right to consult with counsel prior to questioning, but also to have counsel present during any questioning if the defendant so desires." *Miranda*, 384 U.S. at 470; *see also Minnick v. Mississippi*, 498 U.S. 146 (1990). **C is incorrect** because it reflects the interpretation rejected in *Powell*. **D is incorrect** because the exact language from *Miranda* is not required; instead, the warnings must "reasonably convey" the information required by the *Miranda* decision. *Duckworth*, 492 U.S. at 203.

295. This question tests on the adequacy of *Miranda* warnings, with a focus on the right to remain silent.

    A is correct because it is represents the defense attorney's "strongest argument:" by telling the coach that he didn't have to "talk to me if [he] didn't want to," the officer arguably failed to inform the coach of his right to remain absolutely silent, and not speak to anyone.

    B is incorrect because a written waiver of *Miranda* rights is not required. **C is incorrect** because the coach was told of the consequences of waiving his right to remain silent; the first officer's use of the conditional—*i.e.*, the word, "might"—would not be enough to render the warning inadequate. **D is incorrect** because the question asks about suppression, not evidentiary rules.

296. This question tests on the adequacy of *Miranda* warnings, with a focus on the cost of waiving the right to remain silent.

    B is correct because the associate was not informed of the cost of waiving his right to silence, only that his waiver would be "up to [him]."

    A is incorrect because the warnings informed the associate of his right to remain silent and right to counsel. **C is incorrect** because there is no showing that the waiver was the product of coercion or duress, which would render the associate's statement involuntary. **D is incorrect** because the *Miranda* waivers don't have to be clear and unambiguous; instead, *Miranda* invocations must meet that standard. *Berghuis v. Thompkins*, 560 U.S. 370 (2012) (right to silence); *Arizona v. Edwards*, 471 U.S. 477 (1981) (right to counsel).

297. This question tests on the adequacy of *Miranda* warnings, with a focus on the right to counsel. The Fifth Amendment right to counsel includes "not merely a right to consult with counsel prior to questioning, but also to have counsel present during any questioning if the defendant so desires." *Miranda*, 384 U.S. at 470; *Minnick*, 498 U.S. at 153.

    A is correct because the teacher was only informed of her post-charging right to counsel at trial, and not the right to counsel during pre-charging custodial interrogation.

    B is incorrect because the warnings were inadequate and so they didn't "reasonably convey" what *Miranda* requires. **C and D are both incorrect** because each refers to the teacher's waiver of rights, and the "most likely" ruling would focus on the inadequacy of the warnings.

298. This question tests on the adequacy of *Miranda* warnings, with a focus on the right to appointed counsel for indigent suspects.

C is correct because the warnings here did not inform the politician that if he was indigent, counsel would be appointed to represent him.

A is incorrect because it's untrue: *Miranda* requires that the same essential warnings be given to everyone, regardless of income. **B is incorrect** because it's not the "most likely" ruling: although the politician's statement appears to be spontaneous, it was also made directly after he had acknowledged the inadequate warnings. **D is incorrect** because *Miranda* doesn't require a signature on a waiver form, it requires a waiver.

299. This question tests on whether a person can waive the reading of their *Miranda* warnings, using facts derived from *Baltimore City Dep't of Social Services v. Bouknight*, 493 U.S. 549 (1990). The suspect cannot waive a reading of her rights. *Patane*, 542 U.S. at 635 n.1 (government conceded *Miranda* violation where suspect stopped police from reading warnings and asserted that he knew his rights).

B is correct because the officer failed to give full *Miranda* warnings to the mother, so the resulting testimonial evidence—the map and the statement—must be suppressed.

A is incorrect because the map is testimonial. "[I]n order to be testimonial, an accused's communication must itself, explicitly or implicitly, relate a factual assertion or disclose information." *Doe v. U.S.*, 487 U.S. 201, 210 (1988). **C is incorrect** because a suspect cannot knowingly or intelligently waive a reading of her *Miranda* warnings. **D is incorrect** because the mother cannot knowingly or intelligently waive her rights unless they are properly read to her.

300. This question tests on the constitutional status of *Miranda* warnings. The Constitution requires "a procedure that is effective in securing Fifth Amendment rights," not necessarily that "police ... administer the particular Miranda warnings. *Dickerson v. U.S.*, 530 U.S. 428, 440 n.6 (2000).

C is correct because the judge's procedure provides an equivalent to *Miranda* warnings, and so the constitutional requirements of *Miranda* have been met.

A is incorrect because the Fifth Amendment doesn't require *Miranda* warnings; instead, *Miranda* requires that suspects in custodial interrogation be informed of their Fifth Amendment rights. **B is incorrect** because the judge's procedure provides an effective equivalent to *Miranda* warnings and so she is not attempting to overrule the *Miranda* decision at all. **D is incorrect** because *Miranda* warnings are not merely procedural; instead, they are grounded in the Constitution because they inform a suspect of her privilege against self-incrimination—a federal constitutional right.

Miranda Invocations

301. This question tests on the consequences of a Fifth Amendment invocation. If a suspect subjected to custodial interrogation "indicates in any manner and at any stage of the process that he wishes to consult with an attorney before speaking there can be no questioning. Likewise, if the individual ... indicates in any manner that he does not wish to be interrogated, the police may not question him. The mere fact that he may have answered some questions or volunteered some statements on his own does not deprive him of the right to refrain from answering any further inquiries until he has consulted with an attorney and thereafter consents to be questioned." *Miranda v. Arizona*, 384 U.S. 436, 444–445 (1966).

     B is correct because *Miranda* requires that a suspect's invocation be honored, and the suspect here invoked his Fifth Amendment rights.

     A is incorrect because by focusing on waiver, it fails to address the man's invocation and the officer's failure to respond to the invocation. **C is incorrect** because it suggests that the man's invocation was ambiguous, and it wasn't. **D is incorrect** because it's unreasonable to believe that the officer was actually confused by the suspect's statement.

302. This question tests on the standard for the invocation of the right to counsel. "Although a suspect need not speak with the discrimination of an Oxford don, he must articulate his desire to have counsel present sufficiently clearly that a reasonable police officer in the circumstances would understand the statement to be a request for an attorney." *Davis v. U.S.*, 512 U.S. 452, 460 (1994).[1]

     D is correct because the man's request that the officer tell him "more about how [the free lawyer] works" is not a clear and unambiguous request for counsel. Instead, it's a request for information about free lawyers.

     A is incorrect because an officer is not required to clarify an ambiguous reference to counsel: "[i]f the suspect's statement is not an unambiguous or unequivocal request for counsel, the officers have no obligation to stop questioning him." *Id.* at 461–462. **B is incorrect** because the man did not actually request counsel and so the officer was not required to provide counsel in this situation. **C is incorrect** because the "most likely" ruling would address both invocation and waiver.

303. This question also tests on the standard for an invocation of the right to counsel, based on facts derived from *Fare v. Michael C.*, 442 U.S. 707 (1979). "Whether

---

1. *Davis* involved a post-waiver invocation and its holding appears restricted to invocations made in that context. *See id.*, 512 U.S. at 461 ("We therefore hold that, after a knowing and voluntary waiver of the Miranda rights, law enforcement officers may continue questioning until and unless the suspect clearly requests an attorney."). Post-*Davis* however, the Supreme Court has assumed without expressly deciding that the *Davis* "clear statement" rule applies to pre-waiver invocations as well. *E.g.*, *Berghuis v. Thompkins*, 560 U.S. 370, 381 (2010).

it is a minor or an adult who stands accused, the lawyer is the one person to whom society as a whole looks as the protector of the legal rights of that person in his dealings with the police and the courts. For this reason, the Court fashioned in *Miranda* the rigid rule that an accused's request for an attorney is *per se* an invocation of his Fifth Amendment rights, requiring that all interrogation cease." *Id.* at 719.

A is correct because the boy's request for his mother is not the same as an invocation of the right to counsel, as she "is not in the same posture [as an attorney] with regard to either the accused or the system of justice as a whole." *Id.*

B is incorrect because the juveniles have Fifth Amendment rights, the same as adults. **C is incorrect** because what the mother would have done is irrelevant; instead, the proper focus should be on whether the boy properly invoked his right to counsel or not. **D is incorrect** because although the boy may have seen his mother as a person who could protect him, requesting her is not the same as requesting a lawyer.

304. This question tests on the procedure to be followed after a suspect properly invokes his right to counsel. "[A]n accused, … having expressed his desire to deal with the police only through counsel, is not subject to further interrogation by the authorities until counsel has been made available to him, unless the accused himself initiates further communication, exchanges, or conversations with the police." *Edwards v. Arizona*, 451 U.S. 477, 484 (1981).

B is correct because after a suspect properly invokes his right to counsel, police cannot subject him to renewed custodial interrogation the next day. Instead, the invocation must be honored.

A and D are both incorrect because each focuses on the interrogation on the second day, where the focus should be on the failure to provide counsel after the invocation. **C is incorrect** because, "formality" or not, the man invoked his right to counsel and the invocation must be honored.

305. This question also tests on invocations of the right to counsel, using facts derived from *Smith v. Illinois*, 469 U.S. 91 (1984). "Where nothing about the request for counsel or the circumstances leading up to the request would render it ambiguous, all questioning must cease. In these circumstances, an accused's subsequent statements are relevant only to the question whether the accused waived the right he had invoked. Invocation and waiver are entirely distinct inquiries, and the two must not be blurred by merging them together." *Id.* at 98.

A is correct because the woman's statement—"I need a lawyer to help me get through this"—is clear and unambiguous: she is requesting the assistance of counsel during the interrogation process.

B is incorrect because it doesn't respond to the question, which focuses on the invocation and the importance (if any) of the subsequent waiver. **C is incorrect**

because the woman made much more than a "passing reference" to counsel; instead, she properly invoked her right to counsel. **D is incorrect** because "an accused's post request responses to further interrogation may not be used to cast retrospective doubt on the clarity of the initial request itself." *Id.* at 100.

306. This question tests on the longevity of the right to counsel under *Arizona v. Edwards.* "When.... a suspect has been released from his pretrial custody and has returned to his normal life for some time before the later attempted interrogation, there is little reason to think that his change of heart regarding interrogation without counsel has been coerced. He has no longer been isolated. He has likely been able to seek advice from an attorney, family members, and friends. And he knows from his earlier experience that he need only demand counsel to bring the interrogation to a halt; and that investigative custody does not last indefinitely." *Maryland v. Shatzer*, 559 U.S. 98 (2010). For those reasons, the Supreme Court in *Shatzer* held that after a suspect has invoked his right to counsel and was then released from *Miranda* custody, police cannot place him in renewed custodial interrogation for two weeks. *Id.* at 110–111.

     D is correct because it presents the prosecutor's "strongest argument" against suppression: the man's right to counsel did not last indefinitely, but expired well before the police returned to question him six months after the original invocation.

     A is incorrect because *Miranda* rights are not crime-specific. **B is incorrect** because *Shatzer* requires a break in custody and a two-week interval—not just a break in custody. **C is incorrect** because it's not the prosecutor's "strongest argument:" although the man did waive his rights, the prosecutor also needs to demonstrate that the police complied with the procedure set forth in *Shatzer*.

307. This question tests on the standard for the invocation of the right to silence. "[T]here is no principled reason to adopt different standards for determining when an accused has invoked the *Miranda* right to remain silent and the *Miranda* right to counsel." *Berghuis v. Thompkins*, 560 U.S. 370, 381 (2010). Thus, a suspect who wishes to invoke his right to silence must do so "unambiguously." *Id.*

     C is correct because there is no ambiguity in what the man meant when he wrote the word "silent" on the sheet of paper. The word, "silent" is used in the standard *Miranda* warnings ("you have the right to remain silent") and so its use is an unambiguous reference to the Fifth Amendment right.

     A is incorrect because the invocation has to be unambiguous, but that doesn't necessarily require speech. **B is incorrect** because writing the word "silent" is not ambiguous. **D is incorrect** because remaining silent—without more—is considered by the Supreme Court to be an ambiguous reference to the right to remain silent. *Thompkins*, 560 U.S. at 382.

308. This question tests on the procedure to be followed after a suspect properly invokes his right to silence. First, police must "scrupulously honor" the invocation. *Michigan v. Mosely*, 423 U.S. 96, 104 (1975) (police "immediately ceased the

interrogation and did not try either to resume the questioning or in any way to persuade [the suspect] to reconsider his position"). Second, police must wait a "significant" amount of time before re-approaching the suspect. *Id.* (police waited an interval of "more than two hours"). Third and finally, police must provide the suspect with a "fresh set" of *Miranda* warnings, so that he is given a "full and fair opportunity to exercise" his rights. *Id.* at 105, 106.[2]

B is correct because the post-invocation procedure described in *Mosely* requires a "fresh set" of warnings and a waiver, which did not happen here.

A and C are both incorrect because each suggests that police cannot re-initiate contact with the suspect after an invocation of the right to silence. It is only after the suspect invokes her right to counsel that police are completely barred from re-approaching the suspect. **D is incorrect** because it suggests that police must leave a suspect alone for 24 hours after an invocation of the right to silence. Although the Court in *Mosley* did not specify how long a "significant" amount of time might be, the suspect in that case was left alone for "more than two hours," and the Supreme Court found that to be sufficient. *Id.* at 105.

309. This question tests on limited invocations, based on facts derived from *Connecticut v. Barrett*, 479 U.S. 523 (1987). If the suspect makes a clear but limited invocation of the right to counsel, then his access to counsel will be limited according to the invocation. *Id.* at 529 (suspect agreed to speak to police but said he wanted counsel to assist with written statement; Court observed that the suspect "made clear his intentions, and they were honored by police").

A is correct because the discussion between the officer and the suspect made it clear that the suspect only wanted a lawyer for a limited purpose.

B is incorrect because the invocation wasn't ambiguous; instead, it was unambiguous and limited. **C is incorrect** because it fails to recognize that the invocation here was for a limited purpose. **D is incorrect** because "the fact that some might find [the suspect's] decision illogical is irrelevant, for we have never embraced the theory that a defendant's ignorance of the full consequences of his decisions vitiates their voluntariness." *Id.* at 530.

310. This question tests on the procedure to be followed when a suspect makes a vague or ambiguous reference to the right to silence or counsel. While "it will often be good police practice for the interviewing officers to clarify" an ambiguous reference, *Davis*, 512 U.S. at 461, "the police are not required to end the interrogation, or ask questions to clarify whether the accused wants to invoke his or her *Miranda* rights." *Thompkins*, 560 U.S. at 381.

---

2. Courts are split as to whether the second round of interrogation must be about a different topic than the first. Wayne R. LaFave, et al., 2 *Criminal Procedure* § 6.9(f) & nn.103–106 and accompanying text (3d. Ed. 2007 & 2014 Supp.) ("*Miranda*: Waiver of Rights").

C is correct because it addresses the inadequate invocation and the waiver, so it is the "most likely" ruling.

A is incorrect because the police are not required to clarify ambiguous references to *Miranda* rights. **B is incorrect** because it's not the "most likely" ruling: if the police in *Thompkins* were permitted to question the suspect for 2 hours and 45 minutes in a "very, very one-sided ... monologue," *id.* at 393 (Sotomayor, J., dissenting), then the officer's questions here are certainly permissible. **D is incorrect** because it only addresses the waiver, and not the possible invocation as well.

Miranda Re-Initiation

311. This question tests on whether a suspect may ever be interrogated after he has properly invoked either his right to counsel or his right to silence. "[A]n accused, ... having expressed his desire to deal with the police only through counsel, is not subject to further interrogation by the authorities until counsel has been made available to him, unless the accused himself initiates further communication, exchanges, or conversations with the police." *Edwards v. Arizona*, 451 U.S. 477, 484–485 (1981).

B is correct because it accurately describes the events here and recognizes that a suspect can always change his mind about speaking to the police.

A is incorrect because the student's invocation was effective because it was made in response to *Miranda* warnings and because it was clear and unambiguous. **C is incorrect** because the facts show that the student changed his mind, not that he didn't understand his rights. **D is incorrect** because it suggests that the student could never change his mind about his invocation, and *Edwards* plainly holds that he can.

312. This question tests on what must occur for a court to find a post-invocation statement admissible: a court must find that the suspect "re-initiated" conversation with the police. *Oregon v. Bradshaw*, 462 U.S. 1039 (1983) (plurality opinion). Although a majority of justices did not agree as to what would constitute re-initiation by the suspect, the conduct here—the officer re-starting the interrogation, completely on his own and without any indication by the suspect that she wants to discuss the case—would certainly fall short.

B is correct because, however one views re-initiation, it does require some indication from the suspect that she wants to discuss the case.

A is incorrect because the *Bradshaw* plurality did not impose such a rigid who-spoke-first test; only the dissent would have restricted re-initiation to those situations where the "accused himself initiates further communication" with the police. *Id.* at 1053 (Marshall, J., dissenting). **C is incorrect** because the voluntariness—or not—of the arrestee's answers doesn't address the re-initiation

question and whether re-initiation occurs when police simply resume an interrogation that was stopped by a proper invocation. **D is incorrect** because *Miranda*
only requires one clear and unambiguous invocation of rights, not two.

313. This question tests on the standard for evaluating re-initiation. "There are some
inquiries, such as a request for a drink of water or a request to use a telephone
that are so routine that they cannot be fairly said to represent a desire on the
part of an accused to open up a more generalized discussion relating directly
or indirectly to the investigation." *Bradshaw*, 462 U.S. at 1045.

B is correct because it most realistically describes what happened here: the
woman did not re-initiate because she clearly wanted to talk about the noise in
her cell and not her case.

A is incorrect because the issue of re-initiation turns on what the suspect said
to the officer and not on facial expressions. **C is incorrect** because the facts state
that the officer "led" the woman into the interrogation room, so her act of accompanying him can't be interpreted as a desire to speak about the case. **D is
incorrect** because mere contact is not necessarily re-initiation.

314. This question also tests on the standard for evaluating re-initiation. If the suspect's query to the officer "evince[s] a willingness and a desire for a generalized
discussion about the investigation" and "is not merely a necessary inquiry arising
out of the incidents of the custodial relationship," then he has re-initiated conversation with the police. *Id.* at 1045–1046.

A is correct because the man's statement to the officer—that he was bored—was
plainly associated with the "custodial relationship," and so didn't represent the
sort of post-invocation re-initiation that permits an officer to discuss the case.

B is incorrect because the man's request to the guard is not what is relevant
here; instead, the issue of re-initiation will turn on what happened between the
man and the officer. **C is incorrect** because the man's statement about his boredom is best described as a statement of fact, and not an invitation for an interrogation. **D is incorrect** because there could be many reasons why the man
asked to speak to the officer, short of re-initiating a discussion about the case.

315. This question tests on what must also occur for a court to find a post-
invocation statement admissible based on a suspect's re-initiation: the suspect
must waive his rights. "[T]he burden remains upon the prosecution to show
that subsequent events indicated a waiver of the Fifth Amendment right to
have counsel present during the interrogation." *Id.* at 1044. As with any *Miranda* waiver, the waiver must be "made voluntarily, knowingly and intelligently." *Miranda*, 384 U.S. at 444.

A is correct because it cites the correct standard for waiver and accurately describes the waiver here.

B is incorrect because for the woman's statement to be admissible, her waiver
must be more than voluntary—it must also be knowing and intelligent. **C and
D are both incorrect** because the facts don't indicate that the officer did anything

to interfere with the woman's access to her lawyer; instead, the facts show that the woman decided to re-initiate and confess before a meeting with her lawyer could be held.

Miranda Waivers

316. The question tests on the standard for waiving *Miranda* rights. "The defendant may waive [his] ... rights, provided the waiver is made voluntarily, knowingly and intelligently." *Miranda v. Arizona*, 384 U.S. 436, 444 (1966).

    D is correct because it sets forth the proper waiver standard from *Miranda*.

    A and B are both incorrect because each addresses factual circumstances that might be important in the waiver evaluation, not the overall standard for waiver. **C is incorrect** because it states the standard for a voluntary waiver and a *Miranda* waiver requires more than voluntariness.

317. The question tests on what facts are relevant in assessing whether a suspect has validly waived his *Miranda* rights. "[T]he determination whether statements obtained during custodial interrogation are admissible against the accused is to be made upon an inquiry into the totality of the circumstances surrounding the interrogation, to ascertain whether the accused in fact knowingly and voluntarily decided to forgo his rights to remain silent and to have the assistance of counsel." *Fare v. Michael C.*, 442 U.S. 707, 724–725 (1979).

    D is correct because—by referring to the totality of the circumstances—it presents the "strongest argument" in support of the motion to suppress.

    A, B, and C are all incorrect because each addresses only some of the facts surrounding the waiver.

318. The question tests on the meaning of "knowing," in the context of a knowing, voluntary, and intelligent waiver. "[T]he waiver must have been made with a full awareness of ... the nature of the right being abandoned ..." *Moran v. Burbine*, 475 U.S. 412, 421 (1986).

    A is correct because the secretary was not told of her right to remain silent, only that she did not have to speak to one of the four officers in the interrogation room. For that reason, the secretary's "strongest argument" in support of her motion to suppress is that she did not fully "know" what her rights were.

    B is incorrect because there are no facts suggesting coercion and duress—which would render the waiver involuntary. **C is incorrect** because the secretary was told about the consequences of waiver. **D is incorrect** because *Miranda* requires a valid waiver, not necessarily a written one.

319. The question tests on the meaning of "voluntary," in the context of a knowing, voluntary, and intelligent waiver. "[T]he relinquishment of the right must have been voluntary in the sense that it was the product of a free and deliberate choice rather than intimidation, coercion, or deception." *Burbine*, 475 U.S. at 421.

B is correct because the waiver was based on a threat: the officer would remove the woman's children if she didn't confess.

A is incorrect because the woman knew her rights because they had been read to her. **C is incorrect** because the woman understood the consequences of waiving her rights, because that information was included in the *Miranda* warnings that were read to her. **D is incorrect** because nothing in the facts suggests that the woman acted unintentionally. Instead, the facts suggest that the woman acted intentionally, and in direct response to the threat.

320. The question tests on the meaning of "intelligent," in the context of a knowing, voluntary, and intelligent waiver. "[T]he waiver must have been made with a full awareness of ... the consequences of the decision to abandon [the right]." *Burbine*, 475 U.S. at 421.

    C is correct because the man was never informed of the consequences of waiving his rights, only that the arresting officer was his adversary. That is not the same as being told the consequences of waiving the privilege against self-incrimination.

    A is incorrect because the man was told his rights — that he had a right to remain silent and a right to counsel, and that a lawyer would be appointed to represent him if he couldn't afford counsel — and so the "best reason" to grant the motion won't focus on the knowing aspect of the waiver. **B is incorrect** because there are no facts suggesting coercion and duress — which would render the waiver involuntary. **D is incorrect** because the clear and unambiguous standard is applied to invocations, not waivers.

321. The question tests on what information should be evaluated in the waiver assessment, using facts derived from *Moran v. Burbine*. "Events occurring outside of the presence of the suspect and entirely unknown to him ... have no bearing on the capacity to comprehend and knowingly relinquish a constitutional right." *Id.* at 422.

    A is correct because it sets forth the correct standard for waiver and reaches the correct conclusion, given the facts. While it probably would have been helpful for the freshman to know about the professor's call, the freshman's waiver is properly evaluated by examining the facts known to him at the time of the purported waiver.

    B is incorrect because it suggests that a violation occurred and that there is a good faith exception to *Miranda* — both of which are inaccurate. **C is incorrect** because "the privilege against compulsory self-incrimination is ... a personal [right] that can only be invoked by the individual whose testimony is being compelled." *Id.* at 433 n.4. **D is incorrect** because the conduct here is similar to that which occurred in *Burbine*, and which the Supreme Court described a falling "short of the kind of misbehavior that so shocks the sensibilities of civilized society as to warrant a federal intrusion into the criminal processes of the States." *Id.* at 433–434.

322. This question tests on whether *Miranda* waivers have to be in writing. "Some language in *Miranda* could be read to indicate that waivers are difficult to establish absent an explicit written waiver.... The course of decisions since *Miranda,* informed by the application of *Miranda* warnings in the whole course of law enforcement, demonstrates that waivers can be established even absent formal or express statements of waiver that would be expected in, say, a judicial hearing to determine if a guilty plea has been properly entered." *Berghuis v. Thompkins*, 560 U.S. 370, 383 (2010).

C is correct because the recitation of proper warnings ensured that the man's waiver was knowing and intelligent, and the lack of any coercion and duress ensured that it was voluntary.

A is incorrect because the waiver does not need to be in writing. B is incorrect because the waiver does not need to be audio recorded. D is incorrect because it's untrue: the officer did prompt the man when he turned on the tape recorder and said, "okay, start talking."

323. This questions on whether waiver can be inferred based solely on the fact that a suspect confesses after receiving *Miranda* warnings. "If the State establishes that a *Miranda* warning was given and the accused made an uncoerced statement, this showing, standing alone, is insufficient to demonstrate a valid waiver of *Miranda* rights.... The prosecution must make the additional showing that the accused understood these rights." *Thompkins*, 560 U.S. at 384; *see also Tague v. Louisiana*, 444 U.S. 469 (1980) (*per curiam*).

C is correct because the facts don't establish that the officer did anything to ensure that the man understood the warnings, *e.g.*, ask him if he understood his rights.

A is incorrect because it refers only to voluntariness, and a *Miranda* waiver must also be knowing and intelligent. B is incorrect because the factual accuracy of the man's statement doesn't establish that the *Miranda* waiver was knowing, voluntary, and intelligent. D is incorrect because *Miranda* waivers don't need to be in writing.

324. This question tests on the standard for an implied waiver of *Miranda* rights, using facts derived from *Berghuis v. Thompkins*. "Where the prosecution shows that a *Miranda* warning was given and that it was understood by the accused, an accused's uncoerced statement establishes an implied waiver of the right to remain silent." *Id.*, 560 U.S. at 384.

B is correct because there is no proof in these facts that the suspect understood the warnings. In *Thompkins*, by contrast, the suspect was given a written copy of the warnings and read one of the warnings back to the interrogating officers—facts that showed that he understood his rights. *Id.* at 385–386.

A is incorrect because *Miranda* waivers don't need to be express, or in writing. C is incorrect because it refers only to voluntariness, and a *Miranda* waiver must also be knowing and intelligent. D is incorrect because the issue of whether the suspect invoked his rights is separate from the issue of whether he waived those rights.

325. This question tests on whether the validity of a suspect's waiver is affected by whether or not the suspect knows the precise subject matter of the interrogation. "[A] suspect's awareness of all the possible subjects of questioning in advance of interrogation is not relevant to determining whether the suspect voluntarily, knowingly, and intelligently waived his Fifth Amendment privilege." *Colorado v. Spring*, 479 U.S. 564, 577 (1987).

D is correct because the facts here show that the woman's waiver was knowing, voluntarily, and intelligent—even though she did not know the officer wanted to discuss five bank robberies with her, instead of just one.

A is incorrect because the woman was given the critical information she needed to make her choice to waive, *i.e.*, that the officer wanted to discuss bank robbery. **B is incorrect** because *Spring* expressly held that "mere silence by law enforcement officials as to the subject matter of an interrogation is [not the sort of] trickery sufficient to invalidate a suspect's waiver of *Miranda* rights...." *Id.* at 576. **C is incorrect** because the woman's later invocation of the right to cannot be used to show her earlier waiver was valid.

Miranda/Fifth Amendment Remedies

326. This question tests on the basic remedy for a *Miranda* violation: "the prosecution may not use statements, whether exculpatory or inculpatory, stemming from custodial interrogation of the defendant unless it demonstrates the use of procedural safeguards effective to secure the privilege against self-incrimination." *Miranda v. Arizona*, 384 U.S. 436, 444 (1966).

B is correct because it recognizes that if the officer continues to interrogate the man after he invokes his rights—here, the right to silence—the man's resulting statements must be suppressed from the prosecutor's case-in-chief.

A is incorrect because it states a rule opposite from *Miranda*: the confession will be suppressed and cannot be used to establish his guilt. **C is incorrect** because *Miranda*'s impeachment rule extends only to the defendant if he testifies, not to all defense witnesses. **D is incorrect** because it is a Latin phrase— meaning, "I think, therefore I am"—that has no application here.

327. This questions tests on the issue of *Miranda* remedies in the absence of a criminal proceeding. "[T]he absence of a 'criminal case' in which [a person is] compelled to be a 'witness' against himself defeats [a] core Fifth Amendment claim." *Chavez v. Martinez*, 538 U.S. 760, 772–773 (2003) (plurality opinion).

B is correct because the "most likely" ruling is that the privilege against self-incrimination is not violated unless and until the state actually tries to use the woman's testimony against her.

A is incorrect because it doesn't address the fact that criminal charges were not filed against the woman. **C and D are both incorrect** because the woman was subjected to custodial interrogation in the emergency room.

328. This question tests on application of the fruit of the poisonous tree doctrine in the *Miranda* context. "A subsequent administration of *Miranda* warnings to a suspect who has given a voluntary but unwarned statement ordinarily should suffice to remove the conditions that precluded admission of the earlier statement. In such circumstances, the finder of fact may reasonably conclude that the suspect made a rational and intelligent choice whether to waive or invoke his rights." *Oregon v. Elstad*, 470 U.S. 298, 314 (1985).

   D is correct because it recognizes the later confession is not a "fruit" of what happened during the car ride; instead, the later confession was made after the man was told his rights and made the reasoned decision to waive them.

   A and B are both incorrect because *Elstad* rejects application of the "fruits" doctrine for routine *Miranda* violations. **C is incorrect** because it suggests that *Miranda* violations are only "technical" violations, but statements made in violation of *Miranda* are considered to be compelled, even if the suspect "has suffered no identifiable constitutional harm." *Id.* at 307.

329. This question tests on the "question-first, warn-later" procedure considered in *Missouri v. Seibert*, 542 U.S. 600 (2003) (plurality opinion). "The threshold issue when interrogators question first and warn later is thus whether it would be reasonable to find that in these circumstances the warnings could function effectively as *Miranda* requires." *Id.* at 612. To make this evaluation, a court will examine "the completeness and detail of the questions and answers in the first round of interrogation, the overlapping content of the two statements, the timing and setting of the first and the second, the continuity of police personnel, and the degree to which the interrogator's questions treated the second round as continuous with the first." *Id.* at 615.

   D is correct because it recognizes that the first statement should be suppressed due to the *Miranda* violation and that the reading of warnings—at the man's insistence—didn't cure the problem.

   A and B are both incorrect because neither recognizes that the *Miranda* warnings had little chance of being effective, given the circumstances here. Instead, all of the factors that the Supreme Court in *Siebert* found important are present on these facts. **C is incorrect** because, at minimum, the first statement should be suppressed due to the *Miranda* violation.

330. This question also tests on the "question first, warn later" procedure and the types of "relevant facts that bear on whether *Miranda* warnings delivered midstream could be effective enough to accomplish their object." *Seibert*, 542 U.S. at 615.

   B is correct because it is the senior's "strongest argument:" the officer here reminded the senior that he'd already confessed and suggested that purpose of the interrogation was to "fill in the details" of the crime.

A is incorrect because it is not the senior's "strongest argument." A two-hour break may be insufficient in certain circumstances, but it's far longer than the 15-to-20 minute break that was found to be insufficient in *Seibert. Id.* at 605. C is incorrect because—while true and while considered a relevant fact under *Seibert*—it's not the senior's "strongest argument." D is incorrect because age is not a dispositive factor when assessing a person's ability to understand the *Miranda* warnings; instead, the court should evaluate waiver according to the totality of the circumstances. *Fare v. Michael C.*, 442 U.S. 707, 724–725 (1979).

331. This question tests on the impeachment exception under *Miranda*. "The shield provided by *Miranda* cannot be perverted into a license to use perjury by way of a defense, free from the risk of confrontation with prior inconsistent utterances." *Harris v. New York*, 401 U.S. 222, 226 (1987).

C is correct because it recognizes that the prosecutor is properly using the woman's statement to impeach her credibility.

A is incorrect because, according to the impeachment exception described in *Harris*, it would not be misconduct for the prosecutor to use the statement as he did here. B is incorrect because it focuses on the statement's reliability and not its limited admissibility. D is incorrect because the statement may only be used to impeach the woman, and not as substantive evidence of her guilt.

332. This question tests on the scope of the *Miranda* impeachment exception, *i.e.*, whether it applies only to the defendant, or whether it extends to other defense witnesses as well. In the Fourth Amendment context, the Supreme Court has held that "the mere threat of a subsequent criminal prosecution for perjury is far more likely to deter a witness from intentionally lying on a defendant's behalf than to deter a defendant, already facing conviction for the underlying offense, from lying on his own behalf." *James v. Illinois*, 493 U.S. 307, 314 (1990). In addition, "expanding the impeachment exception to encompass the testimony of all defense witnesses likely would chill some defendants from presenting their best defense and sometimes any defense at all—through the testimony of others." *Id.* at 314–315. Although the Court has never ruled on this issue in the *Miranda* context, the reasoning of *James* "is equally applicable to confessions obtained in violation of the Fifth Amendment." Wayne R. LaFave, et al., 3 *Criminal Procedure* s. 9.6(a) n.49 (3d. Ed. 2007 & 2014 Supp.).

D is correct because it recognizes that the *Miranda* impeachment exception most likely does not extend to all defense witnesses, but only to the defendant if she testifies.

A is incorrect because it doesn't address the identity of the witness being impeached. B is incorrect because it doesn't address the impeachment issue. C is incorrect because it is an overbroad statement of the *Miranda* suppression rule.

333. This question tests on whether physical evidence should be suppressed due to a *Miranda* violation, using facts derived from *U.S. v. Patane*, 542 U.S. 630 (2003) (plurality opinion). According to *Patane*, it should not: "[t]he [Self-

Incrimination] Clause cannot be violated by the introduction of non-testimonial evidence obtained as a result of voluntary statements." *Id.* at 637.

A is correct because it recognizes that the photographs are non-testimonial evidence and should not be suppressed because of the *Miranda* violation.

B is incorrect because suppression depends on the nature and extent of the legal violation, not the probative value of the evidence. **C is incorrect** because the photographs may be connected to the *Miranda* violation, but that does not necessarily mean that they should be suppressed as a result. **D is incorrect** because, while the "fruits" doctrine does not apply in the *Miranda* context, the man's statement must still be suppressed due to the *Miranda* violation.

334. This question tests on whether a prosecutor may impeach a defendant with his pre-*Miranda* silence. "The privilege against self-incrimination is an exception to the general principle that the Government has the right to everyone's testimony.... To prevent the privilege from shielding information not properly within its scope, ... a witness who desires the protection of the privilege ... must claim it at the time he relies on it." *Salinas v. Texas*, 133 S. Ct. 2174, 2179 (2013); *see also Jenkins v. Anderson*, 447 U.S. 231 (1980) (prosecutor may impeach defendant with pre-*Miranda* silence).

A is correct because a person does not invoke his Fifth Amendment rights "by simply standing mute." *Salinas*, 133 S. Ct. at 2178.

B, C, and D are all incorrect because they don't respond to the basis of the objection: that the prosecutor's comments violated the owner's Fifth Amendment rights.

335. This question tests on whether a prosecutor may comment on a defendant's post-*Miranda* silence, using facts derived from *Griffin v. California*, 380 U.S. 609 (1965). "[W]hile it is true that the *Miranda* warnings contain no express assurance that silence will carry no penalty, such assurance is implicit to any person who receives the warnings. In such circumstances, it would be fundamentally unfair and a deprivation of due process to allow the arrested person's silence to be used to impeach an explanation subsequently offered at trial." *Doyle v. Ohio*, 426 U.S. 610, 618 (1976); *see also Griffin*, 380 U.S. at 614 (Fifth Amendment "forbids either comment by the prosecution on the accused's silence or instructions by the court that such silence is evidence of guilt").

B is correct because the defendant has an absolute right not to testify at his trial, and the prosecutor asked the jury to infer his guilt based on the exercise of that right.

A is incorrect because the prosecutor didn't mention his witnesses, so he couldn't have vouched for them. **C is incorrect** because the prosecutor's comments about his work ethic may be objectionable, but don't provide the defense with the "strongest" argument for the objection. **D is incorrect** because it's not improper for a party to explain what verdict she is requesting from the jury.

Non-*Miranda* Challenges to Statements

336. This question tests on whether a confession may be challenged outside of the framework established by *Miranda v. Arizona*, 384 U.S. 436, 458 (1966). "Prior to *Miranda*, [the Supreme Court] evaluated the admissibility of a suspect's confession under a voluntariness test. The roots of this test developed in the common law, as the courts of England and then the United States recognized that coerced confessions are inherently untrustworthy." *Dickerson v. U.S.*, 530 U.S. 428, 434 (2000). The Supreme Court has "never abandoned this due process jurisprudence, and thus continue[s] to exclude confessions that were obtained involuntarily." *Id.*

    D is correct because it addresses the fact that the man's confession was linked to being pistol-whipped, and recognizes that the man can challenge his confession outside of *Miranda*.

    A and B are incorrect because neither addresses the fact that the officer pistol-whipped the man and that he confessed as a result. **C is incorrect** because a person presumably can't waive his right to be free from police beatings.

337. This question tests on the standard used to evaluate whether a confession is involuntarily made, using facts derived from *Mincey v. Arizona*, 437 U.S. 385 (1978). The standard "examines whether a defendant's will was overborne by the circumstances surrounding the giving of a confession.... The due process test takes into consideration the totality of all the surrounding circumstances — both the characteristics of the accused and the details of the interrogation." *Dickerson*, 530 U.S. at 434.

    C is correct because it's the most likely ruling: the man was intubated, in pain, taking painkillers, and completely at the officer's mercy.

    B and C are both incorrect because neither takes into account the total of the circumstances — the hospital setting, the fact that the man could not speak and could only blink, and the possible effect of his pain and painkillers. **D is incorrect** because it focuses on the weight of the statement, and not its admissibility.

338. This question tests on the sorts of circumstances that will render a confession involuntary and inadmissible under the Fourteenth Amendment. Such circumstances include physical abuse, threats of such abuse, and threats of future harm within the prison. *E.g., Brown v. Mississippi*, 297 U.S. 278 (1936) (whipping of suspects); *Arizona v. Fulminante* 499 U.S. 279, 287 (1991) ("Our cases have made clear that a finding of coercion need not depend upon actual violence by a government agent; a credible threat is sufficient.").

    A is correct because it recognizes that the officer's statement was a credible threat of future harm, and describes the correct result.

    B is incorrect because the interrogation was never terminated, which would be a pre-requisite for re-initiation. **C and D are both incorrect** because both address the "speculative" nature of the officer's threat; since the officer plainly said that the woman's life depended on her confession, his statement can't be described as speculative.

339. This question tests on whether police deception renders a statement involuntary, using facts derived from *Frazier v. Cupp*, 394 U.S. 731 (1969). Based on the totality of the circumstances, police deception—in the absence of other compelling factors—is not enough to render a confession involuntary. *Id.* at 739 (noting that "questioning was of short duration, and petitioner was a mature individual of normal intelligence").

B is correct because the officer's lie has to be balanced against the other circumstances surrounding the interrogation: the officer only repeated the lie once and the man made his admission relatively early in the interrogation session.

A is incorrect because the man only waived his *Miranda* rights, and the question asks about voluntariness under the Fourteenth Amendment. C is incorrect because it looks at the officer's lie in isolation, instead of examining it under the totality of the circumstances. D is incorrect because it looks only at the deterrent effect of admitting the young man's statement, but if the statement is not involuntary, there is little to deter.

340. This question tests on the use of involuntary statements to impeach the defendant. "Statements made by a defendant in circumstances violating the strictures of *Miranda v. Arizona* are admissible for impeachment if their trustworthiness ... satisfies legal standards. But any criminal trial use against a defendant of his *involuntary* statement is a denial of due process of law...." *Mincey v. Arizona*, 437 U.S. at 397–398.

A is correct because it recognizes that since the woman's statement was made in response to a threat, her statement is likely unreliable and so has no evidentiary value.

B is incorrect for two reasons. First, it doesn't address the impeachment rule. Second, the fact pattern doesn't provide enough information to evaluate the prosecutor's questions and whether he laid a proper foundation. C is incorrect because it fails to recognize that involuntary statements are inadmissible because they are unreliable. D is incorrect because there is no way to measure the accuracy of the woman's statement; instead, since it was made in response to repeated threats, it is most likely inaccurate.

Double Jeopardy

341. This question tests on the core concept behind the Double Jeopardy Clause of the Fifth Amendment. "The underlying idea ... is that the State with all its resources and power should not be allowed to make repeated attempts to convict an individual for an alleged offense, thereby subjecting him to embarrassment, expense and ordeal and compelling him to live in a continuing state of anxiety

and insecurity, as well as enhancing the possibility that even though innocent he may be found guilty." *Green v. U.S.*, 355 U.S. 184, 187–188 (1957).

Under the Double Jeopardy Clause, "once a defendant is placed in jeopardy for an offense, and jeopardy terminates with respect to that offense, the defendant may neither be tried nor punished a second time for the same offense." *Sattazahn v. Pennsylvania*, 537 U.S. 101, 106 (2003). As such, there are "three separate guarantees embodied in the Double Jeopardy Clause: It protects against a second prosecution for the same offense after acquittal, against a second prosecution for the same offense after conviction, and against multiple punishments for the same offense." *Justices of Boston Municipal Court v. Lynon*, 466 U.S. 294, 306–307 (1984).

B is correct because it correctly states the double jeopardy rule, as applied to these facts: the college student was tried and acquitted for the aggravated assault and so the prosecutor cannot re-prosecute him for that same crime.

A is incorrect because it presents a non-legal response to a legal question. **C is incorrect** because the Double Jeopardy Clause bars retrial on these facts, regardless of the subjective reasons for the jury's verdict. **D is incorrect** because it doesn't respond to the legal question—whether re-prosecution would violate the Double Jeopardy clause—raised in the motion.

342. This question tests on when a defendant is placed in jeopardy for an offense, or when jeopardy attaches. "[J]eopardy does not attach, and the constitutional prohibition can have no application, until a defendant is put to trial before the trier of facts, whether the trier be a jury or a judge." *Serfass v. U.S.*, 420 U.S. 377, 388 (1975). In a jury trial, jeopardy attaches when the jury is empaneled and sworn. *Crist v. Bretz*, 437 U.S. 28 (1978). In a bench trial, jeopardy attaches after the first witness is sworn, *i.e.*, when evidence is "actually presented." Wayne R. LaFave, et al., 6 *Criminal Procedure* § 25.1(d) (3d. Ed. 2007 & 2014 Supp.). And when a defendant pleads guilty, jeopardy attaches "at least" when the defendant is sentenced on the crime for which he pled guilty. *Ricketts v. Adamson*, 483 U.S. 1, 8 (1987).

C is correct because it correctly recognizes that jeopardy never attached—the prosecutor filed charges, dismissed them without prejudice, and then later re-filed them—so there is no violation.

A, B, and D are all incorrect because they don't address the question of whether jeopardy attached in this situation.

343. This question tests on when jeopardy attaches, using facts derived from *Martinez v. Illinois*, 134 S. Ct. 2070 (2014) (*per curiam*).

C is correct because it recognizes jeopardy attaches due to an event—here, when the jury was empaneled and sworn—and not on other circumstances associated with the case.

A is incorrect because the prosecutor's refusal to participate in the trial is irrelevant to whether the woman was placed in jeopardy. Instead, she "was subjected to jeopardy because the jury in [her] case was sworn." *Id.* at 2075. **B is incorrect** because the question of when jeopardy attaches is a "bright-line rule: [a] jury trial begins, and jeopardy attaches, when the jury is sworn." *Id.* **D is incorrect** because it doesn't respond to the question.

344. This question tests on when jeopardy terminates. "[T]he protection of the Double Jeopardy Clause by its terms applies only if there has been some event, such as an acquittal, which terminates the original jeopardy." *Richardson v. U.S.*, 468 U.S. 317, 325 (1984). "A primary purpose served by such a rule is akin to that served by the doctrines of res judicata and collateral estoppel—to preserve the finality of judgments." *Bretz*, 437 U.S. at 33.

C is correct because if the two charges are the same and if jeopardy attached and terminated for one charge, the woman cannot be re-prosecuted for the second charge.

A is incorrect because jeopardy terminated on the receipt charge when the woman pled guilty, just as if it would have terminated had she gone to trial and been acquitted or convicted. **B is incorrect** because it suggests that the woman is in continuing jeopardy until her sentence is completed, which would completely undermine the purpose of the Double Jeopardy Clause. **D is incorrect** because it is too broadly worded.

345. This question tests on whether jeopardy terminates when a jury fails to reach a verdict. "Because a jury speaks only through its verdict, its failure to reach a verdict cannot—by negative implication—yield a piece of information that helps put together the trial puzzle.... A host of reasons—sharp disagreement, confusion about the issues, exhaustion after a long trial, to name but a few— could work alone or in tandem to cause a jury to hang. To ascribe meaning to a hung count would presume an ability to identify which factor was at play in the jury room. But that is not reasoned analysis; it is guesswork." *Yeager v. U.S.*, 557 U.S. 110, 121–122 (2009).

C is correct because there has been no finding by a fact-finder, so jeopardy has not terminated for the murder charge.

A is incorrect because the juror's affidavit does not establish anything other than what the juror told the defense attorney. Additionally, "[b]ecause a jury speaks only through its verdict," *id.*, the affidavit is meaningless in this context. **B is incorrect** because dismissal of the jury is not the type of "event" that will mark the termination of jeopardy. Instead, the jury must actually render a verdict on the charges. **D is incorrect** because it focuses on what the defense attorney can "definitively prove," and the question tests on termination of jeopardy.

346. This question tests on when two crimes are the same for double jeopardy purposes, and when they are different. "The applicable rule is that, where the same act or transaction constitutes a violation of two distinct statutory provisions,

the test to be applied to determine whether there are two offenses or only one, is whether each provision requires proof of a fact which the other does not." *Blockburger v. U.S.*, 284 U.S. 299, 304 (1932).

B is correct because no matter how each charge is statutorily defined, arson and murder necessarily will "each ... require proof of a fact which the other does not." *Id.*

A is incorrect because it doesn't respond to the question: the issue here is whether arson and murder are the same crimes, not whether the motion is ripe or not. **C is incorrect** because arson and murder are different crimes; double jeopardy would only bar re-trial if they were the same crimes. **D is incorrect** because it applies the wrong test to determine whether two crimes are the same or different. Under the *Blockburger* test, a court should examine the elements of the offenses at issue, not the factual circumstances giving rise to the charge. *E.g., Texas v. Cobb*, 532 U.S. 162 (2001) (rejecting claim that "factually related" charges are the "same crime" under *Blockburger* in the Sixth Amendment context and observing that *Blockburger* test is applied identically in Double Jeopardy context).

347. This question tests on whether the Double Jeopardy Clause bars retrial on the same charges, after a successful defense-initiated appeal. "The Double Jeopardy Clause is not an absolute bar to successive trials. The general rule is that the Clause does not bar re-prosecution of a defendant whose conviction is overturned on appeal." *Justices of Boston Municipal Court v. Lynon*, 466 U.S. 294, 308 (1984).

B is correct because jeopardy has not terminated; rather, it continues until the charges are resolved on the merits.

A is incorrect because it's a non-legal answer to a legal question. **C is incorrect** because, if true, "[i]t would be a high price indeed for society to pay were every accused granted immunity from punishment because of any defect sufficient to constitute reversible error in the proceedings leading to conviction." *U.S. v. Tateo*, 377 U.S. 463, 466 (1964). **D is incorrect** because the question asked about whether double jeopardy bars retrial, not whether the trial judge erred.

348. This question tests on whether the Double Jeopardy Clause bars re-trial for the same crime after a mistrial has been declared. "[W]here circumstances develop not attributable to prosecutorial or judicial overreaching, a motion by the defendant for mistrial is ordinarily assumed to remove any barrier to reprosecution, even if the defendant's motion is necessitated by prosecutorial or judicial error." *U.S. v. Dinitz*, 424 U.S. 600, 607 (1976).

B is correct because the consequence of the defense-requested mistrial is that jeopardy has not terminated for the capital murder charge, which means that double jeopardy does not bar retrial.

A is incorrect because double jeopardy doesn't bar retrial after a judge *sua sponte* declares a mistrial, assuming there are adequate reasons for the mistrial. *U.S.*

v. Perez, 22 U.S. 579 (1824). **C is incorrect** because it misstates the facts: jeopardy never terminated for the capital murder charge. **D is incorrect** because it doesn't respond to the question and how the judge should rule on the defense motion.

349. This question also tests on the double jeopardy rule and mistrials, but where the mistrial was granted due to intentional government misconduct. "The Double Jeopardy Clause does protect a defendant against governmental actions intended to provoke mistrial requests and thereby to subject defendants to the substantial burdens imposed by multiple prosecutions." *Dinitz*, 424 U.S. at 611. The defendant must show that "the conduct giving rise to the successful motion for a mistrial was intended to provoke [him] into moving for a mistrial." *Oregon v. Kennedy*, 456 U.S. 667, 678 (1982).

D is correct because it accurately describes the prosecutor's misconduct and reaches the correct conclusion.

A is incorrect because it ignores the question and the legal issue presented by these facts. **B is incorrect** because it ignores the prosecutor's role in forcing the defense to request the mistrial. **C is incorrect** because, although the prosecutor did ignore the judge's instructions, the judge never held her in contempt.

350. This question tests on application of the Double Jeopardy clause in the context of serial prosecutions by separate sovereigns. "[A]n act denounced as a crime by both national and state sovereignties is an offense against the peace and dignity of both and may be punished by each." *U.S. v. Lanza*, 260 U.S. 377, 382 (1922).

A is correct because it re-states the separate sovereign doctrine, and properly applies it to the facts.

B and C are both incorrect because each refers to a policy-based reason to bar the second prosecution, and don't answer the legal question presented in the question. **D is incorrect** because, as a re-statement of the general double jeopardy rule, it doesn't recognize the separate sovereign exception presented by the facts.

Grand Jury

351. This question tests on the dual role of a grand jury: "determining if there is probable cause to believe that a crime has been committed and ... protecting citizens against unfounded criminal prosecutions." *Branzburg v. Hayes*, 408 U.S. 665, 686–687 (1972). In its investigative role, "the grand jury has been accorded wide latitude to inquire into violations of criminal law. No judge presides to monitor its proceedings. It deliberates in secret and may determine alone the course of its inquiry. The grand jury may compel the production of evidence or the testimony of witnesses as it considers appropriate, and its operation generally is unrestrained by the technical procedural and evidentiary rules governing the conduct of criminal trials." *U.S. v. Calandra*, 414 U.S. 338, 343 (1974).

C is correct because it recognizes both of the grand jury's functions.

A is incorrect because it fails to recognize the grand jury's investigative role. **B is incorrect** because judges do not preside over the grand jury's investigation. **D is incorrect** because it is too broadly worded: the grand jury's investigative function is limited by its role. *E.g.*, U.S. Dep't of Justice, *U.S. Attorneys' Manual* § 9-11.120 (1997) ("Power of Grand Jury Limited by Its Function").

352. This question tests on whether the Fifth Amendment guarantees a right to indictment by grand jury in the state courts. It does not. *Hurtado v. California*, 110 U.S. 516 (1884).

A is correct because it re-states the holding from *Hurtado*.

B is incorrect because harmless error analysis would only be appropriate if an error had occurred, and there is no error here. **C is incorrect** because the federal right to indictment by grand jury is part of the Fifth Amendment, not the Sixth Amendment. **D is incorrect** because it doesn't address the plumber's claim that he had a federal constitutional right to indictment by grand jury in the state court.

353. This question tests on whether a grand jury indictment can be based solely on hearsay evidence, using the relevant facts from *Costello v. U.S.*, 350 U.S. 359 (1956). "[T]he grand jury's sources of information are widely drawn, and the validity of an indictment is not affected by the character of the evidence considered. Thus, an indictment valid on its face is not subject to challenge on the ground that the grand jury acted on the basis of inadequate or incompetent evidence...." *Calandra*, 414 U.S. at 344–345.

C is correct because it recognizes that the grand jury is permitted to consider a wide range of evidence—including hearsay testimony.

A, B, and D are all incorrect because an indictment can be based on hearsay evidence or evidence that would be otherwise inadmissible at trial.

354. This question tests on whether illegally obtained evidence may be presented to a grand jury. "Whatever deterrence of police misconduct may result from the exclusion of illegally seized evidence from criminal trials, it is unrealistic to assume that application of the rule to grand jury proceedings would significantly further that goal." *Calandra*, 414 U.S. at 351. With that said, a prosecutor may adopt a policy of not presenting such evidence to a grand jury. *E.g.*, *U.S. Attorneys' Manual* § 9-11.231 ("A prosecutor should not present to the grand jury for use against a person whose constitutional rights clearly have been violated evidence which the prosecutor personally knows was obtained as a direct result of the constitutional violation.").

C is correct because it recognizes that the grand jury is permitted to consider a wide range of evidence—including evidence that might well be suppressed from the trial.

A is incorrect because *Calanda* and *Costello* clearly hold that such evidence can be used to obtain a grand jury indictment. **B is incorrect** because the officer has not testified, so she has not committed perjury—assuming she was going to do so in the first place. **D is incorrect** because it doesn't address the issue here.

355. This question tests on whether a prosecutor is required to present exculpatory evidence to the jury. "[R]equiring the prosecutor to present exculpatory as well as inculpatory evidence would alter the grand jury's historical role, transforming it from an accusatory to an adjudicatory body." *U.S. v. Williams*, 504 U.S. 36, 51 (1992). Of course, a prosecutor's office may adopt a more stringent policy. *U.S. Attorneys' Manual* §9-11.233 ("It is the policy of the Department of Justice, however, that when a prosecutor conducting a grand jury inquiry is personally aware of substantial evidence that directly negates the guilt of a subject of the investigation, the prosecutor must present or otherwise disclose such evidence to the grand jury before seeking an indictment against such a person. While a failure to follow the Department's policy should not result in dismissal of an indictment, appellate courts may refer violations of the policy to the Office of Professional Responsibility for review.").

    C is correct because it properly states the role of the grand jury, and recognizes that grand jury proceedings are non-adversarial.

    A is incorrect because, if the evidence does not have to be presented to the grand jury, the prosecutor is not engaging in misconduct. **B is incorrect** because it improperly conflates the grand jury's decision to indict with a determination of guilt. **D is incorrect** because the question asks about a constitutional basis to withhold the DNA evidence from the jury, not the jury's scientific training.

356. This question tests on whether an indictment should be dismissed due to allegations of error in the grand jury's process. "[A]s a general matter, a district court may not dismiss an indictment for errors in grand jury proceedings unless such errors prejudiced the defendants." *Bank of Nova Scotia v. U.S.*, 487 U.S. 250, 254 (1988).

    C is correct because it suggests that the eyewitness's testimony might not have played a significant role in the grand jury's decision to indict, and that the testimony should be evaluated against the other information in the case.

    A is incorrect because *Bank of Nova Scotia* requires a harmless error analysis, despite the use of perjured testimony. *See also* Fed. R. Crim. Pro. 52(a) ("Any error, defect, irregularity, or variance that does not affect substantial rights must be disregarded."). **B is incorrect** because—by referring to "absolutely no limits"—it is too broadly worded. **D is incorrect** because a court does have some limited ability to review the facial validity of the indictment.

357. This question tests on the right to refuse to participate in grand jury proceedings. "Although the powers of the grand jury are not unlimited and are subject to the supervision of a judge, the longstanding principle that the public has a right to every man's evidence, except for those persons protected by a constitutional, common-law, or statutory privilege." *Branzburg v. Hayes*, 408 U.S. 665, 688

(1972). Because of this, "the Fifth Amendment does not confer an absolute right to decline to respond in a grand jury inquiry; the privilege does not negate the duty to testify but simply conditions that duty." *U.S. v. Mandujano*, 425 U.S. 564, 573 (1976).

D is correct because it accurately summarizes the woman's obligation to appear and the scope of her Fifth Amendment privilege against self-incrimination.

A, B, and C are all incorrect because each suggests that the woman doesn't have to answer any questions. Instead, the woman may only properly refuse those questions for which she may assert a Fifth Amendment privilege, *i.e.*, those questions, the truthful answers to which, may tend to incriminate her.

358. This question tests on the right to *Miranda* warnings for grand jury witnesses. There is no right to such warnings. *U.S. v. Mandujano*, 425 U.S. 564, 580 (1976). In addition, "[o]nce a witness swears to give truthful answers, there is no requirement to warn him not to commit perjury or, conversely to direct him to tell the truth. It would render the sanctity of the oath quite meaningless to require admonition to adhere to it." *Id.* at 581–582.

B is correct because if the woman didn't have a right to *Miranda* warnings, she has no remedy for receiving incomplete warnings.

A is incorrect because *Miranda* warnings can be required in non-police settings. *E.g.*, *Estelle v. Smith*, 451 U.S. 454 (1981) (*Miranda* warnings required prior to examination by state psychiatrist for use in capital sentencing). **C and D are both incorrect** because, whatever the prosecutor's error—failure to give complete warnings or to comply with office policy—dismissal of perjury charges is an improper remedy.

359. This question tests on whether a grand jury witness is entitled to be told that she is a target of the grand jury's investigation. "It is firmly settled that the prospect of being indicted does not entitle a witness to commit perjury, and witnesses who are not grand jury targets are protected from compulsory self-incrimination to the same extent as those who are. Because target witness status neither enlarges nor diminishes the constitutional protection against compelled self-incrimination, potential-defendant warnings add nothing of value to protection of Fifth Amendment rights." *U.S. v. Washington*, 431 U.S. 181, 189 (1977). Of course, a prosecutor's office may adopt a different policy. *E.g.*, *U.S. Attorneys' Manual* §9-11.151 (1997) ("It is the policy of the Department of Justice to advise a grand jury witness of his or her rights if such witness is a 'target' or 'subject' of a grand jury investigation.").

B is correct because it recognizes that the accountant doesn't have the right she claims to have.

A is incorrect because it makes no sense: a witness's status as a target depends on the facts, and not on how many other witnesses testify. **C and D are both incorrect** because the question is about the privilege against self-incrimination, and not the due process clause.

360. This question tests on an individual's Sixth Amendment right to counsel while testifying before a grand jury prior to any indictment. There is no right to counsel in such a situation because "[n]o criminal proceedings [have] been instituted..., hence the Sixth Amendment right to counsel ha[s] not come into play." *Mandujano,* 425 U.S. at 581.

B is correct because it properly identifies the start of Sixth Amendment right to counsel.

A and D are both incorrect because they're both untrue: counsel can play a significant role prior to the indictment and the man may have a compelling need for his lawyer's help. However, the question asks about the Sixth Amendment right to counsel, which doesn't begin until the man is charged with a crime. **C is incorrect** because "custodial interrogation" refers to the right to receive *Miranda* rights, not the Sixth Amendment right to counsel.

Sixth Amendment Explanations

Basic Scope of the Sixth Amendment Right to Counsel

361. This question tests on the Sixth Amendment right to counsel: "In all criminal prosecutions, the accused shall enjoy ... the assistance of counsel for his defense." U.S. CONST. AMEND. VI. This right means that "in our adversary system of criminal justice, any person haled into court, who is too poor to hire a lawyer, cannot be assured a fair trial unless counsel is provided for him.... From the very beginning, our state and national constitutions and laws have laid great emphasis on procedural and substantive safeguards designed to assure fair trials before impartial tribunals in which every defendant stands equal before the law. This noble ideal cannot be realized if the poor man charged with crime has to face his accusers." *Gideon v. Wainwright*, 273 U.S. 335, 344 (1963).

    B is correct because it re-states the holding from *Gideon*: an indigent defendant charged with a felony has a Sixth Amendment right to counsel.

    A is incorrect because, by referring to "all people charged with crimes," it is too broadly worded. **C and D are both incorrect** because each suggests that a fundamental Sixth Amendment violation — here, denying counsel because the defendant is indigent — can be balanced against other factors in the case.

362. This question tests on the beginning of the Sixth Amendment right to counsel. The right begins "at the first appearance before a judicial officer at which a defendant is told of the formal accusation against him and restrictions are imposed on his liberty." *Rothergy v. Gillespie County*, 554 U.S. 191, 194 (2008).

    A is correct because the teacher was not charged with a crime at the time the officer interviewed him at his home, so he had no Sixth Amendment right to counsel at that time.

    B is incorrect because it necessarily implies that the teacher had Sixth Amendment rights before he was indicted, and he didn't. Just because the teacher retained counsel doesn't mean that he had a Sixth Amendment right to counsel. **C is incorrect** for two reasons. First, the teacher didn't have a Sixth Amendment right at the time he spoke to the police officer. Second, unlike the *Miranda/* Fifth Amendment right to counsel, Sixth Amendment rights don't need to be invoked; they are automatic. **D is incorrect** because the right didn't begin until the teacher was charged with a crime, and he wasn't charged at the post-arrest probable cause hearing. Instead, the purpose of that hearing was to determine probable cause for the warrantless arrest.

363. This question tests on the scope of the Sixth Amendment right to counsel. "The Sixth Amendment right ... is offense specific. It cannot be invoked once for all future prosecutions, for it does not attach until a prosecution is commenced, that is, at or after the initiation of adversary judicial criminal proceedings— whether by way of formal charge, preliminary hearing, indictment, information, or arraignment." *McNeil v. Wisconsin*, 501 U.S. 171, 175 (1991).

C is correct because it recognizes that the man's Sixth Amendment right to counsel depends on being charged with cocaine-related crimes.

A and B are both incorrect because each suggests that the man had a Sixth Amendment right to counsel to protect him during questioning about the cocaine. Since the man had not been charged with a crime in association with the cocaine, there is no "criminal proceeding" and he cannot claim any rights under the Sixth Amendment. **D is incorrect** for two reasons. First, Sixth Amendment rights do not need to be invoked. Second, the "clear and unambiguous" invocation standard is required for Fifth Amendment invocations. *Arizona v. Edwards*, 451 U.S. 477 (1981).

364. This question also tests on the scope of the Sixth Amendment right to counsel, and "critical stages" of the criminal proceeding. "Once attachment occurs, the accused at least is entitled to the presence of appointed counsel during any critical stage of the post-attachment proceedings ... The cases have defined critical stages as proceedings between an individual and agents of the State (whether formal or informal, in court or out ...) that amount to trial-like confrontations, at which counsel would help the accused in coping with legal problems or ... meeting his adversary." *Rothergy*, 554 U.S. 191 at 212 & n.16.

A is correct because the sentencing proceeding is a critical stage, *Gardner v. Florida*, 430 U.S. 349, 358 (1977), and so the woman had a right to counsel— which was unmet and not waived.

B is incorrect because the constitutional violation did not occur because of a breach of ethics; it occurred because the woman was unrepresented at a critical stage. **C is incorrect** because the fact that the sentence fell within the recommended range doesn't address the Sixth Amendment issue. **D is incorrect** because critical stages do not necessarily need to "involve a determination of guilt." Instead, a critical stage is determined by the defendant's need for the assistance of counsel.

365. This question tests on whether a post-charging line-up is a critical stage. "Since it appears that there is grave potential for prejudice, intentional or not, in the pretrial lineup, which may not be capable of reconstruction at trial, and since presence of counsel itself can often avert prejudice and assure a meaningful confrontation at trial, there can be little doubt that ... the post-indictment lineup [is] a critical stage of the prosecution at which [the defendant is] as much

entitled to [counsel] ... as at the trial itself." *U.S. v. Wade*, 388 U.S. 218, 236–237 (1968).

C is correct because it recognizes that a post-charging line-up is a critical stage of the criminal proceeding.

A is incorrect because the Sixth Amendment right does not depend on the defendant's ability to retain counsel. **B is incorrect** because it doesn't address the Sixth Amendment deprivation. **D is incorrect** because the college senior's appearance at the line-up cannot be construed as a knowing, voluntary, and intelligent waiver of his Sixth Amendment rights.

366. This question tests on whether identification via a post-charging photo array is a critical stage. Because it is qualitatively different from a post-charging line-up, "the Sixth Amendment does not grant the right to counsel at photographic displays conducted by the Government for the purpose of allowing a witness to attempt an identification of the offender." *U.S. v. Ash*, 413 U.S. 300, 321 (1973).

C is correct because it recognizes that the man did not have a right to counsel since the identification procedure did not occur during a critical stage.

A and B are both incorrect because each ties a possible Sixth Amendment violation to what counsel could have done, if present at the demonstration of the photo array. Having counsel at a particular proceeding might be helpful, but the Sixth Amendment right to counsel instead depends the stage of the proceeding being classified as "critical." **D is incorrect** because it suggests that there was a Sixth Amendment violation—and there wasn't.

367. This question tests on whether probation revocation hearings are critical stages. They are not: "the decision as to the need for counsel must be made on a case-by-case basis in the exercise of a sound discretion by the state authority charged with responsibility for administering the probation and parole system. Although the presence and participation of counsel will probably be both undesirable and constitutionally unnecessary in most revocation hearings, there will remain certain cases in which fundamental fairness—the touchstone of due process—will require that the State provide at its expense counsel for indigent probationers or parolees." *Gagnon v. Scarpelli*, 411 U.S. 778, 790 (1973).

D is correct because it states the correct rule from *Scarpelli. See id.* at 789 (distinguishing between "the right of an accused to counsel in a criminal prosecution" and "the more limited due process right of one who is a probationer ... only because he has been convicted of a crime").

A is incorrect because it suggests that there is an absolute right to counsel at probation revocation hearings, and *Scarpelli* holds otherwise. **B and C are both incorrect** because each connects the right to counsel to what the judge told the woman at her sentencing, which is not the proper standard to determine whether the Sixth Amendment applies.

368. This question also tests on Sixth Amendment critical stages. A presentence interview is not a critical stage, although by practice or court rule, a jurisdiction may allow defense counsel to be present. *E.g.*, 44 Geo. L.J. Ann. Rev. Crim. Proc. 781, 832 & n.2220 (collecting cases) (2015). In addition, attendance by counsel, if permitted, may well be good practice.

D is correct because it represents the prosecutor's "strongest argument:" that the defendant did not have a Sixth Amendment right to counsel at the interview.

A and C are both incorrect because neither focuses on the legal issue presented by the question, *i.e.*, whether a presentence interview is a critical stage or not. **B is incorrect** because a defendant's Sixth Amendment right to counsel doesn't end with an adjudication of guilt, and continues through sentencing. *Gardner*, 430 U.S. at 358.

369. This question also tests on Sixth Amendment critical stages, using facts derived from *Estelle v. Smith*, 451 U.S. 454 (1981). A capital sentencing psychiatric evaluation is a critical stage, where the defendant requires "the assistance of his attorneys in making the significant decision of whether to submit to the examination and to what end the psychiatrist's findings could be employed." *Id.* at 470.

A is correct because it re-states the holding of *Smith* on materially identical facts.

B is incorrect because it's untrue; despite facing a capital charge, a defendant still won't have a Sixth Amendment right to counsel at every stage of the proceeding, but only at the "critical" stages. **C is incorrect** because the woman's voluntary participation in the evaluation is not the same as a knowing, voluntary, and intelligent waiver of the Sixth Amendment right to counsel. **D is incorrect** because it suggests that the Sixth Amendment right ends with the guilty verdict, and a defendant still has a right to counsel at sentencing. *Gardner*, 430 U.S. at 358 (sentencing is critical stage).

370. This question tests on the right to counsel at trial, and whether that right depends on the severity of the charge. It does not. Although counsel may be helpful in every criminal case, "absent a knowing and intelligent waiver, no person may be imprisoned for any offense, whether classified as petty, misdemeanor, or felony, unless he was represented by counsel at his trial." *Argesinger v. Hamlin*, 407 U.S. 25, 37 (1972).

B is correct because it recognizes that the right to counsel at trial turns on actual incarceration.

A and D are both incorrect because each ties the Sixth Amendment right to counsel to the severity of the charged offense, and the right depends on whether the defendant is actually incarcerated. **C is incorrect** because the Sixth Amendment right does not depend on whether the defendant would have fared better had counsel been appointed. Instead, it depends on actual incarceration.

371. This question tests on whether there is a Sixth Amendment right to counsel when incarceration is authorized, but not imposed. Since "actual imprisonment is a penalty different in kind from fines or the mere threat of imprisonment," the Sixth Amendment "require[s] only that no indigent criminal defendant be sentenced to a term of imprisonment unless the State has afforded him the right to assistance of appointed counsel in his defense." *Scott v. Illinois*, 440 U.S. 367, 373 (1979).

D is correct because it recognizes that the right to counsel at trial turns on actual incarceration.

A is incorrect because the right to counsel depends on actual incarceration, not the mere possibility of incarceration. **B is incorrect** because it ties the Sixth Amendment right to counsel to proportionality in sentencing, when it instead depends on whether the defendant is actually incarcerated. **C is incorrect** because the man did not have a Sixth Amendment right to counsel to waive when he pled guilty.

372. This question tests on the Sixth Amendment right to counsel when a suspended sentence is imposed. "A suspended sentence is a prison term imposed for the offense of conviction. Once the prison term is triggered, the defendant is incarcerated not for the probation violation, but for the underlying offense. The uncounseled conviction at that point results in imprisonment.... This is precisely what the Sixth Amendment ... does not allow." *Alabama v. Shelton*, 535 U.S. 654, 662 (2002).

C is correct because it recognizes that, for Sixth Amendment purposes, there is no difference between being sentenced to a term of actual incarceration and being sentenced to a suspended sentence.

A is incorrect because it doesn't recognize that the man's suspended sentence is the equivalent of actual incarceration, at least in terms of the Sixth Amendment right to counsel. **B is incorrect** because the holding of *Shelton* doesn't depend on the probability that the suspended sentence will be activated; instead, it depends on a suspended sentence being imposed for an uncounseled conviction. **D is incorrect** because the two sentences are not equivalent; "actual imprisonment is a penalty different in kind from fines or the mere threat of imprisonment ..." *Scott*, 440 U.S. at 373.

373. This question tests on the collateral use of prior uncounseled convictions. "[A]n uncounseled conviction ... may be relied upon to enhance the sentence for a subsequent offense, even though that sentence entails imprisonment.... Reliance on such a conviction is also consistent with the traditional understanding of the sentencing process, which we have often recognized as less exacting than the process of establishing guilt." *Nichols v. U.S.*, 511 U.S. 738, 746–747 (1994).

D is correct because it recognizes that the Sixth Amendment doesn't prohibit use of the prior uncounseled convictions to enhance a current sentence of incarceration.

A and B are both incorrect because both are contrary to the holding of *Nichols*. **C is incorrect** because it doesn't address the Sixth Amendment issue presented by the question.

374. This question tests on the end of the Sixth Amendment right to counsel. The right begins when the "criminal prosecution" begins—*i.e.*, when the defendant is charged with a crime—so it logically ends when the "criminal prosecution" ends. However, ascertaining the end point for the criminal prosecution is can sometimes be difficult. "If the proceeding involves no more than an extension of a challenge to trial ruling, and occurs shortly after trial, as in a post-verdict motion for judgment of acquittal or new trial, it should be treated as subject to the Sixth Amendment. On the other hand, a motion for a new trial based on new evidence, which can occur months after the conviction, might be treated as closer to a collateral attack, which clearly is outside the criminal prosecution." Wayne R. LaFave, et al., 3 *Criminal Procedure* § 11.2(b) (3d. Ed. 2007 & 2014 Supp.).

D is correct because it best describes the situation here: the criminal prosecution against the defendant has ended and, ten years later, he is seeking to challenge his conviction. As such, he no longer has a Sixth Amendment right to counsel.

A is incorrect because it is too broadly worded, and would mean that the Sixth Amendment right to counsel continues indefinitely for some defendants. **B is incorrect** because Sixth Amendment rights depend on "criminal prosecution," not venue. **C is incorrect** because the defendant's Sixth Amendment rights extend into sentencing. *Gardner*, 430 U.S. at 358 (sentencing is critical stage).

375. This question tests whether there is a Sixth Amendment right to counsel on appeal. There is no such right because the "criminal prosecution" is over by the time the defendant appeals his conviction. However, if the state provides a first mandatory appeal of right, the Fourteenth Amendment requires the appointment of counsel for indigent defendants who pursue that appeal. *Douglas v. California*, 372 U.S. 353 (1963).

D is correct because it correctly describes the woman's right to counsel on appeal, and the constitutional source of that right.

A is incorrect because it is incomplete: it only describes the status of the woman's Sixth Amendment right to counsel, but it does not also include information about her Fourteenth Amendment right to counsel. **B is incorrect** because the Sixth Amendment guarantees the right to counsel, not the right to only one lawyer. **C is incorrect** because the woman does have a right to counsel, under the Fourteenth Amendment.

Massiah Doctrine

376. This question tests on the rule that has developed from *Massiah v. U.S.*, 377 U.S. 201 (1964): once adversary judicial criminal proceedings have commenced against a person, the state may not deliberately elicit information from him outside the presence of counsel without a proper waiver. If the rule is violated, the defendant's statements cannot be used in the prosecutor's case-in-chief.

B is correct because the facts here show a clear Sixth Amendment violation: the doctor was charged with a crime and the officer asked her direct questions about the crime outside of counsel's presence and without first securing a waiver.

A and C are both incorrect because each uses language that is associated only with *Miranda*, *i.e.*, custodial interrogation and express questioning or its functional equivalent. **D is incorrect** because suppression will turn on the officer's conduct and not the content of the doctor's statement.

377. This question tests on the start of the Sixth Amendment/*Massiah* right to counsel. "The Sixth Amendment right of the accused to assistance of counsel in 'all criminal prosecutions' is limited by its terms: it does not attach until a prosecution is commenced." *Rothergy v. Gillespie County*, 554 U.S. 191, 198 (2008).

    D is correct because it properly ties the Sixth Amendment right to counsel to charging, rather than some other event.

    A is incorrect because by referring to when the investigation "focuses" on a suspect, it cites the wrong standard. **B is incorrect** because the Sixth Amendment right to counsel attaches automatically at charging, and—unlike the Fifth Amendment right to counsel—does not need to be "clearly and unambiguously" invoked. **C is incorrect** because suspects have a Fifth—not Sixth—Amendment right to counsel during custodial interrogation.

378. This question tests on the scope of the Sixth Amendment/*Massiah* right to counsel. "[W]hen the Sixth Amendment right to counsel attaches, it does encompass offenses that, even if not formally charged, would be considered the same offense under the *Blockburger* test." *Texas v. Cobb*, 532 U.S. 162, 173 (2001). And, under *Blockburger*, "[t]he applicable rule is that, where the same act or transaction constitutes a violation of two distinct statutory provisions, the test to be applied to determine whether there are two offenses or only one, is whether each provision requires proof of a fact which the other does not." *Blockburger v. U.S.*, 284 U.S. 299, 304 (1932).

    D is correct because the man didn't have a Sixth Amendment right to counsel during the discussion in his living room. Also, since the man wasn't placed in custodial interrogation, he didn't have any Fifth Amendment rights either.

    A is incorrect because the man would only have a Sixth Amendment right to counsel during the discussion in the living room if the heroin crime was considered the "same" as the methamphetamine crime. **B is incorrect** because—by referring to "all drug-related crimes"—it is too broadly worded. **C is incorrect** because the man was not in *Miranda* custody in his living room, so there was no need for *Miranda* warnings.

379. This question also tests on the scope of the Sixth Amendment/*Massiah* right to counsel, using facts derived from *Texas v. Cobb*.

    A is correct because arson and criminal homicide are different crimes under *Blockburger*, and so the husband's Sixth Amendment right to counsel extended only to the charged crime of arson.

B is incorrect because the police knowledge is irrelevant to the Sixth Amendment issue; the right attaches when a person is charged with a crime, and not when police become aware that a person can be charged with a crime. **C and D are both incorrect** because the Sixth Amendment right does not depend on the factual connection between the charged crime and the uncharged conduct, *Cobb*, 532 U.S. at 174; instead, the court should apply *Blockburger* to determine the scope of the right.

380. This question tests on deliberate elicitation, using facts derived from *Brewer v. Williams*, 430 U.S. 387 (1977) ("*Williams I*"). Although the Supreme Court has not expressly defined "deliberate elicitation," direct questioning by a police officer of a defendant will surely suffice.

     C is correct because the transport officer's statements to the defendant were "tantamount to interrogation." *Id.* at 400.

     A and B are both incorrect because the officer here "deliberately and designedly set out to elicit information from [the defendant] just as surely as and perhaps more effectively than if he had formally interrogated him." *Id.* at 399. **D is incorrect** because the officer's breach of his promise is unrelated to the Sixth Amendment violation here.

381. This question also tests on deliberate elicitation, using facts derived from *Massiah v. U.S.*, 377 U.S. 201 (1964), and *U.S. v. Henry*, 447 U.S. 264 (1980). In *Massiah*, the defendant confessed to his co-defendant; in *Henry*, the defendant made an admission to another prisoner. In both cases, the defendant was unaware that he was speaking to someone who had already agreed to work for the government. And in both cases, the Supreme Court found that the state had deliberately elicited information from the defendant in violation of the Sixth Amendment.

     B is correct because the undercover officer's conduct constituted deliberate elicitation: as in *Massiah* and *Henry*, the young man had been charged with a crime, didn't know that he was speaking to a state actor, and the state actor asked questions about the charged crime.

     A is incorrect because it doesn't really address the young man's claim: he is complaining that the officer questioned him in the first place, not that the officer used his special training. **C is incorrect** because there is no public safety exception for the Sixth Amendment. **D is incorrect** for two reasons. First, there is no Sixth Amendment covert custodial interrogation exception. Second, the covert nature of the officer's questions actually forms the basis of the deliberate elicitation claim.

382. This question tests on deliberate elicitation, using facts derived from *Fellers v. U.S.*, 540 U.S. 519 (2004).

     D is correct because it addresses what went wrong here: the officer intentionally failed to tell the man about his Sixth Amendment rights, and then questioned him about the charged crime.

     A and B are both incorrect because — by referring to a hearsay exception and voluntariness — neither addresses the deliberate elicitation issue presented in the question. **C is incorrect** because it suggests that the young man wouldn't have spoken to the officer if he'd been told about his rights. That may or may not be true, because a defendant can always waive his rights.

383. This question tests on deliberate elicitation, again using facts derived from *Fellers v. U.S.*

D is correct because it correctly describes the violation here: although the officer told the woman that she'd been charged with a crime, he didn't tell her about the rights that accompany the charge.

A is incorrect because, by offering a non-legal resolution to a legal question, it's not the woman's "strongest argument." **B is incorrect** because while the woman might try to argue that she was in *Miranda* custody because the officer told her that she was going to be arrested, her "strongest argument" would be grounded in the Sixth Amendment, and not the Fifth. **C is incorrect** because, even if the officer had given the woman detailed information about the charge, his actions would still constitute deliberate elicitation assuming he didn't also tell her about her rights and secure a valid waiver.

384. This question also tests on deliberate elicitation, where state actors had absolutely no involvement in obtaining a defendant's statement.

D is correct because it recognizes that when a defendant makes an admission with absolutely no state action—*e.g.*, because the defendant spontaneously admits involvement, or admits involvement to a private party who then takes that information to the state—no prohibited deliberate elicitation has occurred.

A is incorrect because it fails to recognize that the statement was obtained by a private party, not a state actor. **B is incorrect** because the woman's intoxication is not at issue here; state action is. **C is incorrect** because a person can speak voluntarily and still be subjected to deliberate elicitation; the issue here is that the statement was not obtained by a state actor.

385. This question also tests on deliberate elicitation, this time where police simply overhear a defendant making an incriminating statement. "Since the Sixth Amendment is not violated whenever—by luck or happenstance—the State obtains incriminating statements from the accused after the right to counsel has attached, ... a defendant does not make out a violation of that right simply by showing that an informant, either through prior arrangement or voluntarily, reported his incriminating statements to the police. Rather, the defendant must demonstrate that the police and their informant took some action, beyond merely listening, that was designed deliberately to elicit incriminating remarks." *Kuhlmann v. Wilson*, 477 U.S. 436, 459 (1986).

B is correct because the undercover officer eavesdropped on the woman's conversation, but he did nothing to deliberately elicit her to speak.

A, C, and D are all incorrect because eavesdropping can't be characterized as either deliberate elicitation or custodial interrogation, regardless of the merits or wisdom of the officer's actions.

386. This question also tests on deliberate elicitation. While *Massiah* rights are charge-specific, police still must not "act in a manner that circumvents and thereby dilutes the protection afforded by the right to counsel." *Maine v. Moulton*, 474 U.S. 159, 171 (1988).

    D is correct because it best describes why asking about the homicide under these circumstances would not be permitted: because of the overlap between the hit and run charge and the woman's possible *mens rea* for the homicide.

    A is incorrect because, while true, it doesn't really address the fact that the officer can't ask about the homicide without addressing the "hit and run," *i.e.*, without engaging in prohibited deliberate elicitation. **B is incorrect** because it's untrue: prosecutors charge people all the time without first speaking to the prospective defendant about his *mens rea*. **C is incorrect** because the Sixth Amendment right to counsel extends only to charged crimes and others that "would be considered the same offense under the *Blockburger* test." *Cobb*, 532 U.S. at 173.

387. This question also tests on deliberate elicitation.

    D is correct because the officer's response in this particular situation was not intended to prompt an incriminating statement. Instead, it was designed to truthfully answer the defendant's question about the conditions of confinement.

    A is incorrect because there is no proof that the officer's response was "designed deliberately to elicit incriminating remarks." *Kuhlmann*, 477 U.S. at 459. **B is incorrect** because the Sixth Amendment doesn't prohibit police from speaking to individuals charged with crimes; it prohibits uncounseled and non-waived deliberate elicitation. **C is incorrect** because it's not the best answer: it provides a factual description of what happened here, and the best answer will refer to the man's legal argument for suppression, *i.e.*, deliberate elicitation.

388. This question tests on the waiver standard for the Sixth Amendment/*Massiah* right to counsel. The Supreme Court's "precedents ... place beyond doubt that the Sixth Amendment right to counsel may be waived by a defendant, so long as relinquishment of the right is voluntary, knowing, and intelligent." *Montejo v. Louisiana*, 556 U.S. 778, 786 (2009).

    B is correct because the man validly waived his rights: he was informed of his right to counsel ("knowing") and the cost of waiving that right ("intelligent"), and his statement was not coerced ("voluntary").

    A is incorrect because most every statement made by a suspect or defendant will be against penal interest. **C is incorrect** because since the man validly waived his rights, it doesn't matter that counsel wasn't present or had advised the man to stay silent. **D is incorrect** because it refers to the possible use of the statement at trial, and the question asks about the statement's admissibility.

389. This question tests on how a court should assess the circumstances surrounding waiver of the Sixth Amendment/*Massiah* right to counsel. For many years, a waiver of the Sixth Amendment right to counsel was presumptively invalid if the officer approached the defendant to request a waiver; that is no longer the case. *Montejo*, 556 U.S. at 797 (overruling *Michigan v. Jackson*, 475 U.S. 625 (1986)). Now, with the presumption against waiver gone, police may approach a defendant and request a waiver of rights: "[t]he upshot is that ... it would be completely unjustified to presume that a defendant's consent to police-initiated interrogation was involuntary or coerced simply because he had previously been appointed a lawyer." *Montejo*, 556 U.S. at 792.

D is correct because the officer was permitted to approach the woman and ask for a waiver, and the woman then validly waived her Sixth Amendment rights.

A is incorrect because *Montejo* eliminated the presumption against waiver when police approach a defendant and requested waiver. **B is incorrect** because it suggests that a defendant can never waive her rights. **C is incorrect** because the woman's preference isn't what's important here; instead, the question turns on whether the officer violated the woman's Sixth Amendment rights in any way.

390. This question tests on waiver of the Sixth Amendment/*Massiah* right to counsel.

A is correct because it re-states the holding of *Montejo*.

B is incorrect because the officer's right to approach the defendant and request waiver doesn't depend on the defendant speaking in court, or otherwise accepting the appointment of counsel. Instead, *Montejo* gives police an opportunity to request a waiver, regardless of whether the defendant has spoken in court or not. **C is incorrect** because it re-states the holding of *Michigan v. Jackson*, 475 U.S. 625 (1986) — and *Montejo* overruled *Jackson*. **D is incorrect** because the issue here is whether the officer was even permitted to approach and request a waiver, and not whether he tricked him by being too sympathetic.

391. This question also tests on Sixth Amendment/*Massiah* waivers. In the last question, the judge appointed counsel but the defendant did not actually accept the appointment, or say anything in court indicating whether he wanted counsel or not. In this question, woman clearly wants to be represented. Regardless, the rule from *Montejo* is the same: police may approach the defendant once to seek a waiver.

A is correct because if the waiver is valid, the woman's statement is admissible.

B is incorrect because *Montejo* provides the officer with one opportunity to seek a waiver, regardless of what he knows about the Sixth Amendment right attaching. **C is incorrect** for two reasons: there is no Sixth Amendment violation here (the answer presumes that there was) and voluntariness is a Fourteenth Amendment standard, and not a Sixth Amendment standard. **D is incorrect** because, regardless of the officer's intent, if the waiver is valid the woman's statement is admissible.

392. This question tests on the procedure to be followed after police approach a defendant to request a waiver of Sixth Amendment rights. In short, the defendant can either invoke his rights, or he can waive them. In terms of an invocation: "a defendant who does not want to speak to the police without counsel present need only say as much when he is first approached and given the *Miranda* warnings. At that point, not only must the immediate contact end, but badgering by later requests is prohibited. If that regime suffices to protect the integrity of a suspect's voluntary choice not to speak outside his lawyer's presence before his arraignment, it is hard to see why it would not also suffice to protect that same choice after arraignment, when Sixth Amendment rights have attached." *Montejo*, 556 U.S. at 794–795.

C is correct because while *Montejo* allows the officer to request a waiver from the woman, it also requires that he respect her decision not to waive her rights—and her invocation.

A is incorrect because the issue here is not about waiver, but is instead whether the officer could continue to speak to the woman about her case after she reaffirmed that she wanted her public defender's assistance. **B is incorrect** because deliberate elicitation does not require that the officer ask a direct question. **D is incorrect** because it does not respond to the issue: whether the officer was permitted to continue to speak to the woman after she invoked her rights.

393. This question tests on whether *Miranda* warnings are sufficient to inform a defendant of her Sixth Amendment right to counsel. "[T]the key inquiry in a case such as this one must be: Was the accused, who waived his Sixth Amendment rights during post-indictment questioning, made sufficiently aware of his right to have counsel present during the questioning, and of the possible consequences of a decision to forgo the aid of counsel?" *Patterson v. Illinois*, 487 U.S. 285, 292–293 (1988). Because *Miranda* warnings give a defendant the relevant information about the right to counsel and the cost of waiving that right, they are sufficient to inform him of his Sixth Amendment right to counsel. *Id.*

B is correct because the woman was given the essential information she needed to make a reasoned choice about waiving her rights, and so her waiver was valid.

A is incorrect because the Sixth Amendment right does not depend on financial status, it depends on being charged with a crime. **C is incorrect** because it fails to recognize that the woman doesn't need to be told the source of her right to counsel—*i.e.*, Fifth versus Sixth Amendment—but instead that she has a right to counsel. **D is incorrect** because the officer was not required to contact counsel, but was instead required to ensure that the waiver was valid.

394. This question tests on waiver of the Sixth Amendment/*Massiah* right to counsel. Such waivers must be knowing, voluntary, and intelligent. *Montejo*, 556 U.S. at 786.

B is correct because the officer's statement—"I want to talk about a hit and run accident at the mall from six months ago"—led the man to believe that he was waiving his rights associated with a car accident and not for the bank robbery. As such, the man's waiver was unknowing, because he did not know what rights he was waiving.

A is incorrect because it provides a non-legal response to a legal question. **C is incorrect** because the man's waiver was unknowing, and so he couldn't have "validly" waived his rights. **D is incorrect** because the man can ignore his lawyer's advice, but his waiver must still be knowing, voluntary, and intelligent.

395. This question also tests on waiver.

B is correct because the woman knew the rights she waiving ("knowing") and the consequences of her waiver ("intelligent"), and nothing in the facts suggests that her statement was otherwise coerced ("voluntary").

A and C are both incorrect because the officer's failure to witness the woman's signature doesn't necessarily render her waiver invalid. **D is incorrect** because *Miranda* warnings are adequate to inform a defendant of his Sixth Amendment rights. *Patterson*, 487 U.S. at 292–293.

396. This question tests on application of the fruit of the poisonous tree doctrine in the Sixth Amendment context, using facts derived from *U.S. v. Patane*, 542 U.S. 630 (2003) (plurality opinion). "[T]he 'fruit of the poisonous tree' doctrine has not been limited to cases in which there has been a Fourth Amendment violation. The Court has [also] applied the doctrine where the violations were of the Sixth Amendment...." *Nix v. Williams*, 467 U.S. 431, 442 (1984) ("*Williams II*").

A is correct because recovery of the gun is directly related to the *Massiah* violation, *i.e.*, the officer's failure to tell the man about his Sixth Amendment right to counsel and to secure a waiver from the man before discussing the charged crime.

B is incorrect because an officer can also search a home with consent, assuming the consent is valid. **C is incorrect** because it fails to recognize the fruit of the poisonous tree doctrine, contrary to *Williams II*. **D is incorrect** because the man's consent was a product of the *Massiah* violation.

397. This question tests on one of the three exceptions to the fruit of the poisonous tree doctrine: inevitable discovery. "[T]he cases implementing the exclusionary rule begin with the premise that the challenged evidence is in some sense the product of illegal governmental activity.... Of course, this does not end the inquiry. If the prosecution can establish ... that the information ultimately or inevitably would have been discovered by lawful means ... then the deterrence rationale has so little basis that the evidence should be received. Anything less would reject logic, experience, and common sense." *Williams II*, 467 U.S. at 444.

A is correct because the prosecutor is arguing that police would have found the weapon anyway, *i.e.*, that they have a hypothetical, lawful source for the discovery of the weapon.

B is incorrect because the independent source exception requires an actual independent source, and these facts only present the possibility of an independent source. Put another way, because of the possibility of an independent source, the prosecutor is arguing that police would have inevitably discovered the gun. C is incorrect because the officer's bad faith does not matter: "If the trial process was not tainted as a result of [the officer's] conduct, this defendant received the type of trial that the Sixth Amendment envisions." *Williams II*, 467 U.S. at 456. D is incorrect because the wife's generalized desire to help the police doesn't provide a legal basis to admit the gun.

398. This question tests on the second exception to the fruit of the poisonous tree doctrine: attenuation. "Sophisticated argument may prove a causal connection between information obtained through [a constitutional violation] and the Government's proof. As a matter of good sense, however, such connection may have become so attenuated as to dissipate the taint." *Nardone v. United States*, 308 U.S. 338, 341 (1939). (The third exception is independent source. *See Murray v. U.S.*, 487 U.S. 583 (1988) (describing independent source)).

D is correct because the second statement is best described as an indirect fruit of the first.

A is incorrect because, by describing the second statement as a "direct fruit" of the first, it fails to recognize the facts that "attenuate" the connection between the two statements: the two weeks between the two statements and that the woman had her attorney with her when she made the second statement. B is incorrect because it fails to recognize that the woman's first statement was obtained in violation of her Sixth Amendment/*Massiah* rights. C is incorrect because it goes too far by describing the two statements as "completely unrelated."

399. This question tests on the impeachment exception for Sixth Amendment/*Massiah* violations. The Court's "precedents make clear that the game of excluding tainted evidence for impeachment purposes is not worth the candle. The interests safeguarded by such exclusion are outweighed by the need to prevent perjury and to assure the integrity of the trial process." *Kansas v. Ventris*, 556 U.S. 586, 593 (2009).

A is correct because it re-states the proper holding from *Ventris*.

B is incorrect because the judge will overrule the objection on a different basis. C is incorrect because the facts don't give the language of the judge's suppression ruling, so it's impossible to tell if the prosecutor has disobeyed the judge. D is incorrect because it doesn't recognize the holding of *Ventris*, and the existence of the impeachment exception.

400. This question tests on the scope of the Sixth Amendment/*Massiah* impeachment exception and whether it extends to witnesses beyond the defendant. In the Fourth Amendment context, the Supreme Court has held that "the mere threat of a subsequent criminal prosecution for perjury is far more likely to deter a witness from intentionally lying on a defendant's behalf than to deter

a defendant, already facing conviction for the underlying offense, from lying on his own behalf." *James v. Illinois*, 493 U.S. 307, 314 (1990). In addition, "expanding the impeachment exception to encompass the testimony of all defense witnesses likely would chill some defendants from presenting their best defense and sometimes any defense at all — through the testimony of others." *Id.* at 314–315. While the Supreme Court hasn't ruled on this issue in the Sixth Amendment context, the same reasoning would seem to apply to such situations.

A is correct because it is the "most likely" basis for the defense objection, *i.e.*, that the impeachment rule for the Sixth Amendment ought to mirror that of the Fourth Amendment.

B is incorrect because it states the impeachment rule too narrowly; the statement clearly can be used to impeach (at the very least) the defendant. *Ventris*, 556 U.S. at 593. **C is incorrect** because the defense "most likely" will argue that the statement can't be used to impeach defense witnesses at all, and not that it has some impeachment value. **D is incorrect** because the court has already ruled on the suppression motion, and this answer essentially asks to re-litigate the motion.

Right to Counsel and Identification

401. This question tests on one of the two primary arguments for attacking an eyewitness's identification: denial of the Sixth Amendment right to counsel.

    A is correct because the defendant, charged with rape, has a right to counsel at all critical stages of the proceeding. *U.S. v. Wade*, 388 U.S. 218, 236–237 (1967).

    B and D are both incorrect because the Confrontation Clause and Compulsory Process Clause each are trial rights, and don't extend to pre-trial identification procedures. **C is incorrect** because "compelling the accused merely to exhibit his person for observation by a prosecution witness prior to trial involves no compulsion of the accused to give evidence having testimonial significance." *Id.* at 222.

402. This question tests on the Sixth Amendment right to counsel at a pre-charging line-up. There is no such right because "[t]he initiation of judicial criminal proceedings ... marks the commencement of the 'criminal prosecutions' to which alone the explicit guarantees of the Sixth Amendment are applicable." *Kirby v. Illinois*, 406 U.S. 682, 690–691 (1972) (plurality opinion).

    B is correct because it recognizes that the line-up was held before the arrested man was charged with a crime and so he had no right to counsel during the line-up.

    A is incorrect for two reasons. First, it doesn't present a legal basis for the court's ruling. Second, it makes no sense: the eyewitness was only shown one person who matched her description, and so the fact that she identified that person doesn't mean that the procedure itself was without flaws. **C is incorrect** because, despite the flaws in the identification procedure, the arrested man has no right to counsel before he is charged with a crime. **D is incorrect** because it contradicts the holding of *Kirby*.

403. This question tests on the Sixth Amendment right to counsel at a post-charging line-up. Such line-ups are considered critical stages, and so the defendant has a right to counsel. *Wade*, 388 U.S. at 236–237.

D is correct because it recognizes that the line-up was held after the client was charged with a crime and so he had an absolute right to counsel during the line-up.

A, B, and C are all incorrect because the Sixth Amendment right to counsel depends on whether or not the individual is charged with a crime, and not on how desperately the individual needs counsel.

404. This question tests on the role of counsel at a post-charging line-up—assuming the defendant has such a right. Nothing in *Wade* explains the attorney's role at a post-charging line-up; instead, *Wade* holds only that there is a right to counsel during such a procedure. *See also id.*, 388 U.S. at 258–259 (White, J., concurring and dissenting) (expressing concern that presence of counsel will lead to delay in pre-trial investigations and will convert pre-trial procedures into adversarial proceedings).

D is correct because *Wade* holds that a defendant has the right to counsel at a post-charging line-up, but is silent as to the role counsel can and should play.

A and B are both incorrect because the right to counsel under *Wade* doesn't necessarily mean that counsel gets to be an active participant at the line-up. **C is incorrect** because it is too broadly worded: *Wade* doesn't bar the attorney from objecting to the line-up as it is occurring. Indeed, the "presence of counsel itself can often avert prejudice and assure a meaningful confrontation at trial." *Id.* at 237.

405. This question tests on the Sixth Amendment right to counsel in the context of a post-charging show-up: "[t]he practice of showing suspects singly to persons for the purpose of identification, and not as part of a lineup...." *Stovall v. Denno*, 388 U.S. 293, 302 (1967). "The reasons supporting *Wade's* holding that a corporeal identification is a critical stage of a criminal prosecution for Sixth Amendment purposes apply with equal force" to post-charging show-ups. *Moore v. Illinois*, 434 U.S. 220, 229 (1977).

A is correct because the man was charged with a crime and was required to participate in a live identification procedure but without counsel or a waiver of the right to counsel.

B is incorrect because the question asks about the admissibility of the evidence, and not its weight. **C is incorrect** for two reasons. First, the Sixth Amendment right to counsel is not subject to a balancing test. Second, conducting the show-up weeks after the robbery enhances the man's need for his lawyer, and doesn't diminish it. **D is incorrect** because—despite the fact that the charges were amended after the manager died—the man still had a Sixth Amendment right to counsel for the attempted murder charge at the time of the show-up.

406. This question tests on the remedy for a Sixth Amendment violation of the right to counsel during a post-charging eyewitness identification procedure. In such a situation, the eyewitness testimony will be barred—that is, testimony relating to the line-up and any in-court identification—unless the prosecutor can "establish by clear and convincing evidence that the in-court identifications were based upon observations of the suspect other than the lineup identification." *Wade*, 388 U.S. at 240.

D is correct because it states the correct remedy: testimony related to the constitutional violation will be barred unless the prosecutor can establish an independent source.

A is incorrect because "[a] rule limited solely to the exclusion of testimony concerning identification at the lineup itself, without regard to admissibility of the courtroom identification, would render the right to counsel an empty one." *Id.* **B is incorrect** because permitting testimony about the line-up—when counsel was denied at the line-up—serves no remedial purpose. **C is incorrect** because it fails to recognize the possibility of an independent source for the ex-girlfriend's identification.

407. This question tests on the Sixth Amendment right to counsel during the post-charging use of a photo array. There is no such right. *U.S. v. Ash*, 413 U.S. 300 (1973).

C is correct because it re-states the holding of *Ash* as applied to these facts.

A and D are both incorrect because the officer here did nothing wrong: since the defendant had no right for counsel to be present, the officer was not required to inform counsel of the interview with the witness. **B is incorrect** because by referring to independent source, it suggests that the defendant's right to counsel was violated.

408. This question tests on the second primary argument for attacking an eyewitness's identification: "[t]he standard ... of fairness as required by the Due Process Clause of the Fourteenth Amendment." *Manson v. Brathwaite*, 432 U.S. 98, 113 (1977).

B is correct because it recognizes the availability of a Fourteenth Amendment due process claim. *E.g., U.S. v. Ash*, 413 U.S. 300, 320 (1973) ("due process ... safeguards apply to misuse of photographs"); *Stovall v. Denno*, 388 U.S. 293 (1967) (due process challenge to show-up).

A and C are both incorrect because neither provides a legal basis for the attorney's objection, which is what the question asks for. **D is incorrect** because it doesn't recognize that the Fourteenth Amendment provides an alternative vehicle for attacking the identification procedure here.

409. This question tests on the standard to be applied when a defendant challenges his identification on due process grounds. "[E]ach case must be considered on its own facts, and ... convictions based on eyewitness identification at trial following a pretrial identification ... will be set aside on that ground only if the ... identification procedure was so impermissibly suggestive as to give rise to a very substantial likelihood of irreparable misidentification." *Simmons v. U.S.*, 390 U.S. 377, 384 (1968).

A is correct because it re-states the proper standard for a due process challenge to an eyewitness identification procedure.

B, C, and D are all incorrect because each relies on an improper standard.

410. This question tests on the limits of due process challenges to eyewitness identification procedures. "When no improper law enforcement activity is involved, ... it suffices to test reliability through the rights and opportunities generally designed for that purpose, notably, the presence of counsel at post-indictment lineups, vigorous cross-examination, protective rules of evidence, and jury instructions on both the fallibility of eyewitness identification and the requirement that guilt be proved beyond a reasonable doubt." *Perry v. New Hampshire*, 132 S. Ct. 716, 721 (2012).

A is correct because the bank teller's viewing of the video of the woman's arrest was not attributable to the police.

B is incorrect because a harmless error analysis assumes the existence of an actual error. **C is incorrect** because it fails to recognize the absence of state action in these facts. **D is incorrect** because the focus is not whether the officer acted intentionally, but whether he acted improperly.

Ineffective Assistance of Counsel

411. This question tests on the core meaning of the Sixth Amendment right to counsel: "the right to counsel is the right to effective assistance of counsel." *Strickland v. Washington*, 466 U.S. 668, 686 (1984). Because of this, when the Sixth Amendment right is not met—*i.e.*, when the defendant receives the ineffective assistance of counsel—he must be given a meaningful remedy.

B is correct because it best describes the man's right and his remedy, assuming the court finds that his Sixth Amendment rights were violated.

A is incorrect because "it is a general and indisputable rule that where there is a legal right, there is also a legal remedy by suit or action at law, whenever that right is invaded." *Marbury v. Madison*, 1 Cranch 137, 163 (1803) (quoting 3 Blackstone, Commentaries 23). **C and D are both incorrect** because they refer to the wrong relief (money damages) and wrong procedure (filing of a grievance against the attorney) for the enforcement of a Sixth Amendment ineffective assistance of counsel claim.

412. This question tests on the standard for assessing claims of ineffective assistance of counsel. "A convicted defendant's claim that counsel's assistance was so defective as to require reversal of a conviction or death sentence has two components. First, the defendant must show that counsel's performance was deficient.... Second, the defendant must show that the deficient performance prejudiced the defense." *Strickland*, 466 U.S. at 697.

B is correct because it re-states the identical standard from *Strickland*: deficient performance and prejudice.

A is incorrect because it repeats the wrong standard, one employed by some courts before *Strickland* was decided. **C is incorrect** because the man does not have to definitively establish his innocence in order to prove counsel's ineffectiveness; instead, the "ultimate focus of inquiry must be on the fundamental fairness of the proceeding whose result is being challenged." *Id.* at 698. **D is incorrect** because it omits the prejudice inquiry.

413. This question tests on the definition of *Strickland*'s first prong: deficient performance. "[T]he proper standard for attorney performance is that of reasonably effective assistance." *Id.* 466 U.S. at 687.

C is correct because a reasonably effective attorney would not have continued to trial under these circumstances, *i.e.*, after realizing that she didn't have the necessary tools to present her planned defense.

A is incorrect because the facts state that the therapist made the choice to go to trial based on his attorney's advice. If that advice was deficient, the therapist is permitted to claim ineffective assistance of counsel. **B is incorrect** because actual incarceration is the standard for the appointment of counsel, *Scott v. Illinois*, 440 U.S. 367 (1979), not for claims of ineffective assistance of counsel. **D is incorrect** because it suggests that ineffectiveness occurs when the fact-finder doesn't get a chance to see "critical evidence." However, the fact-finder may be denied access to such evidence for legitimate reasons—*e.g.*, due to an evidentiary ruling or a missing witness—and counsel wouldn't be ineffective in such circumstances.

414. This question tests on deficient performance and whether a court should consider factors such as the lawyer's education, experience, and personal life when his assessing performance. "[A] court deciding an actual ineffectiveness claim must judge the reasonableness of counsel's challenged conduct on the facts of the particular case, viewed as of the time of counsel's conduct." *Strickland*, 466 U.S. at 690.

D is correct because it focuses on the attorney's actual performance in the case, which, according to *Strickland*, is the relevant inquiry.

A and B are both incorrect because the events in the attorney's personal life and her relative inexperience would only be relevant if they affected her work in the case. **C is incorrect** because it's untrue: the facts state that the attorney was "distracted" by her divorce and her productivity suffered before trial because of her father's death.

415. This question tests on deficient performance and what standards should be used to evaluate the attorney's performance. "No particular set of detailed rules for counsel's conduct can satisfactorily take account of the variety of circumstances faced by defense counsel or the range of legitimate decisions regarding how best to represent a criminal defendant. Any such set of rules would interfere with the constitutionally protected independence of counsel and restrict the wide latitude counsel must have in making tactical decisions." *Strickland*, 466 U.S. at 688–689. However, at the same time, the Supreme Court noted that "[p]revailing norms of practice as reflected in American Bar Association standards ... are guides to determining what is reasonable, but they are only guides." *Id.* at 688.

     A is correct because it represents the "most likely" ruling: trial counsel decided to reserve his opening statement based on the unique needs of this particular case.

     B is incorrect because an attorney's deficient performance is assessed according to his acts or omissions, not the court rules. **C is incorrect** because *Strickland* rejects a *per se* task-oriented approach to assessing counsel's performance, instead requiring counsel to fulfill certain basic duties to his client and observing that the details of those duties will vary from case to case. **D is incorrect** because it fails to account for the facts of the case. Certainly, what "most trial lawyers" would do is relevant in determining the "[p]revailing norms of practice." *Id.* at 688. Still, the court must also consider the individual case.

416. This questions tests on deficient performance, and whether extra-record facts may be considered when evaluating the attorney's performance. "A convicted defendant making a claim of ineffective assistance must identify the acts or omissions of counsel that are alleged not to have been the result of reasonable professional judgment. The court must then determine whether, in light of all the circumstances, the identified acts or omissions were outside the wide range of professionally competent assistance." *Id.* at 690.

     C is correct because it properly recognizes that the man's ineffectiveness claim is based on an omission—as permitted by *Strickland*. And the only reasonable way to prove an attorney's omission is present the evidence that he didn't.

     A and B are both incorrect because each fails to recognize that an ineffectiveness claim can be either extra-record-based (*e.g.*, that the attorney failed to do something he should have done) or record-based (*e.g.*, that the attorney should have objected at a certain point). **D is incorrect** because the best evidence rule is irrelevant to the question.

417. This question tests on deficient performance and whether and how the attorney's strategy should be considered when evaluating his performance. "[S]trategic

choices made after thorough investigation of law and facts relevant to plausible options are virtually unchallengeable[,] and strategic choices made after less than complete investigation are reasonable precisely to the extent that reasonable professional judgments support the limitations on investigation." *Id.* at 690–691.

B is correct because the attorney's strategy here was not based on an investigation, but was instead based on the attorney's decision to reject investigation in lieu of general experience.

A is incorrect because the success or failure of the strategy is irrelevant; instead, the court should look to the soundness of the strategy. **C is incorrect** because, while the attorney's experience is important, it does not substitute for an incomplete investigation. **D is incorrect** because just having a strategy is not enough; the strategy must also be based on some sort of investigation.

418. This question tests on deficient performance and whether the attorney may rely on client-supplied information in developing his trial strategy. "The reasonableness of counsel's actions may be determined or substantially influenced by the defendant's own statements or actions. Counsel's actions are usually based, quite properly, on informed strategic choices made by the defendant and on information supplied by the defendant ... And when a defendant has given counsel reason to believe that pursuing certain investigations would be fruitless or even harmful, counsel's failure to pursue those investigations may not later be challenged as unreasonable." *Id.* at 691.

C is correct because it accurately describes the relevance of the conversation: it shows the attorney's state of mind and correctly describes the attorney's choice as reasonable based on what his client told him.

A is incorrect because while the attorney has an obligation to conduct a complete investigation, information supplied by the client isn't wholly irrelevant—and the answer suggests that it is. **B is incorrect** because understanding the attorney's thought processes is critical to evaluating a *Strickland* claim. **D is incorrect** because there's no showing that the defendant was wrongfully convicted; instead, the facts simply state that he claimed he was innocent.

419. This question tests on whether an attorney is deficient for refusing to take an unethical act on behalf of his client. "Plainly, [counsel's] duty is limited to legitimate, lawful conduct compatible with the very nature of a trial as a search for truth. Although counsel must take all reasonable lawful means to attain the objectives of the client, counsel is precluded from taking steps or in any way assisting the client in presenting false evidence or otherwise violating the law." *Nix v. Whiteside*, 475 U.S. 157, 166 (1986).

A is correct because counsel cannot be deemed deficient for refusing to break the law, or for insisting on following ethical guidelines.

B is incorrect because it suggests that the attorney made the right choice only because he might have gotten into trouble later. **C is incorrect** because the judge's arrest demonstrates that the politician was correct, not that the attorney was deficient. **D is incorrect** because the attorney can (and should) be a zealous advocate without breaking the law.

420. This question tests on the definition of *Strickland*'s second prong: prejudice. To establish prejudice, "[t]he defendant must show that there is a reasonable probability that, but for counsel's unprofessional errors, the result of the proceeding would have been different. A reasonable probability is a probability sufficient to undermine confidence in the outcome." *Id.*, 466 U.S. at 694.

    C is correct because it recognizes that the verdict here can't be trusted: the only evidence against the man was the eyewitness, and the lawyer failed to impeach that eyewitness with her conflicting police statement.

    A is incorrect because the man doesn't have to show which story was true; instead, he needs to show that he was prejudiced by his attorney's failure to cross-examine the eyewitness with the police report. **B is incorrect** because the lawyer's strategy is relevant to deficient performance, and not prejudice. **D is incorrect** because it gives the wrong definition for prejudice: "[i]t is not enough for the defendant to show that the errors had some conceivable effect on the outcome of the proceeding [because] [v]irtually every act or omission of counsel would meet that test...." *Id.* at 693.

421. This question tests on *Strickland* prejudice and provides an example of the "reasonable probability" standard.

    A is correct because it refers to the reasonable probability standard and recognizes that prejudice is met on these facts: counsel did nothing to prepare for the penalty phase, offered nothing in support of a life sentence, and the defendant can show that he had twenty witnesses who were willing and able to testify on his behalf.

    B and C are both incorrect because *Strickland*'s reasonable probability standard requires that defendant show more that "a possibility" of a different result but also less than a "definitive certainty." **D is incorrect** because the defendant doesn't need juror affidavits to establish prejudice.

422. This question tests on *Strickland* prejudice and the overall purpose of the prejudice inquiry: to determine whether the overall proceedings were fair. *Id.* at 694.

    D is correct because the man's trial was unfair: the girlfriend was not properly cross-examined with her prior statement, and so the result of the proceedings was unfair.

    A is incorrect because it doesn't address the prejudice issue, and because the report would be admissible. **B is incorrect** because it suggests that prejudice is outcome determinative, and it is not. **C is incorrect** because *Strickland* prejudice doesn't require the man to establish the weight the jury would have given to the report; instead, he has to prove that counsel's failure to cross-examine the girlfriend with the information from the report denied him a fair trial.

423. This question also tests on *Strickland* prejudice and its focus on fairness. Under *Strickland*, a prejudice "analysis focusing solely on mere outcome determination,

without attention to whether the result of the proceeding was fundamentally unfair or unreliable, is defective." *Lockhart v. Fretwell*, 506 U.S. 364, 369 (1993). "In every case the court should be concerned with whether, despite the strong presumption of reliability, the result of the particular proceeding is unreliable because of a breakdown in the adversarial process that our system counts on to produce just results." *Strickland*, 466 U.S. at 696.

B is correct because it is the "most likely" ruling: although the first degree murder conviction is inappropriate, the outcome of the case—the defendant's life sentence—would not be changed with a correct verdict.

A is incorrect because an attorney who fails to object to an erroneous jury charge is deficient. **C is incorrect** because it refers to findings of both deficient performance and prejudice, but only deficient performance is present on these facts. **D is incorrect** because the defendant's ineffectiveness claim is based on the allegation that the attorney should have objected, not that he completely usurped the judge's role.

424. This question tests on *Strickland* prejudice and why its focus on fairness can sometimes require a separate inquiry into the overall fairness of the trial. "[W]hile the *Strickland* test provides sufficient guidance for resolving virtually all ineffective-assistance-of-counsel claims, there are situations in which the overriding focus on fundamental fairness may affect the analysis." *Williams (Terry) v. Taylor*, 529 U.S. 362, 391 (2000). Such situations occur when counsel's deficient performance does "not deprive[] [the defendant] of any substantive or procedural right to which the law entitled him...." *Id.* at 392.

C is correct because the man is not entitled to a new trial: the attorney may have been deficient at the time of the trial for failing to object to the instruction, but the omission is irrelevant in the end.

A is incorrect because it fails to recognize that although the reasonable doubt instruction was faulty at the time it was given, the man's trial was not fundamentally unfair because the instruction was ultimately correct. **B is incorrect** because it essentially states that the man can establish prejudice because he received deficient performance—and each prong of *Strickland* is separate. **D is incorrect** both because it relies on an outcome-determinative standard for prejudice and fails to address the facts surrounding the reasonable doubt instruction.

425. This question tests on *Strickland* prejudice, using facts derived from *Nix v. Whiteside*, 475 U.S. 157 (1986).

C is correct because it is factually correct: the attorney didn't restrict the woman from testifying and her testimony—that she reasonably believed her boyfriend had a gun, and not that she actually saw the gun—could have been sufficient for the jury to accept her self-defense claim.

A is incorrect because "[i]f a 'conflict' between a client's proposal and counsel's ethical obligation gives rise to a presumption that counsel's assistance was prejudicially ineffective, every guilty criminal's conviction would be suspect if the defendant had sought to obtain an acquittal by illegal means." *Id.* at 176. **B is incorrect** because "[w]hatever the scope of a constitutional right to testify, it is elementary that such a right does not extend to testifying falsely." *Id.* at 173. **D is incorrect** because it suggests that prejudice can only be established in record-based claims, which is untrue. *E.g., Rompilla v. Beard*, 545 U.S. 374 (2005) (ineffectiveness established where counsel failed to investigate and develop wealth of mitigating evidence, and to present that evidence to the jury at trial).

426. This question tests on whether defendants who plead guilty can allege ineffective assistance of counsel. "[T]he two-part *Strickland v. Washington* test applies to challenges to guilty pleas based on ineffective assistance of counsel." *Hill v. Lockhart*, 474 U.S. 52, 58 (1985).

    D is correct because it re-states the holding from *Hill* and the requirements from *Strickland.*

    A and B are both incorrect because each states that ineffectiveness claims are not available to defendants who plead guilty, and *Hill* holds otherwise. **C is incorrect** because the burden for every defendant who claims ineffectiveness — those who plead guilty and those who go to trial — is the same: they must prove deficient performance and prejudice.

427. This question tests on deficient performance for failure to advise a defendant of the immediate — or "direct" — consequences of a guilty plea. "[C]ertainly the defense attorney is responsible for advising the defendant accurately with respect to the more immediate consequences of a guilty plea — what the risks are as to the sentence if the plea agreement is accepted and a guilty plea is entered, and what prior constitutional violations cannot be appealed if a guilty plea is entered." Wayne R. LaFave, et al., 5 *Criminal Procedure* § 21.3(b) (3d. Ed. 2007 & 2014 Supp.).

    A is correct because the man has a constitutional right to testify on his own behalf and reasonable counsel would have told the man about the constitutional costs and benefits of pleading guilty.

    B is incorrect because the facts don't state that the attorney relied on the judge, just that the attorney conceded that he hadn't properly informed his client about the right to testify. **C is incorrect** because the credibility of the man's testimony isn't at issue. **D is incorrect** because it addresses prejudice, and the question asks about deficient performance.

428. This question tests on deficient performance for failure to advise a defendant of the secondary — or "collateral" — consequences of a guilty plea. "[I]t has often been held that defense counsel is not obligated to advise his client about a variety of collateral consequences (although "gross misinformation" about those consequences can amount to ineffective assistance of counsel if the defendant based his decision to plead guilty upon that advice)." *Id.*

D is correct because the attorney only failed to inform the woman of a collateral consequence of her criminal conviction—*i.e.*, loss of voting privileges—and so didn't perform deficiently.

A is incorrect because disenfranchisement is best described as a collateral consequence, and not a direct consequence. **B and C are both incorrect** because the question asks about the attorney's failure to inform the woman, not whether he failed to perform a task she requested of him or whether he otherwise provided effective assistance.

429. This question tests on failure to advise a defendant of the immigration risks of a guilty plea, using the facts of *Padilla v. Kentucky*, 559 U.S. 356 (2000). "Deportation as a consequence of a criminal conviction is … uniquely difficult to classify as either a direct or a collateral consequence." *Id.* at 366. However, "[w]hen the law is not succinct and straightforward…, a criminal defense attorney need do no more than advise a noncitizen client that pending criminal charges may carry a risk of adverse immigration consequences. But when the deportation consequence is truly clear…, the duty to give correct advice is equally clear." *Id.* at 369.

   D is correct because it re-states the holding of *Padilla* on materially identical facts.

   A and B are both incorrect because *Padilla* rejects the direct/collateral consequences distinction for immigration risks of a guilty plea. **C is incorrect** because the facts are silent as to the attorney's legal research, and so it's impossible to say what research the attorney performed or not.

430. This question tests on *Strickland* prejudice in the context of a motion to withdraw a guilty plea. "[I]n order to satisfy the prejudice requirement, the defendant must show that there is a reasonable probability that, but for counsel's errors, he would not have pleaded guilty and would have insisted on going to trial." *Hill*, 474 U.S. at 59.

   A is correct because it cites the correct standard from *Hill*—which is essentially the same as *Strickland*'s prejudice requirement, placed into the context of a guilty plea.

   B is incorrect because it goes too far by suggesting that *Strickland* prejudice is outcome determinative, and it is not. **C and D are both incorrect** because each refers to what the woman would have "considered," and *Strickland* prejudice requires more than mere consideration.

431. This question tests on *Strickland* prejudice when the defendant has pled guilty. Where the defendant rejects a plea offer based on incompetent advice, he must show that "there is a reasonable probability that the plea offer would have been presented to the court (*i.e.*, that the defendant would have accepted the plea and the prosecution would not have withdrawn it in light of intervening circumstances), that the court would have accepted its terms, and that the conviction or sentence, or both, under the offer's terms would have been less severe than under the judgment and sentence that in fact were imposed." *Lafler v. Cooper*, 132 S. Ct. 1376, 1385 (2012).

B is correct because it re-states the holding of *Strickland*, but within the context of the facts of this question.

A is incorrect because *Cooper* requires the defendant to demonstrate more than a favorable plea offer; the defendant must also demonstrate a reasonable probability that the plea would have gone forward, as it was offered. **C is incorrect** because the defendant's concession that he received a fair trial doesn't address his larger claim that the proceedings in the trial court were unfair. **D is incorrect** because the Sixth Amendment right to effective assistance applies to all critical stages of the proceeding, which includes many pre-trial proceedings, the trial itself, and sentencing.

432. This question tests on how a court may review a *Strickland* claim. "[T]here is no reason for a court deciding an ineffective assistance claim to approach the inquiry in ... order or even to address both components of the inquiry if the defendant makes an insufficient showing on one. In particular, a court need not determine whether counsel's performance was deficient before examining the prejudice suffered by the defendant as a result of the alleged deficiencies." *Strickland*, 466 U.S. at 697.

A is correct because the defendant cannot show prejudice—he has not challenged the DNA evidence—and so the court will not have to examine the lawyer's performance.

B and C are both incorrect because each contradicts the holding of *Strickland*. **D is incorrect** because *Strickland* does set forth guidelines for review: deficient performance and prejudice.

433. This question tests an alternative standard for assessing counsel's performance under the Sixth Amendment—a standard that presumes prejudice. "There are ... circumstances that are so likely to prejudice the accused that the cost of litigating their effect in a particular case is unjustified." *U.S. v. Cronic*, 466 U.S. 648, 658 (1984). These circumstances include (1) actual or (2) constructive denials of the right to counsel; (3) situations where "although counsel is available to assist the accused during trial, the likelihood that any lawyer, even a fully competent one, could provide effective assistance is so small that a presumption of prejudice is appropriate without inquiry into the actual conduct of the trial," *id.* at 659–660; (4) conflicts of interests; (5) situations where the state interferes with the Sixth Amendment right; and (6) situations where counsel completely fails to subject the state's case to meaningful adversarial testing.

D is correct because it recognizes that the man's right to counsel was not recognized, and so the court should presume prejudice and grant a new trial.

A, B, and C are all incorrect because each focuses on how the man was prejudiced by the judge's failure to appoint counsel, and *Cronic* holds that prejudice should be presumed in such situations.

434. This question tests on *Cronic*, using an example of an actual denial of counsel.

B is correct because it recognizes the role of counsel at sentencing, the impact of his absence, and identifies the correct remedy under *Cronic*.

A is incorrect because it suggests that the proper remedy for an actual denial of counsel is a prejudice analysis, and *Cronic* holds that prejudice is presumed when counsel is actually denied. **C is incorrect** because criminal sentencing is a critical stage. *Mempa v. Rhay.* 389 U.S. 128 (1967). **D is incorrect** because the defendant is not required to object in this circumstance; instead, the judge is required to provide him with counsel.

435. This question tests on constructive denial of the Sixth Amendment right to counsel. "Assistance begins with the appointment of counsel, it does not end there. In some cases the performance of counsel may be so inadequate that, in effect, no assistance of counsel is provided." *Cronic*, 466 U.S. at 654 n.11. When counsel is constrictively denied, prejudice is presumed.

C is correct because the lawyer was not relieved of her appointment until after the competency evaluation, and so she had a duty to investigate the man's mental health history and provide that information to the psychiatrist. Because the lawyer didn't do that, the man was constructively denied his right to counsel.

A is incorrect because the man doesn't need to establish prejudice as to the results of his trial; instead, the focus of the man's claim is that he was essentially unrepresented in the weeks before the competency evaluation. **B is incorrect** because the lawyer's reasons for not representing her client support granting the claim, and not denying it. **D is incorrect** because it doesn't respond to the question, which asks about a Sixth Amendment violation.

436. This question tests on another situation where prejudice might be presumed: where "although counsel is available to assist the accused during trial, the likelihood that any lawyer, even a fully competent one, could provide effective assistance is so small that a presumption of prejudice is appropriate without inquiry into the actual conduct of the trial." *Cronic*, 466 U.S. at 659–660.

D is correct because it re-states the holding from *Strickland*, and of the given choices, it will give the officer the "greatest likelihood of success" on appeal.

A is incorrect because there are no facts here to show that this is the type of extraordinary situation where prejudice should be presumed; instead, this appears to be a well-publicized murder trial, but there are no allegations that anything unusual happened at the trial — except for the officer's conviction. **B is incorrect** because the lawyer's admission shows that she felt bad about the verdict, not that the officer was denied counsel. **C is incorrect** because the officer had counsel at trial, and so he can't claim an actual denial of the right to counsel.

437. This question tests a situation where prejudice should be presumed: when counsel labors under an actual conflict of interest. A "defendant who shows that a conflict of interest actually affected the adequacy of his representation need not demonstrate prejudice in order to obtain relief. But until a defendant shows that his counsel actively represented conflicting interests, he has not established

the constitutional predicate for his claim of ineffective assistance." *Cuyler v. Sullivan*, 446 U.S. 335, 349–350 (1980).

B is correct because the man has not shown that "counsel was influenced in his basic strategic decisions by the interests of the employer who hired him." *Wood v. Georgia*, 450 U.S. 261, 272 (1981). Instead, the man has shown only a potential conflict of interest.

A is incorrect because it suggests that a conflict only exists when counsel admits to a conflict, and a conflict may be found in the absence of such an admission. **C is incorrect** because prejudice should only be presumed once an actual conflict is demonstrated, and an actual conflict requires proof of a "division of loyalties that affected counsel's performance." *Mickens v. Taylor*, 535 U.S. 162, 172 n.5 (2002). **D is incorrect** because it doesn't respond to the question.

438. This question tests on another situation where prejudice should be presumed: where the "state interfere[s] with the ability of counsel to render effective assistance to the accused." *Strickland v. Washington*, 466 U.S. at 683.

    B is correct because the woman's "strongest argument" is that the judge's directive interfered with her Sixth Amendment right to counsel.

    A is incorrect because there are no facts to determine whether the judge had an "obvious bias" against the woman and her attorney. **C is incorrect** because it's a plausible argument, but not the "strongest" one. **D is incorrect** because it's unclear whether a denial of due process—assuming one existed—will result in any relief to the woman.

439. This question tests on another form of the constructive denial of the right to counsel: when "counsel entirely fails to subject the prosecution's case to meaningful adversarial testing." *Cronic*, 466 U.S. at 659. "[T]he attorney's failure must be complete." *Bell v. Cone*, 535 U.S. 685, 697 (2002).

    C is correct because it recognizes that the appointment of counsel in this situation was purely *pro forma*, as counsel did absolutely nothing for the woman.

    A is incorrect because it fails to recognize that the attorney did no work on behalf of the woman, and that doing absolutely nothing cannot be considered a strategy. **B is incorrect** because the woman is not required to object to counsel's performance in order to preserve the issue for appeal. **D is incorrect** because counsel was appointed, so the woman wasn't actually denied counsel. Instead, she was constrictively denied her right to counsel.

440. This question tests on the difference between *Strickland* claims and *Cronic* claims. "For purposes of distinguishing between the rule of *Strickland* and that of *Cronic*, this difference is not of degree but of kind." *Cone*, 535 U.S. at 697. In a *Strickland* claim, the defendant alleges that his lawyer performed poorly. By comparison, in a *Cronic* claim, the defendant alleges that he didn't get a lawyer at all.

    C is correct because the man's claim—which alleges specific errors and omissions—falls under *Strickland*.

A is incorrect because the facts don't indicate that the judge had any trouble understanding the man's claim. **B is incorrect** because the judge's jurisdiction over the petition has nothing to do with whether he ruled correctly on the man's claims. **D is incorrect** because, as already established, the nature of the man's allegations falls within *Strickland* and not *Cronic*.

Right to Self-Representation

441. This question tests on the right to self-representation by criminal defendants. "The right to defend is personal. The defendant, and not his lawyer or the State, will bear the personal consequences of a conviction. It is the defendant, therefore, who must be free personally to decide whether in his particular case counsel is to his advantage. And although he may conduct his own defense ultimately to his own detriment, his choice must be honored out of that respect for the individual which is the lifeblood of the law." *Faretta v. California*, 422 U.S. 806, 834 (1975).

    C is correct because it restates the holding from *Faretta*: it recognizes the right to self-representation and the need for a valid waiver of rights.

    A and B are both incorrect because neither recognizes any right to self-representation. **D is incorrect** because it mischaracterizes the rights embodied within the Sixth Amendment.

442. This question tests on whether the Sixth Amendment right to self-representation is absolute. It is not: "[e]ven at the trial level, … the government's interest in ensuring the integrity and efficiency of the trial at times outweighs the defendant's interest in acting as his own lawyer." *Martinez v. Court of Appeal*, 528 U.S. 152, 162 (2000). For example, if a defendant is not capable of adequately waiving his Sixth Amendment rights, or makes an untimely request to represent himself, his request does not have to be honored. *Id.* at 161–162.

    C is correct because it is the best description of the defendant's request: it was made minutes before the trial was about to begin and, because the defendant wouldn't explain his motivation for the request, the most reasonable inference is that he wanted to delay the trial. While the defendant has a right to self-representation, *Martinez* holds that the right is not absolute and must sometimes cede to other interests.

    A is incorrect because it is an incorrect statement of law. **B is incorrect** because it ties the timeliness of the motion to the first witness's testimony, and—in a capital case where the jury has already been selected—that is probably too late. **D is incorrect** because the Supreme Court has not limited *Faretta* to non-capital cases.

443. This question tests on the standard for waiving the Sixth Amendment right to counsel, using facts derived from *Iowa v. Tovar*, 541 U.S. 77 (2004). "While

the Constitution does not force a lawyer upon a defendant, it does require that any waiver of the right to counsel be knowing, voluntary, and intelligent." *Id.* at 87–88.

B is correct because it cites the correct standard for Sixth Amendment waivers, and reaches the correct conclusion on these facts: "[t]he constitutional requirement is satisfied when the trial court informs the accused of the nature of the charges against him, of his right to be counseled regarding his plea, and of the range of allowable punishments attendant upon the entry of a guilty plea." *Id.* at 81.

A is incorrect because if any part of the defendant's guilty plea—a waiver of rights—is invalid, then the plea must be vacated. On these facts, the plea is linked to the waiver of the right to counsel. **C and D are both incorrect** because defendant here was given the core information he needed for a knowing, voluntary, and intelligent waiver of his rights.

444. This question tests on the appointment of stand-by counsel to defendants who waive their Sixth Amendment right to counsel. "[A] State may—even over objection by the accused—appoint a standby counsel to aid the accused if and when the accused requests help, and to be available to represent the accused in the event that termination of the defendant's self-representation is necessary." *Faretta*, 422 U.S. at 834 n.46.

A is correct because it recognizes that *Faretta* permits the appointment of stand-by counsel.

B is incorrect because the judge's motivation for the appointment—as set forth in the facts—was to help the defendant, not because he was concerned about disruptions at trial. **C is incorrect** because it provide a non-legal response to a legal question. **D is incorrect** because the defendant's right to self-representation is not absolute because *Faretta* contemplates the possibility of stand-by counsel.

445. This question tests on whether there is a right to stand-by counsel. "*Faretta* does not require a trial judge to permit 'hybrid' representation," *i.e.*, it does not require the appointment of stand-by counsel. *McKaskle v. Wiggins*, 465 U.S. 168, 183 (1984).

A is correct because it recognizes the correct scope of the right to self-representation: a defendant has a right to counsel and a right to waive counsel, but has no right to something in-between those two options.

B is incorrect because it misstates the facts: the woman's waiver came before the judge denied her request for stand-by counsel. **C is incorrect** because, since there is no constitutional right to stand-by counsel, there is no need for a prejudice analysis when a request for stand-by counsel is denied. **D is incorrect** because the Sixth Amendment right to counsel is tied to actual incarceration and not to the length the defendant's sentence. *Scott v. Illinois*, 440 U.S. 367 (1979).

446. This question tests on the role of stand-by counsel, if appointed. "[T]he right to speak for oneself entails more than the opportunity to add one's voice to a

cacophony of others." *McKaskle*, 465 U.S. at 177. Accordingly, "the *pro se* defendant is entitled to preserve actual control over the case he chooses to present to the jury" and "participation by standby counsel without the defendant's consent should not be allowed to destroy the jury's perception that the defendant is representing himself." *Id.* at 178.

B is correct because, by objecting to testimony in front of the jury, stand-by counsel helped to "destroy the jury's perception that the defendant [was] representing himself." *Id.*

A is incorrect because the defendant's right to self-representation is not absolute, as *Faretta* permits the appointment of stand-by counsel. **C is incorrect** because the question asks about whether stand-by counsel exceeded her proper role and not whether her objections were helpful to the defendant. **D is incorrect** because the defendant's right to self-representation doesn't depend on who did most of the trial work, but instead depends on what the fact-finder perceives.

447. This question tests on the right of access to a law library by a defendant who has waived his Sixth Amendment right to counsel. "[I]t is clear that *Faretta* does not.... clearly establish the law library access right. In fact, *Faretta* says nothing about any specific legal aid that the State owes a *pro se* criminal defendant." *Kane v. Garcia Espitia*, 546 U.S. 9, 10 (2005) (*per curiam*).

A is correct because it recognizes that there is no constitutional violation on these facts.

B is incorrect because it misstates the law: certain law books might be helpful for a defendant who waives his right to counsel, but they are not constitutionally required. **C is incorrect** because the judge would have jurisdiction over the defendant's treatment at the county prison, assuming his rights were being violated there. **D is incorrect** because it provides a non-legal response to a legal question.

448. This question tests on the connection between competency and the waiver of the Sixth Amendment right to counsel. To waive counsel, a defendant must be competent. *Faretta*, 422 U.S. at 835. And the standard for competency to waive counsel is identical to the standard of competency required to stand trial: the defendant must have "sufficient present ability to consult with his lawyer with a reasonable degree of rational understanding and a rational as well as factual understanding of the proceedings against him." *Godinez v. Moran*, 509 U.S. 389, 396 (1993).

C is correct because it recognizes the complete overlap between the two competency inquiries.

A is incorrect because the question asks about competency to waive, and not the relationship between the sophomore and the attorney. **B is incorrect** because the two different competency inquiries are not unrelated—in fact, they are the same. **D is incorrect** because it's not the best answer: while the psychiatrist's report may have only addressed competency to stand trial, the sophomore's incompetency means that the judge may not "properly" allow him to waive his right to counsel.

449. This question tests on the ability of a state to restrict a mentally ill defendant's the right to self-representation. "[T]he Constitution permits judges to take realistic account of the particular defendant's mental capacities by asking whether a defendant who seeks to conduct his own defense at trial is mentally competent to do so. That is to say, the Constitution permits States to insist upon representation by counsel for those competent enough to stand trial ... but who still suffer from severe mental illness to the point where they are not competent to conduct trial proceedings by themselves." *Indiana v. Edwards*, 554 U.S. 164, 177–178 (2008).

C **is correct** because it recognizes that a judge still has some discretion to refuse the woman's waiver of counsel, despite her competency to stand trial.

A **is incorrect** because it contradicts *Edwards*, which holds that the woman's right to waive counsel is not absolute. B **is incorrect** because the woman's ability to "communicate coherently with the court or jury" is only part of the problem here; the woman's delusions will interfere with her ability to handle the trial work herself. In addition, the standard cited here—the ability to "communicate coherently with the court or jury"—was specifically rejected by the *Edwards* Court. *Id.* at 178. D **is incorrect** because it misstates the facts: the psychiatrist opined that the woman was competent, but had reservations about the woman's ability to represent herself at trial.

450. This question tests on whether a *pro se* defendant is entitled to claim ineffective assistance of counsel. "The right of self-representation is not a license to abuse the dignity of the courtroom. Neither is it a license not to comply with relevant rules of procedural and substantive law. Thus, whatever else may or may not be open to him on appeal, a defendant who elects to represent himself cannot thereafter complain that the quality of his own defense amounted to a denial of effective assistance of counsel." *Faretta v. California*, 422 U.S. 806, 834 n.46 (1975).

C **is correct** because *Faretta* forecloses the possibility of an ineffectiveness claim under these circumstances.

A, B, and D **are all incorrect** because they each suggest that a *pro se* defendant can claim his own ineffectiveness, and he cannot.

Index of Cases

Index